Seductress

BETSY PRIOLEAU

S*eductress*
Women Who Ravished the World and Their Lost Art of Love

VIKING

VIKING
Published by the Penguin Group
Penguin Group (USA) Inc., 375 Hudson Street, New York, New York 10014, U.S.A.
Penguin Books Ltd, 80 Strand, London WC2R 0RL, England
Penguin Books Australia Ltd, 250 Camberwell Road, Camberwell, Victoria 3124, Australia
Penguin Books Canada Ltd, 10 Alcorn Avenue, Toronto, Ontario, Canada M4V 3B2
Penguin Books India (P) Ltd, 11 Community Centre, Panchsheel Park, New Delhi - 110 017, India
Penguin Books (N.Z.) Ltd, Cnr Rosedale and Airborne Roads, Albany, Auckland, New Zealand
Penguin Books (South Africa) (Pty) Ltd, 24 Sturdee Avenue, Rosebank, Johannesburg 2196, South Africa

Penguin Books Ltd, Registered Offices: 80 Strand, London WC2R 0RL, England

First published in 2003 by Viking Penguin, a member of the Penguin Group (USA) Inc.

10 9 8 7 6 5 4 3 2 1

Grateful acknowledgment is made for permission to reprint a selection from *Moving Beyond Words* by Gloria Steinem. Copyright © 1994 by Gloria Steinem. Reprinted with permission of Simon & Schuster Adult Publishing Group.

PHOTO CREDITS: 1. Réunion des Musées Natioaux/Art Resource, N.Y.; 2. Goddess of Laussel, 25000–20000 B.C. rock carving, 54 × 36 × 15.5 cm. Dordogne. Collection Musée d'Aquitaine, Bordeaux, France. Inv. 61.3.1. Photo J. M. Arnaud; 3. From *The Prehistory of Sex* by Timothy Taylor, copyright © 1996 by Timothy Taylor. Used by permission of Bantam Books, a division of Random House, Inc.; 4. Statuette of a snake goddess, Greece, Crete. Late Minoan I, about 1600–1500 B.C. or early twentieth century; ivory and gold; H: 16.1 cm (6 5/16 in.). Gift of Mrs. W. Scott Fitz, 14.863. Courtesy, Museum of Fine Arts, Boston. Reproduced with permission, © 2002 Museum of Fine Arts, Boston. All rights reserved; 5. Isabella Stewart Gardner Museum, Boston; 6. Department of Antiquities, Cyprus; 7. Alinari/Art Resource, N.Y.; 8. From *The Price of Genius: A Life of Pauline Viardot* by April Fitzlyon, copyright © 1964 by April Fitzlyon. Used by permission of John Calder (Publishers) Ltd.; 9. © Bettmann/CORBIS; 10. Courtesy of Paul Popper Ltd.; 11. Picture Collection, The Branch Libraries, The New York Public Library, Astor, Lenox and Tilden Foundations; 12. AP/Wide World Photos; 13. Lou Andreas-Salomé Achiv, Göttingen; 14. "Lady Newton," Emilie du Châtelet, c. 1735. By an unknown artist; 15. From *Violet: The Life and Loves of Violet Gordon Woodhouse* by Jessica Douglas-Home. By permission of The Harvill Press; 16. Roger Viollet/Getty Images; 17. Bibliothèque nationale de France; 18. Picture Collection, The Branch Libraries, The New York Public Library; 20. Courtesy of Münchner Stadtmuseum; 21. © Bettman/CORBIS; 22. By Benedetto Gennari. Courtesy of a private collector, England; 23. Roger Viollet/Getty Images.

LIBRARY OF CONGRESS CATALOGING-IN-PUBLICATION DATA
Prioleau, Elizabeth Stevens, 1942–
   Seductress : women who ravished the world and their lost art of love / Elizabeth Prioleau.
     p. cm.
   ISBN 0-670-03166-6
   1. Femmes fatales.   I. Title.
HQ1122 .P75 2003
305.4—dc21   2002069177

This book is printed on acid-free paper. ∞

Printed in the United States of America   Set in Berthold Garamond   Designed by Francesca Belanger

To Phoebe

ACKNOWLEDGMENTS

The subject of the seductress is a siren song drawing everything to it: the whole realm of knowledge, imagination, and personal experience. With a song like that (regardless of the best libraries and inner resources), you need others. Since the idea for the book first dawned on me, through the actual five-year writing process, I've been aided and sustained by an extraordinary group of people.

They've been there from the beginning. The strong *charmeuses* I grew up with in Richmond, Virginia, provided the core inspiration for *Seductress*. My mother, Adeline Howle Stevens, ranks foremost—a sparky man magnet who taught me the ropes and the meaning of feminine sexual pride and fascination. Next were my schoolmates, neighbors, and the formative presence of African American women. From them I learned to boogie and admire female sexual agency in action.

More recently, I have Manhattan College to thank—the students of my "Seductress in Fiction" course and my colleagues, particularly Professors June Dwyer and Mary Ann Groves, who loaded me with information and literature. The most influential of these was Professor Mary Ann O'Donnell—a stellar scholar, counselor, believer, and critical court of last resort.

The path from inception to realization was paved by too many to number. To Dr. Frederick Lane I owe key ideas and the courage to state them. And no one has ever been blessed with better boosters and coaches—Professor Edwin Cady, Sylvia Chavkin, and Sydelle Kramer—or the many informants (some of them strangers on planes) who directed me to potential seductresses. Claudia Thompson introduced me to Violet Gordon Woodhouse; Professor Mike Parker to Catherine Sedley; and Karen Gunderson to Grace Hartigan. Grace herself was a high point of my research—a great creator, great *femme forte*, and generous to a fault with her stories, wisdom, and hospitality. Soprano Kate Hurney supplied priceless information about Pauline Viardot; Sydney Stern about Gloria Steinem; and Dr. Jennie Freiman about contemporary female sexual dysfunction. I am also grateful to New York University for awarding me three productive semesters as Scholar-in-Residence.

Friends from every quarter contributed lavishly of their time and energy throughout the book's preparation. Neide Hucks rescued me from countless time crunches and gave me crash courses on Brazilian and African American sexual mores. Both Ann Gaylord and Smidgie and Alaisdair Macphail ran informal clip services on my behalf, and Barbara Thomas provided invaluable leads and contacts. From my French cousin Nicole Priollaud and Courmes's neighbor Jean-Jacques Celérier, I received critical historical and cultural insights, plus numerous donations of books, articles, and photographs. Bookstore personnel at the Corner Bookstore and Crawford-Doyle also kept an eye out for me and my investigations, as did my oldest friends from Richmond—Kate Roy and Dixon Christian, Frances Lee Vandell, and the late Martie Davenport Reed—who endured long monologues and buoyed my morale.

Without the Allen Room at the New York Public Library, its director, Wayne Furman, and occupants, the book could never have been written. Ella Foshay deserves a halo for introducing me to it. There I had vital access to the library's premier collection, peace and quiet, and the company of learned, helpful colleagues: Gloria Deák, Gretchen Besser, John Demaray, Rita Gelman, and Laura Schenone. All were prodigal with their knowledge, expertise, and encouragement. The Writer's Room at the Mercantile Library was another sanctuary, and I thank Harold Augenbaum for the privilege of working there through one long, hot summer.

While I wrote, I was guided and assisted by a dream team of distinguished professionals. Besides my two translators, Chris Scala (French) and Carlos A. Johnson (Spanish), they include those who read and critiqued my manuscript: John Clubbe and Joan Blythe, Shelley Wanger, and my first editor, Dawn Drzal. Because of Molly Peacock, I found my voice, the figure in the carpet, and the title "Silver Foxes" for Chapter 4. She also revved my confidence and walked me through the rough patches. So did Renata Adler, a wise counselor who went out of her way for me on more than one occasion. My appreciation, too, to Polly Howells and the Women Writing Women's Lives group for inviting me to speak on the *sorcières* and giving me A-1 feedback. Were it not for computer mavens Kevin Meredith and Chris Arnett, I'd have been lost; my PC crashed three times midstream.

Last are the indispensables: Edward Lavitt, my photography procurer; Marc Daniels, my artistic adviser; my agent, Eric Simonoff; and especially Peter Mayer, who believed in the manuscript and launched its publication. Brett Kelly and Jennifer Jackson have been life supports, and my editor, Molly Stern, more than that. To her brains and perfect editorial pitch, she adds the charm and alpha personhood of my seductresses.

The ones, though, who really made this book happen are my daughter, Phoebe, to whom it's dedicated, and my husband, Philip. I wrote *Seductress* for Phoebe and her generation, and if it works, it's because of her guiding spirit. Every page bears the imprint of her critical flair and radiant grand prix personality. As for Philip, there's no beginning or end; he gave me faith in the project and put his whole heart and brilliant mind behind it. That meant sacrifices beyond the call of matrimony: tedious errands, sacrificed weekends and evenings, daily crisis management, incessant manuscript evaluations, and the love and support that kept me and the work afloat. Best of all, he made me feel like a seductress when I was least like one, giving me the pizzazz to persevere, to feed the flame, and finish the job.

PREFACE

It's wonderful what a little determined charm can do. —NOEL COWARD

He that doth play the game best is best loved. —SEIGNEUR DE BRANTÔME

Love despises the lazy. —OVID

Love must be sought, cultivated, and developed by people if we are to make a better world. —ANTHONY WALSH

Search "seductress" on the Internet, and you'll find more than twelve thousand sites, hundreds of starlet and how-to Web pages, and an avalanche of ads for clothes, cosmetics, films, CDs, and escort services. Is there really anything left to say? Haven't we overworked and commercialized this word into an anachronism and tired daytime TV cliché? A whore of all work?

Almost, but not quite. If you scrape off the cultural debris—superstitions, myths, and media cant—you'll see a woman to be reckoned with. The seductress is one of the most potent female personas in existence. Though long misunderstood and ignored, she's the paradigmatic liberated woman, empowered with men and empowered in life. She's a threshold role model who can reinstate feminine sexual sovereignty and holistic happiness and remap the future. And she's not the least as we—or the Internet—imagine.

I came to the seductress, like most people, through the imagination. Raised in a southern belle culture, with a mother who was the Miss Valentine of Richmond, Virginia, I gravitated as a child to stories of man charmers in fiction and fairy tales. Much later I taught a college course on the topic "The Seductress in Literature" that changed everything. First I discovered the dearth of research—few unbiased or comprehensive studies—and second a ravenous appetite among young people for knowledge. In my class, students of both sexes avidly analyzed fabled sirens and tried to scope out their secrets. Afterward, the women flooded my office. Over and over I heard the same laments: elusive bad boys, soulless hookups, sapped confidence, wrecked pride, and total mystification about how to prevail in love.

As I looked around, I realized my students reflected a larger crisis in society. Across the culture, women seemed to have lost the plot erotically and entered the "plague years." Despite equal opportunity sex and babe feminism, guys still hold the whip hand: They have numbers on their side (48 percent women to 43 percent men nationwide); they age better and cling like crotch crabs to their historic prerogatives of the initiative, double standard, promiscuity, mate trade-ins, domination, and domestic copouts. The population of single women, especially middle-aged professionals and first wives, has swelled to one in four, with most wanting and failing to "get married."

In surveys, women en masse report epic demoralization and erotic despair. We say we're "increasingly loved and left," prey to low self-esteem, and "really lonely and really afraid." The orgasm gap—the 15 to 30 percent female success rate during intercourse—continues to widen, as women clamor for a Viagra equivalent and numb themselves with antidepressants. "No one disputes the evidence," writes a *New York Times* reporter, "that many women are unhappy with their sex lives" or that we're engaged "in a frantic search for a role model."

By the end of the semester I began investigating actual seductresses in hopes of finding role models to pull us out of this funk. I cast my nets wide. I read hundreds of biographies; I pumped friends and colleagues; I followed up leads dropped at parties, here and abroad. The list burgeoned; notebooks bulged until at last I narrowed the field to the top players. I defined the seductress as a powerful fascinator able to get and keep the men of her choice, men who are good for her. Rarely discarded or two-timed, she successfully combines erotic supremacy with personal and vocational achievement. That automatically eliminated a number of pseudoseductresses: the eaten and colonized Marilyn Monroe, the oft-dumped flunky Pamela Harriman, and such gofers to male genius as Alma Mahler.

Still, I was left with more *charmeuses* than I could handle, some famous like Cleopatra; others obscure and forgotten, like Pauline Viardot, the "strikingly ugly" soprano who seduced the world: Berlioz, Gounod, and most notoriously, Ivan Turgenev (the literary Brad Pitt of his day), who lived with her and her husband in a forty-year ménage à trois.

In the end I had to limit my study to a mere sample, the worldbeaters. Throughout, I encountered unexpected findings. The great enchantresses, for starters, exploded all the seductress stereotypes. They weren't dim blondes, nothing-without-a-man operatives, sharkhearted vamps, sick narcissists, and comely servile guardians of the hearth. They were myth-busting nonbeauties, seniors, intellectuals, creators, politicas, and bravura adventurers. More dramatically, they shared a constellation of qualities. Androgyny, for example, nonconformity, and Abraham Maslow's criterion of psychological health: supravitality and self-actualization.

Just as strikingly, they followed similar erotic strategies. These, I discovered, mirrored the historic *ars amatoria*. This art of love tradition, which includes dozens of texts from Plato to the present, comprises a core set of erotic principles that have changed little through the ages. Sexologists warn us to beware of any absolutes in the realm of desire: Preferences are unique; tastes vary too much. But some women are universally bewitching, and some truths about romantic passion are timeless—especially the craft of enchanting and keeping someone (the hard part) enchanted.

Not all men of course are won by the identical means. Yet whatever the recipe, the basic ingredients of seduction remain the same. They constitute a kind of periodic table of eros. They can be custom mixed to taste, with some elements omitted—such as fashion flair—and still do the job. They're that potent, rooted in sexual turn-ons that go back to the Stone Age.

Prehistory in fact may hold the key to the whole mystery of the megapower of the seductress and her ancient arts. The best scholarly evidence suggests that a cult of the feminine principle probably existed throughout deep history. Seductresses, I theorize, pack such an erotic wallop because they plug into this ancient archetype embedded in the inherited unconscious of the race. They evoke the goddess, mankind's first love object, and replicate her Seductive Way, the template of the *ars amatoria*. Men, in their libidinal depths, want a divinity to serve and adore and a replay of the sexual themes that arose through goddess worship where the erotic impulse, as we know it, took root. They want to be sent to paradise—bowled over, transfigured, and reborn.

That was one reason the swanky sirens were so alluring; they echoed the all-in-one deity, the life force of the cosmos. Another reason was the primal hit of their lovecraft. They deployed the two branches of the *ars amatoria*—the physical and psychological—the archaic magico-religious way, with all the psychopomp of the earliest cave rites to the sex goddess. That meant shoot-the-works drama in dress, ornament, cosmetics, setting, movement, music, and fireworks in the bedroom.

Their chief artillery, though, was cerebral magic. Seduction is 99 percent mental sorcery, a hijack through the labyrinth to a fifth dimension and the conjuration of a constant state of emotion in motion. Without art, love sinks into stasis and ennui. The seductresses, par excellence, maintained the erotic dynamis, the perpetual light show of alternating solace and anxiety, quiescence and ecstasy, intimacy and distance, pleasure and pain. Like the early eagle-clawed love goddesses, they could be *cruelles*. At the same time, they delivered the balm of nurture and praise and the intoxicants of speech, nonrepression, festivity, and joie de vivre. In short, they restored the life-death ever-whirling Goddess of Everything to men—her Way and the ongoing rapture and transcendence of her cosmic eros. Whether consciously or not, they took their cue from Ovid's first precept, "Do as the goddesses did."

Goddess avatars as they were, though, the love queens were far from perfect. Like all ultravital people, they contained flaws and contradictions and often disported above morality. You wouldn't, for example, want to cross La Belle Otero, who slugged a woman in a hotel lobby, or Ninon de Lenclos, who skewered her enemies with such savage bon mots they became national laughingstocks. Though sometimes great mothers, relatively few excelled at maternity or domestica. They were a fractious, tough lot.

Often the product of dysfunctional homes and early hardship, they had to fight for their lives and place in the sun. In the process they trampled feminine and cultural norms and usually ran afoul of the establishment. Other women included. Despite their outsider status, however, they tried to wise up the sisterhood. Lola Montez lectured for years on erotic artistry; poets, philosophers, journalists, and novelists, and even a comic like Mae West wrote at length about sexual empowerment.

If we anthologized their love wisdom and let them write the preface, what would they tell us today? First they'd marvel at our advantages: financial independence, legal rights, sexual freedom, and cosmetic options. Then they'd fire our courage. It's no coincidence love and warfare share the same vocabulary; seduction demands spunk and "daimonic assertion." "Venus favors the bold!" Next they'd urge us to boost our self-esteem and get high, mighty, and magnificent. And, of course, to discover our genitals, our turbo-charged thrill machines that make us the natural sovereigns of the boudoir.

Finally they'd advise us to tune out the pretty-power propaganda and dial up the neglected psychological arts. They'd direct us to libraries instead of (or along with) gyms, to acting classes, to metacharm schools—whatever it takes to invade men's heads again and hex them into permanent fidelity and fascination. They'd impress on us that this isn't the work of a day, but a sophisticated, complex art form that requires, besides self-drama, "extreme tact, skill, caution, and care." Also antennae, a second sense about tools and timing, and a cool head on the rapids.

This may sound like too tall an order in our already overprogrammed world; the seductresses, too exceptional to emulate. But love mastery is democratic and eminently doable. Not that we need it for fulfillment, as the Hillary Clintons and Martha Stewarts attest. For those, though, who'd like eros under their control, beaux at their bidding, and the upper hand in sex, the know-how is there for the taking. If not a quick fix, it's a kick nonetheless, a route to power paved with valentines, pleasure, and self-development. Rather than a sleazy revenge ride, it actually benefits men. Unless unrequited passion leads them off a tenth-floor ledge, they achieve their fondest dreams in the arms of a seductress, a goddess to venerate who keeps them interested and ignites their inner hero. She leads them to their best self and restores them to true masculinity, their predestined place in the cosmic scheme.

At the same time, she furthers her own cause. Seduction aids and abets individual growth and ambition. Heterosexual love isn't supposed to be the stuff of confiscated egos, stunted careers, 4:00 A.M. panic attacks, tears, and ice-cream binges. We're meant to prevail in sexual relations and cash in on our full gender payoff: erotic primacy and combined success in love, work, and life.

Second-wave feminists of the last century, like their foremothers, labeled seduction a "four-letter word" and reviled seductresses as non-PC sellouts, the "slavish little sisters" of society. As a result, they alienated a generation of women and cast them to the wolves of junk guides and normless, predatory sex. This may have been feminism's dumbest move.

There, beneath their noses, were the first feminists, with men and the world at their feet. Nothing and no one could resist their charm offensive. "Seduction," notes philosopher Jean Baudrillard, "foils all systems of power." And seductresses were the archsaboteurs of patriarchy who infiltrated the hierarchy and upset the applecart. Passé women vs. women rivalries have made them unwelcome too long. They belong at the feminist rally, setting the agenda and steeling our nerves with their silver tongues and big Lady Heartbreaker personas.

If we're amid a nationwide erotic famine at the moment, there are also signs of a recovery. Everywhere, from L.A. to Paris, sexy supremas of all persuasions are love bombing men and getting it together professionally and romantically. Investigators haven't yet analyzed this emergent cadre of *charmeuses*, but if they did they'd see the seductress archetype resurrected and in operation again. They'd see her change-less character and art and the plot lines of tomorrow.

In my book, I've tried to provide a rough guide to this brave new world that will get us and keep us there. It's primitive compared to what will follow and carries no guarantees or promises of earthly bliss. Love resists glib formulas and dot-to-dot diagrams. Some men cannot be had, period. Life's bedbugs will infiltrate the best-designed boudoir: demonic in-laws, infants with issues, illness, fatigue, debt, and death. Seduction won't wave a wand and transport us to Hallmark Heaven with Herr Perfect and happiness eternal.

But it will improve the odds. It gives us back our swerve and sup-plies a program—field tested and anchored in myth and history—that's win-win all the way: personal individuation and achievement, plus absolute sway in love. Seductresses of course were *femmes d'ex-ceptions*, privileged by genes, drive, and destiny, but those who rise in-spire and chart the frontier. If we let them, they can lead us to full liberation, a third sexual revolution (why not?) that recoups the power advantage that belongs to us by biologic and divine decree. Nancy Friday said in *Women on Top* that most women fantasized about the "Great Seductress."

The question now is why retreat any longer into fantasy, that weary strategy of oppressed women for aeons? With a little help from real seductresses and their arts, we can come out of the closet in our shimmering allure and mythic swish and realize our wildest dreams. We can stop men in their tracks, rifle their hearts, addle their brains, and keep them in our pockets for life. We'll get the other good stuff as well: in bed, in the workplace, and in our hearts, souls, minds, and psyches. We'll just be doing what comes naturally. Now it's only a matter of planning—how to prance through the closet door, master-mind the coup, pluck the consorts, stage the coronation, and throw the carnival.

CONTENTS

CHAPTER ONE

Seductress: The Women and the Art

It is not enough to conquer; one must know how to seduce. —VOLTAIRE

We are all seduced and seducing. —ST. AUGUSTINE

A woman with fair opportunities, and without an absolute hump, may marry
WHOM SHE LIKES. *Only let us be thankful that the darlings are like the beasts of the
field, and don't know their own power. They would overcome us entirely if they did.*
—WILLIAM MAKEPEACE THACKERAY

This strength of the feminine is that of seduction. —JEAN BAUDRILLARD

*T*he seductress. She's a scarlet inkblot, a Rorschach of our deepest sexual fears and fantasies. She's the blond bimbette in a string bikini; the stacked vamp in Spandex; the Chanel-suited nymphobitch of Sullivan & Cromwell; the servile artist's muse and maidservant. But we've got it wrong. We've been gulled by chimeras—sleazy, bogus stereotypes that need to be dismantled and replaced by the genuine article.

Real seductresses, those incandescent unditchable sirens who spellbind and keep the men of their choice, belie every popular myth. Forget beauty, youth, vacuity, servility, and shark-hearted rapacity. Seductresses are in fact the liberated woman incarnate. Feminism's biggest mistake was kicking them out of the club. They're futuristic models of female entitlement: independent operators, pleasure claimers, *terroristas* of traditional femininity, and big, classy divas. They recover women's natural supremacy and achieve what most eludes us today—erotic control and a positive union of work and love.

It's time to demystify and rehabilitate this lost tribe of sexy potentates and put them to use. Along with their brains, autonomy, integrity, and high swank, they radiate killer charm and practice the arts of erotic conquest like mahatmas. They can rescue us from the current sexual crisis. They can teach us how to get our groove back, retake the field, and finesse seduction, a forgotten and long-misunderstood art.

These love queens have existed throughout recorded history, although seldom celebrated by the official culture. Social mavericks and mold breakers, many have vanished into semiobscurity or been distorted beyond recognition. For generations they've been trivialized, demonized, and persecuted by the establishment. They strike terror into the insecure male heart; under their black magic all hell can break loose. A man can be pitched into testosterone storm, driven from home and country, led into love bondage, and zapped from a mogul into a mouse.

Yet paradoxically seductresses are often the best thing to happen to a man. Contrary to fable, they're usually *femmes vitales* who put air in a man's tank, conferring growth, creativity, happiness, and authentic masculinity. (For starters, their speed dial orgasmic capacity allays male performance and penis size anxieties.) Most of all, though, the great *charmeuses* are a gold mine for women. They're a secret sorority, never before studied as a group, with a priceless fund of inspiration and seductive wisdom.

In both personality and erotic technique, seductresses show surprising similarities. Although amorous spells vary from woman to woman, with individual mixes brewed for specific times, people, and places, they follow a modus operandi based on an ancient art of love tradition. Their characters, too, tend to conform to a similar pattern, one that flies in the teeth of siren caricatures.

Far from sellouts to patriarchy, for instance, they subvert and sabotage it. They menace male domination. Since antiquity they've roiled the waters and upset the hierarchy, reclaiming women's natural position in love: on top, in command, with swarms of men at their feet. They're the stealth heroines of history. The first feminists.

They're a welcome presence at the new millennium. Despite the sexual bravado and record advances in the workplace, women are stalled out in their love lives. Thirty to 50 percent have difficulty climaxing, a majority rate themselves "below average sexually," and most say they've been humped, dumped, harassed, and "hurt by some guy." We've lost our erotic pride, leverage, and winning edge.

Amid this brownout in female sexual power, men seem to hold all the high cards. Exploiting their social prerogatives in the mating game, they philander with impunity, impose the double standard, preserve the initiative, and cut and run at the drop of a diaper. They grow sexier with age. And given half a chance (as now), they binge out on casual infidelity, wife trade-ins, and hit-and-run sex.

The great appeal of the seductress is that she has always reversed the artificial male advantage and recovered women's innate erotic primacy. "Seduction," says philosopher Jean Baudrillard, restores "female sovereignty." Women are the master sex in sex. Their superiority in love, their absolute sway over men, is hardwired into the human DNA. Unless "subverted by deceit or usurped by force," writes sociobiologist Mary Batten, the female of the species controls the game. Men peacock and petition for her favor while she coolly surveys the competition and picks a mate on the basis of penises, resources, and beauty.

Or mates. To patriarchal dismay, women's sexual plumbing wasn't designed for monogamy and single-family dwellings. Sexier by a mile, they outorgasm, outlast, and outpleasure men and, left to their own devices, gallivant like their nearest cousins the bonobos, stud shopping and sating their eternal-climax machine.

Women's sexual primacy is also rooted in myth. For twenty-five thousand years before there was a male deity, mankind probably worshiped a goddess. More than merely a swag-bellied fertility idol, she was a cosmic sexpot, the be-all and end-all who created heaven and earth and reigned supreme over human destiny. She gave and took life, revived the dead, raised the tempest, ripened the grain, conferred civilization, and reduced her servant, man, to fear, lust, and sublime rapture. He propitiated her with gifts and prostrated himself before the divine one and her wonder-working womb.

Memory traces of this ancient female cult could well be scored deep in the male libido. As the construction of sexuality evolved over time, acquiring refinements and cultural preferences, its intrinsic themes may have remained the same, embedded in the collective unconscious. If so, men can never rid themselves of their first love object or her Seductive Way. Secretly, primally, they pine for goddess women who rattle their bones, woo them with ancient ur-spells, and take them to paradise. By divine right men belong on their knees, and women (sorry), back on the pedestal.

The seductresses of this book are avatars of the original sex divinity. Like the goddess, they're alpha plus women, ladies of strut and accomplishment. They have that numinous shazam we call charisma, combined with the steamy sexuality of the prehistorical deity. In one Neolithic figurine the goddess masturbates with her toes turned up, right hand plunged into her labia and left hand behind her head, Mae West style.

Their erotic siegecraft also mirrors the sexual strategies laid down at the beginning of evolutionary history. They rile, thrill, console, mystify men, and rock their hearts. They deliver the erotic everyperson promised by the archaic deity: mother, daughter, mistress, androgyne, and transcendent divinity. "The open palm of desire," says Paul Simon, "wants everything, everything." A woman who can tap that buried male hunger and provide even a pale reflection of the great sex goddess and a fraction of her "everything" can name her man.

Six Seductress Myths

Since the dawn of patriarchal civilization, seductresses have been enveloped in a pall of myth. They're a little too powerful for patriarchal consumption; hence the campaign to throw women off the scent with a string of siren pretenders. Each chapter targets a different fallacy and treats a group of seductresses in Western history who shatter the stereotype. They fall into six categories: nonbeauties, seniors, intellectuals, artists (not muses), and two commanda types—governmental leaders and high-octane adventurers.

Nonbeauties

The first and most insidious falsehood is that seductresses must be young and beautiful. Temptresses of song, story, and prime TV always have wolf whistle dimensions and cover girl faces. From evolutionary psychologists to image czars, authorities remind us that if we want men, we have to look sensational: big baby blues, flat abs, bazongas, and a perfect waist-to-hip ratio. When we think seduction, we think of lanky blondes stun-gunning a male lineup; we think of supermodels flying first class with money gods.

We hear the folk adages: "The love thoughts of men have always been a perpetual meditation of beauty," and "Love *is* the love of the beautiful." As a result, women knock themselves out cosmetically. Ten times more women than men (more than a million in 2002 alone) have plastic surgery, desperately tucking, lifting, lipoing, and augmenting in hopes of a romantic lotto, a Mr. Right who keels over at the "perfect look" and supplies the Range Rover and suburban dream.

A survey of the tragic love lives of beauty icons and the current singles scene dispels that fiction. In cities everywhere, number ten glamour girls hole up with videos on Saturday nights, sidelined and manless. Many seductresses of course were fabled beauties, but most of the great enchantresses, like the "very ugly" Pauline Viardot or hooknosed Cleopatra, lacked either looks, youth, or both, and often lived in eras more obsessed with beauty than our own.

Seniors

Similarly, the ravages of age didn't deter seductresses from reeling in the most desired men of their times. In popular culture, senior sex appeal is a comedy club oxymoron: the blue-haired granny with dewlaps and stalactite udders in hot pursuit of pool boys. "Hit on a dinosaur," cracks the standup, "the way you would someone in your age range; ask about her prescriptions; ask if she's ever done it in a golf cart."

Contrary to the hag propaganda, however, older women possess some of the most potent erotic weaponry in the book. The goddess in her last phase was an *über*siren. For centuries, cognoscenti have recognized and celebrated the huge allure of "old dames." Anxiety about this amorous megapower in part explains the crone smear campaign. Unface-lifted, unreupholstered, dozens of senior seductresses made conquests that would be the envy of the comeliest nymphet on the man circuit.

Intellectuals

A third libel that bedevils the seductress involves her stupidity. According to this canard, men want airheads who ask all the right questions, play dumb, and keep their mouths shut. Adorable, vapid chicklets populate romantic comedies, and mothers still advise daughters to dumb down and let the guy talk and strut his knowledge. Feminists as diverse as Simone de Beauvoir and Germaine Greer agree that you can't get a man with a brain.

Yet the real manslayers were smart cookies with big mouths. The peerless Greek courtesan Aspasia taught Socrates, founded a school of philosophy, and wrote her lover Pericles's speeches. In fact most seductresses talked brilliantly and knew what they were talking about. Tantric scriptures teach that the highest splendor of the yoni is the flame of "intelligence," and Neolithic goddess cults attributed all known and unknown wisdom to their sex deity.

Artists

Joined to the mindless sex bomb fallacy is the erroneous view of the seductress as a servile man pleaser, a glorified housekeeper, inspiring men to feats of genius. In this fantasy sequence, a negligeed siren rouses the creative giant on a feather bed with the perfectly appointed breakfast tray. What great artist doesn't dream of a domestic menial and muse—to coo approval, fetch his paints, turn down his bed, bend to his whims, and shine in reflected glory?

Plenty, in fact. Seductresses, if they wished, easily entrained artists and other creators into lifelong passions. But rather than decorative, passive, compliant muses, they wrote their own books and lit their own creative fires. They repudiated the traditional submissive parasitic model and appropriated an older female role, the divine mistress of spells.

A whole genus of seductress wielded this goddess-given thaumaturgic power both to enravish men and build major careers. Often they possessed their own covey of male muses, but with typical reciprocity, they delivered as much inspiration as they received. Primordial magic making worked the same way: The goddess's mana infected and transfigured her votaries.

Governmental Leaders

A subset of the ornamental muse/homemaker myth is the pom-pom girl in the man's parade, the politician's gofer, mouthpiece, and prop. Great leaders, claim psychologists, want eager converts and team players who ratify, follow, and diffuse "nonhostile" karma. This tired cliché of the luscious camp follower and senate groupie went out with Monica Lewinsky, the seductress reduced to wipette.

Real seductresses, by contrast, were shakers and movers and often wore the pants politically. The *Machtweiber* (German for "vamppoliticas"), a fifth category of siren, led nations and political factions and exercised equal clout in the throne room and bedroom. Instead of downsexing themselves in office, they played up their erotic allure in order to brew charisma, win consensus, consolidate power, and bespell constituents.

Seduction and politics are natural bedfellows. They potentiate each other and work synergistically. Because men have always known and exploited this, they've tried to turf women out through intimidation and slander. With classic calumny, they branded the sixth-century Theodora a "new Delilah" and a "citizen of Hell stung by the devil's fly." In reality, she governed Byzantium with finesse while putting "forth irresistible powers of fascination." The *Machtweiber* demolish the satanic boss lady stereotypes, winning men and governing with equal proficiency.

Adventuresses

A sixth chapter takes on another deep-dyed fallacy: the Madonna-whore fiction. This old chestnut won't go away. Biobehaviorist Richard Wright still warns darkly that the dichotomy between the domestic angel and the quick-trick Jezebel is "rooted firmly in the male mind." Ultrafeminine, virtuous homemakers inspire love everlasting. Hellrakes who invade the male domain of high action and sexual adventure get laid, forgotten, and scorned. Nobody gets serious over a woman on the move and make. She's the whore-hearted hussy and shark goddess, the one you don't marry. Romantically minded women have to be crazy to leave home and hit the high seas of sex, thrills, ill-gotten gains, and fun in the wild zone.

Crazy like a fox. The most fabulous *charmeuses* of history—idolized and adored to the grave and beyond—were rakish adventurers and sex professionals. Descended from the first prehistoric love goddess, Inanna, the out-for-kicks wanderer and prostitute, they buccaneered through life, fortune hunting, daredeviling, and raiding male hearts. They didn't, it's true, win Sunday school medals, but they were neither better nor worse than other women and actually liked men and aided their fortunes.

Patriarchy stigmatized siren-adventurers as vile, unmarriageable tramps for a reason. Their escape from domestic captivity was too seditious; their sexuality, too unbounded; and their siren song of the open road, too strong. Men can't resist them; the urge is rooted deeper than the Madonna, in the first roving, roistering sex goddess.

Seduction: The Art

Seduction, the art of enchanting and holding men, has been obfuscated just like the seductress herself by a miasma of myth. The *ars amatoria* have all but disappeared, debased into *Rules* primers, flirt guides, sorority scuttlebutt, and a Victoria's Secret version of man-killing. Intelligent women everywhere equate lovecraft with "a second-rate skill," the duplicitous wiles of low-rent Cosmo girls.

The secrets of fascination, however, don't come cheap. They're an advanced, serious discipline. "It takes a hundred times more skill," said archtemptress Ninon de Lenclos, "to make love than to command an army." The art of seduction is a "complex, learned system," with a consistent set of principles, detailed in dozens of forgotten books. Its precepts go back to prehistoric goddess worship, when the core themes of sexuality were fused into the human libido, and have changed little over time, despite fluctuations in sexual tastes. They're the real rules, the power book of love.

Deep mystical impulses infuse seduction. In love songs men pray to earth angels and find salvation and seventh heaven in their embraces. That's because sexuality and the sacred were united for most of human history. Men seek in women what they sought twenty thousand years ago in cave shrines and yearn for the same rituals. Along with heart's ease, they want awe, mystery, terror, and cosmic extravaganza when they fall in love. They want to be carried away, led on a magical mystery tour through the labyrinth. They want to see stars. Love means never having to say what else is new. Satiety and boredom kill the most ardent passion. After the first fireworks subside, the show must go on. And the show must follow the ancient scenario, the Seductive Way of the goddess and the *ars amatoria*.

Physical Arts

Too much has been made of physical lures in seduction. Alone they can't arrest men for eternity; psychological love spells always pack the big magic. But seductresses and their physical appeals remind us that we neglect them and drab down at our peril.

Dress, Ornament

Ornament and costume—the more dramatic the better—entered sexuality from the start. Stone Age shamans and priestesses glammed up to channel the goddess's cosmic sex energy. For their sacred ceremonies they wore masks, skins, and hip-slung diaphanous string skirts, frayed at the hem and lavishly decorated. Intricate designs of chevrons, whorls, lozenges, dots, and dashes covered goddess figurines from head to toe.

Seductresses dressed for parade, with look-at-me excess and over-the-top opulence. Many plain sirens edged out beautiful competitors through the originality and "emotional assault" of their dress. With time, dress became more erotically sophisticated, telegraphing sexual preferences, subtle power cues, and provocative mixed messages. Madame de Maintenon, for example, intrigued and piqued men with her crossed sartorial signals—deep mourning embellished with co-quettish furbelows and yards of expensive lace. When we gird up for love, we do well to heed the Spanish proverb, as good today as in pre-history: "Only God helps the badly dressed."

Cosmetics, Hygiene

In the realm of seduction, the natural look may be inherently antierotic, an innate turnoff. "He who is not painted," say the Cadu-veo tribesmen, "is stupid." Just as cavewomen ritually bedizened their bodies with complicated divine motifs in honor of the goddess, priest-esses seven thousand years ago coated their nipples with gold, stained their nails, and painted their faces with ocher, blue-black lipstick, ver-milion rouge, kohl eyeliner, and green eye shadow made from crushed beetles. In classical times *kosmētikos* constituted a respected art form. Grecian toilet boxes contained razors, scissors, tweezers, eye pencils, ceruse, curling tongs, and hair dyes, and the hetaerae made them-selves up as elaborately as geishas. Cleopatra, Lola Montez, and Eliz-abeth I all went heavy on maquillage and wrote books on the cosmetic arts.

Natural body odors, notwithstanding the libidinal kick of pheromones, have never fared well in the history of seduction. Even in eras when bathing was verboten, seductresses kept scrupulously clean. Scent bypasses the thalamus and strikes directly at the oldest stratum of the brain, the rhinecephalon, source of memory and emo-tion. The goddess's votaries steeped themselves in costly spices, gums, and aromatic woods and burned incense to their deity. Cleanliness, scents, and unguents have been routine with sirens for millennia, a tribute to the earliest incense offerings to the sex deity.

Setting

Sacred space is one of the keystones of religion, the place of divine revelation, and the cave shrine, the archetypic seductive setting. Approached via twisted, tortuous labyrinthine paths over a mile long, these cavernous rooms were spectacular stage sets. Glowing tapers lit the mystic womb chambers, which were filled with dramatic drawings, statues, and cornucopias of food offerings—fruits, vegetables, and specially prepared cakes.

"Every woman," say the erotic experts, "should know how to arrange her own setting." Seductresses arranged theirs according to the primordial blueprint, to awe, delight, and fascinate. Cueing into the food-sex connection, they also laid excellent tables and served the choicest, most aphrodisiacal cuisine.

The sex goddess was the patron of animals, incarnations of the life force. Seductresses picked up on that too and accessorized their surroundings with menageries of pets—gazelles, monkeys, squadrons of cats, and, in one case, a grizzly bear. The house of love has its "poetics of space," which the *grandes amoureuses* mastered like design swamis, clairvoyantly replicating the most erotic and earliest sanctum sanctorums.

Music, Dance, Body Language

According to archaeologists, the first religious services looked like rave clubs full of Ecstasy trippers. Cave dwellers beat out rhythms on crude instruments as worshipers holy-rolled, stamping and miming sex in ecstatic circle dances. Music and dance lie at the heart of sexuality.

Music is depth charge weaponry; it goes straight for the pleasure center, the primeval inner cortex of the brain and source of the strongest emotions and urges. After Ivan Turgenev heard Pauline Viardot sing in a voice like "amber flowing over velvet," he deserted Rus-sia and followed her around in a ménage à trois for forty years. Mu-sic's power to soothe the savage beast is only half the story; it also awakens the savage, the earliest sex worshiper in orgiastic communion with his deity.

At those prehistoric rites celebrants danced themselves into delir-ium. They rocked their pelvises in copulatory rhythms and gyrated in dervish circles to summon the goddess's cosmic energy and lose themselves in lust. The female form in motion plugs smack into the male libido, reigniting the old sacred sex dances. Women in the busi-ness of fascination learn how to hold the floor, to move with grace, style, rhythm, and slam dunk sensuality. From the *Kama Sutra* on down, seduction bibles extol the mystical properties of dance and women's mesmerizing powers when they swing their hips and "grace-fully sway in time." Some seductresses, such as Josephine Baker and La Belle Otero, were professionals, and most burned up the ballroom.

As eros evolved through history, body language gathered an aphrodisiacal power of its own. Sirens were prima donnas of gesture, but not of the kid glove, touchy-feely persuasion. They fogged win-dows with their entrances; they made sheet lightning with their "devilish eyes"; and they addled minds with contradictory cues—submissive shrugs and aggressive self-caresses. "'Twas surely the devil," warned church fathers, "that taught women to dance." Or they might have added, to work such diablerie with their bodies. The teacher, however, wasn't the devil but a she-devil, the heretical creatrix herself.

Sexpertise

Before the advent of higher civilization, female orgasms weren't prob-lematic. Given women's naturally souped-up sexual anatomy, how could they have been? We're endowed like Mazeratis, built for multi-ple orgasms, powerful spasms, incessant excitement, and numerous partners. Among the other goddess qualities they revered, men in pre-history worshiped this sexual prepotency. As study after study proves, they still do; deep in their loins they want a pleasure claimer, a wild thang, and the caterwauls of double-digit orgasms.

The love queens of history were raunchy sexperts. Hot, randy, and wanton, they were accomplished bedmates, skilled in getting a full return on their hypersexuality and playing every note and half note in the sexual score. The Sumerian sex goddess Inanna summoned Dumuzi to the royal bed with a lusty "Plow my vulva, man of my heart!," then treated him to a smorgasbord of gourmet delights, including "tongue-playing," phallus-kissing, and "holy churn[ing]." One nineteenth-century enchantress mastered the esoterica of Arabian eroticism: *hez* (a system of hip movements), *jedhb* (vaginal muscle control), and twenty-five coital positions.

Feminists used to say that the discovery of the female orgasm in the 1960s was "the biggest single nail in the coffin of male dominance." But female orgasms go back much farther, to the Stone Age, when they didn't need to be discovered; they came and came and inspired a culture of sexual technique that made men sit up and beg, and raise hosannas to the deity.

Psychological Arts

Physical beguilements alone, however, carried to whatever heights of refinement and proficiency, can't cut the mustard in seduction. To entrance a man for life, a woman has to use her head. Love, even the most soul-bonded and heaven-scaling, won't, alas, remain frozen in amber. It's a dynamis, emotion in motion, just as the goddess and her universe constantly flux, cycle, and dance the dance of the cosmos. It's a "continuous courtship with a continuous progression," a constant interplay of the deity's multiaspects: solace and fear, quiescence and rapture, intimacy and mystery, pleasure and pain.

In this ongoing enravishment, psychological appeals are the A-weapons, the heavy artillery of love. Sex originates in the mind. Archaeologist Timothy Taylor attributes human brain size to the "sexual fix" of mental charms and cultural attainments 150,000 years ago. Cerebral lures consequently permeated the cult of the sex goddess and shaped the erotic impulse, a thing "of imagination all compact." Philosopher Jean Baudrillard takes the extreme view that "the real has never interested anyone" in eros and blames the current impasse in women's sex lives to an atrophy of mind spells. Seductresses suffered no such atrophy. They plied psychological charms for all they were worth, idiosyncratically and unsystematically, at full concert pitch.

Obstruction, Difficulty, Anxiety

Everyone loves the fantasy of love in the tranquil zone, a hot tub bath of mutuality, reciprocity, and blissed-out togetherness. But desire, perversely enough, doesn't work that way. Love goes brackish in still waters. It needs to be stirred up with obstruction and difficulty and spiked with surprise.

The great goddess was not easy of access. Pilgrims reached her shrine through a long, dark, circuitous, labyrinthine passage, a sacred journey commemorated in the meander and spiral designs on their relics. With the labyrinth as the paradigm of seduction, seductresses made themselves difficult. They led men a dance, provoking, teasing, thwarting, and disappearing around the next bend.

Programmed to this arduous archaic Seductive Way, humanity puts no value in erotic prizes easily won. Love philosophers belabor the point: "What's granted is not wanted"; "Dearness gives value to the meat"; "We scorn too easy a victory in love"; "We still consider that one fairer and more worthy in which more obstacle and risk is [*sic*] offered."

The first sex goddesses, after all, were "austere and merciless" taskmistresses and required blood sacrifices at their rites. Anxiety is the "food of love"; pain, its spice. Desire and aggression share the same neurocircuitry; a pinch in the soft place heightens love on a now-and-then, mild-to-moderate basis.

Compliant, eager-to-please yes girls not only give off the BO of need, they fail men at a gut level. Men may dream of consensus, calm, and peace on the home front, but they long for a little action. They crave intrigue, caprice, the tang of distress and fear—a tortuous treasure hunt, with a numinous, ever-fascinating queen at the end.

Maternal Nurture, Intimacy

At the same time, men require the primal gratifications of the great goddess strewn along her labyrinthine way. Central to the cult of the goddess was woman the creatrix. She gave birth to the universe, watered the heavens and earth with her life-giving milk, and spawned and nurtured humanity.

Mother love underpins all desire. The rocking, stroking, sucking, and nuzzling of lovemaking imitate the first caresses of infancy, and the love object—if she answers male prayers—restores the mom to the man.

With a qualifier. While men yearn for the lost delights of maternal succor and at-oneness (intensified by the forced renunciation of them in boyhood), they're also skittish, fearing engulfment and annihilation. The great goddess killed her consort-son each year; mermaids sucked men underwater and drowned them in amniotic fluid.

Seductresses therefore played the mommy card with discretion. They defused the fear by balancing intimacy and TLC with nonmaternal sizzle. The backdrag to mother and her maternal sweets is inherent in eros, a powerful, primordial pull. Yet it coexists with female autonomy and sex appeal and may even depend upon them for peak efficiency. The goddess wasn't just a *magner mater;* she was a blowtorch sex queen and mage of a million charms.

Ego Enhancement

Connected to the maternal draw of seduction is a passion for self-inflation. In love, everyone seeks an ego boost—and not a small one. At the depths of our being, we hanker to be number one, a god, just as our cave ancestors became "divine" in the presence of the deity. Psychologist Theodor Reik thought that the ego drives in love are older and stronger than sexual ones; we'll crawl over broken glass for the lover who lifts us out of ourselves into a nobler, grander, classier identity. To pull this off, though, the lover must be a winner, which explains why the praises of toadies and errand girls never work as their mothers promised. Only the applause of valued people carries any value.

The sirens' Olympian egos made them natural praisers; they instinctively projected their inflated sense of self onto others. After first applauding herself, her "wondrous vulva," and endless accomplishments, the cocky Inanna trained her accolades on Dumuzi and recited his superhuman virtues. We go for the ego burn, an apotheosis, and no ordinary woman will do. She must have the swish of the first goddess and her divine powers of transfiguration.

Conversation, Comedy

By tradition, the best way to build men up is to listen, listen, listen. Guys love laugh track girls and loopy ingenues who ask all the right questions. But in truth they're sent into orbit by silver-tongued talkmeisters. The queen of the cosmos brought the cultural arts to mankind, and her successors were divas of speech: Inanna the "eloquent," "Aphrodite the Persuasive," and Isis the "Lady of Words of Power."

Primitives believed in the magical power of words, and anthropologists speculate that sexual enchantment might have been one of the first functions of language. Ever since Scheherazade's verbal veil dance in *The Arabian Nights,* men have always been seduced by the "smooth tongue of the adventuress." All the traditional love texts recommend conversational prowess.

In ancient Greece eloquence was a sine qua non for hetaerae who mastered classical learning and "hundreds or thousands" of "appropriate ways of expressing things." Renaissance courtesans studied *bel parlare* (seductive speech) as assiduously as lute playing and bedcraft and reviled "dumb of mouth" whores. Before the recent ascent of mute babes, "every woman to be well loved" had to "possess good powers of speech."

Contrary to the lonely clown propaganda, comedy is a strong aphrodisiac, and the funny bone, a high-explosive erogenous zone. Aphrodite was the "laughter-loving goddess," and her descendants through the ages joked and quipped their way to men's hearts. "What is more seductive," say the love philosophers, "than a stroke of wit?"

In the ballad "Just the Way You Are," Billy Joel instructs his inamorata not to make "clever conversation," and the hero of *9½ Weeks* commands the heroine "not to talk." They're begging for mercy. Sword without *s* spells "word," the siren's sharpest weapon. As Jean-Paul Sartre observed, "Seduction *is* fascinating language."

Festivity, Nonrepression

Men never lose an atavistic appetite for license—the release of social and temporal constraints and ecstatic abandon. Seductresses were mistresses of misrule, carnival queens who cast off repressive shackles and declared a public holiday. The goddess Inanna decreed, "Let all of Uruk be festive!" Once a year at the sacred marriage ceremony she ordained a gala free-for-all of feasting, cross-dressing, game playing, and promiscuous fornicating.

We cannot bear too much reality; bound, gagged, and led in chains by custom and civic authority, we demand that eros set us free. Love guides since antiquity have urged women to loosen up, "be festive," and provide "moments of organic relief." The French cocottes at the turn of the century were maestras of disinhibition and unbuttoned frolic. With *Quid nihi* (To hell with it) for their motto, they lit cigarettes with bank notes, talked dirty, threw *transvesti* balls, and danced with pet pigs.

Among the many other tunes in their songbook, sirens sang of parties—of frolic, joy, masquerade, and anything goes abandon. Love jumps the turnstiles. In Shere Hite's study of male sexuality, men said what they valued most about sex was being allowed to be "totally out of control, to release the pent-up emotions they were taught they 'should' repress at all other times." Here they echo their prehistoric male ancestor *Homo festivus*, who cut loose when he worshiped the sex goddess: cross-dressed, caroused, and let the deity take possession of him.

Vitality, Plentitude, Androgyny

Since the primordial sex deity personified life energy and totality, including the union of both sexes, seductresses played up their ultravitality, inner plentitude, and androgyny. The lure of gender synthesis, with its "superabundance of erotic possibilities," exerts a potent fascination on the libido. Feminists have long crusaded for a more androgynous definition of womanhood, without realizing how sexy it is. "The indistinctness of the sexes," amorist scholars agree, "is seductive."

Sirens deliberately traded on the appeal of the androgyne. Venetian courtesans wore pants under their overskirts and adopted a "masculine mode" of behavior and lifestyle, while others, like the omnisexual first goddess, engaged in love affairs with both sexes. Androgyny, no secret to these women, amps sex appeal. As a French connoisseur observed in the seventeenth century, "A beautiful woman who has all the good qualities of a man is the most wonderful thing in the world."

Another secret weapon enchantresses deployed was joie de vivre, the goddess's yes energy that animated heaven and earth. Fictional heroines may be loved for their bovine placidity and gravitas, but the women who inflame men are live wires. Vitality creates an aphrodisiacal whirlpool around a woman. The goddess created out of superabundance, a sacred power surge, and all her avatars radiated the same ultraélan. Ninon de Lenclos, the empress of courtesans, took for her motto "Joy of spirit is the measure of its force," and Lola Montez careened through life exclaiming, "I must live before I die!"

This aliveness, if genuine, emanates from inner health, a full to brimming psychic wholeness and "plentitude of being" like the deity's. Sirens have been endlessly typecast as neurotics and sick souls, but they were saner, if anything, than other women. They gave off that "plus-feeling of power," that assurance, creativity, complexity, and rage to grow we associate with robust egos. Great swaggering queen bees, they had self-concepts to match the deity—the stuck-up mistress of the universe, the life principle, and the "eternal image of the whole."

Impact, Drama

Whatever her fascinations, physical or psychological, the seductress pizzazzed them up. Eros is the great stirrer-upper, a mover, shaker, and drama maker. When the sex goddess of ancient Sumer made an entrance, the earth trembled, the kettledrums rolled, and men stood dumbstruck. "Clothed with the heavens and crowned with the stars," she drove in on a chariot drawn by lions, bearing a staff entwined with snakes and brandishing her eagle wings like parasails.

Love that lasts never neglects the old éclat; it needs wake-up calls and limelight to stave off the natural drift to satiety and blahsville. It needs vital tension, a kaleidoscopic play of sedate and elate. The *grandes amoureuses* were doyennes of dazzle, showboaters, and scene stealers. Too muchness was the goddess's signature, "all that's fascinating, terrible [and] overpowering." They kept things in motion and threw off *électricité*, the star power that sends shock waves through a room. When Richard Burton first saw Elizabeth Taylor on a pool chaise, he hyperventilated. "She is famine, fire, destruction and plague, she is the dark lady of the sonnets, she is the only true begetter . . . in short, too bloody much."

Although we've been groomed to supporting roles and self-deprecation, the women who enthralled men and kept them on their toes punched up their style with drama, self-parade, and excitement. The sex goddess didn't sit out the ball in her all beige personality; she was "shinning bright and dancing."

Summary: Art of Seduction

These ancient seductive arts are so effective, so fire-powered that they work without a blanket application. Seductresses practiced them piecemeal and selectively and seldom employed the full spectrum of spells. Lou Andreas-Salomé, for instance, hated music and cosmetics, Eva Perón lacked a sense of humor, and Martha Gellhorn and Grace Hartigan refused to mother men. Seduction is an art, not a science, requiring different mixes for different men and a fingertip feel for mood, timing, and hidden tastes.

Then, like any human endeavor, the best-laid assaults can go awry. Some men are just siren-resistant, slow on the sexual uptake, well married, cryptogay, or scared, and would push the snooze button if

Cleopatra climbed into bed with them in a G-string and pasties. Similarly, no "right" combination of physical and psychological moves delivers the goods every time.

Nevertheless, the seductresses and their lovecraft provide a premier field guide to sexual empowerment—time-proven, reality-tested, and grounded in ancient wisdom. It's a liberation front waiting to happen and death to male dominance. Enchantresses blow the hatches. They subvert patrilineal succession, female monogamy and submission, and give women the scepter and throne.

Seductress: Resistance

Obviously patriarchy hasn't taken this minx to its bosom. Throughout recorded history, she's been stigmatized, ostracized, and persecuted. She's been villainized as "the terrible goddess [who] rules over desire and seduction," a bloodthirsty ball breaker like Salome and Circe, and the antithesis of virtuous femininity. Lilith, Eve's predecessor, is the prototype: a promiscuous jilt who refused to accept the missionary position and dumped Adam for an eternity of revolving door sex with satanic superstuds.

To eradicate this dread specter of female autonomy and power, men have gone to heroic lengths. They've hyped female asexuality, inflicted the double standard, broken women on the wheel of domestic servitude, and punished sirens to the limit of the law, mutilating and burning them as witches in cultural panic attacks.

Sadly enough, women have all too often joined the witch-hunt. Like subjugated people everywhere, they've internalized the master's beliefs and colluded in their own oppression. Competition for a Few Good Men has only fueled the hostility. With marriage a woman's life support system for centuries, the seductress represented a real death threat. At any moment she could break and enter, swipe your guy, and sack your very existence. Athena, Jupiter's stooge, turned the too sexy Medusa into a revolting monster, and women still demonize and assail fascinators. Often more viciously than men—just as the status quo intended.

Seductress Redivivus

But nothing has worked. Seductresses can't be stomped out. They're stronger than the law and foil "all systems of power." Like their divine progenitor, they're a tough breed with a big sense of Me and serene indifference to criticism and persecution. Mae West mocked the court when she was arrested for corrupting the morals of minors, and Martha Gellhorn drove Ernest Hemingway's car into a ditch during one of his sexist rampages and let him walk home. Sirens snapped their fingers at authority and went their own way, the Seductive Way.

Women today are better positioned for erotic sovereignty than at any time in memory. Educated and sexually liberated, we have an array of advantages denied to previous generations: money, mobility, independence, leisure, cosmetic options, and feminism's legacy of equal entitlement. We don't have to seduce for our supper anymore; now it's about the perks of choice and romantic success.

The will to seduce is there. Women from business queenpins to rocker chics are demanding a single standard, sexual agency, and the "hard dick" and "tight butt" of their pick. In her *Bitch* manifesto, Elizabeth Wurtzel says she'll "scream, shout, race the engine . . . and throw tantrums" until she gets a free, fulfilled sex life. Summarizing the current campaign for sexual empowerment, pop diva Courtney Love concludes that "it's like any frontier, there's going to be all sorts of doors to kick down and all sorts of people to kick in the head." Men, however, can't be brought around by "tantrums" and blows to the skull. For this one, we need charm, cunning, and an operating manual that works.

Just as important, we first need to junk the old myths and prejudices, then gun out. Seduction isn't what it's been cracked up to be by the media. What's left of the revered art has fallen into the wrong hands—beauty shills, love coaches, and idiot how-tos—and alienated intelligent women. The art of love, though, is consistent with the highest principles of feminism. It promotes self-development, autonomy, and liberation and expands our options. Instead of pushing back the clock, love mastery *is* the future. It frees women from the naive no games, total candor ethos of the 1960s (one of the cleverest shell games in sexual politics) and maps a path to erotic preeminence. From sex object to sex subject.

Although the *ars amatoria* doesn't read like a cookbook with step-by-step recipes, it provides the ingredients and techniques, and encourages us to concoct our own love spells according to personal taste. This is a potent cocktail. But power in love doesn't have to be malign, destructive, or manipulative; it can preserve and improve a good thing.

The practice of seduction, though, takes moxie. "Venus favors the bold." At present women seem to have wimped out. Pollsters find epidemic demoralization and "an undercurrent of fear" in our sexual dealings. We've let the playground bullies spook us. We're afraid of being sidelined, trashed, dumped, name called, and punished if we aspire too high and break too many hearts. We're afraid of self-loss, humiliation, and a thousand bedroom no-no's.

The dashing seductresses, with their imperial command of men and eros, save us from this sorry plight. They juice up our sexual pride and nerve and show us what's possible with a little love savvy. They recoup our ancient prerogatives of sexual supremacy and recover the power base. They blow all the false seductress myths out of the water. They prove we can have our cake and eat it, romantic *and* professional power, without any of the fabled sacrifices.

Wowing men coexists with and enhances worldly success. Georg Simmel observed more than a century ago that the most seductive women were also the most "domineering." His feminist contemporary Ellen Key argued further that they had the strongest identities and best shot at happiness, a finding confirmed by a recent sex survey that linked "happiness with partnered sex" with "happiness in life." Of course, even seductresses took some knocks. But their triumphs outnumbered the losses, and their reverses left them intact and at the top of their form.

Complex pinwheel personalities, enchantresses had supersized egos and a don't-give-a damn bravado. They bucked the tide, invented their own characters, and lived outside the pale of convention with divine amorality. They were unzipped originals, bellwether belles who blazed new feminist territory, reclaiming women's native domain. We belong in seduction country in command of the whole power turf—love, work, and our own destinies.

Glamorous heroines of this stripe should lead us to tomorrow. The feminist pantheon is only half full; the standard role models—the Eleanor Roosevelts, St. Teresas, Virginia Woolfs, and Hillary Clintons—have served us well, but we need new blood, women who can take us, tangoing their hips, through the postmodern sexual minefield and tell us we can have it all. Activists say that the problem of "how to be a woman in this culture and be sexual too" ranks as the number one issue today. Seductresses solve it with panache; they take back the boudoir and reinstate women as victors, both in the battle of the sexes and in life.

Freud, then, should have asked not what women but what men want. The traditional answers, it turns out, are false. Men have been blowing smoke at us. The women who light their fires and keep them lit are supremas of clout and charm. That they were irresistible makes sense. We're naturally magnetized by powerful personalities with superior individuation, wholeness, and "unconflicted psyches." But men have deeper reasons to adore queens of the hill. Their libidos were engineered at the beginning of time to swoon over sexy magnificas, to quake in their presence, and glorify, honor, and serve them. Pushovers, bubble brains, and penthouse pets therefore disappoint them at a primal, biochemical level.

The following seductresses—the mythic archetypes of the first chapter and the stereotype smashers of the next six—rewrite the book of love for women. They turn control of the plot over to us, give us the best lines, the starring role, and a happy ending: wonderful men and all the homage we can handle. The action and dialogue aren't prescripted, but we have a master plan to follow.

Many women of course couldn't care less. They're perfectly content with career rewards, social status, community service, motherhood, and apple pie. "This dance," as rapper group Salt 'n' Pepa say, "isn't for everyone. Just the sexy people." But the sexy people are starting to mass, cropping up everywhere, like rocker Liz Phair and Undersecretary for Public Diplomacy and Public Affairs and former

CEO Charlotte Beers, who "wants to seduce" and "is a woman, a woman, a woman."

Robert Graves believed that goddess worship was the "repressed desire" of patriarchal civilization, destined for a comeback in the future. The future is now. With the seductresses to guide us and teach us the steps, let the dance begin. Ladies' choice.

CHAPTER TWO

The Seductress Archetype

Thou, goddess, thou alone rul'st over everything. —LUCRETIUS

Studied alive, myth . . . is not an explanation in satisfaction of a scientific interest, but a narrative resurrection of a primeval reality. —BRONISLAW MALINOWSKI

Every historical man and woman carries on, within themselves, a great deal of pre-historical humanity. . . . The mind uses images to grasp the ultimate reality of things. —MIRCEA ELIADE

Do as the goddesses did. —OVID

*I*f the seductress hadn't existed, she would have been imagined. Since the Ice Age men and women have envisioned Goddesses of sexuality and worshiped them. These were no bloodless Madonnas with eyes cast heavenward, but creatures of flesh and appetite, adored for their erotic power. Their sacred insignia was the pubic triangle, like the cross in Christianity. Charity, fidelity, modesty, and selfless domestic service had nothing to do with their appeal. Female sexuality alone—in all its majesty and mystery—inspired these early cults.

The goddess religions, historians speculate, lasted for twenty-five thousand years, much longer than the reign of male belief systems. With the ascent of patriarchy, the female deities were demoted to supporting roles and specialized functions, and their powers co-opted by gods. The strongest were demonized. But the first sex goddesses still exert a strong pull on our psyches. They established the archetype of desirable womanhood that continues, with subterranean tenacity, to govern passion today. They defined the seductress persona.

Throughout history the women who've enchanted men resemble these ancient deities to an uncanny extent. Inconceivable as this may sound, it makes perfect sense to mythologists. Archetypes, they say, never vanish from a culture but work stealthily and subversively beneath the surface, especially on the libido. They "take hold of the human personality as a whole, arouse it and fascinate it," despite every precaution.

The early goddesses have usually been seen as simple Great Mothers whose birth-giving powers struck awe and terror in the primitive mind. But woman in toto was the true *objet de culte,* the almighty Lady of Everything: cosmic totality, death and rebirth, and the sex energy of existence. Women who echo these archaic images of desirability, however faintly, are the ones who send men over the moon. The déjà vu sentiments in love may be only memory traces of the first prepotent goddess and all she incarnates.

Her archetype reveals not only the anatomy of the seductress but also the infrastructure of sexuality. The core themes of sexual desire evolved through goddess mythology. Out of those primordial beliefs and rituals arose the construction of the erotic—who and what excite us and why we mate as we do. It's the paradigmatic Seductive Way, incised in the human collective unconscious and resistant to change, despite fluctuations in sexual tastes and mores.

The Prehistoric Goddess

From the Pyrenees to Siberia archaeologists have unearthed hundreds of mysterious Stone Age (30,000–10,000 B.C.) female statuettes and carvings. Without any male ones to speak of—except diminutive stick figures—these Venus images have generated a storm of speculation. Some scholars contend they were fertility fetishes; some, porn toys; others, sacred relics of an aeons-old matriarchal religion. In the absence of written records, we'll never know for sure. But no one denies the sexual content of these busy, hippy figurines with their high-profile vulvas or discounts the possibility of their cultic significance. Historian Richard Rudgley, one of the most impartial investigators, thinks the female body almost certainly held for early man a mythological and "metaphorical" meaning suggestive of a primitive cosmology.

Through myth, the explanatory stories and dreams of the race, we can imagine the general drift of such a prehistoric cult. Most mythologic systems mention an earlier protomyth inherited from deep history, in which a creatrix formed the earth and heavens and ruled the cosmos. Given woman's miraculous sexual biology—her menses in rhythm with the moon, her inordinate orgasmic capacity, her ability to give birth and sustenance—it makes perfect symbolic sense.

This ur-divinity, by tradition, embodied the life force, contained opposites—male and female, change and changelessness—and regenerated the dead in the "great round of her being." The first peoples envisioned her as the moon, a dynamis in motion, cycling constantly through growth, decay, and rebirth. Female sexual power drove the wheels of the universe.

The Venus carvings, etched with strange signs and scattered throughout Eurasia, clue us to her multiple meanings for early man. Although they come in every shape and size, from rail thin to Rubenesque, none even approached the neo-Darwinists' gold standard of feminine sex appeal, the 0.70 waist-to-hip ratio. Yet they were sex incarnate. The famous Venus of Willendorf is swallowed up in mountains of femaleness. Her double D breasts flop on a monumental belly, and her saddlebag hips hold her prize feature in parenthesis, "the most carefully and exquisitely carved realistic vulva in the entire European Upper Paleolithic." To our ancestors the vulva was the holy of holies, carved on every surface as chevrons, triangles, and semicircles and symbolic not just of sexual desire but of maternity and divine creative energy.

Another queen-size goddess, the imperial Venus of Laussel, points with one hand to her vulva and holds in her other the allegorical equivalent of the "child at the breast of the Virgin," a bison's horn, curved like the new moon and notched with the lunar months. This proclaims her the "Perfect Mind," the cosmic mistress of intelligence. To the Ice Age nomads on those dark, frozen continental wastes, the moon (from the Indo-European *manas,* mind) conveyed a sense of time, measurement, and order. Prehistoric humankind never set any value on the dumb beautiful female ideal.

Zombie babes wouldn't have excited them either. The earliest-known female figurine, Fanny the Dancing Venus of 31,000 B.C., depicts a woman with motion in her ocean. She stands like a flamenco dancer poised for takeoff: left leg cocked, hand on hip, right arm raised high over her head, with one lush breast caught mid-swing. The goddess personified action, movement, the propulsive, ever-cycling, whizzing energy of existence. With her, "there [was] no stagnation."

Nor was there gender division. A figurine found in the Grimaldi cave has full breasts, a plump love cushion, and an erect penis. A later statuette from a Neolithic temple in Malta pays tribute to an equally important source of the deity's prestige—women's magical, seemingly inexhaustible orgasmic capacity. The bosomy lady this time is portrayed deep in the throes of masturbation: legs splayed, toes turned up, and hand sunk into her swollen labia.

The discovery of this X-rated figurine in a temple is no coincidence. Unlike the Flintstones, prehistoric people didn't live in caves but used them as shrines for elaborate magico-religious rites. Though better known for their animal paintings, these caves were filled with female sexual symbolism, hundreds of vulva designs and enough statuettes (footless to be staked in the earth like crosses) to persuade Joseph Campbell of a widespread goddess cult. If the Venus images suggest the contours of the mythic Perfect Woman—the seductress archetype—the earliest ceremonies structured desire as we know it.

From the scenarios re-created by archaeologists, the rites began with an arduous trek into the bowels of the cave, perceived as a "vulvar/vaginal/womb" pilgrimage. To reach the innermost shrines, celebrants had to endure a treacherous assault course more than a half mile long, clambering through a labyrinthine maze of blind passages, sudden drops, thin ledges, and long narrow, coffinlike tunnels. The deity's path was perilous, designed to instill awe, terror, and the *mys-*

terium tremendum of the almighty. This is the template for the love journey.

Once at the interior temple chamber, pilgrims joined in an ecstatic quest to draw the goddess in their midst and appropriate her powers and sexual energy. Conjuring her through sympathetic magic, they imitated her Being. Like the creatrix, they created. They painted her sacred animals on walls, sculpted her visage, and carved an array of erotic objects, such as phallic batons, one with a lioness licking a gigantic human penis.

Their faces daubed in red-ocher spirals (emblems of rebirth and menstrual blood), they dressed as the goddess would. Which meant they "were adorned rather than clothed." Some of the early Venuses look like rock stars run amok in a tattoo parlor, incised with meanders, whorls, and zigzags and rigged out in hip-slung aprons and animal masks.

Stone Age women likewise wore plumed headdresses on braided coiffures and red and black-striped bell skirts hitched up in front, their arms and necks decked with shell bracelets and necklaces. They circle danced topless to throbbing drums, rattles, and rasps, miming coitus with men.

They were in the business of rapture—a "sail away" epiphany, as Norman Rush says of erotic possession. On the basis of hemp seeds found on location, they might have used psychoactive substances to help them. More too than grain offerings might have been sacrificed to the goddess. Underscoring the archaic link between sex and pain, one cave contains hundreds of stencils of mutilated hands.

When votaries reached a state of collective delirium, they entered a mystical union with the goddess. Transfigured, reborn, they merged with the Most High. She recharged them with her cosmic vitality, fecundity, and libidinal force and sent them off larger than life, imbued with her divinity. All of which might have led to a sacred orgy where women (to judge from the number of in situ dildos) sated their heaven-born mega-appetites.

These primeval rites and the mythic goddess who inspired them form the matrix of desire. As eros evolved through Western history, it merely elaborated on these core leitmotivs: An overscale goddess woman who has it all, observes the "tortuous path principle" and exerts the same fascinations, from dance, music, setting, and costume to intelligence and plentitude, even pain. She pitches us into ecstasy (*ecstasis*, out of ourselves), takes us to paradise, and regenerates and redeems us.

"Sex," in essence "is religion and vice versa." When the hero of Philip Roth's *Sabbath's Theater* can think of no other way to describe the ultimate woman, he compares her to the "fat little dolls with big breasts and big thighs unearthed all the way from Europe down to Asia Minor and worshipped under a dozen different names as the great mother of the gods."

The Snake Goddess

One of her dozen names in later prehistory was Snake Goddess, the curvaceous deity of Minoan Crete, the first high civilization of Europe from 2500 to 1000 B.C. In contrast to the zaftig, ill-proportioned Stone Age Venuses, she has the designer body of a supermodel in all her statuettes—*Penthouse* breasts, tiny waist, and slim greyhound hips.

She stares at us with obey-me kohl-rimmed eyes, two writhing serpents in her upraised arms, in full coronation regalia. She wears a towering crown or wreath of roses and a dog on her head, a frontless jacket cinched at the waist by a tight belt, an ornamental double apron, and a tiered skirt. But she's a "direct inheritor of Neolithic culture," a sex goddess of the same cosmic grandeur, totality, and ever-evolving, restorative life force.

Her snakes, which undulate up her arms and in some cases enwrap her entire body, signified a wealth of divine powers to the ancient Minoans. It was a "seminal symbol" for the goddess, incorporating her vital energy, regenerative magic, maternal consolations, sexuality, and almighty wisdom. At the deepest level the serpent, coiled on itself with its tail in its mouth, connoted her wholeness, her primordial union of "male and female, positive and negative" in the uroboric "Great Round."

Her snakes, associated with the moon since earliest times, also betokened immortality with their uncanny ability to shed their skins and renew themselves. Their lunar connections too made them emblems of ceaseless motion and activity. In one gold ring seal the Cretan goddess whirls down a mountaintop, head inclined to a gigantic snake, her hair flying behind her.

The Snake Goddess wasn't the Minoan deity's only incarnation. Although the details of Cretan mythology remain murky, we can see the Cretan deity in frescoes, seals, and figurines in many guises: Goddess of the Animals, Mistress of the Sea and Fruits of the Earth, Lady of the Wild Places, Lady of the Labyrinth, and Queen of the Mountain. But the "glorification of the meaning of sex" informs all her personas. It was also the heart and soul of her worship services.

The libido unbound—joy, action, gusto, and frank physicality—was the hallmark of Cretan culture and its religion. Sexual iconography pervaded the goddess and her cults. Celebrants adorned the caves and mountaintops where the first rites took place with tributes to the deity's sex power: figurines of mating couples, amatory doves on her sacred pillars, and phallic stalagmites inscribed with her holy logo, the coital double ax. Its paired triangles with a shaft thrust through the middle could be an ideogram for copulation.

As in the Stone Age, access to her presence was fraught with difficulty, fear, and breathless wonder. Initially votaries navigated cave passages or scaled steep mountain crags to reach her altars and later simulated this tortuous path in the labyrinthine design at the Palace of Knossos. The route to the goddess's sanctum sanctorum took them on a convoluted, thrill-inspiring trip through a maze of halls that wound in and out of light and darkness, around Piranesi-style staircases, down twisted corridors to the dim shrines of the goddess in the crypt.

On the ceilings and walls, Minoans, like their ancestors, painted goddess images to elicit her presence and divine eros. Art, for the Cretans, merged indissolubly with ritual and was both the first attempt at naturalism and "the most inspired of the ancient world." Every fresco pulsates with the divinity's cosmic élan and generativity. Dolphins leap, flying fish cavort in gravity-free space, blue monkeys pick flowers, deer bound over rocks. A Cleopatra-eyed priestess sways back to pour libations on a trussed bull while a man pipes furiously in the background.

Just as the Snake Goddess was "the one and the many," so a variety of ceremonies honored the Divine Feminine in ancient Crete. All, though, shared the identical goal—mystical fusion with the goddess and personal and social transfiguration. Through cultic magic they sought to tap into her "principle of life-energy" and reanimate the world, to seize rebirth from the jaws of death. The Snake Goddess idols, with their stoned, bugged-out eyes, raise their arms in a gesture of epiphany. Reincarnation, holy madness, rhapsodic self-abandon: these were the aims of every religious rite.

Minoans made no distinction between the secular and sacred in their rites, most of which resembled carnival in Rio. The new year's festival, the supreme drama of rebirth and transformation, took place when Sirius, the dog star, rose for the summer solstice at the end of the honey harvest. High on fermented honey (mead) and opium, they danced out their religion to music in a state of primal theater.

Costumes rivaled court dress at Versailles in glamour and sophistication. Women wore bright boleros open to expose their breasts, gold belts, embroidered rainbow skirts, and acres of pendants, chains, beads, bracelets, and rings. They had the big hair of a mafioso bride: a whorl of braids and curls on top with ringlets erupting in front of their ears and flowing in long tendrils down their backs. Hypergroomed and depilated, they painted their eyes and faces with thick powders ground on special palettes.

Instead of the primitive crotch thrusting of earlier peoples, Minoan dancers performed a mystic round dance that imitated the labyrinthine way. To the hypnotic strains of lyre, harp, and double pipe, they wound and unwound in concentric circles, replicating the journey to the goddess and drawing dancers into rapturous contact with her spirit of "indestructible life." Perhaps the new year's celebration also included bull dances. At these gymnastic spectacles, men and women—cross-dressed in tribute to the deity's androgynous powers—somersaulted and vaulted over charging beasts with death-defying bravura.

The festivities proceeded inexorably to the climactic holy mysteries at the altar. After food and honey offerings to the goddess, the bull, symbol of the divinity's creative power, was killed with the double ax and sacrificed. As before, pain and violence were at the very marrow of the sexual experience. With the ritual bloodletting, the miracle of Parousia occurred. The goddess made herself manifest, filled devotees with her transcendent presence, infused land and sea with new life, and resurrected the dead. Images of votaries (some nude) in ecstatic abandon, their long black fusilli curls streaming out at right angles, suggest the kinds of revels that succeeded this divine possession.

Later in Minoan culture, the bull, once an icon of the deity's androgynous nature, acquired a masculine character. Eventually he became the goddess's young son/lover, a proto-Dionysus, doomed to annual death and rebirth. Man's place in the Minoan cosmology was strictly second class. He existed, as the palace frescoes attest, to serve and honor female sexual power. In one low relief a lady of resplendent authority receives a delegation of nearly a hundred handsome tribute bearers. So much for women's instinctive asexuality and monogamy. A seal shows a man with his arm raised in salute, his eyes shaded against the radiance of the goddess, who stands on a mountaintop, flanked by lions, brandishing a swagger stick.

An heiress of the primeval creatrix, the Snake Goddess continued the divine line of cosmic queenship. She was the almighty "it"— the great unity, melder of sexes and opposites, the all-knower, and a perpetual-motion machine that woke the dead and spun the earth on its axis with her erotic energy. The Cretans played their own riffs on her personality and refined her Seductive Way, but the mythic underdrawing stayed intact: the supreme she-god awhirl in her heaven, men and beasts in adoration at her feet.

The invading Greeks who conquered the Minoans had to construct a myth to put her prepotency to rest. In the story of the Minotaur, Ariadne, a goddess avatar, saves the captive Theseus by leading him out of the labyrinth and follows him to Greece. Like a good Greek patriarch, Theseus ditches her en route and marries a docile child bride in Athens.

But Ariadne and her Snake Goddess archetype couldn't be dispatched so easily. In another myth, she elopes with Dionysus, the divine consort and god of sexual excess, and migrates to Cyprus, where she founds the cult of Aphrodite Ariadne. She is the goddess who will not die, the erotic prima donna absoluta of the universe.

Inanna/Ishtar

Before the reign of the Snake Goddess, another divine seductress inspired one of the most enthusiastic cults of the ancient world. Inanna, goddess of sexual allure and desire, was the supernova of Near Eastern deities. She originated in Sumer during the fourth millennium B.C. and, renamed Ishtar by the Babylonians, held sway for four thousand years. This time written records authenticate her stature and the scope of her sovereignty.

Although Inanna shared her power with a tribune of ruler gods, she outranked and outfoxed them all. She cut a formidable figure. Wearing a towering horned headdress, flounced skirt, lapis lazuli jewels, and a zodiac-tooled belt, she stands with one foot on a lion and carries a staff of intertwined serpents. Wings, tipped with buds and maces, flare from her shoulders. Above her shines Sirius, "the shape-shifting dog of the Great Goddess."

Despite the goddess's role reduction to the sphere of sexuality, Inanna retained the cosmic authority of the prehistoric deities. Like them, she was the "Totality of What Is," the "Lady of Blazing Dominion," who contained multitudes and contradictions and presided over life, death, and regeneration. Her numerous names reflect her myriad aspects: Queen of Heaven, Great Mother Cow, Princely Inanna, Lady of Vegetation, First Snake, First Daughter of the Moon, Lady of Raging Battle, and Bearer of Happiness. But her defining quality was her prodigal, hot-bodied female sexuality. She incarnated raw erotic desire, beyond societal laws and human control.

She is known as mythology's "ultimate femme fatale." She thumbed her nose at proper femininity and walked on the wild side, snaking men and slaking her voracious sexual appetite. But she was really the seductress writ large and at large. In a society that subordinated women to their husbands and punished female adultery with death by the iron dagger, Inanna represented the principle of female sexual empowerment.

She repudiated Sumerian sexism and demanded free use of her allure and holy vulva. The original rambling rose, she refused to stay
put and restlessly roamed the neighborhood in quest of erotic adventures. Often she sat at the tavern door decked in gaudy beads, casing
the goods and carrying off the comeliest men. When Inanna finally
agreed to marry the young fertility god Dumuzi, she still wouldn't toe
the line. She insisted on no women's work—weaving, dyeing, or child-
bearing—and an equal place at the table.

Inanna not only violated social norms, she transcended gender
divisions. Perpetuating the twin-sexed nature of the archaic goddess,
she had *la-la,* "the vigor of a young man in his prime," and enjoyed
masculine pursuits, warfare and liaisons with women if she wished.
Nothing, no cultural constraints, could curb Inanna's all-inclusive,
runaway carnality. She changed men into women and the reverse at
her pleasure, confusing the sexes and casting the ancient spell of the
androgyne, the promise of gender fusion and completeness. Devotees
cross-dressed at her rituals, with women in the male robes of power
and men in brooch-pinned gowns.

Her sex drive came straight out of prehistory, unmediated by civilized ideas of feminine sexuality. She adored her supercharged equipment and didn't let it idle in neutral. After she crowned herself Queen
of Heaven, she leaned against the apple tree in the Sumerian Garden
of Eden and rejoiced in her "wondrous vulva." Then she set off with
her "ardent desire" and "holy water–bathed loins" and took them to
town—to the marketplace, temple, brothel, and home front.

A proactive love goddess, she made the moves and got her way.
She bragged to Dumuzi of her physical enticements and sexual skills—
precious caresses "more savory than honey"—and commanded him to
stroke her pubic hair and to "plow my vulva, man of my heart, plow
my vulva!" This hyperphilic lust, however, had a cosmic significance.
Inanna's sex energy generated all growth and productivity on earth
and made the heavens dance. She was the *hi-li,* the sexual joy of the
universe, the life force of creation. She was the deity who "loved to
laugh," who bid Sumer sing, carouse, and "be festive!"

Inanna, though, by her very nature, was as variable, as motile as
the primordial moon goddess, her ancestress. Unpredictable, full of

contraries, she was always in motion, now this, now that, sometimes everything at once. One minute she strapped on her sandals and became the "whirlwind warrior," smashing skulls and soaking the earth with blood; another, she kissed babies and dispensed loving kindness. If she struck terror into human hearts with her tempests and carnage, she delivered the ultimate consolations of "Great Mother Cow." Suffering she would not tolerate. As mistress of the "art of lamentation" she wept, wailed, clawed her thighs, and tore her hair to intercede for mercy. She held the most extreme oppositions in dynamic tension: deceit and straightforwardness, travel and domestic stability, strife and concord, dark and light. Under her bed, scene of honeyed amorous delights, she kept a scorpion.

Inanna's mercurial, complex nature resulted not from her instability but from her supernal wholeness and maturity. To underscore the point, the Sumerians constructed a myth of her passage to ultimate adulthood. During her ordeal she descended—in classic heroic fashion—to the underworld, where she was stripped of her robes and breastplate emblazoned, "Come Man Come!," hung on a hook, and left for dead like a piece of "rotting meat." At the end of three days the gods came to her rescue. She arose, rid herself of her demons, and resumed her reign with redoubled authority.

Not only did Inanna personify the perfectly evolved psyche and unitary principle—the unmoved mover and welder of opposites—but she occupied the clout position in the pantheon. She seized the "world-ordering power" and put "all gods, all creatures" under her dominion. She was the quintessential powerfrau, "the goddess of sovereignty."

In one of the coolest coups in mythology, she unseated the god of wisdom. Over a dinner date at the table of heaven she got him so drunk on beer and flattery that he gave her the entire *me's* (all human knowledge), with the double meaning "power" and "laws of civilization." Earthly wisdom became her province, from the arts of leadership and heroism to eloquence, crafts, and "Truth!" Included in the package was erotic knowledge: "The art of lovemaking! The kissing of the phallus!" and "tongue-playing."

The sacred marriage ceremony that celebrated Inanna's romance and union with Dumuzi in the holy temple adhered to the basic pre-historic paradigm and repeated the themes of the Seductive Way, with a Sumerian twist. Dumuzi's courtship of Inanna, which set the stage for the wedding rite, established the goddess as an erotic adept. Before she accepted the handsome shepherd, she goaded him to fever pitch with her circuitous wiles. She backed and filled and made him walk over hot coals, taunting him with a competitor, deriding his appearance, and finally baiting him into a quarrel. Only when she had him sewed up, amenable to all her demands for superior treatment, did she turn up the volume and sing to him of all the delights in store.

This moment and their subsequent coupling carried such numinous significance for the Sumerians that they staged it each year with the priestess and king enacting the parts. Again, the objective was apotheosis, to be remade in the image of the goddess, to channel her divine sex energy and redeem and regenerate the earth. Accompanied by tigi music, the congregation wound up the spiraling ziggurat to the chapel at the top. Women, as usual, dressed with holy flamboyance—flounced, form-fitting one-shouldered kaunakes with gold hoop earrings, diadems, and stacks of bracelets.

The priestess who played Inanna, the *nugig* (woman of highest rank), wore the most spectacular attire and dramatic makeup and smelled like a living censer, having bathed and perfumed herself for days beforehand. Her hair, a huge turn-on for Sumerians, was coiled in a wreath of thick braids, surrounded by "small locks" and gold ribbons. Once within the high altar, the *nugig* accepted the king's gift offerings, then serenaded him with lascivious verses, praising her "honey-man's" erection, and itemizing how she would "holy churn" and pleasure him.

At the climax of the service they repaired to a bed on the dais and copulated, to the ecstatic cries of the assembly. Inanna had revealed herself, charged the king with semidivinity, and reinvigorated the world. A blowout carnival of license followed. Possessed by their goddess, the "one-who-is-joy," the community joined in a rhapsodic orgy of games, feasts, dances, music, intoxicants, and wholesale coupling.

After the Babylonians adopted Inanna and renamed her Ishtar, she began to lose her luster among Sumerian divinities. As the archfascinator Ishtar in *The Epic of Gilgamesh*, she failed to conquer the hero, even though she deployed all of Inanna's wiles and added extra enticements. Despite her bribes of endless wealth, political power, and jeweled chariots, the mighty Gilgamesh stood his ground. He scorned her lures and sex appeal and read her a long lecture on her loose morals. At this point in mythology the seductress began her metamorphosis into the femme fatale. With all the fury of a woman scorned, Ishtar declared war on Gilgamesh and destroyed him. Ishtar became an icon of predatory female sexuality, the mantis lady red in tooth and claw.

But unofficially Ishtar's cult persisted and prospered for centuries. Inanna/Ishtar was too compelling, too magnetic an archetype to be swallowed up by patriarchy without a trace. Excavations in one city, Alalakh, contained temples to her at fifteen different levels, and throughout the ancient world she resurfaced with new names: Astarte, Asherah, and finally, in a slightly altered form, Aphrodite.

Aphrodite

Unlike her sister Athena, Aphrodite did not spring full blown from Zeus's head but developed incrementally from a mélange of earlier goddesses. She came late to the Greek pantheon, a Near Eastern import who smuggled a powder keg into Attic culture–she-power and the raging tumult of sexual passion.

The patriarchal Athenians did what they could to curb her. They limited her job description to romantic love, restaged her myths, frowned on her festivals, and prettied her up, but she burst through their definitions and became "the most potent goddess." A PC Grecian makeover couldn't efface centuries of worship. An amalgam of the archaic Serpent Goddess and Inanna, she threw Olympus into confusion and attracted one of the most enthusiastic cults of classical times.

Although the Greeks demoted her from her central place in the cosmos, Aphrodite preserved much of her earlier all-inclusive preeminence. In the original story of her birth she united the powers of heaven and hearth and inherited jurisdiction over both. After the sky god's semen fell on mother ocean, Aphrodite arose miraculously from the foam. She supervised mankind as queen of the world and sailed through the empyrean as empress of the great above in a chariot drawn by swans.

The sea birth also signaled her regenerative powers. As statues of her with snakes coiled on her arms indicate, she was a resurrection goddess of life renewal. Wherever she stepped, roses, crocuses, hyacinths, and lilies sprang up in her path like a magical May Day processional. She was a walking "cosmic generative force," the joyous energy of procreation, who fecundated earth and sea and reanimated existence. She inspired art; she "postponed old age."

Celestial superstar that she was, she carried a large entourage in her wake, advertising her primordial, mythic attractions. Along with Eros, Himeros (desire), the Seasons, Graces, and Persuasion, a throng of amorous creatures followed her everywhere. Attended by bees, doves, sparrows, goats, "insatiable panthers," wolves, and dolphins and trailed by a swarm of children from each of her affairs, she announced her divine kinship with the Mistress of the Animals and Mother Goddess.

Of all the Greek goddesses, none approached her multinatured complexity and plentitude. Despite the loss of the creatrix's total wisdom, she still possessed a formidable "mind that ruled over" the gods and got the best of "even the wise." Like her prehistoric ancestress, she "resolved opposites" and "made pale very sort of partialness" with her triumphant wholeness. Besides sensuality and maternity, she combined compassion and vengeance, peace and war, candor and guile, and male and female. She gave birth to the twin-sexed Hermaphroditus, and her rites featured gender bending and an androgynous Aphroditus.

With divine variability, the "shifty-eyed" Aphrodite changed moods and personas as unpredictably as her mother, the sea. By turns cruel and kind, she unleashed hideous persecutions with her blessings. She fomented the ten-year bloodbath of the Trojan War, put her daughter-in-law, Psyche, to the torture, and afflicted the Lemnian women with such a bad smell that their husbands deserted them. At the same time, she saved sailors from the deep, arranged happy marriages, and adopted orphans.

Her most salient trait, though, like Inanna before her, was her gangbusters sexuality. Although the Greeks attempted to domesticate her, she incarnated "*sex,* the sheer amoral drive" of lust and attraction. Misogynistic mythmakers married her off to the hunchbacked Hephaestos and made her guardian of conjugal love. Sculptors subjected her unruly sexuality to Apollonian law and order, freeze-framing her in ideal visions of symmetry and "beauty without extravagance."

But she behaved with supreme disregard for Attic sensitivities. Repudiating respectable femininity—servile marital fidelity, house arrest, and nonpersonhood—she cat-prowled the premises in search of buff gods and men. The second part of her name, *hodites,* means "wanderer." Never raped in a culture that celebrated rape in hymns and odes, she aggressively pursued lovers and took her pleasure with unapologetic "extravagance." She went by the epithet "laughter-loving," a pun on "penis-loving."

She was a lioness on the loose in the Olympian firmament. There was "no resisting her." She could lead astray the "mind of Zeus himself." Warriors dropped their swords, men's knees buckled, and the immortals "gawked" in her presence. When Hera wanted to recapture her husband, Zeus, she turned to Aphrodite for help: "Give me love and desire, the powers by which you yourself subdue mankind and gods alike."

Contrary to modern expectations, Aphrodite didn't zap Hera into a willowy blonde. Proving that she relied on more than her beauty to bewitch men, Aphrodite provided her subjects with a whole system of love artistry. This "complex, learned discipline" incorporated some of the basic precepts of the Seductive Way.

Of the five separate areas of expertise, the first treated the most elementary: the movements and positions of lovemaking, with special emphasis on the ultimate Greek delicacy, *kelēs,* the female-superior "racehorse." Second came singing, dancing, cosmetics, and hygiene, then persuasive speech, followed by the more advanced arts of poetry and recitation. Finally, there were the virtuoso psychological skills: empathy, sensitivity, and all the ruses, "wiles and charms of amorous relations."

To the consternation of the ruling patriarchs, Aphrodite plied her love arts to her heart's content with impunity. Her seductions were no cheap candlelight and negligee affairs. When she went after a man, such as the shepherd Anchises, she rolled out the big effects. She had the Graces bathe, oil, and perfume her and deck her in operatic finery, a gown "brighter than fire-flesh," caught at the waist by a belt figured with sexual scenes, and ornamented with fabulous jewelry. Her necklaces, brooches, earrings, and spiral ringlets—their goldenness proclaiming her associations with honey and seminal fluid—shone before the astonished Anchises "like the moon" when she surprised him on the mountaintop.

A shepherd greeted in such circumstances on the wild scarps of Mount Ida required deft handling. Aphrodite, the "weaver of wiles," did not disappoint. She appeased him with arch flattery, then beguiled him with her golden tongue. Another Scheherazade, she spun an account of herself so colorful, picturesque, and expertly crafted that Anchises listened in rapt fascination. Posing as a virgin princess, she told him she'd been kidnapped by a god to be his bride and accord him honor, riches, and prestige. Filled with "sweet longing" by her words, Anchises bore her to his tent, where she ravished him on a bearskin rug.

At this point Aphrodite, as part of Zeus's revenge, should have become the shepherd's love slave. Instead she resumed her divine identity and shot up to the ridgepole of the tent in all her eight-foot glory. The terrified Anchises reacted with the same thrill of terror as his ancestors in the presence of the goddess—with a Grecian difference. Panicked by the specter of female sexual power, he begged not to be castrated. The obliging Aphrodite reassured him, promised him the consolation prize of a heroic son, and rocketed back to Olympus in a blaze of special effects.

Aphrodite foiled Zeus's attempt to shackle her and thwarted every other patriarchal takedown. When her cuckolded husband, Hephaestos, invented an invisible iron net to capture her flagrante delicto for eternity, her philandering days seemed over. But as soon as the panel of gods saw her in bed with Hermes, they were so overcome with lust they voted to free her. The state proved just as ineffectual in curtailing her power.

Her rites, the most popular in the Mediterranean, proliferated in dozens of forms despite their unofficial, unsanctioned status. All honored different aspects of Aphrodite inherited from past goddesses, with the same riotous abandon to mystical intoxication, revelation, and transfiguration. At one, girls reenacted Inanna's maturity passage, filing through a tunnel to Aphrodite's temple with secret objects on their heads. This likely duplicated ceremonies in which the objects were phalluses, and the celebrations, revels with dildos. (The Greeks took female hypersexuality as an unfortunate given and thought it exceeded men's tenfold.) Another cult restaged the death and annual resurrection of the consort god, Adonis, with the traditional bacchanals afterward.

By far the best known and attended, though, was the spring *aphrodisia*, which commemorated the goddess's birth from the sea. Hundreds of rose-garlanded devotees wended down to the harbor, where an Aphrodite surrogate stripped and submerged herself in the water, thereby summoning the divinity into their midst and revivifying the earth.

After the procession to her temple and tributes of incense and apples, the *pannychis* began: a rapturous carouse of wine drinking, opium taking, feasting, dirty dancing, sambyke and flute playing, and fornicating. Aphrodite's chosen people, the hetaerae, sold their favors that night for a pittance in a diluted, wholesale version of the sacred marriage ceremony. Other festivals ran to greater extremes, including lesbianism, transvestitism, flagellation, and self-castration.

Aphrodite was not the marble poem in symmetry so dear to Greek aesthetes, arrested in an attitude of demure passivity, a hand in front of her pubis and a foot on a tortoise, symbol of female silence and domestic immobility. She was an "awesome power," "greater than a god," who epitomized the tempestuous force of sexual passion in all its splendor and terrible might.

A blood sister to Inanna and her kin, she ran roughshod over patriarchal institutions—a rambling, slick-talking voluptuary and law unto herself. She turned the Greek pantheon and polis upside down and ruled her way, with men in adoration and women released to themselves and their almighty sexuality.

Although downgraded over time into a pale copy of herself,

Aphrodite and her archetype prevailed. There are more figurines of her in the Louvre than all other goddesses combined. Even the Judeo-Christian campaign to eradicate her never completely succeeded. Her capital city, Aphrodisias, was reduced to rubble, her name erased from nearly every surface. By 1357 the Siena residents had smashed her statue to pieces and buried the fragments in neighboring Florence.

She seemed to have been left for dead at last, written out of Western history. But she survived in occultism, magic, folklore, fairy tales, and the erotic imagination—persistent as the tides. Whether we use her name or not, we still petition her, like the ancient Greeks, in our secret erotic prayers: "Give me the kind of song that seduces, please."

Lilith: The Demonization

Since Aphrodite, it's been all downhill for the sex goddess. One of the worst threats to male domination, she's been declassed to a sex toy and slut or demonized as a fiend. With Lilith we can track her mythic decline. According to talmudic lore, Lilith—a big, splashy goddess woman who sneered at female subordination—was Adam's wife before Eve. She insisted on equality, rejected the missionary position, and at last fled in disgust. "Why should I lie beneath you," she demanded, "when I am your equal since both of us were created from dust?"

In high dudgeon she soared off to the Red Sea, where she assembled a crew of male demons more to her liking. Unleashing her female supersexuality, she copulated around the clock, giving birth to a hundred monsters a day. Finally three angels appeared to put a stop to her lascivious living, and she agreed to give up her sex marathon if she could plague mankind for eternity. As the antitype of the divine life force she became the death bringer incarnate. She prowled through the night and throttled children after playing with them. She infested men's dreams so that they spilled the seed of life; she killed them with her kisses.

In one myth, she again preyed on Adam. When he escaped to the desert to atone for his sins, she dogged his steps and tormented him with wet dreams. Not that she felt any nostalgia for him or monogamy. Lilith required the entire population of the Near East to glut her rapacious appetite; she even stooped to Gentiles. Although she began inauspiciously, she eventually worked her way into the bed of God himself. She cast such a potent spell on the almighty that he abandoned his lawful wife, Israel, and set Lilith up in her place, thereby precipitating the destruction of the Temple of Jerusalem. Folk tradition decreed that only the coming of the Messiah would put an end to her depredations. We're still waiting; Lilith and her train of femmes fatales have struck deep roots in Western culture.

Lilith systematically reversed all the positive sexual attributes of the earlier goddesses. Her magic became black; her promiscuity, manic; her supremacy, despotic and satanic. Aphrodite's bestiary, setting, goldenness, and roses turned malevolent. Lilith's animal entourage consisted of jackals, hyenas, and carrion-eating kites, and her preferred oceanic habitat was a "Sea of Blood." Instead of Aphrodite's billowing blond hair, Lilith wore a kind of fright wig, long, snaky tendrils dyed rose red.

As with other erotic deities, Lilith melded genders. But her bisexuality arose from hell and only increased her iniquity. In one account of her birth she sprang to life from the dregs of a satanic wine like an evil hermaphroditic genie. Entwined with her in a single rose-colored shoot was her male half, Samael, with whom she formed a perfect "image of the androgynous deity." But their male-female fusion potentiated their nefarious natures so that they spread villainy tenfold throughout the earth when they separated.

Lilith also preserved traces of the love goddess's totality of being. With protean wizardry, she could assume myriad identities and had the name "mother of a mixed multitude." However, her personas were infernal, and her infinite progeny, the cancerous metastases of an unholy womb. Like the sex goddesses before her, she fancied younger men and took the dominant role. Her preference, though, for little boys, which began in "sport" and ended with asphyxiation, were pedophilic and homicidal.

Lilith perverted the goddess's stewardship of nature as well. Instead of spring verdure, she dispatched diabolic weather fronts from her command post on the Mountains of Darkness. Her name Lil meant "dust storm."

Lilith also dragged the love arts through the mud. As the original saddle tramp she debased and caricatured the principles of erotic attraction. She possessed Inanna's and Aphrodite's seductive eloquence—a suave tongue and words as "smooth [as] oil"—but her blandishments led men to their doom. Behind their backs, she resumed her "real" voice, shrieking so loud the earth shook.

In private she also danced the dance of the damned with her female minions in the desert. Rather than divine roundelays, these demonesses whirled and gyrated with berserker fury, then fell upon one another in pitched battle. Lilith put Aphrodite's wiles to the most depraved purposes. She enticed victims with "the sweet, sensual sounds of cymbals" and feigned a coy virginity that she later disproved with a vengeance. Once bedded, her prey found himself in the clutches of such rarefied sexual delights that he could never be satisfied again. Usually, though, Lilith solved the problem for him by making him impotent or killing him altogether.

Her appearance was as two-faced as her character: beautiful in front, hideous behind like the Frau Welt figurines in medieval cathedrals with their lovely facades and putrescent backsides. Instead of rebirth, she brought decay and annihilation. In one terra-cotta relief, she rises nude, half female, half bird of prey, on the backs of two monkeys. Bewinged and crowned with a tiered tiara, she makes a stop sign with her outstretched arms and fixes us with a Gestapo stare. Death everlasting, all who enter here.

When she dressed up, she pulled another demonic fraud. She stationed herself at the crossroads costumed in goddess wear, a flaming gown with forty ornaments—six earrings in each ear and ropes of Egyptian necklaces. But as soon as she'd ensnared and ravished the unwary, she transmogrified into her terrible self, a tower of fire, denuded of all her trinkets and charms. Sometimes, with a satanic inversion of the deity's snake imagery, she took the form of a serpent, aflame from the waist down, with a dragon and second serpent on her back.

What Lilith gained in gothic frisson and melodrama, she lost in interest and complexity. Without the variegated personas of the earlier goddesses, their contradictions and caprices, Lilith became a cardboard cutout. She was stripped of the seductress's most potent aphrodisiac, her full personhood, her "plentitude of being," with all its mystery, depth, and complication.

Monster of depravity, "Spirit of Defilement," queen of mean, Lilith wore only one color, black. She personified Evil Womanhood and with her Dragon Lady forefinger, pointed mankind to the inevitable holocaust attendant on female sexual autonomy and freedom. Cartoon vamp that she is, though, she has taken up stubborn residence in the Western psyche. Until the nineteenth century people wore amulets to ward off her infernal machinations; her legends circulated for four thousand years, and her demonic stereotype still rears up in films and fiction or whenever a woman takes her sex power too far.

Despite a Gen Y tide of postfeminist sex avengers—bad girls ransacking bars and frat houses—the Lilith model is played out, a passé remnant of old-guard male-dominant societies. There are sexier, happier, more adult erotic exemplars for the twenty-first century. Just as we've cleansed the temple of cipher wives and dumb floozies, we need to exorcise Lilith and recall the sex goddesses.

Whether men admit it or not, these mythic queens of creation are their dream women, and the Seductive Way, established through millennia of goddess-worship, the royal road to their hearts. Since the dawn of history, men have not been content with hog-rutting, soulless carnality. They've hungered for an ideal love object, cut to the divine pattern. Far from the nubile childbearer of neo-Darwinian theory, she was a flashy, hell-on-wheels Ms. Big, Our Lady of Lust.

If archaeology and prehistoric lore are to be believed, she once occupied the catbird seat of the cosmos. She made and contained all that was, jump-started creation, and kept it rolling from death to rebirth with her divine sex energy. A mental titaness, she knew everything and merged multitudes and contraries in her being: masculinity and femininity, maternity and sexuality, consolation and aggression, and constancy and variability. She came on strong, with thunderclaps and kettledrums, and struck awe and wonder into mankind. Men, deep in their erotic circuitry, still crave a woman of her cosmic scale and impact, a charged-up Somebody who electroshocks them with the life spirit and transports them elsewhere. They want the transcendence and redemption of the old ecstatic rites, according to the primordial sacral script.

The Seductive Way might seem antiquated in an age of Turbotongue vibrators, designer faces, insta-sex, image doctors, and love coaches, but it endures in the erotic pathways of the subpsyche. The women who sow heartbreak and love madness trade in charms established at the genesis of sexual desire, when the idea of eros crystallized around a mythic goddess and was played out in her worship services. Men cannot escape the tidal pull of her physical magic: pyrotechnic costumes, lush settings, high maquillage and body care, and hot dance, music, art, and sexpertise. Nor have they lost their thirst for mind spells, the delights of "infinite variety," and the labyrinthine "tortuous path." They prefer the most circuitous, arduous, unexpected, and complicated route home, a "latticework of anticipation," succeeded by a cannonade finale that stands their hair on end. Anything less is blahsville and June Cleaver.

Men may tell us they want a living doll in a hostess apron and quiescence on the home front, but they're programmed otherwise. Their receptors are primed for a numinous empress of excitement, a life pump, and a mover and shaker. Their love lights dim and wink out unless a grandmistress of eros takes them in hand: an ever-variable "Mother Cow" or "Loud Thundering Storm," a replete, holographic charismatician who keeps them as transfixed and fascinated as the mythic goddesses aeons ago.

One of the uses of an archetype is that it provides a "self-portrait of the instinct." The archetypic sex goddesses, with their consistent character traits, symbols, and rites, give us a diagram from Gray's Anatomy so that we can view desire from the bones up. We can see how ego enhancement, maternal nurture, and pain, for example, infiltrated sexual passion and why we're subliminally moved by scent, speech, and food offerings.

Better still, we can read the makeup of the ultimate desirable woman with CAT scan clarity. And she explodes every bimbo-in-bustier image of sex appeal that men have created to suppress us. The mythic archaic seductress defines woman as subject and restores control and pride. Autonomous, smart, proactive, she has no truck with submissive norms and incarnates complete personhood par excellence. A paragon of mental health and maturity, she contains opposites with energy to spare. She plants the flag of female sexual power and flies it from the battlements of heaven and earth.

Psychiatrists have long recognized the therapeutic value of identification with mythic figures, which helps explain the runaway popularity of the goddess movement. But the goddesses usually held up for our admiration are crones, oracles, Amazons, great mothers, and angry fiends like Medusa.

The seductress deities, if and when they're treated at all, have been given short shrift and cleaned up for PG consumption, their sexuality muted and sugarcoated. Most Inanna scholars avert their eyes from her hungry vulva and phallus kissing. In one feminist re-vision of the Lilith story, Lilith washes her hands of sex altogether after she leaves Adam and bonds platonically with other women.

The mythic seductresses not only give our egos a shot in the arm; they purge feminism of this puritanical legacy. They were queens of raunch, vulva-proud divinities who reveled in their hypersexuality and ran with it. Cosmic reminders of women's sexual supremacy, they took charge, reaped the fruits of their anatomy, and put the male population at their mercy.

Feminist critic Mary Ann Doane argues that "everyone wants to be elsewhere than in the female position." It depends on how you see it. If we look at sex goddesses through the ages, they show us another position for women: on top, studs at our feet, aglow with superior personhood, total empowerment, erotic allure, and postcoital bliss. As the hapless singleton in the pop British novel *Dear Goddess* discovers, "It was time to reclaim my pedestal, bring it down from the attic, polish it up, and clamber back on."

CHAPTER THREE

Belles Laides: *Homely Sirens*

Everyone will decidedly prefer and eagerly desire the most beautiful individuals.
—ARTHUR SCHOPENHAUER

Beauty's the thing that counts in women; red lips and black eyes are better than brains. —MARY J. ELMENDORF

The ugly may be beautiful, the pretty never. —PAUL GAUGUIN

The greatest treat for a connoisseur is l'amour d'une laide. —WILHELM DINESEN

You don't have to be born beautiful to be wildly attractive. —DIANA VREELAND

*I*n the farewell dinner scene of Martin Scorsese's *The Age of Innocence,* Michelle Pfeiffer reigns over the table like Aphrodite at a church potluck. Her lover, married to a homely socialite, devours her with his eyes and decompensates when she walks out of his life forever at the end. It's just the opposite, however, in the novel. There the wife, not the other woman, is the picture-perfect beauty. On that final night the real Ellen Olenska looks old, ravaged, and "almost ugly," but her adorer "had never loved her as he did at that minute."

Such a role reversal profanes every romantic sanctity in our culture. It couldn't be more obvious: Ugly women get the short straw in love. They're the dogs, douche bags, gargoyles, and double baggers of comedy club fodder, a synonym for sexual revulsion and women's worst fear. Wherever we turn we hear the stentorian voices of scientists and experts, insisting that beauty delivers the erotic goods, the hunks, and the homes in the Hamptons. Like it or not, biology decrees the survival of the prettiest, the girls with symmetrical baby faces and wolf whistle curves. As Nancy Etcoff and others warn, "If you're unlovely, you're unloved"; "in the sexual domain, the importance of looks cannot be overestimated."

Actually they can and are. Despite the messianic cult of good looks, babes don't have a corner on seduction. In fact, many of the most fascinating and successful seductresses in history were zeroes, with every defect from hooknoses, receding chins, and thin lips with overbites to big bottoms. Their cultures were not less beauty-fixated than our own, but they muscled out the pinups and won the choice men of their age. Although plain, there was nothing drab about them. The French call them *belles laides,* homely women whose charisma, fire, and charms of character transform them into beautiful sirens. They unsettle all our beauty dogmas and reveal an insidious truth: Love is nine-tenths imagination and has "no more to do with lovely than like with likely."

Evolutionary psychologists argue that men choose comely blondes over plain Janes because our earliest ancestors sought the most reproductively fit breeders. But as prehistorians and scholars remind us, eroticism was "primarily a religious matter" to early mankind rather than a copulatory contest for hale offspring. Paleolithic peoples knew a pretty face when they saw one. The 36,000 B.C. Brassempouy Lady has the sweetheart features of a computer-generated FacePrint fantasy: symmetrical, wide-set doe eyes, short straight nose; and tiny jaw. Anthropologist H. R. Hays believes these people were probably a "very handsome" race.

But the objects of their sexual worship lacked any trace of conventional beauty. The relics recovered from temple sites are a lineup of malproportioned goddesses, symbolically distorted to proclaim their divine sex energy and cosmic grandeur. Buttocks balloon from stick torsos, mountainous breasts flop over Michelin Man bellies, and thunder thighs bracket vulvas the size of footballs.

By Neolithic times these idols had acquired faces, but they were grotesque snakes' and birds' heads that depicted the deity's animal incarnations. If evolution decreed babes for transient impregnations, it decreed these "unshapely, weird," and asymmetric goddesses for love objects. They, not pretty breeders, were the images that snared men's hearts, fired their loins, and vaulted them to mystical union with the almighty. Nor has this primordial fascination disappeared; it persists underground in the collective unconscious, in folk tales and art, ready for access.

Belles laides, then, slipped past the beauty screen and surprised men at the precivilized depths of the libido. They also laid the biggest mind trip. Without the standard attractions of looks, they sank their resources into the Seductive Way. Its ultimate test case, they prove, without question, the supremacy of lovecraft and disprove every canard about the natural triumph of artless blondes in romance. To replace beauty, they constructed characters, each of which bore an uncanny likeness to their mythic archetypes, the Neolithic beast goddesses.

Isabella Stewart Gardner, 1840–1924

The "Serpent of the Charles," she stood at the top of a massive horseshoe staircase. Dressed in skintight black velvet, the infamous Isabella Stewart Gardner, "the idol of men and envy of women," presided over the 1903 gala opening of her museum palace, Fenway Court. It was a classic Isabella moment. One by one the august Boston Brahmins mounted the steep stairs and climbed down again to pay their respects. Waiters served champagne and doughnuts as the Boston Symphony played Mozart overtures. Then at the climax of the "party of the century" Isabella strode through the great hall with her entourage of "Museum Boys" and flung open the double doors. A collective gasp went up from the crowd. Inside they found a tropical wonderland, a soaring three-story courtyard lit by the moon and red lanterns and filled with palms and statuary. The psychologist William James described it as a religious moment, a "gospel miracle."

But it was a miracle from no Christian Gospel. Isabella Stewart

Gardner loosed the pagan snake goddess into the Boston temple of high culture. An avatar of the Stone Age lunar serpent deity, she incarnated the disruptive, dynamic principle of life energy and creativity. She was, as her doctor noted, a mythic "corpse reviver"; she regenerated the dead. Like the earliest images of this divinity, she was nonpretty to an extreme. In an age that deified feminine pulchritude and preached that nothing was "more powerful . . . than personal beauty," she looked painfully plain: a fisted-up simian face, asymmetric pale eyes, and a thin, downturned mouth. Her nickname, Belle, seemed a cruel joke.

Yet this homely woman with a sad-sack, lusterless face had a serious "way with men." Not only did she hook Boston's prize catch, Jack Gardner, who idolized her throughout their long marriage, but she attracted a permanent Praetorian guard of strapping bluebloods and prominent artists. Wherever she went, admirers swarmed around her, memorializing her in books and paintings and loading her with love tributes. "She throws out her lariat," said a newspaper of her strange allure, "and drags after her chariot the brightest men in town, young and old, married and single."

Besides virtuosic seductive arts, Belle's secret weapon was her goddess-born vitality. "I may not be so beautiful as Diana," boasts her alter ego in a novel, "but I am sure I am much more alive than she is." Such raging high spirits did not make for a tranquil childhood. Despite her aristocratic pretensions, Belle came from a bourgeois Brooklyn family that made good in ironworks and lavished its newfound fortune on their only daughter. Her father's favorite, she was indulged in all her whims—gymnastics, music, language, dance lessons, and "fine clothes." Even so, she was an obstreperous rule breaker and troublemaker. She ran off to join the circus, walked home from church in her bare feet, and generally raised cain, roughhousing with boys and throwing temper tantrums.

By her teens she was a devil for men. She hit on her Italian professor and seduced one of the most sought-after undergraduates at Harvard. The rich, stunning Jack Gardner had never met anyone as plain as Belle when his sister introduced them in Paris. But he underestimated her "glorious vitality." Before he knew it, she'd bewitched him with her quick movements and bright conversation and made him roar with laughter. Defying his family, he dropped out of Harvard and married her on the sly, an escapade later covered up by a full-dress wedding in 1860 and suppressed for generations.

Bringing Belle back to Boston was like introducing a bucking bronco into a Back Bay china shop. She systematically smashed every time-honored custom. She slept until ten, snubbed the sewing circle, and violated the sacred code of female immobility: She rode, swam, and worked out. More heinously, she claimed a room of her own and entertained gentleman callers at all hours, including a prizefighter just to "feel his flexed muscles."

In this bastion of American prudery, she told off-color jokes in mixed company, smoked Turkish cigarettes, and brazenly flirted. She arrived at cotillions decked in corsages from admirers and hogged the floor, dancing in the center of the ballroom (a practice called chandeliering) with "all the festive stags."

After the tragic death of her infant son she began the practice of biannual trips abroad. On these binges, her husband bought her whatever her heart desired: artworks, rare pearls (in a string that eventually hung to her waist), and a Worth wardrobe that included clingy black décolleté sheaths at a time when ladies wore cameo chokers and crinolines. Amid his wife's flirtatious romps, Jack remained the smitten, faithful paladin. Only once did an extracurricular amour try his patience.

The man was "one of the handsomest men" on two continents, the novelist and bon vivant Francis Marion Crawford. Frank met Belle, thirteen years his senior, on an 1882 trip to Boston to find a wife, and ended up in her clutches for two years. In this liaison Belle deployed two other primordial lures of the Snake Goddess: intellect and mother love. At their daily tête-à-têtes in her "boudoir," she talked literature and history and read Dante to him in her "musical, mellow voice." Just as seductively, she encouraged his literary talents and nursed him through his first novel, which she bound in lavender and fastened with silver buckles.

Under the horrified gaze of Proper Boston, they rode out in public, monopolized each other at balls, and behaved like lovers. Very likely they were. They spent the summer together at her Beverly estate, made unchaperoned visits to New York, wore identical bracelets with erotic Italian mottoes, and destroyed their letters. Frank said his "only worth" was that "he loved her so dearly," wrote sonnets to her "beauty," and featured her in a novel as "the most charming woman in the world," a plain, fiery seductress who plots to leave her husband for a dashing lover. Maybe they contemplated some such move.

In any event, Jack snapped out of his uxorious swoon and broke up the affair. This, though, seems to have been Gardner's last stand as a dragon at the marital gate. Afterward he withdrew discreetly to the sidelines, content to plan Belle's parties, provide her with jewels and affection, and fund her passions.

At midlife these took a fresh turn. Shedding and assuming identities like snakeskins, Belle moved from muse to genius and social anarch to a creator herself. America's first "lady architect" and "proto-interior designer," she designed not only a "startling," award-winning garden in Beverly but an Italian palace that pioneered an entirely "new kind of museum in America." At Fenway Court great paintings were hung for the first time in an intimate setting with fine furniture and decorative art amid connecting galleries, each with its distinct character.

With creative reciprocity, Belle continued to foster and promote other artists. Her intimate friend Henry James immortalized her as Isabel Archer in *Portrait of a Lady,* and painters Anders Zorn and John Singer Sargent did their best portraits of her. Sargent's *Woman—An Enigma* captured all her erotic numinosity and created such a scandal it had to be removed from St. Botolph's Club. Belle stands in a plunging gown before a gold mandala with a Mona Lisa half smile on her parted lips.

Unlike many plain-featured women who grow handsome in age, Belle deteriorated physically. "Battered, depleted, [and] disfigured," she worsened the effect with a blond wig, pancake makeup, and bizarre costumes that included a pair of diamonds on long antennas that bobbed from her head. But she was still "the very incarnation of life" and catnip to men.

On her travels, flocks of liege men succumbed to her "spell" and accompanied her everywhere. In Venice a blond artist-god squired her through the palazzi, and in Bombay seven men motored out to her ship with gold and silver gift baskets filled with chocolate Champagne bottles. At home she acquired so many devotees that wits called them the Isabella Club and the Museum Boys. An observer remembered seeing her in the center of a ballroom with "ten or a dozen of the leading male members of Boston society, just like flies around honey." One wrote her: "I shall always worship you as . . . the most life-enhancing person, the most lovable person on earth."

Time did not mellow this fractious "specimen of vital nature." She promenaded down Beacon Street with a lion named Rex, appeared at a costume party in Persian dress on the back of an elephant, and barreled through town in her automobile, scattering terrified pedestrians and swearing like a stevedore in four languages. She championed tabooed causes—the gay and African American communities—and alone defended Karl Muck, the composer, against false charges of being a German spy.

She profaned the first law of ladyhood: "Never *ever* behave with pride, self-confidence, and self-conceit." She wore the crown of the Snake Goddess with lofty hubris and complete indifference to female hostility. She traced her ancestry to Mary, Queen of Scots, identified herself with the two great Isabellas of history, and orchestrated a royal funeral for herself with her coffin carried "high—as for a queen."

Bernard Berenson called Belle "a miracle." With her "proclivity for the primitive and archaic," she might have glimpsed her primordial appeal. She played the moon goddess in an amateur theatrical and treasured a poem her last lover wrote to her comparing her to the moon, the emblem of the dynamic, self-renewing she-serpent. She placed a mosaic of the Medusa's head at the center of the courtyard of her museum. This misunderstood "ugly deity" actually was a Snake Goddess whose "lovely terrible face slew [men] by the eye; it fascinated." Belle Gardner may not have lived up to her full seductive potential. She probably got less sex than she wanted and failed many character tests. She was a snob, a robber baroness, an autocrat, a histrionic, and an insufferable bully. But she fascinated. As a local paper put it, "the spell of Mrs. Jack's enthrallment cannot be broken." Beauty was beside the point.

The second most common images of the primordial goddess after snakes were birds, grotesque beaked idols with popped eyes, anthill breasts, and wings or winglike epaulets on their shoulders. Sometimes they had elongated bodies with vast, ovoid buttocks, designating the deity's role as creatrix, layer of the cosmic egg. In her avian guise, the goddess again embodied the life force and libidinal energy of creation; bird-masked figures in one cave painting dance around a man with an erection. As the divinity evolved, distinct species—owls, hawks, and waterbirds—assumed different aspects of her being.

Waterbirds, for example, represented her healing and life-giving properties, with special emphasis on material goods and happiness. In this category, swans led the flock, incarnating desire (with their phallic necks), poetry, and the power of transformation. One group of swan figurines from prehistoric Greece compresses these meanings and suggests another—the spirit of comedy, that most primal of aphrodisiacs. The bell divinities were the holy clowns of the prehistoric pantheon; their goofball heads with jug ears and bug eyes tower up on necks attached to domed bodies with pea-size breasts.

Catherine Sedley, 1657–1717

Catherine Sedley, wag and wench extraordinaire, might have taken these antic idols for her mascot. In a charitable light, Catherine looked merely humorous. A flat-chested string bean, she was the antitype of the Stuart England beauty ideal—plump butter blondes with snub noses, rosebud mouths, and full *poitrines*. She had dark hair, a long nose, an unfashionably big mouth, and a walleye that made her squint. "The weapons at her disposal," writes her biographer, "included neither beauty nor any other attraction to the outward eye." To a man, everyone found her "very ugly." But with her artillery—the id-seeking missiles of laughter–she needed little else. Through her comedic charms, she conquered any lord she wanted, including James II, whose passion for her bordered on lunacy.

Catherine was born in 1657 into a household that would have knocked the stuffing out of a lesser being. The only daughter of Restoration hellrake and poet Sir Charles Sedley, she grew up both "notoriously plain" and party to an incessant donnybrook of brawls, bacchanalias, and violent parental squabbles. While her father roistered around England, her mother spiraled into insanity until she entered a madhouse in Catherine's early teens. At this low point in her life Sir Charles consoled his daughter by introducing a common-law wife into the family and ejecting Catherine from the house.

She landed a job with a beautiful Italian princess her age, Mary of Modena, who'd just married James, duke of York, heir to the British throne. Before long the scampish Catherine had made a name for herself at court. Having inherited her father's poetic and hedonistic proclivities, she became known as the "shocking creature"–"none the most virtuous but a witt." Her glaring defects of face and figure did not affect her popularity with men; she received more than her share of marriage proposals, including one from a prosperous, well-heeled widower.

But the brazen jade, unenchanted by the seventeenth-century marital bargain in which women surrendered their legal identities, money, and autonomy to husbands, rejected them all. She even backsassed suitors with impunity. When a dumpee, Lord Dorset, avenged her with satiric verses, accusing her of hurting men's eyes with her ugly face and nasty squint, she fired back with a stinging pasquinade of her own. One of his slurs, however, hit the mark: Catherine's "cupid" was no angelic cherub but a "Black-guard boy," an uncouth, foultongued, insurrectionary street urchin.

This seems to have been just the sort of ruffian imp designed to mug her employer. The forty-four-year-old duke of York was handsomer, braver, kinder, and a more avid womanizer than his brother Charles II, himself a world-class Casanova. James stood six feet two inches and had a long roster of conquests, some famous beauties. But Catherine threw him for a loop. She supplied a tonic he could not live without, the liberation of laughter. Casting the curative spell of the archaic bell divinities, she released him from the royal straitjacket.

She serenaded him with her father's lewd drinking songs on the virginal, mocked his Roman Catholic pieties, bombarded him with coarse zingers, and roasted him to his face. "We [James's mistresses] are none of us handsome," she wisecracked, "and if we had wit, he has not enough to discover it."

While the beautiful Mary of Modena pined away in jealous melancholia and his priests and advisers stormed, James could not be parted from Catherine or her bed. Whatever she did there, she clearly had her patron deity's appetite. In James's absences, she disported with the keeper of the privy purse, a young beefcake named Colonel James Grahame. She gave birth to at least two children during these coterminous affairs, one (who died) by James and another, a girl, by the colonel. Characteristically, she needled her daughter. "You need not be so proud," she gibed, "for you are not the king's but old Grahame's."

Once installed in office, James II faced a massive campaign to oust Catherine. The combined forces of church and state descended on him with horrendous threats and admonitions. To no avail. He settled a huge pension on her and gave her a mansion on St. James's Square, which she fitted out with carte blanche splendor, hiring the best artists and craftsmen in England. When he made her countess of Dorchester and Baroness Darlington, though, he went too far, and a goon squad bundled her off to Ireland. After six months she sneaked back to the king who continued to see her in secret.

His abdication in the 1688 Glorious Revolution should have sent her to the Tower. But the doughty Catherine sweet-talked his enemies and demanded her pension and property back. Because of the "favor" (perhaps amorous) she found "in the eyes of King William" and her persuasive powers in Parliament, she succeeded in both.

By now, in her late thirties, Catherine's looks were a shipwreck. Rail thin, her "wither'd" features caked with white paste and cochineal, she prowled the social scene festooned in yards of "embroidery, fringe, and lace." Diamonds spangled on her, jested a courtier, like rancid spots on rotten veal. Except for her comic spark, she had few ostensible feminine charms, not even a fortune. Again, though, her "wit and humor" carried the day. She promptly captured the star bachelor in the kingdom, Sir David Colyear, a kind, charming Scottish baronet with "a great deal of wit" himself.

Their marriage ushered in a new phase in Catherine's off-color, irreverent career. Appropriating the swan divinity's transformational privilege, she morphed into a loving wife and mother, the archetypic creatrix, "giver of life, nourishment, warmth, and protection." Wealthy and adored, she gave vent to her innate tenderheartedness, championing the poor and doting on her two sons. Neither her sex appeal nor her humor deserted her. When she dispatched her boys to boarding school, she quipped, "If anybody calls either of you the son of a whore you must bear it for you are so: but if they call you bastards, fight till you die; for you are an honest man's sons."

With the mythic waterbird's command of material goods, she astutely managed the family business, attracting more than professional admiration from the master of the mint. On one of her husband's brief absences, a Mr. Conduitt wrote honeyed verses to console her. Rigged out in "great splendor," she tottered around Bath until 1717 and survived to skewer the archbishop of Canterbury at George I's coronation. When he asked the consent of the people, she barked, "Does the old Fool think Anybody here will say no to his Question when there are so many drawn swords?"

Stuart England was no playground for women. Derided as the "softer sex" and "weaker vessel," they were at the legal mercy of their husbands and condemned to silence, passivity, niceness, and mindless household pursuits. With every strike against her, including a gothic childhood, the walleyed, nonpretty Catherine Sedley pulled a stunning gender break and brought down the prize men.

She mesmerized James II into the strongest passion of his life and won a dream husband, all the while making a mockery of female norms, the double standard, and male oppression. A caustic loudmouth and pushy virago, she saw herself with perfect clarity. She swanned around, sure of her superiority and the "extraordinary part she played in English history."

Lord Dorset, her ex-suitor, lashed her with scurrilous verses for decades. "What strange mysterious spell," he snarled, could she have possibly cast on "sacred James"? It was a spell more ancient than he could have imagined and more sacred than kingship: the charm of the harlequinesque bird goddess with her divine life, loin, and health-reviving laughter.

Besides swans and waterfowl, owls haunted the primitive religious imagination. With their eerie shrieks, soundless flights through the night sky, and deadeye vision, they personified the goddess as death wielder. In the archaic cyclic scheme of things, of course, this included the miraculous power of rebirth. The prehistoric idol, the Owl-Headed Madonna of Cyprus, cradles newborn life in her arms, a tadpole creature that gapes at her in helpless adoration. She stares straight ahead with artillery-target eyes, decked in high-fashion regalia. She wears three stylish chokers, a geometrically patterned bikini (to mark her overly endowed libido), and four hoop earrings in double-pierced Minnie Mouse ears.

Wallis Windsor, 1895–1986

This obscure Bronze Age figurine, better than all the psychospeculations, contains the clue to the outlandish sexual power of Wallis Warfield Simpson. She was just as bizarre and ungainly looking as the Cypriot Madonna—"flat and angular," with "large startled eyes" and an à la mode wardrobe. She had a strong sex drive, drew a stern bead on her goals, and clutched to her breast the same babe, the duke of Windsor, who abdicated the throne for her sake. Maternal owl deity charms, however, didn't account for Wallis's entire allure; she deployed seductive arts of an advanced order. For a *belle laide* of such admitted limitations—superficiality, intellectual arrest, to name a few—her hit list of inamorati strains credulity. Wallis, almost literally, could peg any man she wanted.

Since she invented social X-ray chic, she seems less plain now than she did seventy-five years ago, when curvy, whipped cream Kewpie dolls were the rage. Nicknamed Minnehaha, she had an Aztec nose, hatchet jaw, bushy eyebrows, and a "masculine figure."

Homeliness wasn't her only problem. Born out of wedlock in 1895 to a Baltimore couple who married seventeen months later, Wallis lost her father to tuberculosis at two and spent the rest of her childhood on the move with an impecunious mother. Dependent on the charity of in-laws, her mother sewed for the Women's Exchange and took in boarders in a modest apartment house.

Thanks to a generous uncle, Wallis attended fashionable schools, but she grew up with the sting of financial insecurity and a poor relative complex. A scrappy tomboy, she was a preemptive striker with a will to climb. Instead of "Mama," her first words were "me-me" and her dolls, named Mrs. Astor and Mrs. Vanderbilt. Under her mother's tutelage, she learned the guerrilla arts of southern charm—flattery, flirtation, small talk, and rococo self-presentation. Vivacious and quick-witted with an intriguing bad-girl edge, she "oozed sex appeal like an old-fashioned burner stove radiates heat."

Beginning in grade school, she attracted boys "the way molasses attracts flies." At fifteen she made her first conquest. Although the "least pretty" of her friends, she enamored the designated dreamboat of the group, a patrician high school senior. When she "came out"—courtesy of a blackmail threat to her uncle—she collected "more beaux than any other girl in town." Harsh-featured and plain as she was, she managed to decorate the front of her stylish gowns with fraternity pins and snag Baltimore's premier bachelor, Carter Osborne, who loved her "wildly" and considered himself engaged to her for three years.

Yet for all her lovecraft and primordial dazzle, Wallis lacked the owl goddess's clear vision. In a heated moment she picked Mr. Wrong. Soon after her 1916 marriage to air ace Earl Winfield Spencer, she found she'd acquired an alcoholic, a bounder, and a sadistic wife beater. As their union unraveled over the next eight years, Wallis man-shopped, seducing a succession of Washington diplomats—an Italian ambassador, an Argentinean playboy, a naval attaché, and a future foreign minister—and living in China in a ménage à trois with Herman Rogers, who thought her "the great love of his life."

A divorce and several conquests later, she married a second time. Ernest Simpson, a starchy shipping magnate with a pseudo-English accent, left his ailing wife for Wallis and moved with her to England. In London, flush at last, Wallis upclassed herself into a Lady who Lunched, hobnobbing with nobility and throwing chichi parties. At her celebrated dinners she provided jaded British aristocrats with piquant cuisine—southern soul food—and an unbuttoned ambiance that made them feel like "boy[s] let out of school."

Inevitably the most incarcerated boy in Britain found his way there as if by psychic radar. David Windsor, next in line to the throne and international heartthrob, lived in a correctional institution called Buckingham Palace. Neglected and bullied as a child, he was a lost soul trapped in the body of a prince. Wallis held the master key. The moment he met her, she cut through the ceremony and protocol and answered his polite inquiry about British heating with a sharp wisecrack: "Every American woman who comes to your country is always asked the same question. I'd hoped for something more original from the Prince of Wales."

After that she became his "oxygen"; he "could not breathe without her." He dropped his beautiful mistress and practically moved in with the Simpsons. In Wallis's company he bloomed; her frank country bluntness dissolved pretense, her relaxed style dispelled inhibitions, and her risqué jokes and parodies of the royal family made him laugh out loud. Sexually he was reborn. Underendowed and prey to obscure dysfunctions and perversions, he'd never been fully satisfied until Wallis came along with her Fang-Chung Shu and Taoist Kegels. To commemorate a particularly raunchy session in the bathtub, he gave her a gold bracelet inscribed with intimate code words.

But her chief fascination for David was her maternal allure. Famished for parental affection, he basked in her motherly ministrations and affections. On his visits to her London flat she treated him like a favorite son: She plumped his cushions, concocted special highballs, and led him to the kitchen for home-cooked midnight treats. Later she micromanaged his health with the solicitude of a supernanny, bundling him up against the cold and leaving a typed schedule of his daily activities on his plate each day. With her deft ego massage and empathetic ear, she released him from the stranglehold of his neuroses. "Home," he always said, "is where the duchess is," and he died in Wallis's arms with the word "mother" on his lips.

After David's abdication of the throne in 1936 to marry "the woman he loved," their life together devolved into a long café society odyssey signifying nothing. Night bird that she was, Wallis dined and danced her evenings away with titled swells. Without the visionary faculty of *intelletto,* without the rebellious punch of her youth, she succumbed to a dreary status grope and reinvented herself as a "beautiful person." Unlike most seductresses, she shirked the job of self-growth and wasted her substance in bridge, shopping, best-dressed lists, seating charts, and superhousekeeping. As to be expected, such betrayal took its toll. With age, the "rending beak and flashing eye" of the owl goddess grew more prominent. She became testy and shrill with the duke and subjected him to a sordid five-year passade with the bisexual Woolworth heir Jimmy Donahue, noted for such pranks as placing his penis on restaurant tables and requesting the chef to cut it thinly.

Yet despite all this—Wallis's ferocity, infidelities, and developmental failures—the duke remained "as much in love with her as ever" for forty years. He showered her with one-of-a-kind jewels, catered to her wishes, and called her "the perfect woman." With typical seductress conceit, she agreed with him and regarded herself as a "surrogate queen." She weathered royal censure, media smears, and banishment to Eurotrash purgatory with her ego unfazed. "It would take four ordinary duchesses," she said airily, "to make one Duchess of Windsor."

Of course she asked for it. Yet she's been savaged more brutally than almost any woman of the twentieth century. Like the bad wife of Welsh folklore turned into an owl for her adultery, Wallis has been villainized as "the ugly, miserable bird hated by all the others." She and the original owl goddess were demonized for the same reason—too much female sovereignty, in too strange a vessel. "She got him by witchcraft," snorted her beautiful female rival; "there's no other explanation." True, Wallis wasn't the "perfect woman," but there was an "explanation": the mythic Owl-Headed Madonna with her beak, jewels, sharpshooter eyes, and captive boy child clasped to her chest.

Tullia d'Aragona, 1505–1556

An earlier avatar of this Cypriot Madonna escaped Wallis's failings and surpassed her on every count. Truer to the owl goddess's archetype, Tullia d'Aragona was the "Intellectual Queen" of sixteenth-century Italy and "the most celebrated" of Renaissance courtesans—a fully realized seductress. Without Wallis's social and erotic myopia, she saw clearly the lay of the land and homed in on her own happiness, freedom, and self-actualization.

The unsightly Tullia chose her time and place badly. Renaissance Italy, seized by beauty mania, believed looks mirrored the soul and enshrined lovely women as divinities. "Overly tall," Tullia had no curves and a long face with a large, thin-lipped mouth and hooked nose. Beauties of the idolized variety—petite, bosomy Botticelli blondes—crowded her chosen métier, the sex trade. But she outstripped them all. Nearly every important figure of the cinquecento fell in love with her, poets lauded her, and the populace treated her like a celebrity.

Tullia was born to Giulia Ferrarese, "the most famous beauty of her day," and the cardinal of Aragon. Her mother, herself a courtesan, must have wept bitter tears over her homely daughter, but the cardinal took her in hand and educated her as a boy, permitting Tullia to pass "her childhood in diligent study." She proved an infant prodigy; when her mother's "very learned" guests visited, they listened to her "arguments and disputations" with nothing short of "stupor."

Mental precocity, however, didn't pay the bills. As Tullia matured, her mother supplemented her studies with master classes in the arts of seduction—a dynamite combination. Her first foray into the field at eighteen couldn't have been worse timed. Rome, just sacked by Charles I's marauding army, was swept up in a tide of penitential prudery, and swarmed with pretty girls from the provinces. Amazingly, though, Tullia prospered in this miserable climate. With shrewd perspicacity, she niche marketed herself as the "intellectual courtesan" and reached the top of the profession within four years.

More than cerebral fascinations alone accounted for Tullia's astonishing rise. Like other *belles laides,* she worked her fashion sense, an age-old substitute for natural beauty. When pile-it-on excess—fringed high clogs, gold brocades, and stem to stern jewelry—was in vogue, she dressed more "divinely" than anyone. As Moretto da Brescia's portrait of her illustrates, she cultivated signature elegance: She wears a pale blue dress with an ermine throw knotted roguishly on one shoulder and holds a royal scepter like a quill. Instead of earrings or ornaments, ropes of pearls and blue ribbons enlace her braided coiffure.

Her eyes, as befitted an owl goddess, were her strongest feature. Sparkling with "devilish" animation, they "skipped about [and] inflamed men's hearts." Although she lavished maternal succor on lovers, who hymned her as "home," "womb," and "repose," Tullia had a sharp beak. In seduction she played rough. She lured senior intellectuals to her salon, charmed them with her conversation and lute playing, then refused to deliver in bed. She made all her clients suffer a "thousand trials." The maximum difficulty principle paid: Suitors and beaux followed her around town "like hungry greyhounds," and the most distinguished thinkers, poets, and diplomats besieged her. "She knows everything," they proclaimed, "and she can talk about anything that interests you."

In 1531 Tullia landed the beau ideal of the Renaissance world, Filippo Strozzi, a Florentine banking magnate who'd broken the heart of Italy's loveliest courtesan, Camilla Pisana. With Tullia, however, he met his match. She so unstrung him that he shared state secrets with her, neglected his diplomatic negotiations in Rome, and had to be recalled to Florence. None of his "other mistresses" ever exerted more "influence" over him. Other picky womanizers followed Filippo. Ippolito de' Medici adored her and wrote her love sonnets, and a young hotspur, Emilio Orsini, founded a Tullia Society of six cavaliers for her honor and protection.

After six banner years Tullia left Rome and moved to Firenzuola, where she had a child of unknown paternity. Her next venue was Venice, easily the most competitive stage in Europe. Almost a hundred thousand courtesans cruised the canals, catering to the Venetian taste for the "bottom, breasts and body" of fifteen-year-olds. Tullia, at thirty, was thinner and uglier than ever.

Once more, though, she prevailed and bagged the top artistic gun of the city, poet Bernardo Tasso. When a local dramatist featured them in a dialogue (then the literary rage), Tullia gained nationwide fame as the penultimate courtesan, renowned for her brains and "charm of manner." Her part in the dialogue puts her in a ravishing light. Tart, smart, and salty-tongued, she carries her learning lightly and debunks her partner's high-flown theories of love and courtesanry. "Let's leave out the poetry," she chides, then details the hazards of the job and proposes a sense-based love philosophy.

The next year Tullia tackled an equally brutal theater of operations, Ferrara, the festive capital of arts and culture. In this siege she displayed her genius for public relations. She saturated the city with advance publicity, rented the finest villa, and talked, sang, and entertained so magnificently that citizens raved that no "man or woman in these parts [was] her equal."

On the first Sunday of Lent she stopped traffic by sweeping into church in penitent's robes with a retinue of adolescent boys and followed it up with a rebuke in verse to the priest for his invective against pleasure. The campaign worked. Italy's two literary lions, Girolamo Muzio and Ercole Bentivoglio, both fell in love with her. Muzio regarded her as the woman of his life and wrote five passionate eclogues to "Thalia," his "beautiful Nymph." When Muzio left Ferrara, Bentivoglio stepped in with perfervid verses of his own, carving Tullia's name on every tree on the Po River. By the time she left Ferrara four years later, at least one man had attempted suicide over her.

Tullia finally ended up in Florence after a brief marriage to a nameless Sienese. Now dispossessed of her wealth and approaching forty, her luck seemed to have run out. *Volupté* blondes on the make overran this brilliant banking and cultural center, and she was without letters of introduction, with a daughter and mother to support.

Tullia, though, astutely targeted the intellectual kingpin of Florence and bombarded him with flattering sonnets. Benedetto Varchi bit and was soon joined by the rest of the cultural elite. Once more the "Queen of Courtesans," Tullia filled her coffers and turned her home into a philosophic academy for the cognoscenti. She took up serious writing and published a dialogue and two well-received verse collections.

So much concentrated power—intellectual, social, and erotic—in a woman who desecrated aesthetic sanctities cried for punishment. Twice enemies denounced her to the authorities, and twice friends got her off, but a third time she wasn't so lucky. Only an abject appeal to a Florentine duchess saved her from disgrace and the stigmata of the yellow veil. Still, most people thought her a witch; a famous poet claimed to have seen her in a black robe, throwing handfuls of salt on a fire and incanting the names of the hearts she wanted to incinerate.

Tullia, without a doubt, worked magic. A shot of her primordial voodoo and lovers saw her as a raving beauty. "You are young and beautiful," one wrote in her late thirties; "your face resembles that of the first angel." That "first angel" was the prehistoric bird deity.

Tullia, "more queenly than the queen," prided herself on her long, noble lineage, not guessing how long or noble. "Monster, miracle, sibyl!" a poet called her. Descendant of the earliest monster goddess and later sibyl, she was a miracle of her time, an ugly stepsister who englamored herself, won all the princes, and transcended her age and feminine destiny.

Thérèse Lachmann, 1819–1884

No one has ever found an explanation for the paranormal sex appeal of the Second Empire courtesan La Paiva, née Thérèse Lachmann. "Fierce and hawk-like," she was thick-waisted and grim-visaged without a shred of standard female charm. But she exercised a fatal fascination on nineteenth-century men, becoming the "queen of kept women" and the beloved wife of the richest man in Europe. Her uncanny sexual pull ran deep; like other *belles laides,* she tapped into the primitive wellsprings of the male libido.

Just as her critics charged, she was a "monstrous archetype"—another death deity, the carrion-eating she-vulture. Her Neolithic icon, the Bird-Headed Goddess of 6000 B.C., is not meant for calm contemplation. "Ugly, elegant, and remote," it has the chilling aspect of a thief in a nylon stocking mask: torpedo breasts, a fat phallic neck, and a bullet-shaped face with slit eyes. Yet this eerie creature paradoxically incarnated the "lusts of the flesh"; "desire [was] her charioteer."

While the she-vulture personified the erotics of death—the link between sex ecstasy and extinction—she also served a host of positive functions. With the ur-goddess's characteristic ambivalence, she transmuted base metal into gold, epitomized the maternal spirit, and raised men from the dead. The goddess Isis beat the breath of life into her dead husband with her flaring hawk wings. Carrion divinities too could transform themselves; the crows, hawks, and vultures that wheeled over battlefields often assumed the shapes of beautiful young maids.

La Paiva looked just as forbidding as her mythic noir counterpart. She had jet black hair and a crudely modeled face with a male jawline, froglike eyes, and a thick, bulbous Mongolian nose. She hated dogs, cats, and children, worshiped Mammon, terrorized employees, and bored guests with her vulgar braggadocio. She came almost literally from the gutter, where she was conceived, said enemies, by a witch and a broom handle.

Her parents, poor Jewish weavers, raised her in a squalid Moscow ghetto without education or prospects and married her off at seventeen to a consumptive tailor. After the birth of her first child in 1837, Thérèse broke and ran. She moved to the red-light slums of Paris where thousands of prostitutes scrambled like crabs in a bucket for survival. Without entry-level looks, she faced certain ruin. Thérèse, however, believed in the spoon-bending power of will. She spent three years locked in concentration in her garret, willing her success into being. "All of my wishes," she said, came "to heel, like tame dogs."

The first was a thoroughbred. In 1841 she descended on a spa in Ems in a borrowed wardrobe and nabbed the famous, wealthy concert pianist Henri Herz. Thanks to her three-year seduction-intensive and "rare, disturbing" sex appeal, she held on to him for half a decade. The affair would have lasted longer except that when she brought Henri to the brink of bankruptcy, his parents intervened and forcibly drove her from the premises.

After a lean stretch Thérèse remobilized her willpower. The night before her campaign, the writer Théophile Gautier found her surveying her "arsenal of clothes" like a general before battle. "I am not badly equipped, am I?" she said. But "I may misfire," and asked for a vial of chloroform in case she failed.

Failure, however, wasn't in Thérèse's vocabulary. On her first night in London she landed Lord Stanley in the next box at Covent Garden. He led to bigger game—namely, a Portuguese marquis, Albino Paiva, who fell "madly in love with her" and married her. His wedding night, though, held a diabolic surprise. Spreading her hawk wings, Thérèse told him she'd attained the position she wanted whereas he'd acquired a prostitute. "You go back to Portugal," she commanded. "I shall stay here with your name and remain a whore."

The obliging Albino trundled home and later committed suicide. La Paiva meanwhile widened her offensive and hauled in ever-richer princes, dukes, and captains of industry. As aggressive a "snatcher" as her tutelary deity, she stalked her prey with craft, cunning, and guile. To win Count Guido Henckel von Donnersmarck, a "magnificent human stallion" worth billions, she logged months on the road and spent three hundred thousand francs. She trailed him from St. Petersburg to Naples, pretending to ignore him and making herself as conspicuous as possible.

When no respectable women wore makeup, she powdered her black hair blond and painted her face like a "tightrope-dancer." She wore *bouchons de carafe* (diamonds the size of decanter stoppers) and furs thrown over cashmere gowns with shoulder straps designed to fall off and reveal her deep cleavage and the "reddish hair under her arms." Transfixed by her "strange and voluptuous beauty," Guido at last came around and fell "in love to such an extent, to such a degree" that he offered her his entire fortune if she would live with him. Her bedcraft probably sweetened the pot. So renowned were her sexual performances that one man agreed to a session lasting until ten thousand francs in notes burned in her grate.

When La Paiva accepted Guido, he lived up to his end of the bargain and made her "the greatest debauchee of the century." In keeping with her mythic persona, she had a Midas touch. A hawk-eyed businesswoman, she multiplied Guido's fortune to such proportions that she "couldn't ruin herself if she tried." She tried. She bought a sixteenth-century château and built a gaudy "temple dedicated to the worship of physical pleasure" on the Champs-Élysées.

At this ornate shrine to the "Golden Calf," with its alabaster staircases and Baudry murals, La Paiva feted the upper crust of intellectual Paris. Though entirely unschooled, she held up her end of the table with "witty" persiflage and encouraged "sparkling, original" talk on a variety of outré topics, such as the colors of emotions. Celebrities like Delacroix, Sainte-Beuve, and Gautier were regulars at these lavish feasts, which cost five hundred francs apiece. The door was barred to bores—and other women.

La Paiva, rivaling the bitch bosses of pulp fiction, ruled her domains with a bullwhip. She fined gardeners fifty centimes for every leaf she found on the lawn, forbade fires in winter, and killed a horse with her pistol when it threw her. The doting Guido uttered no protest. He eventually married her and tagged behind her like a faithful "trainbearer," never swerving in his adoration. It must have been tried on occasion. In 1870 she earned the lasting contempt of the French when she turned her home into a German espionage center during the Franco-Prussian War. Hissed in the street, she was publicly tarred in a Dumas *fils* play as the diabolic Césarine, a "foul, adulterous, prostituting, infanticidal" "beast."

The countess von Donnersmarck, smug on her mountainous millions, gave less than a damn. She had a leviathan ego. Ultimately, though, her enemies got the better of her and banished the Donnersmarcks to their estates in nether Silesia. There La Paiva batted around a drafty castle in solitary grandeur with all the mirrors destroyed. When she died of a stroke at sixty-five, Guido was so devastated that he bottled her body and stashed it in his closet, where his second wife discovered it bobbing around in a vat of alcohol.

La Paiva's tacky vulgarities, despotism, and rapacity blaspheme the romantic Traviata visions of Second Empire courtesanry. On the other hand, she avoided La Traviata's pathetic lot, the usual fate for sex professionals in nineteenth-century France. Plug-ugly, mean, and domineering, she nevertheless had her way. With her primal erotic spell and seductive willpower, she gained wealth, men, and celebrity and in the process convinced everyone she was a "beauty." Dumas *fils*, though, saw her aright; she was a "beast," an eruption from prehistory—the carrion sex goddess with her eerie fascination, cruel claws, and regenerative and transformational diablerie.

Rather than disappear, the Neolithic bird of prey divinities went underground in folklore and folk religion and resurfaced in classical Greece as *keres*. These were "man-seizing" spirits with "distorted ugly faces" who pestered humanity with plagues and uncontrollable lusts. The Sphinx, Gorgons, Harpies, and Sirens belonged to this tribe. Though later beautified by mythologizers, Sirens looked grotesque, with Toulouse-Lautrecian hawk bottoms concealed below their female faces. They sang the song that lured men to destruction (of forgetfulness and perfect knowledge) and symbolized the demonic undertow of unreason and erotic madness. By the same token, they contained the opposite power of resurrection and brought "things to birth."

Edith Piaf, 1915–1963

The squat, pint-size Edith Piaf might not have resembled a modern sex siren, but she was the spitting image of the archaic one. She fetched up so many men on the rocks with her voice and "extraordinary powers of seduction" that she lost count. Onstage she gave just the reverse impression, wailing of love gone wrong and failures with men. This, however, was a classic siren ruse to waylay the unwary. No man in fact "disappeared from her life until she ordered him out of it"; "she was the one in charge in any sexual situation."

Her early life was a "little girl lost" parable of lovelessness and neglect, perhaps explaining her lust for erotic control. Abandoned by her mother at six, Edith was sent to live with her grandmother, a cook in a Normandy brothel. Several years later her father, a circus performer, plucked her up and took her with him on the road, where he palmed her off on a succession of "mothers." Always one step ahead of destitution, Edith began singing for handouts while her father performed acrobatic tricks in public squares.

When they moved to Paris in her teens, she was considered too plain for prostitution, so she and her half sister sang ballads on street corners for sous. Her voice, raw, ragged, and untrained, had a strange hypnotic spell. Throngs of "young guys" clustered around her, once blocking a road in the faubourg to hear her. Soon a nightclub owner discovered her and made her the cabaret sensation of Paris. Known as the Little Sparrow, she became a twentieth-century cult figure and national logo with her little black dresses, Punchinello face, and break-your-heart torrid chansons.

She should have been called the Little Sparrow Hawk instead. Like her siren precursors, she was an aggressive, dominant, and promiscuous bird of prey. Looks were deceiving. At first sight she looked like a dismal orphan with a syndrome. Only four feet ten inches tall, she had a boxy build and an oversize head with a thick neck and wide-set Pekinese eyes.

"I'm ugly," she conceded. "I'm not Venus. I've got sagging breasts, a low-slung ass, and little drooping buttocks." But, she added defiantly, "I can still get men." In both work and love this homely waif woman seized what she wanted and managed her affairs with fight, panache, and the "authority of a dictator."

While still on the street corners of Paris at fifteen, Edith took control of her sex life. She strung guys along and left a tiresome live-in lover after their child died. At one point she juggled three partners simultaneously and almost didn't live to tell about it. An aggrieved inamorato caught her on the cheat and shot at her, grazing her ear. For three years she remained relatively faithful to a Pygmalion figure, Raymond Asso, who spruced up her act and redressed her neglected education. But Edith couldn't be man- or housebound.

Footloose and polyamorous, she migrated from lover to lover. One of her best known was Yves Montand, then an anonymous crooner of cowboy songs. Encountering this swarthy hunk at an audition, she snapped him up with a classic whipsaw maneuver. First she panned his act in brutal street French; then she praised his handsome build and told him he'd be "the greatest of them all" if he submitted to her instruction. For a coup de grace, she made him listen to her sing. Like the sirens on an Etruscan lamp encircled by Silenuses with hard-ons, she gave performances that drove men crazy. She stroked her body with her "tenacious, lizard-like hands" as she sang, and the males in the audience "leaned forward in their seats as though they wanted to take her in their arms." She "grew beautiful."

Totally blown away, Yves conceived a violent passion for Edith that lasted for years and escalated into desperate marriage proposals. Edith's departure left him "seared," unable to forget their good times together. Contrary to the Piaf *lacrimosa* legend, she was a jokemeister and prank player who laughed "a lot" and "well."

Unlike her character in the sentimental Claude Lelouch film in which she spins in aphasic circles, she could also talk a good game (she followed a rigorous self-study program) and bring any man around with her tongue. Her landlord during World War II, a prominent madam, said that "there was no escape" when Edith "set her cap at some handsome young man" and chatted him up. She knew in seconds "what you had to say to a man to get him to like you" and assailed him with vivid anecdotes, dramatic confessions, and poetry, her own and others.

After Yves and a succession of men, Edith found her grand amour, celebrity boxing champion Marcel Cerdan. When he died in a plane crash two years into their affair, she plunged into near dementia. Her superhuman, mythic-fueled vitality, however, saved her. A lover of those post-Cerdan years, a champion cyclist, said that "forty-eight hours with Piaf [were] more tiring than a lap in the Tour de France."

Part of this stupendous energy included a high-heat libido. Like the Sirens (emblems of female hypersexuality with splayed crotches), she was a lech-hearted dickhound. She believed you never knew a man until you slept with him and once astonished a hotel maid by throwing back the sheets and asking her to admire the nude body of actor Eddie Constantine.

Eddie, who left his wife and child for Edith, thought she possessed occult seductive powers. "One look from her," he said, "could pull down a ten-story building." With Eddie, as with other favored paramours, maternal solicitude accounted for some of this occult appeal. Although militantly antidomestic and bored by decor and cuisine, she loved mothering men. She bought them expensive Italian suits and shoes, knitted them sweaters, and overhauled their characters. During their two-year affair she gave Eddie a total makeover, from gold cuff links to voice training. "She made me believe I was somebody," he later reflected, "so that I'd become somebody"; "she had a kind of genius for bringing out and strengthening a personality."

By the fifties Edith's taste had shifted to celebrities at least as famous as herself. In the singing world, that left only one man, Jacques Pills, the "Monsieur Charme" of Paris, whom she married in 1952. Doomed from the start by her drug, alcohol, and adulterous excesses, the marriage lasted five years. Afterward she provided herself with a "club" of lovers, the "Piaf Boys."

Among these were a young actor, an Egyptian guitarist, and a songwriter in his twenties. Even in her final illness, her face swollen and disfigured with cortisone treatments, she ensnared a Greek Adonis twenty-five years her junior, who married her and cared for her until the end. The end of course was no Silhouette Romance fade-out. She died at forty-seven, ravaged by substance abuse and a farrago of illnesses, chiefly rheumatoid arthritis.

Edith hardly qualifies for superheroine status. She was riddled with flaws, complexes, impulse control disorders, and self-destructive passions. At the same time, she was more than the sum of her weaknesses and "poor me" public postures. She'd have laughed at the thought of herself as a Gallic love-jinxed Judy Garland or suggestions that she "lacked confidence as a woman." "I had a very high opinion of myself," she declared, "perhaps with good reason."

There were plenty of good reasons: the iconic voice and persona, superstardom, defiant grit, and seductive genius—all against ridiculous odds. "A woman who gets herself dropped," she sniffed, "is a poor sap." Early in her career a rival taunted, "You're short, badly dressed, and you haven't got a bosom. Who are you going to attract?" With her acquired charms and mesmeric siren song, *toute le monde.* Jean Cocteau rightly called her a "sacred monster." As her half sister put it, "I never saw a man who could resist Edith."

Pauline Viardot, 1821–1910

Russian opera lovers remembered the night of November 3, 1843, for generations. After a fifty-year ban Italian opera had returned to St. Petersburg. Music-starved aficionados, some suspended from the cupola at risk of their lives, packed the aisles and boxes to hear the coloratura soprano Pauline Viardot (1821–1910) in *The Barber of Seville*. On the last note of Rosina's aria "*Una voce poco fà*" the house exploded in a thunderous, show-stopping avalanche of applause. From the topmost bleacher one man, his face rapt with pentecostal ecstasy, outshouted the rest; it was the "turning point" of his life.

The man was twenty-five-year-old Ivan Turgenev, and the woman who caused this epiphany, one of the plainest seductresses on record. Everyone who saw Pauline Viardot pronounced her "very ugly," "strikingly ugly," or "atrociously homely." Dark and crude-featured, she had hooded eyelids, a receding chin, a wide mouth with a heavy underlip, and an H-shaped figure.

But after that night Turgenev, a gifted, aristocratic heartthrob, fell so irrevocably in love with Pauline that he abandoned Russia and followed her from pillar to post for the rest of his life. For forty years he lived with the Viardots in a ménage à trois and loved her "with an unswerving loyalty such as few women have had the fortune to inspire."

As a siren Pauline was closer in spirit to the archaic archetype than Edith Piaf; hence her superior power and stature. She sang the original siren song—of knowledge and intelligence—and lived truer to her *ker* pedigree. Self-controlled and directed, she arrowed in on her goals without once losing sight of her best interests. A multitalented woman of extraordinary gifts, she achieved a life from the gods—or goddess: long life, happiness, self-actualization, domestic and professional success, and the abject adoration not just of Turgenev but of some of the most distinguished men of her age.

Pauline's prospects as a girl, however, looked poor to nil. The ugly duckling of a glamorous opera family, the great Garcias, she grew up in the shadow of a gorgeous older sister, "La Malibran," the "Enchantress of Nations." Her father, the Pavarotti of his times, trained Pauline on the piano and made her his special pet. Nicknamed the Ant for her concentrated work habits, Pauline distinguished herself intellectually and artistically, mastering drawing, five languages, and musical composition.

But when she was fifteen, her career as a professional pianist derailed. Her sister died in a freak riding accident, and overnight she was assigned to take her place. The most concerted, expert training failed dismally. Pauline had a flawed, second-tier voice and subpar looks. In a period of fascistic looksism in the theater, "exceptionally plain" singers were given no quarter.

Her debut at eighteen, however, was the surprise of the season. She seemed to possess some transcendent star quality—exquisite technique, combined with passion torqued to breaking point. She also parlayed her plainness into striking originality. When she strode onstage for the first time with her "fine carriage," jaded Parisians sat up; she wore a plain white dress, black chain necklace, and a solitaire diamond on her forehead.

Then she sang in a way that "made people forget her looks" altogether. It was a voice with a strange, hallucinatory spell, saturated with sensuality, emotion, and "consummate intelligence." Critics compared it to "amber flowing over velvet," "the taste of wild fruit," and jungle scenes. Like Dante's siren-ogre of *The Purgatorio,* she became "almost beautiful" as she sang.

Her aesthetic wizardry extended to eros. She enchanted men into seeing beyond her "unfortunate features" and falling in love with her. The Byron of Paris, romantic idol Alfred de Musset, preferred her over all the official beauties at his disposal. He praised her in reviews and love poems, proposed marriage, and adored her so fervently that he "could not exorcise her spirit from his mind" for many years.

Amid this adulation Pauline, with sirenic self-possession, chose a man designed to serve and further her best. Louis Viardot, a theater impresario twenty-one years her senior, offered her a climate-controlled conservatory for her "genius": moral support, calm, security, and "a love which was profound, lasting, unselfish, and generous." They married in 1840, but this did not stop the stream of infatuated men. One of the most ardent, painter Ary Scheffer, arrived thinking her "terribly ugly" but left "madly in love" and remained her lifelong acolyte. On the St. Petersburg tour Pauline attracted an entire claque of suitors, the "Four Paws" club, who assembled in her dressing room after performances and vied for the spot of "favorite" on the paws of a giant bearskin rug.

After a furious siege on her affections that fall of 1843, Turgenev won a coveted spot on her rug. For him, it was a "life-and-death" passion; for her, less so, though a passion. Young, hot-blooded, and ensconced in a tepid marriage of convenience, she could not have been indifferent to a man of Turgenev's caliber. He was six feet one inch tall, vibrant, charming, with Paul Newman eyes and "almost hypnotic" powers over the opposite sex.

Since they destroyed their letters, no one will ever know the precise details of their affair. But in 1845 Turgenev left Russia to be with Pauline and installed himself in the Viardot household. Except for periodic breaks and journeys home, he never strayed from her side. He treated her four children as his own (as indeed several might have been) and loved her "like an eighteen year old" until he died.

Her voice was a drug for him; he wept at her concerts and installed a pipe to his study so that he could hear her practicing. Pauline, though, possessed a wealth of other fascinations. She had a personality, said friends, that "conquered her physical ugliness." Brilliant, scintillant, well read, and artistic, she wrote Turgenev enravishing letters that made him think of avenues of green trees, alive with birdsong. At the same time, she critiqued his work and helped him become one of Russia's premier writers.

In his novels he portrayed her over and over again as a seductress who bewitches men with her conversational charm. She talked "like a princess"—with eloquence and sparkle. She told her St. Petersburg audience that despite "thirty degrees of frost," she found in them "thirty-five degrees of warmth" and repeatedly schmoozed enemies into abeyance. One huffy Russian remembered how she turned him into a "docile lamb" as soon as she spoke; "instead of being cold with her," he said, "I would, on the contrary, be most amiable."

Like many raconteurs, Pauline brought out the best in others and

deftly baited Turgenev so that he shone at gatherings. She also encouraged him to let down his hair; her parties were cut-loose affairs
with impromptu comic concerts, games, feasts, and amateur theatricals (admission: one potato) in the attic. Her up-tempo buoyant spirits drove out his Slavic gloom. "Laugh," he beseeched her, "laugh
heartily . . . [and] show all your teeth."

How heartily she dispatched herself in bed can only be guessed.
She was secretive and delivered a mixed message: On the one hand,
she spoke of her volcanic sexuality; on the other, of ascetic self-denial.
"Ah," she said, "I too had my gypsy instincts to combat."

Unlike Piaf, Pauline kept a strong hand on her emotional tiller.
Husbanding her resources and guarding her ego integrity, she refused
to let her passions run away with her. In the interests of self-
preservation, she once banished Turgenev for three years and hedged
her erotic bets with a throng of other beaux. These included some of
the leading lights of the artistic world: Maurice Sand (son of the author) and composers Charles Gounod and Hector Berlioz. The latter
endured "agonizing physical and mental sufferings" on her behalf and
said she'd made him lose his bearings "like the needle of a compass in
a typhoon."

Throughout all this Turgenev was steadfast in his affections. He
dreamed of her every night and "quite simply could not live without
her." So complete was her hold on him that he believed she trafficked
in black magic. "There have always been witches," he once said. "They
have some sort of inner power over people, no matter what one says,
and there's nothing to be done about it."

With her husband supplying domestic support, and Turgenev
valentines, Pauline soared creatively. "One of the greatest artists in the
history of opera," she set the standard for numerous parts (such as *Or-
phee* which she performed 150 times), and won an idolatrous following.
"She is perfect," said a critic, "as far as it is possible to attain perfection, both as a singer and an actress." After her voice deteriorated prematurely at forty, she taught, performed privately, and brought her
other considerable talents into play: piano, composition (she published three music collections), and drawing. She died in 1910 at

eighty-nine with a "contented smile" on her face, surrounded by a loving family and eulogized by the music world.

Among her many excellent sketches is a self-portrait in which she looks like a long-lashed beauty, every irregularity softened and modified. Objectively she resembled a "bizarre mélange" of Spanish busboy and Olive Oyl. But Pauline Viardot, a master illusionist, made people see her as she saw herself, a beautiful, svelte stunner. That was her specialty. When Turgenev drew her fictional likeness in *Spring Torrents,* he made her a blond, gray-eyed bombshell, and just before he died, he surveyed his pictures of her in the room and exclaimed, "What marvelous features."

"Transformation," say folklorists, "is a power of privileged beings." To look at this clutch of homely women, few would guess they were babe shapeshifters or privileged beings. Biologically, they should have been the most underprivileged of society: the despised, shunned, and undated, the outcasts at the high school geek table.

Belles laides weren't accorded any magical immunities or advantages at birth. They belie the psychological wisdom that beauty can be loved into ugly children by the devoted parental gaze. Only Isabella Stewart Gardner and Pauline Viardot were fathers' favorites; the rest grew up the dysfunctional way, acquainted with familial strife and neglect and the gall of homeliness. Plastic surgeons weren't on hand to make it all better; with few career options beyond male patronage, it was beauty or bust. They scaled the heights through go-getter spine and chutzpah, creating their dazzle and transformative hoodoo from scratch.

Of the seductresses, *belles laides* were the overachievers. Without the passe-partout of a pretty face, they tried harder. They turned themselves into erotic fighting machines. They developed their characters, mined the Seductive Way for the strongest munitions, and intuitively exploited their primordial charms. Erotic guerrillas, they tunneled beneath the beauty checkpoint and took the enemy off guard. They knew—who better?—that amour is an illusionist game, "of imagination all compact." For that reason, they played up the necromancy of the senses, especially the ancient beauty substitutes of fashion, cosmetics, and image. Whatever other physical appeals they could muster, they did—with a vengeance: dance, gesture, music, voice, *volupté* settings, and hot and heavy sex.

Not surprisingly they stressed mind spells. Accentuating their archaic attractions, they laid on ego strokes and maternal beguilements and blazed with goddess brio. When they talked, they took eloquence one better and traded in comedy, laser-guided weaponry that strikes at the "animal unconscious," the involuntary matrix of desire. The sex goddess is "laughter loving"; she hits below the belt—smack at the id. They also aimed for the biggest bangs in love. With their elemental, no prisoners' personalities, they designed their love labyrinths on the thrill park model, for maximum intensity. They delivered the *mysterium tremendum* of the first cave rite in all its heartstopping awe, terror, surprise, and rapture. This was strong medicine, not the pap of pretty girls. Symmetry, as George Santayana points out, elicits "domestic peace" and "delights without stimulating." It expresses no "vitality."

Disproportion and irregularity, on the other hand, exert the opposite effect, something closer to the punch-to-the-solar-plexus of passion. *Belles laides* knew their style: the "beauty of the Medusa," which disorients, electrifies, whiplashes us with ambivalence, and transports us to an "estranged," irrational world. That world is the world of myth; the word "grotesque" comes from *grotta* (cave).

Plain women, then, are less accursed than they think. Not only do their defective faces and figures contain an unsuspected mythic charge, they can transfigure themselves into seductive supremas with a little love savvy. They can redefine beauty as radically as Bosch or Picasso.

There are two ways, according to George Sand, of handling ugliness: You can either submit to public consensus or ignore it and get on with the business of personal greatness and enchantment. In the latter case, the erotic impact doubles. A *belle laide* "wins the heart" and deliciously "shocks the senses." Shock and ecstasy are what men seek in love, not the stasis, regularity, and calm of clueless lovelies.

In fact men may not be as excited by pretty girls as they'd have us

believe. Many seasoned connoisseurs have brushed them off. "Prettiness suggests nothing," carped George Moore; "Whoever looks at it
twice when it has been in the house three days?" growled George
Bernard Shaw. In Bertrand Blier's film *Too Beautiful for You*, Gérard De-
pardieu ditches his cover girl wife for a plus-size secretary, and in
Thomas Mann's *The Magic Mountain*, the plain, flat-chested Clavdia
Chauchat enamors all the men on the mountain while comely guests
madly circulate the book *The Art of Seduction*. A whole subgenre of literature and film celebrates homely seductresses.

In Marcel Proust's view, "pretty women ought to be left to men
without imagination." He might have added "boys." Psychiatrists and
sexologists point out that perfect tens appeal primarily to adolescents
and insecure men. Living dolls are fetishes, defenses against performance anxieties and the frightening swamps of female sexuality. If
you're not careful, a woman can hurtle you headlong into precivilized
madness, into the maw of nature, where sexually she can't be beaten
or contained.

So when we swallow looksist propaganda and sink all our resources into beautification, we're accommodating nervous half men
who want to divert us from sexual empowerment. A gorgeous face and
figure, to be sure, cause a momentary power surge, but it's momentary, exactly as chauvinists want it. A cupcake can't sink her claws in
your heart; an armpiece stays on your arm, not in your head.

The beauty chase is a wild-goose chase, leading us to look for love
in all the wrong places. Salons, spas, gyms, boutiques, and ORs can
take us only so far; without self-cultivation and amorous artistry we're
lunch meat in the mating wars. While plastic surgery soars to over a
million cases a year and feminine self-esteem sinks proportionally (80
percent of women report disliking their looks), we're slip-sliding romantically, unable to get a grip on men or our love lives.

Belles laides suggest a better way. They lassoed the top-of-the-line
lovers and held them, without body work or personal compromise.
They didn't sand down their edges. Faithful to their prehistoric style,
they were audacious sex mahatmas who defied social norms and dared
to be themselves. All but Wallis Simpson and La Paiva (you have to be
careful of the metamorphosis you wish for) brewed the love philter of

personal excellence and self-actualization. At the same time, they cultivated their primordial attractions, finessed seduction, and restyled themselves into *belles des belles*. They prove the hoary adage that beauty is subjective, an experience rather than an objective quality.

Washington Irving, an old hand with women, recognized this. "Divinity within," he said, "makes divinity without." The *belles laides'* divinity was no angel. She was the masked Neolithic sex deity in her grotesque, zoomorphic form: death bringer, life regenerator, cosmic superpower, and goddess of a thousand faces. She's the Loathly Lady of the folktale that preserved her myth through the ages, the ugly Lady Ragnall, who zeroes in on the handsomest knight, subjects him to character tests, then turns into a nubile beauty when he measures up and grants her sovereignty.

Naomi Wolfe wrote that "stories don't happen to women who are not beautiful." But Zsa Zsa Gabor came closer when she said, "There are no ugly women." Just those who don't know the story, the one about the primeval beaked goddess with her numinous powers, metamorphoses, cosmic sex appeal, and triumphant plots of conquest and seduction.

CHAPTER FOUR

Silver Foxes

Old women must take on anybody, for no one will have them. —KATHY ACKER

The hell of women is old age. —LA ROCHEFOUCAULD

An old hen doth make better broth. —PROVERB

How many men there be which do love old women for many reasons better than young. —SEIGNEUR DE BRANTÔME

Oh, there's life in the old girl yet. —GRAHAM GREENE

*A*bigail Adams, the young wife of future President John Adams, received a rude shock when she first arrived in Paris. At Benjamin Franklin's suggestion she attended a dinner party to meet one of the legendary French seductress-*salonnières*. Imagine her horror, she wrote, when a shriveled old lady in moth-eaten finery bounded in and carried on like a "very bad" *fille de joie*.

"Where's Franklin?" the brazen creature bawled out, then raced over and planted three kisses on his cheeks and forehead. At dinner she hogged the entire conversation, lacing and unlacing her fingers with Franklin's and sometimes throwing her arm on the back of Mr. Adams's chair! Worse followed. She flopped on a settee, "showed more than her foot," and proceeded to kiss her lapdog on the mouth.

When the dog peed on the floor, she reached down—mid-sentence—and wiped it up with her petticoat. "I own," wrote the indignant Abigail, "I was highly disgusted, and never wish for an acquaintance with any ladies of this cast."

Ladies of this cast, like Franklin's "bad" *salonnière,* were—unbeknownst to Abigail—the height of fashion in prerevolutionary France. They captured the choice men with their conversational brilliance and mature charms and decided important questions of state at their influential salons. Debutantes powdered their hair white to emulate these Silver Foxes, just as seniors today color up to look young.

Contrary to myth, elder seductresses have never gone out of style. The powers of fascination in a fascinating woman only potentiate with time. In maturity women gain formidable allures denied to the young. They cast perhaps the biggest spells of all—the aphrodisiacs of a fully developed character, an enriched mind, sexual freedom and experience, maternal mana, status, money, and a what-the-hell closing time joie de vivre.

They're surprisingly populous. Ancient Greek chroniclers list dozens, and the sixteenth-century Brantôme recounts the exploits of at least fifty "old vixens." Most great seductresses bewitched men until they died. The aged Jane Digby, for example, held a young Bedouin prince captive for twenty-five years, and Isabella Stewart Gardner had a fan club of Museum Boys who swarmed around her like "flies to honey." As the French (historically predisposed to eldersirens) say, "At vespers the feast is sweetest."

If so, why the universal animus against older women? For centuries in Western culture, postchildbearing women have been stigmatized as repulsive hags, morphing at the stroke of menopause into grizzled Ma Joads, asexual frumps, and comedy club figures of fun. "What's ten, nine, eight, seven, six? Bo Derek growing old." Or: "What's wrong with being Grandpa? Having to sleep with Grandma."

It doesn't take a genius to see the motive behind this mudslinging. Older women unnerve younger female rivals and alarm men. Like seductresses in general, they menace their hegemony. Besides their innate sexual magnetism, senior *amoureuses* have a dangerous liberty, the freedom of the postreproductive female to flit about and fornicate and escape domestic captivity. Unlike their male counterparts, they lose none of their libidinous marbles. They're hotter to trot, if anything, often rendered raunchier by a testosterone boost to their sex drives. As a recent survey discovered, women between sixty and ninety-one reach orgasm 72 percent of the time, as opposed to 50 percent for their younger counterparts. The mature woman, in short, is too big for masculine comfort—too free, too strong, too orgasmic, too mom-run-wild and must pay for it. Demonized as a crone and Miami gargoyle, she must be cut from the dance, with her daughters and granddaughters seconding the motion.

Ironically, however, she belongs at the head of the dance, enthroned on the royal dais, queen of the mythic prom. The mature sex goddess was a powerhouse; "crone" and "crown" share the same etymology. She incarnated motherhood and the accumulated knowledge of existence and possessed a volcanic libido. Prepatriarchal societies invested her with an aggressive "active sexuality" and surrounded her in their myths with an honor guard of young, lusty hunks. She was so dynamic, so potent in her final form that she could metamorphose in a flash, transforming herself into cats, birds, and beautiful young women.

Since the goddess represented an active life-and-death continuum rather than a static entity, she didn't convey the usual linear idea of senescence and decline. Instead the old lunar deity was a font of regeneration that magically resurrected the dead in her cosmic cauldron and restored them to new life. She possessed the secret of the fountain of youth, conferring immortality and eternal rejuvenescence.

Men, then, to their intense confusion and fear, are attracted to older women at a deep, archetypic level. They can't help themselves; it's soldered into the inherited structure of the psyche. Beneath their seamed faces, Silver Foxes serve them a straight-up *goblet d'amour,* the concentrated charms of the seductress at her peak and the primordial pull of the senior goddess with her potent enchantments: wisdom, plentitude, maternal nurture, seismic sexuality, and the power of rebirth and the elixir vitae.

Minette Helvétius, 1719–1800

With Minette Helvétius, Franklin's beloved Silver Fox, the prevailing charm was her contagious, restorative cosmic vitality. Like Demeter, the old fertility goddess who transformed Pelops into a handsome young hero in her cauldron, Minette had a magical effect on men: She turned back the clock and gave them back their youth. Around her the seventy-year-old Franklin felt "like a little boy," as did the other infatuees who flocked to her Auteuil salon on the edge of the Bois de Boulogne. At sixty-one, covered in wrinkles and moles, Minette looked both raddled and "no longer young." She "didn't know it," though, and carried on as if she were a grisette.

Her weekly salon was a jamboree. Statesmen, philosophers, historians, poets, and "the wittiest and most sought-after talkers" in France poured through the gates of her walled garden into a large blue and white parlor overrun by twenty Angora cats in ribbons and sateen coats. At the center of the hubbub stood Minette in girlish short petticoats, greeting men with shrieks of joy.

After a boisterous supper, guests repaired to the aviary, carved mottoes in the furniture, and milled in and out of the dining room, where the conversation continued full cry. "Gaiety" resounded until deep into the night, with Minette's comic anecdotes ringing "through the whole house."

Minette's life seemed little calculated to inspire gaiety. Born the tenth of twenty-one children to an impoverished noble family, she grew up hungry, neglected, and uneducated. On the plus side, she escaped the pernicious consequences of eighteenth-century education, the instruction in female timidity, obedience, silence, and artificiality. Still, she faced the likelihood of lifelong dogwork and destitution.

Early hardship, however, a common siren theme, often steels the siren's soul, especially when combined with a redemptive mentor. For Minette the mentor was a fairy godmother unimaginably ahead of her time. A rabid advocate of women's rights, Françoise de Graffigny wrote for a living, cultivated such seductresses as the brilliant Émilie du Châtelet, and crusaded for a new system of feminine education that instilled "strength of character," independence, and "accomplish-ments of the mind" in women.

When a patron offered Françoise lodgings at the court of Lor-raine, she invited two of her nieces along. The ten-year-old Minette was her favorite. For five years, while Françoise occupied herself with salons, balls, and polyamorous intrigues, Minette developed into a *charmeuse*. As "cunning and smart as a cat," she roguishly flashed her calves at cavaliers and looked like a diminutive Cather-ine Deneuve, with blond braids coiled at the back of her neck and wide sapphire eyes.

But before she could put her powers to a test, Minette was placed in a convent, compliments of a charitable cardinal. Life sentence to a spinning wheel would have been preferable. An expensive club for abandoned ladies and *laiderons* (girls scarred by smallpox), these clois-tered retreats were stultifying sinks of domestic drudgery, masses, embroidery, and parlor readings. Miraculously, however, Minette sur-vived with her spirits intact.

When she reemerged fifteen years later at the cardinal's death, she bewitched all Paris with her fetching joie de vivre. Christened the "light of the house" of her aunt's Left Bank salon, she infatuated men and women alike. (Queen Marie Leszczynska found her so delightful she gave her an expensive dress and a purse of louis d'or.) Her first beau, a handsome student seven years younger, became one of the greatest French statesmen. But at the time the twenty-three-year-old Anne Robert Jacques Turgot was too poor to marry her and contented himself with an *amour platonique*.

The man she did accept surpassed even Turgot. Claude Adrien Helvétius, the reigning male pinup of Paris, was the stuff of ancien régime wet dreams. Philosopher, writer, actor, self-made millionaire, and winner of twenty duels, he plowed through women like *petites madeleines*. Every morning his valet brought him his "service girl," and every afternoon and evening he worked his way through the aristoc-racy, ending with the famous actress Mademoiselle Gaussin.

The thirty-year-old Minette, however, stopped him in his tracks. Proclaiming her his "icon," and "divinity," he forsook his paramours and lived with her in perfect marital fidelity and devotion for twenty years. They moved to a country estate, practiced philanthropy, and lived at the height of gaucherie, treating each other with bourgeois intimacy and raising their two daughters democratically.

At forty Minette presided over their weekly salon in the city and broke hearts again. Still a *ravisseuse*, still the life of the party, she pitched gamely into highbrow debates (despite her lack of formal education), and jollied suitors along—too kind to say no. Her most serious conquest, the ninety-year-old Enlightenment celebrity Bernard de Fontenelle saw her seminude at her toilette by accident and sighed, "Ah Madame, if only I were eighty years old." Ex-flame Turgot visited her every day.

When Helvétius died unexpectedly in 1771, the fifty-two-year-old Minette bounced back and created herself anew. She gave her homes to her daughters, bought a cozy estate in the Paris suburbs, and threw herself into senior seduction with gusto. Reconstituting her salon on newer, more ambitious lines, she turned her Auteuil residence into a "sacrosanct chapel" for the intellectual and political elect of the day. The best minds, as Franklin said, gravitated to her "as straws about a fine piece of amber." In time it became an underground command post for both the French Revolution and the later Republic.

Once within this cloistered sanctuary, few could resist the enchantment of its resident life force. In a backyard "Philosophers Pavilion" lived three myrmidons—Abbé Morellet, Abbé de La Roche, and the young Pierre-Jean-Georges Cabanis—who provided Minette with "unremitting adulation." Turgot renewed his marriage proposals, and though they practically lived in each other's houses, she refused him because she enjoyed her independence too much.

Franklin's passion for her should have surprised no one. Almost a male counterpart of Minette, he was high-spirited, whimsical, and amorous, and he preferred older to younger women. A heartthrob even at seventy, Franklin, like Helvétius before him, caused an erotic firestorm among the young Parisian lovelies who created coiffures in his honor and beat down his bedroom door.

Yet after seven weeks in France he was so besotted with the sixty-one-year-old Minette that he told friends that he intended to "capture her and keep her with him for life." Nearly every day he trudged over to Auteuil, where she relieved him of the American puritanical corsetry he detested so much; she made sure he kicked back and "was always feted." Minette shrieked with approval at his defenses of atheism and joined him in rowdy drinking songs and "gay nonsense." He gorged on her thick whipped cream and played the harmonica for her circle of acolytes.

Minette herself fell very much in love with Franklin but repeatedly refused to marry him, citing her devotion to her salon and personal freedom. He composed a last-ditch plea on his own printing press, "To Our Lady of Auteuil: A Descent into Hell," a witty jeu d'esprit in which he imagined their ex-spouses married in the afterlife. "Let us *avenge ourselves!*" Franklin implored. To no avail.

She and Franklin, though, remained ardent lovers. They exchanged mash notes and regular visits, kissed in public, and praised each other abroad; he said if he were summoned to paradise, he'd pray to remain on earth for another of her embraces. When he was at last summoned back to America from his diplomatic tour, he wrote sadly, "It seems to me that things are badly arranged in this world when I see that two beings, so made to be happy together are obliged to separate."

After Franklin left, other equally illustrious men took his place: noted author and orator Sébastien Chamfort and Comte Destutt de Tracy, a philosopher and revolutionary activist. As the nation hurtled toward revolution, Auteuil became a "horrifying nest of ideologues," harboring the masterminds of the future republic. Thanks to them and her husband's populist sympathies, Minette was spared the ravages of the Terror.

By eighteenth-century standards Minette lived to an astonishing age of eighty-one. Like Roald Dahl's Grandma Georgina, she seemed to age backward, awakening with the birds, throwing open her windows to smell the flowers, and romping with the caretakers' children. As "light and lively" as a twenty-year-old, she still drew admirers. Even Napoleon paid a call. She died of a chest cold in 1800, her longtime companion and backyard "philosopher" Cabanis beside her. At her deathbed he sobbed, "My dear mother!" To which she replied, "Yes, I am. I always will be."

Cabanis, like others, instinctively invested her with mythic dimensions. Both Franklin and Fontenelle equated her with the moon goddess, sacred archetype of the senior siren and divine regenerator. Fontenelle likened her to a moon that rose for him, and Franklin, to an old moon whose castoff fragments created her "star" children.

Abigail Adams, with thirty-something pique, set Minette down for a "very bad" woman, and she was. She broke the patriarchal old lady mold and came out blazing with life, noise, and razzmatazz sex appeal. She belonged to the wrong club, a sorority of uppity, obstreperous love queens, life spirits beyond good and evil. Franklin's drinking song, which he dedicated to her, acknowledged as much: "Fair Venus calls, her voice obey!"

As Cabanis's tribute to Minette acknowledges, maternal allure often figures into the elder siren's attraction. In her later incarnation, the Mother of All Being reached her apogee. Men at a preconscious level know it; for them the older woman is always "mother," a source of terrifying dependencies, authority, and incest taboos. Also, of course, a source of tremendous appeal. The cagey Silver Foxes handled this high-intensity aphrodisiac with finesse, artfully mixing nurturer and sex queen so as to neutralize oedipal anxieties and maximize the maternal hit. Through the adroit deployment of the *magner mater*, two French "old dames" captured younger kings who adored them to the end and made them de facto queens of France.

Diane de Poitiers, 1499–1566

In 1543 the first of these "old dames" lay with her royal lover on a turkey carpet at Fontainebleau. They gamboled in "wanton" abandon, she throwing off her shift, he covering her "beautiful" body in hot caresses. She was the forty-four-year-old Diane de Poitiers, and she was being watched. From the ceiling above, a tear-streaked young woman peered through a peephole: Catherine de' Medici, wife of the prince on the carpet.

For nine years she'd tried unsuccessfully to lure her husband to bed, a failure neither she nor her minions could fathom. Catherine epitomized Renaissance feminine desirability; she was nubile, plump, docile, and sweet and wore the costliest, sexiest clothes at court. What black magic explained the appeal of this ancient strumpet? Advisers knew how to handle it–sulfuric acid to the jade's face. But Catherine preferred to "wait and hate." With a middle-aged rival it was just a matter of time.

Wrong. It would be another fifteen years before Diane de Poitiers was displaced, a decade and a half in which she became the queenpin of France. And her appeal for Henri was no mystery. Throughout his traumatic youth she'd been his protectress and shoulder to cry on. When Henri came back from a four-year captivity in Spain, the twelve-year-old dedicated his first feats to Diane and wore her colors. She initiated him sexually at seventeen and ruined him for other women. He neglected his wife, and when he became king in 1547, he invested her with power, riches, and influence beyond those of any *maîtresse en titre* in French history.

Diane had been bred for this. Born in a turreted castle on the banks of the Rhône, she was raised for no ordinary destiny. Her father's favorite (like so many female achievers), she eschewed traditional feminine employments for riding and hunting, and acquired a masculine taste for "magnificence." Instead of being browbeaten out of it through the usual training, she spent her adolescence at a finishing school for women of majesty. Her teacher was one of Europe's boldest iconoclasts, the "ardent feminist" Anne de Beaujeu. She'd governed her own kingdom for eight years and taught her demoiselles to rule. They learned classical literature, medical lore, grace, civility, the art of conversation, and the importance of "great doing." There men addressed ladies on bended knee.

When Diane turned fifteen, Anne, a firm believer in the advantages of widowhood, provided her with a rich husband forty years her senior. While married to Louis de Brézé, an indulgent Burgundian baron, Diane bore two daughters and served as a matron of honor to the French queen.

At Fontainebleau she won her spurs in seduction. François I had just imported Renaissance culture to France and imposed Castiglione's charm school precepts on the court. Women had to fascinate: dress rakishly in extravagant gowns trimmed with guipure lace, swing their hips when they walked, half close their eyes, and know "how to dance," talk, and "be festive."

Eldersirens catch on early; Diane soon made her mark. She sang a profane De Profundis to great applause and stole the balls with her graceful gaillards. Her conversational gifts, burnished by Anne de Beaujeu, rapidly drew the king's attention. He summoned her to his private Pavilion St. Louis for long parleys and probably more. His jealous mistress hired poets to savage Diane, rumors ran rife of an affair, and the king inscribed her portrait with a sentimental tribute, "Good to look at, pleasant to be with."

Although sycophants called her "the beauty of beauties," Diane looked more like one of Cranach the Elder's burgher women—a long face with thin lips, narrow, lashless eyes, and a Nixon nose. But she made herself "pleasant" through an outré technique, washing daily in cold water and cleaning her teeth with a rag soaked in vinegar. She also had that rarity of rarities in the sixteenth century, a clear complexion unscarred by smallpox.

When her husband died after their fifteenth anniversary, Diane assumed the role for which she had been groomed, chatelaine of their Burgundian estate at Anet. Rich, commanding, and at the crest of her charms, she had the whole older woman power package. That, with her accumulated maternal charms, made the seventeen-year-old Henri fall completely under her spell.

From the start of their affair he submitted to her guidance. Although a prize jouster with an action figure physique, Henri was morose, withdrawn, and socially challenged. Under Diane's tutelage, he came out of his shell and became a suave operator. He read Machiavelli at her insistence and grew affable and vivacious. A visitor recalled a lively evening in his company soon after. Henri played the guitar with Diane in his lap, stopped to fondle her breasts, and turned to the company and asked if they'd ever seen a more beautiful woman.

By her forties Diane looked at least twenty years younger. In a time when most women her age tottered toothless to the grave, she boasted a slim, lithe figure that she accentuated with tight gold riding costumes and décolleté black and white gowns. But she'd never pass for a debutante. A midlife portrait shows her with marionette lines, eye pouches, and a wattle. Even Henri admitted it wasn't her "beauty . . . as much as [her self] that pleas[ed] him."

The self that pleased him so much was more than a nurture mom, though she was that too. She was the mother goddess in all her totality and swank. Diane, crackling with sex appeal, combined divine élan and a heady mélange of opposites—Renaissance prince and courtesan, abbess and bawd, lady charity and hardball powerfrau. She thought herself the ne plus ultra and signed her name, celebrity style, Diane. Shrewdly identifying with the divine regenerator of youth, she took Diana (ancestress of Hecate, the senior moon deity) as her patron deity and hired artists to immortalize her as the eternally nubile goddess of the hunt.

Caught in this mythic undertow, Henri thought her semidivine. When he took the throne in 1547, he went public with his passion. He insisted on Diane's presence beside him at the coronation and, failing in that, redesigned the royal robes with their paired initials, "DDH," on the embroidery. He made her duchess of Valentois, gave her the crown jewels, and, in the first years of his reign, funneled a quarter of the national revenues into her account. He taxed the churches to pay for a renovation of her estate at Anet, prompting Rabelais to crack that "the king had hung all the bells in the kingdom around the neck of his new mare." He wore Diane's black and white colors with her coat of arms and a new motto on his justaucorps: "My devotion shall be known throughout the world."

He didn't need to spell it out. She "ruleth the roost," groaned the English envoy. The palace matriarch, Diane replaced ministers with her satellites and joined the king's private council, an unprecedented event in French history. Yet Henri II was no royal wuss. He initiated administrative reforms and successfully pursued his father's war against the Holy Roman Empire. Still, he never made a decision without first consulting Diane, a maven of statecraft. As his chief adviser she instigated peace treaties, forged alliances, handled his correspondence, and persuaded him to sleep with Catherine to ensure heirs.

The "Dissimulation Queen," however, was not moved to gratitude. The moment Diane came down with a menopausal malady, Catherine de' Medici opened fire. She invited Henri to an erotic ballet and instructed one of the comeliest dancers to seduce him. The dancer succeeded and bore a child, but the plot failed. Henri wearied quickly of his pretty piece and returned to Diane with redoubled ardor.

When Diane recovered, he said he couldn't "live without her" and gave her Chenonceaux, the romantic château that spans the Cher River. Faithful to her credo "You must dazzle," she imported celebrity artisans, artists, and gardeners from all over Europe and transformed the château into "the most prized jewel of the sixteenth century." Through wise acquisitions (fifteen more properties plus three houses in Paris), tight bookkeeping, wholesale taxation, and a fleet of lawyers, she built up one of the largest estates in France.

She may also have paid Henri back in kind. According to rumor, he surprised her one day in her boudoir and discovered a "very handsome, intelligent, and ambitious courtier" under the bed.

After Henri died of a lance wound in a tourney, Catherine de' Medici, who'd waited and hated thirty years, sharpened the long knives. She seized Chenonceaux, repossessed the crown jewels, and went for blood. But the provident Diane had crisis-proofed herself with powerful allies and retired in peace to Anet, where she administered her estate and dispensed charity, building a hospital for the village and refuge for homeless women.

Brantôme, who saw her before she died at sixty-six, said she was as seductive as ever, full of "grace," majesty, and gallantry. Her "winter," he claimed, "was more glorious than the spring and summer of any other." Yeats's poetic tribute to ageless charm, "When You Are Old," was based on Ronsard's "When You Are Old, at Evening," written for Diane.

At her death she left instructions for a spectacular memorial mass, an invitation-only service with a hundred white-robed paupers filing in, singing paternosters. The eternal grandstander, she designed her mortuary chapel with an ornate sarcophagus in the center, a sculpture of her youthful self in prayer attended by a statue of love writing the history of her life on marble tablets.

Her history was written instead with poison pens. Her elder enticements, not surprisingly, disquieted everyone; the sexual allure, power, money, "plentitude of being," and, most of all, maternal sway over Henri. Textbooks portrayed her as a man-eating ogress who despoiled France with her greed; folktales, as a witch—the standard rap for spellbinding sirens.

Diane, according to folk tradition, hexed Henri with diabolic spells and potions of potable gold. The very gates of her home were bewitched. On the pediment she placed a clock flanked by two bronze hounds that barked on the hour and a stag that tapped out the time with its hoof. Whenever it chimed, the townspeople said demons were at work; the resident goddess was up to her old tricks, bespelling men and time.

Françoise de Maintenon, 1635–1719

A century later another eldersiren made an equally astounding conquest of a king, in this case, the John Kennedy of French monarchs, Louis XIV. Like Diane de Poitiers, the suprafascinating Françoise de Maintenon was also accused of witchcraft, but hers was a different maternal voodoo, tailored for another age. There were no torrid scenes on the turkey carpet, no flamboyant festivities and castle renovations. With the ascendance of Puritanism and its impact on the Counter-Reformation, a Madonna cult swept through France, exalting docile, gentle, self-sacrificing homemakers and mothers.

The Silver Fox this time was a lily pure nanny on the cusp of forty without money, magnificence, or (overtly) the slightest interest in sex. That alone ought to disqualify her since sirens are known by their carnal zest. But Françoise deserves honorable mention because she shows just how prepotent a trained senior enchantress can be, especially when she unleashes the divine mother.

As a boy, Louis's favorite bedtime story was *"Peau d'Âne"* (The Ass's Skin) about a prince who marries a princess disguised in a dress made of an old ass's skin. In Françoise he found his lady of disguise. Subjected to a miserable childhood, with a mother who hated her and an aunt who forced her to scrub stairs in wooden sabots, Françoise d'Aubigné learned early to dissimulate for her keep. At seventeen, faced with incarceration in a convent, she married a hopeless cripple of forty-two, Paul Scarron. Though immobilized by rheumatoid arthritis and strapped to a wooden box on wheels, Scarron ran the rowdiest, bawdiest salon in Paris, a kind of seventeenth-century Animal House.

During this eight-year marriage Françoise walked a tightrope between mistress of revels and sainted nurse. Fortunately she had superb rabbis, male and female. Her husband, a court poet, educated her in letters and *bel parlare* so that she could hold her own and amuse the company, while the great Ninon de Lenclos taught her to captivate men without compromising her stellar image. Françoise went further and combined it with a stainless reputation. "Nothing," said this cunning vamp, "is cleverer than irreproachable conduct."

Françoise was, if not conventionally pretty, a disturbing presence. Lovelocks spilled to her shoulders in long corkscrew curls, and her black eyes, "the most splendid in the world," flashed like hot coals, eclipsing her Gallic nose and small wire-drawn mouth. "It was a fight," she later recalled, "who would have me." "I was universally loved." Amid her sister of mercy ministrations to Paul, she loved them back. She trysted with Maréchal d'Albret and the duc de Villars and used Ninon's bedroom for assignations with the marquis de Villarceaux, the darling of the adultery circuit. Yet few, except Paul, suspected. "You are as much a little devil as you are spotless," he fleered.

After he died and left her penniless, Françoise dug in further behind her pious facade. In the mid-century prudery backlash, charity depended on stainless respectability. Although rumored to have entertained troops of lovers, she lived for nine years in a convent, ingratiating herself with the aristocracy by performing domestic services.

One of these aristocratic ladies, Athénaïs de Montespan, hired Françoise in 1668 for a delicate mission: to nurse her illegitimate children by the king at a secret hideaway. Nothing could have seemed like a safer bet. La Veuve Scarronique was the picture of middle-aged stolidity and domestic virtue. Louis at first found Françoise (three years older than he) "difficult in every way," and Athénaïs, a proficient sexpert and witty, curvaceous glamour girl, had the king wrapped up, some said under a love spell.

But Athénaïs, not the swiftest seductress, didn't know her man. Louis had a secret fixation, like many rakes, on mother women. Not only did he love children, he idolized his pious mother and hungered for maternal solace, support, and ego ratification. Beneath his autocratic formality he harbored deep insecurities. Childhood wounds still festered: inadequate nourishment as a baby, inferiority feelings from an irregular education, and the lasting trauma of the Fronde revolution in his youth. When he saw the "pure" older Françoise, then, in the garden one day in a pietà posture with his three children, she hit him where he lived. "She knows how to love," he said famously. "It would be pleasant to be loved by her."

In less than ten years Françoise had supplanted the divine Athénaïs. Increasingly Louis visited his children to talk to her. Nicknamed the Thaw for her disinhibitory effect on others, she permitted him to feel "perfectly free" and "wholly at ease." She amused him so much with her "delicious talk" that he told Athénaïs not to gossip with Françoise after he left because she'd find her conversation more entertaining than his own. She called him a "hero," listened and consoled, and provided him with excellent advice.

By the time Athénaïs caught on, it was too late. She rounded on Françoise with wildcat fury and fired her. But Louis XIV, who'd already made Françoise Madame de Maintenon, appointed her second lady-in-waiting to the dauphin's wife to have her closer at hand. By 1680 the court placed its bets on the "rise of the elderly *gouvernante* with the magnificent black eyes." Françoise now passed Athénaïs on the stairs at Versailles and quipped, "You are going down, Madame? I am going up."

Three years later Louis XIV married the fifty-year-old Madame de Maintenon in a secret ceremony. Courtiers feared for his sanity. To have singled out an old fossil from a mosh pit of young blondes bespoke a sorcery deeper and darker than Madame de Montespan's. As with so many senior sirens, Françoise was called the "old witch," the "black spider." More uncanny still, Louis, a confirmed horndog, remained faithful to her for over thirty years. He monopolized her time, could not bear to have her out of his sight, and referred every important question to "Madame Reason." "However much you love me," the king declared, "my love for you will always be greater."

Undoubtedly Françoise *did* love the king—in her fashion. She put up with Athénaïs only "for the love of him" and dedicated her very existence to mollycoddling him. But her reign at court was a "veritable martyrdom." Although she was genuinely domestic and maternal (unlike most seductresses), her libido wasn't in it. The king sapped her energy with his gargantuan needs and demands and left her cold in bed.

Wearily she put herself through her seductive paces like an old circus pony, organizing fetes, forcing herself to shine, charm, and mother well into her seventies. She outlived Louis by four years, and ended her days at St.-Cyr, the female academy she founded, in the company of her favorite "turbulent" girls. She died at eighty-three and achieved her last wish—"to remain an enigma for posterity."

She may not look like an eldervixen surrounded by Bibles and crucifixes in her hawkish portraits. She may not have cashed in on the seductress rewards: sexual happiness, self-actualization, and independence. In the end her dissimulation racket backfired and trapped her in her own hall of trick mirrors. She lost her groove to a Madonna game. She nevertheless pulled off one of the most stunning seductions by an older woman in Western history. She rose from nothing—poverty, disgrace, and a checkered past—to the highest position in France. She always credited her extraordinary rise to a "miracle," "a work of God." She should have said "goddess," specifically the one at the foot of the grand staircase at Versailles, Latona—the derivative of Lat, the archaic all-in-one maternal deity in her last, most powerful phase.

Besides maternal allure, men gravitate to Silver Foxes for their wisdom. Again this is primordial, beyond conscious control. The archaic mistress of the universe, the cosmic sex bomb, knew it all, and her avatars, like Inanna, conferred language and learning on mankind. According to ancient myth, the goddess's brainpower peaked with age. Because of her retention of menstrual fluids (a sort of smart juice), she had Wise Blood. She persists in the archetype of the Wise Crone, though in a castrated form. Rather than a bifocaled postsexual fogy, however, she was a dishy dame as well as the "Perfect Mind," delivering sex appeal and wisdom with equal shazam.

Gnathaena and Glycera, c. 400 and 300 B.C.

The ancient classical world was no Elysium Estates for older women. The misogynistic Greeks relegated the overaged to the slag heap of society, stigmatized them as loathsome hags, and bombarded them with a hail of invective. Yet this viciously ageist civilization produced powerful Silver Foxes, some of whom engineered their triumphs through mental prowess.

Of the twelve senior courtesans in Athenaeus's Grecian chronicles, two of the most successful were wise women, gifted with Aphrodite's deadliest weapon, "verbal power." Gnathaena and Glycera, both topflight elder hetaerae, "thought very highly of themselves," "apportion[ed] their time to learned studies," and "were quick in making answers."

Gnathaena's bon mots outnumber everyone else's on record, and her book *Rule for Dining in Company* competed with philosophers' tracts on the subject. Admirers jammed her pricey carriage trade, and the comic poet Diphilus loved her to distraction.

A generation later Glycera retired to Athens to enjoy the fruits of her career in courtesanry, which had included a queenship and her own goddess cult. But she attracted so many beaux with her wit and learned persiflage that she opened shop again and attracted such celebrity lovers as the playwright Menander. Until she died, she held this ex-playboy writer in thrall, just as she "ruined" the many other young Athenians with her autumnal, mind-spun charms.

George Sand, 1804–1876

In 1852 the British poet Elizabeth Barrett Browning made a pilgrimage that was a de rigueur rite for every major intellectual of the day. She visited George Sand, the "Good Woman of Genius" and icon of senior wisdom. The encounter left Elizabeth visibly shaken. "La Sand," the seeress of romantic thought, looked shockingly unethereal—ugly, in fact. She had the face of a jowly Sioux warrior with buckteeth, a beaked nose, and a "deep olive" complexion. More startling was her company. Surrounding the "priestess" sat a "circle of eight or nine men," all of whom "adore[d] her *à genoux bas* [on bended knee]."

A "female Don Juan" in her youth, George didn't quit in her twilight years. With the sizzle conferred by her intellectual fame and accrued knowledge, she attracted even better men. "Old women," she announced after a particularly successful catch, "are more loved than younger women."

Which is saying a great deal. From her early teens she drew adorers like iron filings. Born to seduce, George (christened Amandine-Aurore-Lucie Dupin) was the product of a match between a professional Parisian mantrap and a hot-blooded aristocratic father. Her grandmother's unorthodox training augmented her genetic inheritance.

After Aurore's unstable mother abandoned her, this enlightened grande dame taught her literature and the pleasing arts of dance, music, and drawing, then handed her to an eccentric ex-abbé, who educated her like a boy. Under his tutelage, she learned medicine, agronomy, and estate management and galloped through the Berry countryside in men's clothes. The boys who accompanied her on these jaunts, one by one, fell in love with her.

But at eighteen, with her grandmother dead and no one to advise her, she made an ill-fated marriage. She accepted Casimir Dudevant, a dull, conventional minor squire of twenty-six. By the third year and birth of one child she snapped and sought satisfaction elsewhere— with a magistrate (who said her "mind" spoiled him for mere "pretty" girls) and with a group of neighborhood blades, one of whom fathered her daughter. Five years later she flung down her celebrated gauntlet: She defied Casimir's marital authority (which was absolute under the Napoleonic Code), demanded an allowance, and fled to Paris with her lover and children.

Her audacious gamble paid off. Her first novel, *Indiana,* under the pen name G. Sand, was a succès de scandale, a scathing "manifesto" that assailed feminine marital bondage and masculine privilege. This was followed by a spate of other books, all messianically radical and produced with manic industry. Over a lifetime she accumulated a staggering 150 volumes: 70 novels and novellas, 25 plays, a dozen collections of essays and miscellany, an immense autobiography, and 40,000 letters. Although praised for its sensuous musicality, George's writing was informed by a "passion for the idea." Everything she wrote was a cri de coeur for reform, for a new socialist, egalitarian order that influenced thinkers from George Eliot to Karl Marx.

Never beautiful—even in her "bachelor" heyday in Paris—George not only swayed men's minds through the "fascination of her genius," she totally captivated them sexually. With an "odalisque's authority," she chose and beguiled her lovers, often two or more at a time. These affairs were conducted *con furioso.*

All Europe followed her soap opera amour with celebrity poet Alfred de Musset with bated breath. She handled this spoiled womanizer like an erotic maestra. At the zenith of her fame she invited him to her apartment, where he found her in a Turkish negligee inundated by admirers, smoking a pipe. While he caressed her babouches, she warned, "Do not speak to me of love." He did, according to plan, and spirited her off to Venice, where George checkmated his night of brothel hopping with a grand slam infidelity of her own. When she threw him over, he tore out his hair in tufts and cried, "Tell her that I love her with all my heart, that she is still the most womanly woman I have ever known."

With maturity, George's erotic heft increased. Wiser in love and learning, she floored it romantically. Under cover of a maternal, one-of-the-guys persona, she assembled a squadron of male admirers who "were more or less in love with her." A seasoned enchantress by now, she throttled up the elder aphrodisiacs. Making the most of her ripened, unfathomably complex personality, she drove a handsome Swiss poet to public tears at a soiree. "This complicated being is unintelligible to me," he cried. "Oh siren!"

Her hold on the twenty-eight-year-old Chopin was partly due to her senior diablerie. A prim salon idol chased down by young lovelies, he looked twice when the literary lioness attended his concert in one of her androgynous costumes. "Is she indeed a woman?" he asked. Afterward she slid a note, "You are adored," into his score and propositioned him through friends.

In addition to the perfected sex, she understood his music with a developed ear (she played the piano well), buoyed his spirits with her evergreen joie de vivre, and loosened him up with her "Rabelaisian" foolery. And he swooned into her maternal embrace.

Without dropping a stitch professionally, she bathed his fevered brow and nursed him through his physical and creative crises. In 1848, with his health and sexual performance on the wane, he staged a series of jealous tantrums that effectively ended their nine-year relationship.

His jealousy had not been unfounded. In the final lap of their romance she had affairs with two leading socialists. "There are some infidelities," she temporized, "which do not destroy love." She went on to achieve a "hale, honored, and triumphant old age"–with all the erotic perks of the senior goddess. Flocks of young men migrated to her Nohant headquarters and hung on her radical pronunciamentos and wise aphorisms. Like Morgan le Fay, she morphed into a "better" fascinator than in her "youth."

She could be picky. "To preserve my love and esteem," she said, "a man must hold himself very near perfection." After working through two prime paramours–a political activist and German pianist–she settled on a handsome engraver thirteen years her junior. Alexandre Manceau sweetened her bed with his "skilled" hands and pampered and adored her for fifteen years. She in turn rejuvenated his life. "I have laughed more," he said of their time together, "cried more, *lived* more than in all the thirty three preceding them. . . . What a joy!"

Her Wise Blood surged. "Brainwork," she said, came to her as easily as "to a child," and between 1857 and 1862 she wrote thirteen novels, two volumes of essays, and three plays. The blood went straight to her loins. Still "not exclusively any man's," George left Manceau for a weeklong honeymoon with a hulking painter two years younger than her son. After Manceau's death she had a final fling with her "Great Big Springtime" before she called it a day and re-created herself as "the Good Lady of Nohant"–grand old Wise Woman and oracle to the young. She died at seventy-two of an intestinal obstruction, a life regenerator to the last. Her final words were "Let green things–[be]."

Although women never cottoned to George Sand (and vice versa), she saw herself as the "Spartacus of women's slavery." Today we've struck off most of the shackles she had in mind except age anxiety. "To know how to grow old," she said, "is the masterwork of wisdom." With age, George rocked out: a juicy, "large-brained," abundant Silver Fox who reclaimed the divine privilege of eternal youth and allure.

Crowned with supraconfidence, "she spoke," said one observer, "with the large utterance of the early gods." That it was really the early goddesses explains her tarnished image. For a century after her death she was called "Chopin's bloodsucker," a "seductive, seditious devil," who practiced "black magic," and every man's nightmare of a sexed-up Mother Hubbard. As Sainte-Beuve told her, "Your genius, your devil is to be forever young."

Colette, 1873–1954

George Sand's modern successor is another tribute to the French sweet tooth for cerebral older women. At forty-seven this rotund woman with a frizzled aureole of gray hair watched her comely stepson of sixteen on a Brittany beach through kohled, predatory eyes. At 180 pounds, she looked like a Goddess of Willendorf in her tight black 1920s bathing costume. And goddess-wise she was about to ensnare a consort—in the shape of Our Lady of Words of Power.

Colette, the celebrated French author, was on the brink of a sexual "vintage time." After squandering her youth under the yoke of adulterous despots, she metamorphosed in midlife into one of the "beautiful, authoritative female demon[s]" of her fiction, a take-no-prisoners siren. This wasn't a freak mutation. Her whole life had been a long rehearsal.

Her mother and first mentor, herself a siren manqué, raised Colette in a female-dominant, sexually permissive household. Ensuring that her daughter developed a huge sense of self, she idolized her "Jewel of Pure Gold" and allowed her free rein. Colette's two marriages, though ordeals in feminine subjection, toughened her and honed her seductive edge.

The subsequent years as a stage performer were instructive too. She learned self-presentational savvy as a stage performer, experimented sexually and bisexually, and studied the great courtesans at close range, La Belle Otero in particular. By her late forties, then, when she'd reached the apogee of her literary fame, she was ready to strike.

Her stepson, Bertrand de Jouvenel, was so awed by the author of *Chéri* (the story of an older woman's seduction of a young man) that he trembled uncontrollably at their first meeting. Now, on the beach in Brittany, he trembled again as Colette sidled over and placed a practiced hand on his wet back. Later she cornered him in a stairwell and deflowered him, beginning an affair that lasted five years. The entire time Bertrand remained totally enrapt by his "voracious, expert, and demanding" "professor of desire."

At fifty-two Colette scooped up another young literary fan, a handsome bachelor who'd long admired her writing and fantasized about marrying her. Maurice Goudeket, a dark smoothy of thirty-five, dealt in pearls, symbol of the lunar goddess and trope for Cheri's attachment to the elder Lea. He too was electrified by the Great Author. Seated beside him at dinner, she gave him the full seeress treatment, fixing him with her "all-seeing" midnight blue eyes, then sprawling insolently on the sofa "like a great cat."

Afterward she surprised him on the Riviera and bore him off. For thirty years he loved her unconditionally and gave her the support and stability she needed to become France's premier writer. She "saved" him, he said, with her "vitality."

Colette returned his adoration, married him in 1935, and referred to him as her darling Satan. Their friends called him more graphically Mr. Goodcock. Their sex life was athletic and passionate, and their marriage, a movable feast of intellectual, artistic, and sensuous pleasures. To Colette, the arrangement could not have been more comme il faut; a young man's passion for an older woman, a doyenne of cerebral dazzle, was utterly "natural."

No amount of kohl and rouge could make Colette glamorous in old age. She barreled around Paris in Grecian sandals like Hagar the Horrible with a bad perm. But she had something more, the mantle of Circe (down to her sandals)—the "inconceivably old" "goddess of human voice" who transformed herself into a beauty and her captives into tamed beasts. Her persona, though, goes back farther still, to the first sex goddess, the "Knower of All Wisdom" and seducer of all mankind. When she was elected to the Académie Goncourt for her lit-erary achievements at seventy-two, Colette said her greatest pleasure was finding herself in her preordained place, "the only woman sur-rounded by a tribunal of men."

Mae West, 1893–1980

Of modern eldersirens, Colette admired Mae West most. This "impu-dent woman," she wrote, "alone does not experience the bitterness of the abandoned older woman." These soul sisters, both smart, sexy di-vas, threw different senior spells. Mae trafficked in the older deity whose erotic authority and appetite topped out in maturity.

The crone goddess of early myth possessed a "powerful appetite for sex" and copulated with abandon. She roamed the night skies in lascivious disguises and seduced young men through trickery or "sheer charisma." Her force field was no joke; few could withstand her torrid sexuality and superior sackcraft.

Beneath her self-parodic hypervamp facade, Mae West was the genuine article, the elderbabe with a cortege of pretty boys and allure to burn. "Just kiddin'," she purred as she cocked her hip and lobbed her pleasure queen zingers: "Too much of a good thing can be won-derful"; "Is that a gun in your pocket or are you just glad to see me?"; "I've been on more laps than a napkin"; "Find 'um, fool 'um, and for-get 'um." Through comedy, the oldest contraband in the book, she smuggled the repressed senior sex goddess, with her runaway appeal and appetite, into mainstream American culture.

Mae was nearly forty before she began her Hollywood career as a sexpot, four years older than the age-phobic Marilyn Monroe when she killed herself. But Mae West had been a "sex queen regnant" all her life. She seemed endowed with a rogue genome that "automati-cally" showed her "what to do."

"I can't help it"–she shrugged–"these guys pop up and there it is." By the time she reached her teens she'd established her lifelong erotic pattern: multiple men with one or more on permanent hold.

Like Colette, she also had an unusual mother-mentor to thank for her siren power. Matilda West was an anomaly in the turn-of-the-century Brooklyn of Mae's youth. A Bavarian corset model, Matilda held an advanced Continental view of sexuality, encouraging her daughter to play around, avoid marriage, and preserve her self-possession.

Her ideas on child rearing were equally iconoclastic. In defiance of conventional wisdom, she exempted her "favorite" from punishment, denied her nothing, and allowed her to quit school in the third grade for a professional stage career.

As a consequence, Mae developed into a boundary-smashing original with a stupendous ego. She hogged the limelight with nervy shticks on the vaudeville trail and, inspired by a dream of a bear with a four-inch penis (modest then in her demands), sexually sampled the neighborhood.

Terrified, as seductresses often are, by the prospect of maternity, she protected herself with a sponge attached to a silk string. She looked ill suited for the part. A lean scrapper of just five feet, she was an unremarkable brunette with a slight overbite, square jawline, and strong eyebrows like two virgule slashes.

During her apprenticeship in the theater, though, she restyled herself into a glamour girl. "There's nobody in my class," she boasted. "I'm my own original creation." She blondined her hair, redrew her eyebrows into penciled arcs, and floozied up her wardrobe, undulating on five-inch platforms. From female impersonators she took her hyperfemme mannerisms and whipcrack repartee; from African American dancers, her slo-mo pelvic rolls and the "shimmy shawobble."

She cruised for trouble and got it. She caused a riot in New Haven for her lascivious cooch dancing. And her plays up-yours'd the establishment. Beneath the hoochie-mama packaging, Mae was a serious cultural saboteuse, an inspired wordsmith whose four plays and eight movies lampooned bourgeois prudery. *Sex,* the story of an unrepentant prostitute, landed her in jail for corrupting minors, and the others (one about a woman with "voracious sexual demands") generated two raids, a lawsuit, and a tsunami of critical outrage.

While Mae was "inventing censorship" on the stage, her private life was just as transgressive, a reel-to-reel blue movie. During a brief marriage to a fellow vaudevillian, she locked him in his room on tour and accumulated the highest fines in the troupe for forbidden trysts with townies.

Convinced that a "thrill a day kept the chill away," she flipped the double standard and helped herself to chorus boys, cabbies, boxers, fans, and theater bigwigs. A matinee idol wanted to marry her, and a flashy entertainment lawyer, Jim Timony, who called her "Helen of Troy, Cleopatra, and Duse," left his practice to manage her career.

Mae handled her next career move, though, alone. With her play *Diamond Lil*, she discovered a way to sneak her flammable subject matter past the censors. Through nostalgia and self-parody, she made her lurid tale of white slave trade, sex, and prostitution palatable to puritanical America. The lewd lowlife seemed quaint in turn-of-the-century New York, and the siren suprema, harmless in the guise of a cartoon hussy with a swan bed and line of comic patter. The play was so wildly successful that Hollywood hired her for the movies.

In 1932, at a superannuated thirty-nine, she made her debut as the sex bomb in *Night After Night*. The macho studio moguls did a double take. This was outside their repertoire—a bossy broad who rewrote her lines and played a smartmouth, triumphant vamp. *She Done Him Wrong*, a diluted version of *Diamond Lil*, made Mae West a superstar, the biggest box-office draw in the country, and a household name.

Ten years and eight films later she was finished. Despite her ingenious cover—the jokes and sentimental scrim—the purity police caught on and sanitized her off the set. By the time Paramount canceled her contract, she'd been neutralized into a pale *Good Housekeeping* version of herself.

But nothing, not all the engines of social repression, could curb Mae's private life. The studs kept coming, often handpicked at boxing matches, where she'd signal her choice to an accommodating bookie. Rich, famous, and at her sexual and seductive peak, she could "pick and choose." In her mid-fifties she looked decades younger and took fabulous care of herself: no late nights, alcohol, cigarettes, or sunlight and lots of exercise, health food, and bottled water. So orgasmic she could climax in thirty seconds, she practiced kegels each day with her dumbbell reps and gave men a ride for their money.

On the road in *Catherine the Great* and *Diamond Lil* (two post-

Hollywood plays), she feasted on cast members, once with a sexual athlete who climaxed twenty-six times in twenty-four hours. But she liked the sauce of male adoration with her sexual gourmandizing. Besides her ever-faithful lawyer/manager, she collected a ménage of impassioned devotees: black boxer Chalky Wright; her bodyguard; a costar; and one poor cast member who cracked mentally when she refused to marry him.

Mae applied a deliberate system to these conquests. Physically she went for broke—the glamour, hells-apoppin' sex, and a setting that looked like a temple to Venus of Vegas. The living room was a riot of polar bear hides, nude statuettes, and white satin; the bedroom, a mirrored rococo playpen with a round lace-skirted bed in the center.

The imagination, however, was her real strike zone. "Let 'um *wonder,*" she told women; spook men's minds with humor, surprise, distance, and mystery. Flex your egos, she said, and take command of love. Men were like apes trying to play the violin; women ought to run the sexual show.

Run the show she did. On the verge of seventy she chose a chorus boy from her Vegas "muscleman act" and found "ultimately what every woman wants," a senior erotic dream. Thirty-three, blue-eyed, and abulge in all the right places, Chester Ribonsky changed his name to Paul Novak to please her and believed God had put him "on this earth to take care of Miss West."

He cooked for her, supervised her exercise, and spent romantic weekends with her at a Malibu beach cottage that housed two pet monkeys and murals of naked men and golden phalluses. At "seventysex," her libido still smoked. She rewrote the screenplay of *Myra Breckenridge* so that *she* (and not the other way around) put a young student in the hospital after a tumble, and she grabbed Paul's crotch at dinner when he denied her dessert and said, "This is one thing you're not going to tell baby she can't have." She died at eighty-seven, an eponym for *bambola* and an icon on the scale of Marilyn Monroe, who, as she pointed out, couldn't "even talk."

Unlike Marilyn, Mae was "genuinely dangerous." She dredged up one of patriarchy's worst nightmares and shoved its noses in it: the older woman unchained. Promiscuous, multiorgasmic, dead attractive to the opposite sex, and triumphant over them. "I was the first liberated woman, y'know," she shrewdly observed. My "message [was] a little too premature." She was drummed out of Hollywood and reduced to a comic caricature, but no one could beat down this mythic senior manslayer.

Several contemporaries grasped her numinous significance. One critic associated Mae with "a vanished race of regal sirens"; Mussolini called her a fertility idol, and Fellini wanted her to play the old "erotic witch" in *Satyricon,* the only woman sex-wise enough to give the jaded hero an erection. Dalí painted her as a modern goddess of desire, her face superimposed on a scarlet wallpapered shrine, her hair looped over a curtain rod in long blond temple veils.

Mae, though no student of mythology, wouldn't have disagreed. "I'm the woman's ego," she trumpeted, a "regal" "sex personality that requires multiple men." Or as her *Diamond Lil* book proclaimed, "Ancient Babylon in all its glory had no Queen of Sin to equal her. Sex was her scepter and she knew how to use it."

Mae would have credited another spell, besides sex, to her erotic sway: money and status. Wealth, she loved to say (as one of Hollywood's richest stars), "is stronger than a love-potion." Erotic texts through the ages have celebrated the aphrodisiacal impact of cash. "No loadstone so attractive," wrote the sixteenth-century Robert Burton, "as that of profit." And it can be a sizzling turn-on in older women, who often gain riches, authority, and rank with age.

We associate alpha sex appeal with men, but women create the same power buzz. The first goddess, after all, was a divine *ganze,* an almighty mistress of the universe who owned the real estate, cornered the money market, and called the shots. The legendary Celtic crone Morgan le Fay of Glamorgan (origin of "glamour") sat in the CEO's seat at the Green Knight's table and controlled the show.

Mrs. Frank Leslie, 1836–1914

Late-nineteenth-century America, of all places, produced a mogul Silver Fox who made out like a bandit with men and money. She used a man's name, Frank Leslie, and stormed the world with the lust of a robber baron. When women her age shuffled into the sunset to hook antimacassars, Mrs. Frank Leslie, "the colossus" of "publishers' row," ran a newspaper empire and raked in husbands, lovers, and admirers. Only older women, she declared, had the "gift of fascination," a gift in her case that traded heavily on clout and capital.

At the apex of feminine invisibility in public life, she was the "most famous and successful woman" of her time, author of seven books and nearly fifty articles, and head of Frank Leslie Enterprises, the biggest publisher of books and periodicals in the nation. She was also a hell of a *femme d'un certain âge.*

In her sixth decade a marquis and a prince came to blows over her in Hyde Park, a noted poet eulogized her, beaux crowded her box at the opera, and a young literary swell became her fourth husband after a four-day courtship. No modest matron, Frank identified with Napoleon, swanked around like an "undisputed queen," and reinvented herself goddess-wise, changing her name a total of eight times.

Frank (née Miriam Florence Folline) had good reason to reinvent herself. Although she fantasized a New Orleans childhood of lazy days on grillwork verandas, she grew up as seductresses tend to—off the curve, in hardship. She was born illegitimate and lived a poverty-stricken existence in an aberrant household.

Her eccentric father, however, a failed cotton broker, absolved her from a southern belle's education in genteel idiocy. In a crackpot scheme he grilled Miriam from age three for a "spectacular and exalted career," subjecting her to dumbbell workouts, cold plunges, and a crash course in Western culture. By ten she was fluent in four languages.

Her precocity didn't stop with academics. When her family moved to New York City to run a boardinghouse, she traded sexual favors for borrowed diamonds from a jewelry clerk named David Peacock. Her mother forced the couple to marry, and at eighteen the "Young Aspasia of the South" was already a divorcée, wise in men, jewels, and book learning and ramping for adventures beyond the classroom.

At this juncture she found the siren's classic open sesame, a guide and guru. After Miriam's brother committed suicide over a failed affair, the penitent ex-mistress appeared on the Folline doorstep and offered to employ his sister. The mistress was none other than Lola Montez, perhaps the most brilliant "mankilling spectacle" of the century. Fandango dancer, international heartbreaker, and fomenter of riots and a Bavarian revolution, Lola had just launched a theatrical tour of the East Coast.

She rechristened Miriam Minnie Montez and cast her in playlets as a "noble, rich, and beautiful widow" who ruins men. She primed Miriam for the part. As the archmaven of seduction she taught her "sister" the ropes, from the basics—hygiene, costume, conversation, and sexpertise—to the bravura moves of erotic brinkmanship and prestidigitation. Always a quick learner, Miriam seduced a married congressman after two months on the road and moved to his love nest in New York City.

There she plotted her next move and waited for her cards to turn up. The card in question was no king of diamonds, but he sufficed for a starter marriage, an almost universal feature of seductress's careers. Ephraim Squier, an archaeologist fifteen years her elder, had written the definitive book on serpent symbolism and knew a divine avatar (the moon goddess's ageless snake mascot) when he saw one. They married in 1857, and for four years Miriam kept a low profile, translating two French books and founding a New York Spanish newspaper.

Then the swarthy Frank Leslie arrived on the scene and hired her husband for his newspaper. It was instant fireworks. Frank, the father of American tabloid journalism, published three blockbuster newspapers and pulsated sex appeal. When he took the Squiers to Lincoln's inaugural ball, Miriam went in for the kill.

Though unpretty by any gauge—a face with cigar store Indian's nose, square chin, and pinched little putto mouth—Miriam "took down" all the ladies at the dance. She wore a white décolleté tulle gown that made the most of her lavish curves and an ivy wreath around a tumbling mane of copper curls. Her "beauty," wrote Frank in his newspaper the next day, "bewitched the crowd"; her "grace" and "sprightly and intellectual conversation" ravished dignitaries. She was, in short, the "acknowledged belle of the ball."

Two weeks later Frank left his wife and children and moved in with the Squiers, where he took up residence in a room adjoining Miriam's boudoir. The ménage à trois lasted for ten sensational years. Once the lovers jumped from a carriage on the way back from the theater and let Ephraim ride home alone; another time they bolted for a two-week "honeymoon" in Paris and abandoned him in a Liverpool jail to serve out Frank's unpaid debt.

During this heated triangle Frank put Miriam in business. He made her editor of a failing women's magazine, the *Ladies Gazette,* which she turned around overnight, replacing drab Civil War sagas and household hints with punchy fun-and-fashion features. In less than a year she salvaged a second magazine and netted six figures.

By 1873 she'd added a third to the list and published her translation of Arthur Morelet's *Travels in Central America.* The same year Frank's divorce went through, Miriam rid herself of Ephraim, who spent the rest of his life in a lunatic asylum.

At the advanced age of thirty-eight she wed for the third time, wearing a knuckle-length solitaire diamond. As Mrs. Frank Leslie she re-created herself into a high society doyenne. The Leslies opened a posh Fifth Avenue salon for "the most cultured and refined of the city" and bought a baronial Saratoga estate with its own lake and steamship, where they entertained the social elite.

Although Miriam now possessed her dream man and the most uxorious of husbands, she kept her options open. She wore the "lowest of low necks and shortest of short sleeves" and came on strong. When the Don Juan "Poet of the Sierras" Joaquin Miller hymned her as a goddess propitiated by ten thousand men and as the heroine of a romantic novel, *The One Fair Woman,* she rewarded his esteem with rendezvous. Some said Rome; others, Saratoga.

At the height of the party the roof caved in. A vindictive journalist exposed her amorous history in newspapers nationwide. Then the stock market crashed. Frank Leslie lost his shirt and, with satanic timing, contracted throat cancer. He died in 1880, enjoining his wife with his last breath to "do his work until [his] debts [were] paid."

Never one to strike tragic postures, Miriam changed her name to Frank Leslie and sprang into action. In less than a year she paid off creditors and turned a profit through aggressive makeovers, timely scoops, and modernized equipment. The astonished business world called her a "Commercial Joan of Arc," a miracle "moneymaker," as well as "the most fascinating newspaperman in America."

At forty-five she knew what to do with her senior sex appeal. The "belle," she wrote in one of her advice books, is "apt to be a widow" who upstages ingenues with her seasoned social charms, "perpetual youth," and "intellectual and conversational powers."

These were no idle boasts. Men packed her "Thursday Evenings" wall to wall and wooed her relentlessly. The rakish marquis de Leuville, a distant relative of Louis XIV, composed a sequence of love poems to her that he called his rosary, shot her initials on a wood plank, and stalked her for years with marriage proposals. But she refused to give up her "role of enchantress."

The marquis was followed by Prince George Eristoff de Gourie, a tall ripsnorting Russian fifteen years her junior. When the prince and the marquis crossed swords over her in Hyde Park and proved unequal to her regard, she dropped them both and kicked off a gala lecture tour across America. En route a Minnesota magnate nearly married her.

Frank, however, had other plans and set her sights on a literary trophy boy, Willie Wilde, Oscar's thirty-nine-year-old brother. She was fifty-five, with a full purse and a full pack of seductive wiles, including "Odic" kisses and the "secret of fascination." In less than a week he succumbed and wed her.

But the honeymoon was short-lived. Willie got drunk at the wedding supper and stayed that way, rising each day at one and toting up triple-digit liquor bills. After six months Mrs. Leslie-Wilde shucked him. "He was of no use to me either by day or by night," she quipped. "I really think I should have married Oscar [who was gay]."

Through all these romantic escapades Frank minded the store. She churned out copy at lightning speed—books, features, a play adaptation—and rescued Leslie enterprises from bankruptcy a second time, posting a sixfold profit in four months.

With a Scarlett O'Hara–on–steroids management style, she dressed in tight black gowns with ruffled organdy aprons, blended masculine steel with "feminine charm" and treated employees like a "queen with her court."

To better reflect her "Empress of Journalism" title, she renamed herself baroness de Bazus at the turn of the century. Emblazoning her coat of arms on every surface, she turned her Thursday evenings into quasi-royal levees. With a brace of terriers in tow, she swished out in full-dress satin, festooned with jewelry—a bracelet with her name in diamonds, a ruby-eyed serpent brooch, and a Venetian chain of three thousand diamonds that contained a secret vial for poison.

Overrouged and overpowdered, the septuagenarian Frank Leslie still had the old "gift of fascination." Two serious beaux occupied her golden years: a founder of a chain of coffee stands and a Spanish poet, scholar, and gentleman-in-waiting to the king who died just before their wedding. For the rest of her life Frank wore his gold key to the king's bedchamber on a chain around her waist. When her health failed in her late seventies, a devoted doctor gave up his practice to nurse her.

A showwoman to the last, she surprised everyone at her death by leaving her money to none of the promised legatees but to women's suffrage. The behest guaranteed the passage of the Nineteenth Amendment. Not that feminists thanked her; she was too sexy and ahead of her time.

A twenty-first-century visionary, she believed in female superiority and in combined erotic and professional power. The same "habit of command," "self-confidence," and "weight of will" worked in the marketplace and the "battle of the sexes." Go for the clout, she encouraged, strip off the "swaddling bands," become "queen of your position and he will make you queen of his."

Age just added jewels to the crown. In her view the seductress was always the elder deity, the sex goddess in her ageless, serpentine form. "The fascinating woman," she wrote, is like a "beautiful serpent" with "a dangerous power, a magnificent power, a fatal power, a blessed power . . . a power before which all others must wane and pale." Frank Leslie's carpets were woven with heart designs, and when a guest at one of her latter-day soirees noted that they were right under her feet, she tartly replied, "Quite their proper place."

*   *   *

Mrs. Frank Leslie dreamed of the day when the fifty-year-old woman would become a sex symbol. Her day has come. With women's increased longevity, freedom, power, and cosmetic options, the manslayer is just as likely to be sixty as twenty. We're witnessing, reports the *New York Times,* the "apotheosis of the older woman" in our generation.

Joan Collins posed nude for *Playboy* at fifty, Tina Turner became the first rock sex icon of sixty, and the perennial Elizabeth Taylor and Catherine Deneuve sold more perfume with their faces than any two women in history. Cher staged a rip-it-down comeback in her fifties and, like so many nouvelles Silver Foxes (Madonna, Mary Lou Whitney, et al.), seized the male prerogative of the young armpiece.

When does it end? More and more seventy and eighty mean fifty. Graham Greene envisions a boudoir queen on the wrong side of seventy in *Travels with My Aunt,* and the film *Harold and Maud* dramatizes (believably with the bewitching Ruth Gordon) a love affair between a boy and an octogenarian. Surrealist artist Beatrice Wood attributed her 105 years to "chocolate and young men." "Honey," said Lena Horne on the cusp of eighty, "sex doesn't stop until you're in the grave."

That's the good news. Unfortunately not enough are cashing in. Because of poor demographics and cultural bogeys, many, if not most, older women today feel "grayed out," bitter, and shelved. With a negative sex ratio approaching sixty-five men to a hundred women after age fifty and twenty-five to a hundred after seventy-five, life in sunset villages can be a Darwinian catfight for a few viable geezers. Men, the weaker sex, have an inconvenient way of dying off. A woman's chances of remarrying after fifty are only 17 percent, compared with 77 percent for men.

Some of course *do* beat the odds; a select few, like the great eldersirens, have always known how to get theirs. The rest, though, have no instruction manuals, except pack-it-in cronehood directives, gray power pep talks, and plastic surgery guides—and no "role models."

Silver Foxes come along just when we need them most. With their examples and lessons, they show older women how to claim the love lives they deserve. They explode the fallacies and myths that bedevil the Third Age and demystify senior seduction. As we've seen, they transcend the tastes and prejudices of specific eras and extend throughout recorded history.

For all their idiosyncrasies they have much in common. Defying the child development primers, they grew up "wrong," without normal parents, schooling, gender role orientation, social adjustment, or realistic egos. Grandiose mavericks, they broke rank, seized male privilege, and defied convention.

Along the way (or at the start), revolutionary mentors gave them the means and the marching orders to haul out. What these mentors taught them isn't in *Saving Ophelia*—sass, brass, sexual liberty, and the craft of seduction. If times and marriages were tough, the early Silver Foxes didn't pick their scabs; they remembered their worth and lessons and muscled up.

Seductresses in their youth, they continued strong as older women. They smashed senior citizen stereotypes and reframed the idea of age. Because they followed futuristic antiaging regimes, they remained physically fit and active and pushed the envelope, pursuing new projects and challenges and living as if there were no tomorrow. They didn't leave it to the young folks; they blatantly plied their senior charms: vitality, wisdom, money and status, maternal allure, and sexual firepower.

They scored big with men for a reason. They touched a mythic nerve. They reinvoked the archaic first sex goddess in her mature phase, the elder deity whom men cannot forget. Each Silver Fox dramatized a different facet of this divinity, although most contained the full complement of crone *über*charms. What they all had was the magic of metamorphosis and the goddess's most signal characteristic: complete, manifold, enriched-by-time identities. Jean-Paul Sartre called this ultimate turn-on the "plentitude of absolute being." Ripeness really is *all*, an all-powerful magnetic field for the hungering male soul.

In addition, vintage vamps play a shrewder hand at love. Time confers the craft and wisdom to excel. They've been around the block and realize that with age, strategies shift. While less significant, physical lures gain in symbolic strength. Ornament becomes more important, and settings grow more evocative of prestige, wealth, and myth—walled gardens, plush wombs, and Our Lady of the Animals.

Seduction, they knew well, is the ultimate head game. That explains why they edge out nymphets so easily. With maturity, seductresses ratchet up the psychological appeals: conversation, élan, disinhibition, ego strokes, festivity, and the art of the labyrinth. Past mistresses of the game, they're adept at stoking desire through circuit, delay, and difficulty and staving off satiety through a thousand and one enchantments.

Traditionally, older women are the official instructors of youth. We've heard about them ad nauseam, those sibylline postsexual frumps with their vats of borscht and wise mutterings. Now we need less dated models, sexy guides like those who mentored the seductresses, who'll teach us what counts—sexual mastery and life mastery until we die. Silver Foxes inhabited no kitchen corners peeling beets. They looked half their age, kept their waistlines, and wore diamonds as big as the Ritz. They mouthed off, cha-chaed through the corridors of power, courted the limelight, celebrated themselves, and refused to follow cultural instructions. Self-created originals, they kicked down the door of convention and of the future. They made a feminist racket, too much for the patriarchs.

The male chauvinist of Ovid's *Art of Love* lays a curse on one of these senior renegades, the old erotic witch Dipsas, who instructs women in how to get the upper hand in love. "May the gods," he howls, "give her old age no fire and many long winters." The pioneer Silver Foxes have lifted the patriarchal curse. The withered Dipsas has metamorphosed (as the elder, shape-shifting sex goddess loves to do) into a fire-eating dame, a twenty-first-century manslayer mama with sexual confidence and smarts and all the mega-allure of the first deity in her prime.

Morgan le Fay, the crone of Celtic legend, has taken back her original identity in the new millennium, that of the elder seductress-queen who lives in a golden palace at the bottom of the sea and grants her favored lovers unimaginable delights, sometimes immortality. Above the entrance to her Fortunate Isles an inscription reads: "Morgan the Goddess is her name and there is never a man so high and proud but she can humble and tame him."

CHAPTER FIVE

Scholar-Sirens

A fair body, if it have not a fair mind to match, is more like a mere image of itself or idol than a human body. However fair it may be, it must needs be seconded by a fair mind. —SEIGNEUR DE BRANTÔME

He who teaches a woman letters feeds more poison to a frightful asp. —MENANDER

Let women not by any means aspire at being women of understanding, because no man can endure a woman of superior sense. —MARY ASTELL

I always thought a tinge of blue improved a charming woman's stockings.

—R. M. MILNES

$\mathcal{M}$ary Wollstonecraft, eighteenth-century savante and author of *Vindication of the Rights of Women,* raced from home one rainy night in a state of suicidal despair. For a second time she'd caught playboy Gilbert Imlay, the father of her illegitimate child, in bed with another woman. She paced the London streets until her skirts were waterlogged, then jumped from a bridge into the Thames where a stray bystander fished her out.

For women of mind, as they used to be called, romantic misery went with the territory. Women who burned the midnight oil, played the scholar, and "unsex'd" themselves couldn't expect happy love lives and male adoration. We've all heard the nerd stories: how

they've been two-timed and dumped à la Mary Wollstonecraft or co-
opted like Mileva Einstein and recruited into lifelong gofer duty.
Some were even martyred. The fifth-century Egyptian philosopher
Hypatia was dragged from her chariot by a male mob and hacked to
death with oyster shells. Scared off the erotic preserve, others have re-
treated to Boston marriages and bitter singlehood.

"Men hate intellectual women," thundered the poet Tennyson.
The loathsome stereotype glowers out from every comic strip and
lowbrow comedy: the top-knotted schoolmarm with an upraised
ruler, staring daggers through her hornrims and breathing the halito-
sis of too much learning.

But when you scratch the surface, this male hostility to female intelligence turns out to be a hoax, a smoke screen for sexual fear. Our
Lady of Learning in fact is too alluring, too erotically potent for masculine comfort. Knowledge is not only power per se; it's a devastating
aphrodisiac. Especially for men. If Carl Jung is right—that the oldest
myths reign eternal in the human subpsyche—then men are programmed at the deepest level to turn onto and adore smart women.

In the first creation myths a goddess, a "Perfect Mind," created
the earth and heavens through her stupendous intellect. As the all-
inclusive Divine Being she also incarnated holy lust. For that reason the
sex divinities of early antiquity were deities of both wisdom and eros.

The Sumerian love goddess, Inanna, possessed the entire corpus
of human knowledge, having cozened it from the god of wisdom in
a drinking match. According to legend, he drank so much beer during her toasts and challenges that he gave her the *me*'s, which she do-
nated to society. They included erotic arts ("lovemaking, kissing of
the phallus," and female "allure") along with five kinds of intellectual
prowess: persuasive speech, judgment giving, psychological acumen
and counseling, logical analysis and record keeping, and philosophic
wisdom. Brainpower for Inanna incorporated sexual power and potentiated it.

Even after patriarchy had demoted the original goddesses and
subdivided them into specialties, the link between sex appeal and intelligence lingered. The Roman "Lady of Wisdom" Sapientia, for example, poured the wine of enlightenment from her breasts and rose

from the sea like crowned Aphrodite. Seduction preeminently is not for dummies.

While none of the seductresses lacked a quick mind and agile tongue, some were avowed intellectuals. They were also among the most devastating heartbreakers in Western history. Being smarter than average, they tended to be "globally gifted" (like the mythic creatrix), but each displayed a different sort of intelligence, roughly equivalent to Inanna's five types. Their style was early sex deity. Glamorous, gaudy, self-sovereign, sexed up, and footloose, they put their learning in the service of seduction and vice versa. They got it together goddess-wise: sage and siren, queen of smarts and queen of hearts.

Veronica Franco, 1546–1591

In the movie *Dangerous Beauty*, Veronica Franco's mother, a retired courtesan, tells her daughter the secret of seduction. "Desire begins in the mind," she says, then explains how to feign emotions, flatter codgers, and provoke imaginations by fellating bananas. Even in the sexist sinkhole of sixteenth-century Venice, no girl—especially Veronica—would have heeded such moronic advice.

Veronica Franco, a brilliant operator, knew to a scudo the aphrodisiacal value of her mind and worked it for all it was worth, becoming "the most famous and gifted courtesan" of her time. Her forte was verbal power, Inanna's "forthright and adorning speech."

The ruling elite took pains to keep this high explosive out of most women's hands, muzzling 80 percent of the population with enforced illiteracy. "Rhetoric in all its forms," declaimed the authorities, "lies absolutely outside the province of women." Those who rebelled were forced into marriageless obscurity and social exile. All except the Venetian courtesans. These renegade birds of paradise knew a hot turn-on when they saw one and "cultivated the verbal arts" as assiduously as bedcraft. Men paid separate fees just for their conversation, which was informed, learned, and spiked with lightning repartee.

Of these, Veronica Franco took the palm. She so far outrivaled the competition that she occupied a class by herself, as a peer of the city's intellectual elite and recognized grand mistress of speech. A polemicist, poet, and rhetorician, she published three breakthrough books of verse and letters, argued down the Inquisition in court, and defeated the reigning literary stars at public sparring matches.

She didn't speak in the low, dulcet strains of feminine modesty. She paraded her knowledge and pulled out the oratorical stops. Men traveled throughout Europe to see her and fell in love with her by the score. Nearly every important figure of the day numbered among her lovers, and she could name her price and men.

Veronica's educational background baffles every axiom of female achievement. Rather than with supportive parents and kid glove instruction, she grew up in an impoverished bourgeois family with a courtesan mother, a worthless father, and no schooling beyond what she picked up secondhand from her three brothers.

Unlike the movie, her mother never took her by the hand and ushered her into a vaulted library. Determined to "educate herself and follow scholarly pursuits," she scrounged what she knew through sheer rage to learn. Hardly out of adolescence, she married a local doctor, but by eighteen she was already ensconced as a courtesan, wielding her brains and sex appeal with the panache of another Inanna.

She was beautiful in the preferred cinquecento style—an oval face with a widow's peak, auburn curls, large, soulful eyes, and a bowed, bee-stung mouth—but she gilded the lily. She braided her dyed blond hair in an artful crested wreath, softened her skin with sugared alum and ass's milk, and hung dangling gold earrings from rouged earlobes. She wore embroidered high clogs and ornate, impearled gowns of satin, silk, and crushed velvet.

A maestra of the seductive arts, she threw marvelous parties: gondola sing-alongs through the canals and cozy suppers where she sang, played the harpsichord, and dined "without pomp and ceremony." She prided herself on her boudoir skills. She bragged that she performed so well "in bed" that all her "singing and writing [were] forgotten."

No one, however, forgot her voice for long. Early in her career she infiltrated the all-male literary ridotto, which served as her university, public forum, and personal fraternity house. Shrewdly plotting her career moves, she befriended Domenico Venier, the intellectual kingpin of Venice, and joined his elect salon of leading scholars and writers. At the ridottos, Veronica honed her mind and eloquence and established her persona as the "Honest Courtesan."

Rather than be a decorative accessory, she took the high ground and the offensive. In her poems, debates, speeches, and letters, she demolished courtesan stereotypes and positioned herself as a moral paragon, social critic, and patriot nonpareil. In masked contests she competed with and bested male poets with her erudition and flashing wit. Domenico's patronage ensured that she got published and heard, the rarest feat for a woman.

Instead of intimidating men, however, as popular wisdom would have it, Veronica's in-your-face verbal brilliance did just the opposite. She scored her wins with such rhetorical charm—ironic wordplay, humor, homey idioms, erudition, and erotic allusions—that men didn't know what hit them and lined up ten deep.

An "expensive mouthful," whose kiss alone cost five scudi, she drew the glitterati of the day. (Each of her six children was fathered by a different magnifico.) When the future French king Henri III visited in 1674, he only wanted to see her. Two hundred dancing girls in diaphanous white dresses had been procured for his pleasure, but he spent the entire time with Veronica, discussing literature and making love. He left with her portrait and two sonnets she'd written in his honor.

These verses, like much of her work, address the theme of eros—subversively so. Her sonnets to Henri rewrite the myth of Zeus and Danaë so that instead of a rape, the coupling is mutual, and Danaë, an active, equal participant.

All her poems proclaim her erotic authority loud and clear. She's the one in charge, the archsiren who taunts a heel-dragging beau with her "charm," "beauty," and list of "noble" suitors. Playboys, with their perfidious cruelties, get short shrift. She challenges one miscreant to a life-and-death combat in her bedroom, where she goes on the attack and wins:

> I'd not give in to you even an inch;
> instead, to punish you for your rotten ways,

I'd get on top and in the heat of battle,
as you grow hotter still defending yourself,
we'd die together shot down by one shot.

Later, in a series of elegies, she envisions a revolutionary solution to the battle of the sexes. At Fumane, a lover's country estate, she imagines an erotic earthly paradise where lascivious murals decorate the walls, desire and friendship merge, and the sexes live in equality and sensuous harmony. In such a utopia the courtesan redeems society with the "positive power of her love."

But by 1580, in the wake of plague and war, courtesans had lost their prestige and become social scapegoats and pariahs. Veronica was arraigned before the Inquisition on charges of witchcraft, whoredom, and satanic love spells. She mounted a brilliant suit in her own defense. Through calculated about-faces, artful counterattacks, faux submissions, and an array of rhetorical coups, she swayed the jury and won a reprieve.

She died not long after of fever at forty-five. In her will, written with her customary flair and colloquial frankness, she displayed characteristics not usually associated with seductresses. Devoted to her children and extended family, she divided her assets among them and included a handsome provision in the event of a granddaughter.

Although abhorred and shunned by her sex, she cared deeply about the plight of women. She bequeathed part of her estate to poor, undowered girls and twice petitioned the government with plans for a home for fallen women. One letter urged a friend to keep her daughter from courtesanry at any cost. "Of all the world's misfortunes," she wrote, "this is the worst."

But it was not the worst. Had Veronica married the biggest swell in Venice, she would have been shackled, gagged, and lobotomized. Despite the occupational hazards of her job (which were considerable), she was able to slip the feminine traces and reinvent herself as a suprema. With her silver tongue and seductive moxie, she scaled the Venetian heights, attaining independence, acclaim, and a mind and deluxe identity of her own. Not least, she entranced the whole city. Her devotees called her "divine," a "goddess." They little knew how nearly she approximated the first one, the cosmic queen of lust and "words of power."

Ninon de Lenclos, 1623–1705

The imperious Louis XIV was notoriously indifferent to the views of his advisers and peers, but he never changed a mistress without asking, "What does Ninon say?" In seventeenth-century Paris, Ninon de Lenclos was the last word in the court of public opinion, the high arbiter of manners, morals, and behavior. Like Inanna's alter ego, the wise, sexy Nimsum who ruled contests between sacred kings, Ninon possessed the gift of judgmental acumen, "the making of decisions."

The tastemaker of her times and lady of the level head, Ninon earned equal renown as a "priestess of Venus." So celebrated were her seductive exploits that for years after her death the women of Versailles petitioned her beribboned skull for erotic success in a secret chapel. The most distinguished men of the *grand siècle* found her irresistible and awaited (often unsuccessfully) her "caprice." They also bowed to her brains, stepped to her intellectual measure, and lapped up her "magnificent erudition."

Such a power mix did not come naturally to seventeenth-century women, two-thirds of whom could not sign their names. Silence, docility, chastity, piety, and vacuous domesticity defined the compass of proper femininity. Ninon was born in 1620 into the most proper of circumstances. Her genteel family belonged to the minor nobility of Touraine, and her mother personified female orthodoxy.

Ninon blew the feminine mold to flinders. As a child she sided with her fun-loving, libertine father against her mother and persuaded him to educate her as a boy. She learned languages, science, history, philosophy, and lute playing and rode with him through the Bois de Boulogne in breeches and doublet. By thirteen Ninon was a hardened blasphemer. She sequestered Montaigne in her prayer book at church and once brought the service to a horrified standstill by singing a bawdy ballad in the middle of a Holy Week sermon. When the curé scolded her, the independent-minded Ninon "saw clearly that religions are nothing but inventions" and washed her hands of organized Christianity. A few years later she discarded the last shreds of feminine modesty. Defying her hysterical mother, she dressed in flimsy, décolleté gowns and promptly "ruined" herself with one of the most notorious rakes in Paris.

At that point Ninon's life veered off into uncharted territory. Rather than the traditional recourse of compromised ladies—marriage or convent—she struck out as a free agent, deciding that since men had "a thousand privileges that men do not enjoy," she "would turn [herself] into a man." And no ordinary man, but an *honnête homme*, the beau ideal of honor, gallantry, and truth. A feminist trailblazer, she invented herself from scratch, without paradigms or role models. She moved to Paris, ditched the double standard, and put her philosophy into practice, choosing lovers for pleasure and wealthy *payeurs* (to whom she denied boudoir privileges) for profit.

Ironically, she got her start in society through her unprepossessing appearance. Although she became a byword for beauty (with Ninon creams and powders peddled throughout the nineteenth century), she gained access to Marion de Lorme's famous salon because she posed no threat to the famous courtesan. Even her flattering portraits portray Ninon with a long nose, heavy Joan Crawford brows, and a double chin. Her most besotted beaux admitted that "her mind was more attractive than her face and that many would escape her toils if they confined themselves to just looking at her."

Yet few escaped. With her uncommon mental and erotic fascinations, Ninon soon eclipsed and superseded the glamorous Marion. At barely twenty, she spellbound the salon with her fund of knowledge and wisdom. She engaged in Latin repartee with the Great Condé, skewered received truths, and expounded her philosophy, an Epicurean skepticism based on the pleasure principle and golden mean.

Ninon, though, confounded every she-pedant cliché. Unlike the priggish, affected *précieuses* of the day, she was a full-blooded voluptuary who believed, with Kierkegaard, that "it is not enough to be wise, one must be engaging." Her "enchanting" conversation was considered the wittiest, freest in town. *Toute le monde* repeated her quips, such as her dig at a minister who ennobled his mistress like Caligula "when he made his horse consul." Queen Christina visited her just to hear her talk, and a poet apostrophized her:

> Your conversation is magnetic
> I find nothing to equal it,
> It could console a king
> For the loss of a battle.

A live wire, she believed the "joy of spirit was the measure of its power." She presided over gay parties, where she danced, played her lute, and dined until all hours on gourmet cuisine. During one merry feast a guest threw a chicken bone out the window and hit a passing priest on the head. No less uninhibited than her guests, she swam nude and talked about sex as openly as a libidinous Dr. Ruth, once asking a friend to recommend a "spicy" bedmate.

She reportedly brought into play a refined and "prodigious erotic technique." "The bed is a battlefield," she once said, "where victories are won only at great cost." But her biggest sexual secret may have been less about vaginal love locks than cleanliness; when bathing was considered heretical, Ninon washed precoitally with soap and water and applied a light lemon scent.

She also broke with tradition by taking the lead in love. Cavalier-style, she cruised the Cours-la-Reine (a one-mile promenade ground) each day in her silk sedan chair, selected the keepers, and propositioned them with billets-doux. True to her inner sex goddess, she required numbers and variety. "Love with passion but only for a few minutes," she preached, and limited her amours to three months, always ending the affair at full boil.

Contrary to modern playgirls, though, she put her conquests in her power, entangling them in her love nets. Most of the desirables of the day adored her: three generations of the Sévigné family, Gaspard de Coligny, the war hero duc d'Enghien, seigneur de Charleval, Le Grand Madrigalier, and scores of other notables. She was, penultimately, "the type that left and was not left."

Mid-career, however, Ninon about-faced and became monogamous for three years. Too much her own person to seek self-completion in another, she chose a nonintellectual Adonis and found mental stimulation elsewhere. The man was the marquis de Villarceaux, the "slim-hipped wolf" and premier womanizer of the realm. Physically magnetized by each other and equally matched in spirit and libido, they retired to the country, where Ninon studied the "articles of her belief" with a resident scholar while Villarceaux hunted. They had a son together, whom Ninon (in another surprise move) loved tenderly and promoted throughout her life.

When Villarceaux's lowbrow interests wore thin, Ninon moved back to Paris, with her spurned lover hard on her heels. He took a house across the street and fell into a fever when he saw a light on in her bedroom and suspected rivals. To hasten his recovery, Ninon cut off her hair and presented it to him, creating a national vogue for the short bob, *cheveux à la Ninon*. He remained unappeased and unconsoled but eventually, like all her lovers, forgave her and became her loyal friend.

The Paris Ninon encountered on her return in 1655 had changed since the libertine glory days of the regency and succumbed to a wave of puritanical zeal. As usual in these cases, courtesans paid the price. A coalition of the church and Ninon's numerous female enemies mobilized and succeeded in sentencing her to a convent for wayward women for eight months. But Ninon swayed the nuns in her favor and stage-managed a protest demonstration by her beaux outside the walls that forced the king to rescind the decree.

After a triumphal reentry into Paris Ninon reopened her salon and secured her position as the city's intellectual and moral touchstone and courtesan queen. The major figures of the day—Racine, La Rochefoucauld, Saint-Évremond, Jean-Baptiste Lully, and Molière—flocked to her exquisite parlor and sought her imprimatur. Molière tried out all his plays on her first and credited his "Leontium," the Epicurean courtesan of ancient Greece, with the inspiration of *Tartuffe*. Her version, he claimed, was superior to his.

During this period Ninon produced her own small but distinguished literary oeuvre: poems, a character sketch, and a full-length satire savaging lecherous prudes, *The Coquette Avenged*. With her friend Saint-Évremond, she also solidified her Epicurean principles, the pursuit of happiness through moderation, reason, and strict morality. Ninon did not drink or indulge in anything to excess and was known as a model of rectitude. She reserved a year's income for those in need and gained the epithet "the beautiful keeper of the casket" after she guarded a friend's fortune for many years and returned it intact.

At midlife she opened an academy where she taught her enlightened Epicureanism and arts of love to aristocratic youths, with special emphasis on pleasing women. Lovers, including two bluebloods half her age, filled her dance card in later years. She swore off sex, though, at fifty-two and consoled herself with philosophy, reading, and friendship.

Shunned all her life by respectable women, Ninon was nonetheless "the century's leading feminist," in both example and precept. She mentored like-minded protégées (such as Madame de Maintenon) and condemned the plight of the feminine masses. They were tyrannized by lovers and husbands, she charged, "set upon by members of their own sex," and rendered stupid in love. She urged them to wise up erotically and, as per the goddess, play the field. "A woman who has loved but one man," she counseled, "will never know love."

Uncharacteristically for a courtesan, she died comfortably of old age, with a valedictory poem on her lips. A radiant well-being accompanied her to the end, the result of a mind-heart sagacity cultivated to a perfect pitch. After her death mythmakers transformed her into a sex icon, the subject of twenty-three plays, dozens of novels, and hundreds of old wives' tales.

But none perceived the true source of her supra-allure. One suggested that her combination of "beautiful woman" and gentleman made her the "most delicious of all." Ninon, however, pushed a hotter button and embodied a more "delicious" combination: the sex goddess and all-wise goddess, the judge of man and arbiter of culture and morality.

Lou Andreas-Salomé, 1861–1937

When Lou Andreas-Salomé arrived in Vienna in 1912 to study psychoanalysis with Freud, few would have guessed they had a seductress in their midst. She was a stout, fiftyish matron who wore no makeup and looked so much older than her age that she'd been mistaken for her lover's mother. She had the coarse face of a Muscovy peasant: a square chin, wide, fleshy mouth, beetling brow, bulbous nose, and deep-set eyes. But this plain Mother Hubbard, with her dirty blond hair pulled back in a bun, was one of the leading femmes fatales of her time and all times. More than one man committed or threatened suicide on her account, and Freud's circle went into an electron spin the moment she set foot in his lecture hall.

Although love spells involve a complex mélange of lures, Lou's chief aphrodisiac was her psychological genius. "Her mind was her charm center," said one conquest, "captivating beyond compare, stimulating beyond compare." But it was a mind with a special bent: insight into the human psyche, Inanna's "perceptive ear" and the "art of counseling." Few intellectual gifts are sexier. One of our deepest erotic wishes, as amorist writers and psychiatrists attest, is to be known and validated for our true selves.

Lou Andreas-Salomé, the "great understander," knew this and put it to astute account in love. The god-men of her generation ate from her hand and tranced out beneath her "magnificent tiger-gaze" that plumbed and affirmed their core identities. The same depth charge perception also paid off professionally. A celebrity writer, thinker, and psychiatrist, she wrote twenty influential books and more than a hundred essays, articles, and reviews.

As one of the founding mothers of psychoanalysis, Lou was her own best subject. From childhood she deliberately fashioned her character into a paragon of mental health. With an acute sense of her nature and needs, she orchestrated her life for maximal happiness, becoming one of Abraham Maslow's self-actualized exemplars before there was a name for it. Her titanic ego—vitality, courage, nonconformity, and swerve—inspired Nietzsche's theory of the superman and prompted Freud's rare concession that she was "beyond human frailty." But the achievement of this wunderself didn't come without a struggle.

Like other seductresses, Lou had to strike off the fetters of convention. She was born, by coincidence, in Russia on the day the serfs were emancipated, February 12, 1861, the last child and only daughter of the aristocratic Salomé family. From the start Lou was locked in mortal combat with her mother over correct behavior. But her sexagenarian imperial father indulged Lou and treated her like an infanta. Secretly opposing his wife, he allowed her to do as she wished, run wild, and roughhouse with her three brothers. When she found school and her classmates distasteful, he withdrew her, with a preemptory "Lou does not need compulsory schooling." When she later rebelled and flatly rejected the tea party circuit, her mother gave up in exhaustion.

Worse was to come. After her father's death the seventeen-year-old Lou tacked up her ninety-five theses. She hunted down a swashbuckling preacher, Hendrik Gillot, and defected from the family faith to the Dutch Reformed Church. More shocking still, she studied the history of Western philosophy in his private apartments, sometimes perched on his knee. Only after he seized her in a mad embrace and said he'd made plans to marry her and divorce his wife did things come to a head.

The horrified Lou fled from St. Petersburg and enrolled (in another act of apostasy) at the University of Zurich. She'd fled, not for the first time, from sexual passion. With all her intellectual precocity, she was a sexual late bloomer, perhaps the latest of any siren on record. But she ignored convention, heeded her own clock, and remained a virgin until she was ready for surrender with autonomy and satisfaction guaranteed.

In the interim she churned up some of the highest romantic dramas and greatest scandals the staid European intelligentsia had ever witnessed. After her studies in Zurich, where professors proclaimed her an intellectual "diamond," Lou moved to Rome and ingratiated herself with the feminist doyenne of the day, Malwida von Meysenbug. Lou persuaded her of their affinity, invaded her salon and promptly grabbed Malwida's prize exhibit, the philosopher-genius Paul Rée.

Paul, a brooding nihilist of thirty-two, was staggered by Lou. On their long talks during midnight strolls through Rome, she listened intelligently and challenged his ideas with breathtaking skill and vigor.

He proposed and was so smitten he agreed to her preposterous coun-
terproposal that they live together platonically with another like-
minded philosopher.

Enter Friedrich Nietzsche. From the moment he met her,
Friedrich felt he'd found the one woman who "understood him as no
one else." Lou's clairvoyant grasp of his thoughts, combined with her
defiant, life-affirming character, convinced him he'd at last discovered
a "sibling brain" and alter ego.

To public stupefaction, he, Paul, and Lou settled into a threesome
that they called the holy trinity, with the two friends secretly vying for
Lou's affections. Throughout this turbid ménage, Lou held her
ground and refused to be engulfed by either philosopher-king, intellectually or erotically. A photograph of the time shows her firmly at
the controls, whip in hand behind Paul and Friedrich, who were harnessed to a donkey cart.

In the end it was too much for the high-strung Friedrich. He commandeered her on a mountain expedition, kissed her wildly, and demanded marriage. When Lou declined, he went to pieces. With the
fury of a "jilted schoolboy," he took an opium overdose, challenged
Paul to a duel, cursed Lou, and excoriated the whole female sex in
Thus Spake Zarathustra.

Afterward Lou moved in with Paul in a sexless *à deux.* He called
her "Her Excellency" and made her well-being the "sole task of his
life" for five years. She bloomed intellectually under these hothouse
conditions, publishing an acclaimed novel about female freedom and
attracting the best minds to their avant-garde salon. One regular said
her book alone made his "love for Lou burst into bright flames."

Her novel had a similarly inflammatory effect on a middle-aged
professor en route through Berlin. Friedrich Carl Andreas, an exotic
Orientalist, scholar, and world traveler, conceived such a passion for
Lou that he planted himself on her doorstep and would not leave until
she married him. Moved by a mysterious inner command (perhaps related to increased security), she agreed in 1888, with her usual proviso:
no sex. Although she invited Paul to join them, he scrawled a wild note,
"Be merciful, don't look for me," and disappeared, never to be heard of
again until workmen found his body at the base of a cliff years later.

The marriage was as unconventional as everything else about Lou. Friedrich, after an abortive attempt to rape her, moved downstairs with the housekeeper and gave the upper floor to Lou, who came and went as she pleased. The union lasted forty-three years, during which Friedrich lovingly played caretaker-to-genius, colleague, confidant, and domestic anchor.

Lou thrived. She traveled and wrote steadily: reviews, fiction, philosophic essays, and two daring full-length psychological critiques. One, perhaps the first psychobiography, explained Nietzsche's philosophy through his inner pain and conflicts. In the other, she examined Ibsen's plays and came up with revolutionary dynamite. Women, she argued, are the superior sex, happier, hardier, sexier, better integrated, and naturally polygamous. They don't "need the man in *any* sense." Her fictional heroines began to change soon thereafter. During her mid-thirties they suddenly coruscate with allure, lay men out, and exult in the "marvel of sexual passion."

Any number of suitors might have been responsible for Lou's late-life sexual initiation: a Russian "giant of a man" who spirited her off to an Alpine hut for a week; the noted socialist Greg Ledebour; or two playwrights, Gerhart Hauptmann and Frank Wedekind, who dramatized her as a femme fatale. But she woke up with a bang, hypersexed and plurally inclined for the rest of her life, except for one monogamous passade.

The affair was a long romance with Rainer Maria Rilke, then an unknown poet and thirteen years her junior. Lou saw with X-ray clarity his potential and called herself his wife for four years. Under her tutelage he remade himself. He changed his name from René to the more masculine Rainer, learned the art of "festiv[ity]," and acquired confidence, psychic stability, and intellectual discipline. Their life together was "an unprecedented period of inspiration and creation for them both," with shared studies and gay excursions to Russia and the countryside.

For Rainer she embodied a mythic divinity, a goddess of "blessed comprehension," his "magnificent one," his "June night of a thousand paths," his muse, "mother and home." Then, on the cusp of forty, Lou wearied of Rainer's desperate idolatry and dropped him for more lovers and greater freedom. Like her other victims, he never got over her and said on his deathbed that she alone knew who he was.

In middle age Lou was no Brigitte Bardot. Heavy, plain-faced, and dressed in shapeless gray shifts, she seemed hardly a power vamp. Yet she was inundated with lovers. The most serious, handsome Dr. Friedrich Pineles (known as Zemek), squired her around for a dozen years and almost certainly got her pregnant. (Lou, averse to motherhood, miscarried, perhaps on purpose.) Despite Zemek's popularity with women, he never married and died in 1936 with Lou's "picture [still] in his heart."

Throughout her fifties Lou continued to burn through men. She not only infatuated Freud, who sent her flowers and "sweet letters," but enrapt his apostles. Victor Tausk, a tall, young "beast of prey," fell passionately in love with her (only to commit suicide later), and a married Swedish psychoanalyst mooned over her for two years. She'd bewitched him, he believed, with her diabolic gift for "entering completely into the mind of the man she loved." Another inamorato attributed her witchcraft to her "archaic" sexuality, her insatiable appetite and lascivious speech. "The reception of the semen," she'd say en passant, "is for me the height of ecstasy."

In psychoanalysis Lou found the ideal métier for her combined erotic and psychological gifts. With her usual independent-mindedness, she challenged Freud and developed her own theories, specifically on anal eroticism (still the standard on the subject), narcissism, love, and female sexuality.

A self-exalter herself, she anticipated post-Freudians, like Norman O. Brown, and valorized narcissism as the true source of love and vitality. Expanding on her female chauvinism, she claimed that women were not only the hornier, hotter, polygamous sex but also erotic multitaskers who performed a dozen roles at once in love: "lover, sibling, refuge, goal, defense, judge, angel, friend, child, and mother." Male envy of this sexual superiority explained the angel-whore split and misogyny in general.

On sex she waxed mystical. Through intercourse, she wrote, lovers merged with the unity of all creation and recovered their innate bisexuality. Satiety and infidelity, though unavoidable, could be averted through love artistry or personal charisma. Some "geniuses" of seduction, she concluded, have "an unwonted aura of majesty" and entrain men forever.

Unquestionably she had herself in mind. "Yes, *I am* a femme fatale," one of her fictional alter egos says, "and I shall sit back and *enjoy* being it." Enjoy she did. Ignoring female hostility (housewives called her the "Witch of Hainberg") and social coercion, she achieved the rarest of human fates: self-actualization, happiness, acclaim, and the adoration of men. At the end, half bald and sallow with renal disease, she enamored a young acolyte who nursed her and devoted his life to sorting her papers. She didn't exaggerate when she referred to herself as the "fortunate animal."

Others—Freud, Rilke, and assorted lovers—went beyond her self-assessment and equated her with a "mother goddess of the stone age," a "daemonic [and] primordial" "force of nature." She tapped a fantasy, buried deep in the genetic memory of the psyche, for a supreme she-deity of desire and wisdom to whom all hearts are open, no secrets hidden. At the same time, she used her "dangerous intelligence" for her own ends, to know herself cold and become what she was—the "Lou phenomenon," sovereign in love, learning, and life mastery—and in the bargain, to find an "existential joy" of unparalleled, even mythic proportions.

For all of Lou Andreas-Salomé's psychological brilliance, she couldn't compute. Unable to calibrate her fees against the declining German mark, she would have starved as an analyst if Freud hadn't sent her periodic handouts. "The Fairy godmother who stood at your cradle," he chided, "apparently omitted to bestow on you the gift of reckoning."

But this gift was one of Inanna's prime contributions to civilization and an innate female talent: "the holy measuring rod and line." Inanna's deputy, the sexy grain goddess Nisaba, governed writing, accounting, surveying, and the "cubit ruler which gives wisdom." Although usually considered a male left-brain function, logical and mathematical intelligence stems from the feminine principle. Paleolithic peoples learned to calculate by observing the cycles of the moon, the goddess's imago. The twenty-two-thousand-year-old Venus of Laussel holds a bison horn aloft in her right hand notched with the thirteen months of the lunar year. Inevitably, two of the premier manslayers of Western history were queens of reason, analytic thinkers and surfers of factual reality.

Émilie du Châtelet, 1706–1749

The first, Émilie du Châtelet, was a woman cut to a superhuman scale. "A genius in virtually every realm of mathematics," she outsmarted the leading male scholars of her day. In addition, she looked like a celebrity model, loved like a Lotharia, and lived like a sultana. "The wench," said a Romeo of the age, "is formidable." "The most brilliant member of her sex in Europe," she was also a "passionate," magisterial siren who captured and held the two *beaux du jour* of Paris, the duc de Richelieu and Voltaire.

Yet few parents have ever held out less hope for a daughter. The youngest of four children in a titled, wealthy family, Émilie was an ugly duckling, a plain, gangling tomboy whose mother rejected her in favor of her two tractable sisters. Her father, a pompous court official, had an equally dim view of Émilie's prospects, but he took a shine to her and gave her an uncommon education. She received the finest tutors and athletic instructors and proved a prodigy, in sports and languages, math, and metaphysics. "No great lord will marry a woman," groaned her father as she approached maturity, "who is seen reading every day."

She proved him wrong. When she arrived at Versailles for her "debut" with crates of texts and philosophy books, she set the jaded court gallants back on their heels. They took bets on who'd have her, but she fought them off, literally, for two years until she found the right husband, dueling a cavalier in the courtyard and gambling the others under the table through "prodigious feats with numbers in her head."

Unexpectedly she'd become a stunning beauty. A five-foot-nine-inch blonde, she had a full *poitrine* and a piquant face: wide-set eyes, a high forehead, and a fetching pointed chin. She wore her thick hair unpinned to her waist and dressed in gold and silver *robes volantes* with such low necklines she created a fashion for rouging nipples.

At nineteen she discovered the marriage partner best calculated to serve her purposes. The marquis du Châtelet-Lomont measured up not only physically (at over six feet) but practically; as a general he spent most of his time in the field, leaving Émilie free to follow her own devices.

After an obligatory three children, Émilie took wing. She hired the best math and physics professors from the Sorbonne, studied maniacally (sleeping only two to four hours a night), and worked out original theorems. Determined to talk shop with her peers, she cross-dressed in breeches and frock coat and gate-crashed the all-male scientific club, the Café Gradot.

She threw herself just as furiously into high society. Overdressed, overperfumed, and histrionic, she was the center of attention of every gathering, quoting Descartes and flouting feminine decorum at every turn. She attended the theater, she bathed nude in front of her male servants, she took lovers. With one, she feigned suicide to get her way; with another, she discussed "the nature of man in relation to himself and his universe" in bed.

The duc de Richelieu, however, was of a different caliber altogether. This national hero and *homme fatal* "with all womankind at his feet" equaled Émilie in brains and libido and transformed her life. "Fascinated by her mind," he encouraged her ambitions, guided her studies, and taught her emotional restraint. The affair lasted longer than any in his life, a year and a half, and ended only when he introduced her to Voltaire.

They made an odd couple. Émilie stood a head taller than Voltaire, then the intellectual dynamo, gadfly, and salon darling of eighteenth-century Europe. But they were made for each other. Both larger than life, both geniuses, they shared a passion for learning and social defiance. Before the night was out, they had fallen madly in love, Voltaire for the first time at thirty-nine.

They retired to Cirey, a Châtelet château in Lorraine that Émilie transformed into a voluptuous think tank and love nest. The library rivaled a small university's, secret passageways connected their studies, and drawn curtains kept the rooms in perpetual twilight for mental concentration. Each, competitively whetted by the other, worked at fever pitch on separate projects, joining at dinner for long, guest-filled banquets.

Émilie descended the staircase for these dinners in full court dress, her hair upswept and decked with diamonds, her hands bejeweled and stained with ink. As dumbwaiters (the first in France) delivered courses of gourmet food, Émilie and Voltaire jockeyed volubly for attention. They fired off erudite screeds, argued at top volume, traded bon mots and insults in gutter French, then stopped abruptly and burst into laughter.

The revels continued beyond the dinner table. They staged play productions and impromptu poetry readings at 4:00 A.M. and once mounted a midwinter picnic to a frozen creek, where they sat on satin cushions in the snow and debated politics and drama all afternoon. Sometimes Émilie entertained the company with entire operas, which she played on the harpsichord, singing the parts from memory.

The Cirey years marked a period of prodigious intellectual output. The high-tension sexual and mental ambiance—the mutual admiration, challenge, and stimulation—spurred them both to massive achievements. Although most of Émilie's work has been lost, she wrote the definitive book on Newton during this time and a three-volume study of Leibniz that earned her an international reputation as one of the leading minds of her time. She launched hundreds of scientific experiments and bested Voltaire in a science competition that argued the opposite thesis. The academic establishment anointed her "Lady Newton," while Voltaire hymned her as "the most extraordinary woman in France" and his "divine mistress."

A man of parts himself—poet, philosopher, historian, dramatist, and moralist—Voltaire was hard put to keep up with her. Émilie worked with the frenzy of an eighteen-armed goddess. Before even beginning her real work, her scientific and mathematical studies, she spent six to eight hours each day on other pursuits. She wrote poetry, translated Latin and Greek (her *Oedipus* remained a classic for over a century), designed a darkroom and indoor kitchen, and mastered law to defend her husband's interests in court.

For fun, she wrote the first how-to, *On Happiness*, which became a best-seller and went through six editions. In it she told women how to be as happy as she was. They should, she advised, cultivate "strong passions," savor the pleasures of the flesh, enrich their minds through study, and make themselves mistresses of the "metaphysics of love."

Although she didn't expatiate on this metaphysic, she plainly understood the arts of love. Along with the erotic and mental fireworks she delivered, Émilie monitored Voltaire's life like a stage mother. She oversaw his diet, drove off pests and distractions, and reconciled her fractious lover to Louis XV with the "finesse and cunning" of an experienced diplomat. During their thirteen years together women scrambled to get their hands on Voltaire. But he was content to remain her "willing slave," immune to temptation throughout his extended leaves in Paris and Prussia.

Nevertheless, these volatile geniuses drifted apart in the late 1740s, he to his niece, she to the arms of a glamorous poet ten years her junior. With him she became pregnant and died in childbirth at forty-three. When Voltaire heard of her death, he sobbed so violently that he struck his head on a post and fell down a flight of stairs. "I have lost half of myself," he raved, and eulogized her as the ultimate woman, "a very great woman whom ordinary women knew only by her diamonds."

Women knew more of her than her diamonds, of course—more than they liked. They sniggered at her behind their fans, cut her, and called her a "sorceress." The clearheaded Émilie, who had an exact sense of her own worth, recognized her superiority and paid them no heed. "When I add the sum total of my graces," she noted with mathematical precision, "I confess I am inferior to no one." "The light of my genius," she promised Voltaire, "will dazzle you." It was a light no man, certainly no alpha man, could resist: the primordial lunar light of the goddess who bestowed numerical calculation, along with divine lust and the sex energy of creation.

Martha Gellhorn, 1908–1998

The divine Nisaba's accounting skills extended beyond numbers to language. She was the mistress of "Scribal Knowledge," the fact gatherer and record keeper of society. Martha Gellhorn, her modern successor, took the measure of the twentieth century with pitiless accuracy. The first female war correspondent and a superb reporter, she wrote seven prizewinning collections of journalism, eleven books, and was known as one of the best witnesses to our age. She was also known as "the blonde peril" and "Magnificent Martie," a killer siren who wowed men, notched up the choice honeys on her garter belt, and walked out of three marriages.

Martha Gellhorn's upbringing could be a template for the making of a seductress. She was born into a permissive and unconventional family, the only daughter in a household with three brothers. Her mother and father, prominent St. Louis community leaders, raised their children on a diet of praise and positive reinforcement, with a religious respect for independence, nonconformity, and knowledge. During dinner debates, children were required to follow *Robert's Rules of Order* and prove their points with evidence from books and journals. Living in the company of boys, Martha grew up feisty, rebellious, cocksure, and precociously smart.

When her private girls' school threatened to make a lady of her, the Gellhorns transferred her to a progressive, coed school that they cofounded. Later, at Bryn Mawr, she escaped the "curse of respectability" again, leaving after three years for a career in journalism. With burn-your-boats bravado, she declined money from home, traveled to Albany, barged in on a newspaper editor, and demanded a job. For six months she covered the morgue and social events for the *Times-Union*, then bartered her way to Europe on a steamship in exchange for a magazine story.

Her career as a foreign correspondent had begun. Also as a seductress. She was tall, blond, and svelte, with chorine legs and a Breck girl face. She dangled a cigarette between her fingers in a "gesture of the brothel" and wore heavy maquillage and Schiaparelli samples. Already a veteran of an affair with a St. Louis poet (who'd written a sonnet about her "golden head" on his pillow), she had the sheen of experience and a stock of practiced love arts. Uninhibited, sensuous, fun-loving, and flirtatious, she "could talk the birds off a tree."

As soon as the journalist Bertrand de Jouvenel met her, he simply walked out on his wife. This magnificent man was no tyro. Initiated and groomed by his stepmother, Colette, he was a world-class lover and serious activist who edited the leftist magazine *La Voix*. He shared Martha's passion to "look and learn" and toured Europe with her, analyzing the body politic and lobbying for world peace. They married in 1933, but Martha, a chip off the goddess block, found monogamy and settled domesticity too big a "sweat" and divorced him two years later.

At that point Martha got her first journalistic break as a field investigator with the Federal Emergency Relief Agency. Her record of the Depression fallout across rural America, delivered in "precise," "evocative" prose, made her famous. Her picture ran on the cover of the *Saturday Review of Literature*, and *The Trouble I've Seen* drew praises from the toughest reviewers, one of whom compared her with Hemingway.

They seemed destined to meet. One afternoon in Key West she wandered into Sloppy Joe's Bar, and there sat the thirty-seven-year-old author in a stained T-shirt and cutoffs belted with a piece of rope. Martha might have walked out of his *Sun Also Rises*, another Lady Brett femme fatale. She wore a black silk sheath and heels and, when she slid over to talk to him, spoke with wit and arch worldliness in a "husky, eastern-seaboard-accented voice."

They left the bar together and conducted a torrid affair under his wife's nose, calling each other Mooky and Scrooby and trysting openly. Later they reunited in Spain, where Martha finagled an assignment on the Spanish Civil War. Invading the no-woman's-zone of war reportage, she stationed herself with Ernest in the thick of enemy fire and wrote dead-on dispatches that surpassed his in "intensity, focus, and unity."

Their nine-year romance was one long erotic arm wrestle. They used each other as copy, not always flatteringly, and fought like matched champions. Deaf to Hemingway's pleas to do his bidding, Martha went her own way, and when they married in 1940, she refused to take his name, play muse-wife, or stay home. From Finca Vigia, their Cuban villa, she flitted around the world on assignments and drove Ernest to distraction. He "would be destroyed," he told Archibald MacLeish, if anything happened to her.

As he grew by turns more irascible and possessive (to the accompaniment of twelve whiskeys a day), Martha consoled herself with a handsome jai alai player and suffered no shit. After one of Ernest's drunken exhibitions in public, she ran his favorite Lincoln into a ditch and let him walk home.

Without a qualm she left to cover World War II and beat him to the punch. Not only did she get there first, but she outclassed him in courage and coverage. She walked through minefields, flew a night-bombing mission in an unpressurized Thunderbolt, and stowed away on a hospital boat on D-Day and sneaked ashore as a stretcher bearer. Her powerful pieces, with their savage accuracy and clinical eye for significant detail, were masterpieces, "miniatures of war." When the liberators arrived at Dachau, she was there to record it with chilling precision.

By the war's end her marriage to Ernest had tanked. Martha filed for divorce and paired up with a war hero, General James Gavin, of the Eighty-second Airborne, while Ernest went off the deep end. Having never been dumped before, he stalked and harassed her throughout Europe, once hysterically breaking into her hotel room with a bucket on his head.

During the postwar years Martha took a sabbatical from "writ[ing] and tell[ing] what she saw." She retired to a village in Mexico, where she raised an Italian boy she'd adopted, and freelanced stories and articles. As always, there were men, notably Dr. David Gurewitsch, a thinking woman's Casanova, who fell deeply in love with her and pleaded with her to move with him to New York City.

But in 1952 she broke it off, moved to England, and found another beau to her taste, Tom Matthews, a handsome, debonair ex-editor of *Time*. They married in 1954, and for the first few years chemistry and good times held Martha's wanderlust in check.

Eventually, though, she shoved off and divorced him too. A "female flying Dutchman," she required movement, change, and novelty—new events to chronicle. With her portable typewriter in hand, she lived on the wing, setting up a base of operations in Kenya and investigating Poland, Israel, Germany, and seven other countries.

While fact finding, she wrote two story collections and a novel

1. Paleolithic "beauty": the Brassempouy Lady,
C. 21000 B.C.

2. Mistress of intelligence: the goddess of Laussel with her notched lunar bison's horn, 25000–20000 B.C.

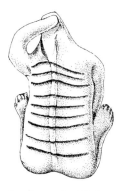

3. Masturbating woman, drawing of a Maltese figurine, c. 4000–3000 B.C.

4. Minoan snake
goddess statuette,
C. 1600–1500 B.C.

5. John and the "plain" Isabella Stewart Gardner, 1861.

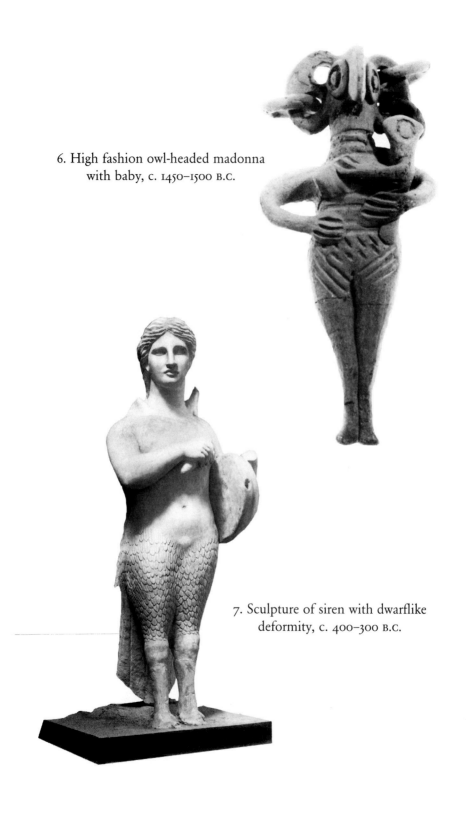

6. High fashion owl-headed madonna
with baby, c. 1450–1500 B.C.

7. Sculpture of siren with dwarflike
deformity, c. 400–300 B.C.

8. The "terribly ugly" siren,
Pauline Viardot, 1871.

9. Wallis Warfield
Simpson, the duke's
"Perfect Woman,"
1940.

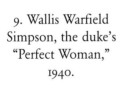

10. Mae West at sixty-three with two of her musclemen, 1956.

11. "The Empress of Journalism," Mrs. Frank Leslie, at fifty-seven, 1893.

12. The "Blonde
Peril," Martha
Gellhorn,
at work, 1946.

13. Lou Andreas-
Salomé with
whip in hand
and two suitors,
Paul Rée and
Friedrich
Nietzsche, 1882.

14. "Lady Newton,"
Émilie du Châtelet,
c. 1735.

15. Violet Gordon
Woodhouse with
three of her four
"superhusbands."
From top: Bill
Barrington,
Max Labouchère,
and Gordon
Woodhouse,
c. 1915.

16. OPPOSITE:
Josephine Baker
in action, Paris,
1926.

17. Coin image of Cleopatra VII,
c. 30 B.C.

18. Caricature of Catherine the Great, the "Imperial Overstepper," c. 1792.

19. Agnès Sorel, mistress of Charles VII of France,
in her signature dress, c. 1447.

20. The "mankilling spectacle," Lola Montez, 1847.

21. Lady Lioness, Beryl Markham, 1936.

22. OPPOSITE: The "Queen of the Amazons," Hortense Mancini with her entourage, c. 1684.

23. "Suicide Siren,"
La Belle Otero,
in her prime,
c. 1900.

that brutally dissected sexual love. With methodical ruthlessness she laid bare the dynamics of eros and showed where the old arrangements led: to stasis, suffocation, and mutual destruction. Traditional "soft and helpless women" either cannibalize their lovers or disgust them with their stupidity, sometimes both. Another breed of woman, however, held out hope for a new and improved erotic order in her fiction. These swanky sexpots—replicas of herself—devour men "like ice cream" and win them with a charm that comes from "deft lechery" and from "talking, moving, seeing, [and] being wide awake."

Through middle to old age, Martha ferreted out humanitarian causes to champion and roamed the hot spots of the world like a recording angel of the apocalypse, covering Vietnam, Nicaragua, El Salvador, the Arab-Israeli conflict, and, at eighty-one, the U.S. invasion of Panama. Increasingly anti-American, she expatriated to Britain, where she commuted between a cottage in Wales and a London apartment, bearing a "gaggle of young chaps" in her wake. She remained a pistol to the end, full of piss and vinegar, bravado, blazing energy, and sex appeal. After she died in 1998, a longtime inamorato slipped a dozen roses into the Thames with her ashes.

Not everyone loved Martha Gellhorn. Hemingway's cronies thought her a "mercenary bitch," and feminists, peeved by her glamour girl edginess, cut her from the honor roll. There was plenty to hate: her barbed tongue, swelled head, and lousy marks as a mother. But she undoubtedly pushed the frontier. More "ambitious than Napoleon," she smashed gender norms, succeeded by dint of grit and hard work, and stepped out boldly—into the line of fire. With the goddess's writing stylus, she wrote "what she saw and how it was," leaving a merciless document of our times. As the deity's modern reincarnation she also acted her appropriate sexual part, the restless, man-collecting empress of seduction, "the one who is joy." She once said, "I'm overprivileged. I've had a wonderful life." By the goddess's reckoning, not "over," simply a woman's just deserts.

When it came to learning, the love goddess Inanna demanded the whole enchilada. Truth: nothing less. Like the mythic creatrix, the light of all intelligence, she possessed ultimate knowledge, the wisdom of eternity. Despite male claims to the philosophic domain, woman was the "original seeress, the lady of wisdom." She was also, with no contradiction involved, the cosmic queen of lust. Hence the sexual charge (as one amorist put it) of a "brilliant philosophic performance" and the plethora of philosopher-sirens throughout history.

Aspasia, c. 420 B.C.

In ancient Greece, for example, the elite courtesans, the hetaerae, included the study of metaphysics in their armamentarium. One of them, Aspasia, took it further and achieved such fame as a philosopher that she became the female Socrates of fifth-century Athens. The only historical woman to be included in Plato's dialogues, she taught Socrates, lectured publicly, and formulated a revolutionary philosophic system, the Aspasian Path. With perfect consistency, she ran a profitable "house of joy" at the same time, instructing her charges in the finer points of love artistry. She was not an *erotodidaskalos,* erotic master teacher, for nothing. She reached the heights of the profession, conquered the top statesmen, and won the lifelong adoration of the peerless Pericles.

In her only extant portrait, a mortuary herm, Aspasia looks more like an irate soccer mom than a sultry vamp. Heavy-featured and matronly, she wears a kerchief and scowls from her pedestal with hollow, implacable eyes. As a result, academics have long assumed that she was probably "quite ordinary in appearance." But even if the bust were authentic (an unlikely possibility), Aspasia could not, under any circumstances, have been "ordinary in appearance."

Extraordinariness was the hetaerae's trademark. When they strolled the agora and swept into symposium parties, they made a drama of themselves and outflaunted one another in flash and originality. At the very least Aspasia whitened her face with ceruse, rouged her cheeks, blackened her eyes, and dressed in see-through tunics of "gaudy colors, with much gilt work."

Beyond that, she would have fashioned a signature look, perhaps with rows of sausage curls drawn up in a "melon coiffure" or with eye-stopping jewelry: chandelier earrings festooned with bells and swans, gold finger ornaments of jasper and chalcedony, and necklaces hung with scent-filled vial pendants.

When Aspasia arrived in Athens at twenty, she was already a virtuoso of self-presentation, a polished professional, and an adept in love and knowledge. She'd trained first with her father at her home near Miletus in philosophy and classical learning, then later with the great Thargelia, a *ravisseuse* of powerful men. Added to these accomplishments, she had a lively "animated" spirit. Plutarch says that within months she'd "entangled with her love the chieftest rulers and governors" of the time. Attracted, according to report, by her "rare" "wisdom," Pericles at last swam into her orbit.

Pericles, nicknamed the Olympian, was then the biggest potentate in the Mediterranean, a brilliant empire builder of Apollonian dimensions, who erected the Parthenon and ushered in the Athenian golden age of prosperity, peace, and artistic supremacy. He became so "absolutely besotted" with Aspasia that he divorced his wife and lived with her for thirteen years. His passion for her exceeded all the acceptable limits of *philia*. He kissed her, an unprecedented intimacy, when he returned home each day from the agora and underwrote and supported her philosophic ambitions. Without his encouragement, she might never have developed as she did into a "key figure in the intellectual history" of Greece.

Like Socrates, Aspasia left no formal, written account of her thought. Contemporary philosophers, however, recorded her teachings, which she elucidated at salon-type gatherings in her home. Socrates, one of her students, sent a disciple there for further instruction, insisting that Aspasia could "enlighten [him] more fully than [he] could." She excelled in rhetoric. So impressive were her powers of persuasion and oratory that Plato included her speech in his *Menexenus*. A canny performance, this eulogy to the war dead both redefines the Athenian state and insinuates the primacy of the maternal principle.

Marshaling the same argumentative dexterity, Aspasia methodically mapped out a philosophy that put a whole new spin on Greek love. Her idea, in contrast to pie-in-the-sky Platonic idealism, was an associated eros: equality between the sexes and a union of mind and body, virtue and sex, self and community. With revolutionary pragmatism, she proposed a *techne* for passionate, happy relationships, prescribing continuous self-culture and complementary sex roles. She also spelled out a strategy for seduction. The seducer, she explained, must arm him- or herself with a protean personality, "charming language," honest praise, an "element of enchantment," and customized charisma.

This was volatile stuff, especially in the hands of a woman who held the illustrious Pericles love hostage and freely disseminated the Aspasian Path among her hetaerae, who "learn't so much from her that their names were uttered with awe."

It was only a matter of time until the patriarchs girded for action. They hauled her into court, accused her of heresy, and sentenced her to death. Only a grandstand effort by Pericles, who burst into tears in her defense, saved her life.

It didn't stop the character assassination. Playwrights assailed her as a "cock-sucking slut" and ball buster, and historians blamed her for the war with Samos. But the case-hardened Aspasia went on about the goddess's business unfazed. After Pericles died, she married a wealthy sheep dealer, bore another child (she'd had one with Pericles), and turned her new husband into a prominent politician.

PC scholars condemn the "sexualization of Aspasia's intellect" and believe she should be reevaluated on her cerebral merits. Judy Chicago accordingly honored Aspasia as a "woman of achievement" rather than a "courtesan" in her 1978 installation *The Dinner Party*. But the sexpot-sage division is passé and false; Aspasia's name in Greek means "welcoming." And she comes as a welcome presence to the postfeminist table, as an envoy of Inanna, goddess of "allure" *and* "Truth."

Germaine de Staël, 1766–1817

In early nineteenth-century Switzerland, a noted German poet returned in a state of erotic euphoria from the "Shrine of St. Aspasia." The lady, he rhapsodized, "worked miracles for the salvation" of men. Salvation or damnation, depending on the source. For most of her lovers Germaine de Staël resembled a she-devil, a "veritable female

roué" and "serpent." This vamped-up opera queen version of Aspasia
sowed heartbreak and ecstasy through every corner of Europe. "A dictionary of the great men of her time," writes her biographer, "would
serve as a list of her worshippers."

Intellectually Germaine de Staël created just as big a stir. She
molded public opinion in politics, history, literature, and gender relations and was "consulted like the Bible" on every issue of moment.
Heavyweights from Goethe to Byron were provoked by her ideas,
artists painted her as "Apollo's priestess," and a generation of Roman-
tics took their inspiration and themes from her work.

Germaine's appearance was ludicrously at variance with her
achievements, amorous and otherwise. Broad-beamed and stout, with
fat legs and a chambermaid's gait, she lacked any semblance of beauty
or intellectual ethereality. Her face looked like a photograph taken
with a fisheye lens: Gallic nose, protuberant eyes, and buckteeth. She
only worsened the effect with her eccentric, unbecoming dress, a confection of oriental robes and striped turbans crested with huge feathers. As she talked, she fidgeted, compulsively rolling and unrolling
small strips of paper.

Yet all was forgotten—looks, dress, and nervous tics—under the
spell of her conversation. She suddenly metamorphosed, said one ad-
mirer, from an "unpleasing" apparition into someone "irresistibly seductive." Her huge black eyes flashed with intelligence, and her
musical voice wove a siren song as she spun from subject to subject
with the speed of a "shuttlecock." "Beautiful? Ugly?" said one after
hearing her. "I do not know." Another sighed. "If I were a queen, I
would order Mme. de Staël to talk to me always."

Germaine learned to combine brains and seductiveness at her
mother's breast. The only child of an ambitious French *salonnière*, Germaine was taught to please through intellectual achievement. She was
force-fed learning like a Strasbourg goose, denied dolls, friends, and fri-
volity, and compelled to perform for the admiration of guests. At five,
already joining mind and eros, she asked an astonished marquise her
opinion of love. For the young Germaine, mental brilliance procured
not only public applause but also her father's. In classic oedipal fashion, she competed with and detested her mother, courting her father,

financier Jacques Necker, with displays of precocity and treaties on law and history. "Of all the men in the world," she wrote in her adolescent diary, "it is he I would have wished for a lover."

Lovers, alas, didn't besiege the dumpy, bookish teenager, so at last the Neckers rustled up an impoverished aristocrat, Baron de Staël, the Swedish ambassador, to marry her. But Germaine, like so many sirens, turned a lackluster first marriage into a springboard for seduction. With her father's fortune at her disposal, she opened a glittering salon that she used to attract the gratin and showcase her charms.

"No one could escape [her] fascination" when she wheeled into action. "The most brilliant talker of her time," she deployed conversation like a four-front offensive. She homed in on her listeners' interests and spoke, accompanied by balletic arm movements, on a dazzling array of topics, from gossip to constitutional law. She flattered, teased, declaimed, harangued, and bandied aperçus, fizzing with vitality and bringing out the "best in everyone."

Within two years she'd snaffled the prize diplomats of Paris: Talleyrand, Mathieu de Montmorency, and, above all, Viscount Louis de Narbonne. Her five-year affair with Narbonne, during which they had two sons, was a classic Staëlian grand amour. A disciple of the roiling boil school of love maintenance, she subjected this handsome lady-killer to a perpetual *crise* of death threats, panegyrics, recriminations, and fourth-act scenes. When he fled to England after the French Revolution, she bombarded him with tragic letters, while simultaneously cultivating two other suitors who'd "fallen madly in love with her." The upshot was a concurrent liaison with all three.

Throughout these operatic affairs Germaine's intellectual labors proceeded uninterrupted. During the Terror she moved to Coppet on the shores of Lake Geneva, where she held forth to a "Circean menagerie" of distinguished men. She customarily received in her bedroom and discussed metaphysics or politics deshabille, once interviewing a male pundit with her bare leg suspended in the air for a pedicure. Always with a green morocco folding desk under her arm, she wrote on the fly and on the sly, even at breakfast, and generated an impressive output: a novel, books of philosophy, and literary criticism.

By the time Germaine met the man of her life, Benjamin Constant, she was, at twenty-eight, Europe's "leading woman of letters." Benjamin, an intellectual giant in his own right, explained his *coup de foudre*. "Her mind dazzled me," he recalled; "within an hour she had secured over me the greatest sway that a woman can gain over a man." Unlike her usual male lineup, Benjamin was nothing to look at: a tall, rawboned Ichabod Crane of a man in green glasses, with curly red hair tied back in a pigtail. But he fascinated women and rivaled Germaine in ego, genius, and high-decibel drama.

For ten years they were locked in a tempestuous tango, with Benjamin raving that she'd magically enslaved him with her voice. They had a daughter together, but parted in a mad dog flameout when Germaine refused to marry him after the baron's death. Still, over the ensuing years she had only to snap her fingers or stage one of her breast-bearing arias to bring him back "a conquered man." He moaned, "No one will ever appreciate my mind as completely as she does."

Their furious melodrama, rather than sapping Germaine's mental energies, fueled them. During their roller-coaster romance, while Germaine trifled with lovers on the side (three noblemen a decade her junior, an Italian poet, an Australian officer, and a scholar who declared himself her "slave" and accompanied her everywhere for the rest of her life), she produced her major philosophic works.

As she loved, so she thought. All the themes of her epoch-making books were of apiece with her erotics. Even her intellectual methodology, the alternation between engagement and detachment, mirrored her back-and-fill seductive style. Her ideology was a still closer fit. In both *On Literature* and *On Germany,* her masterpieces, she fused brains and eros and exalted women and feelings. Criticism should be an "act of love," fiction should privilege emotions, the "superior woman" should reign supreme, and the governing sensibility of society should be liberal, imaginative, and passionate.

Her two fictional heroines, Delphine and Corinne (modeled on herself), introduced a revolutionary new woman to Western culture: a rebellious, autonomous, high-souled queen of thought who seduces men with her brains and conversation. If she's killed off at the end, it's a mere pro forma ploy to allay anxieties about female superpower. Germaine, on the other hand, charged ahead with her heaven-storming ambitions, immune to opinion. Her range was goddess size, encompassing every discipline from drama to theology and every interesting man on the Continent.

With age she reached her zenith. As a philosopher she held a "position comparable to Voltaire's"; as a seductress, "Cleopatra's." Banished to Switzerland by Napoleon because of her pernicious influence, Germaine escaped to England in 1813 with her male entourage. Included this time in the retinue was a "splendid animal" half her age who'd seen her across a crowded ballroom and declared he would "love her so much she [would] have to marry him."

The twenty-three-year-old John Rocca wooed Germaine (then a blowsy forty-four) with such fanatical resolve—challenging Benjamin to a duel and scaring off her acolytes—that she married him after the birth of their child. But her happiness was short-lived. Soon after their first anniversary and the publication of some of her best work, she died of a brain hemorrhage at fifty-one, followed swiftly by the inconsolable Rocca.

Her death stunned the men whose lives she'd "transformed and dominated" and shattered Benjamin Constant, whose spirit was permanently "extinguished." Such an arrant diva, however, could not have been universally mourned. Her male detractors, who called her an "infernal slut" and "witch emerging from a sabbat," heaved a sigh of relief. So did her countless female enemies, fed up with her insufferable sideshows and love thefts.

Germaine loved to harp on her social persecutions and griped that brilliant women were always envied, loathed, trashed, and dumped by men. Both of her fictional *femmes savantes* are annihilated by public disapproval and male perfidy. Love and brainpower cannot coexist, she stormed. But she knew better. It was just smoke and camouflage to conceal her true sexual authority and disproportionate share of the spoils.

In actuality she had an ego the size of Gibraltar and ballyhooed her self-integration, brains, and seductive feats to anyone who'd listen. "Monsieur," she told Henry Crabb Robinson, "I understand everything that deserves to be understood and what I do not understand is nothing." To her beaux, she bragged of her sexual fascinations and body count, and she never doubted her right to both erotic and intellectual conquest.

She saw herself as a sibyl reborn, not Apollo's hireling but her earlier incarnation, priestess of the fertility goddess. In Corinne's climactic scene, she wears sibylline robes and lectures a group of entranced men on the great truths at the mouth of the Cumean cave, originally known as the "marriage bower." These truths, like Inanna's, derive from a "descent into" and "ascent from the underworld," a maturity passage of exile and persecution.

But Germaine emerged from her trials, such as they were, a fulsomely happy woman, even by her own exacting definition. She transcended her looks, developed her "abilities," reconciled "love and Euclid," and won the love of the best men with her "magic gift of seduction." "One must adore her," said a Russian Casanova who knelt before this "Sultana of Mind" and wept.

By all rights, the scholar-siren should now be in her element. With women's assimilation into the intellectual mainstream, sexual liberation, and seductive parity, Our Lady of Learning should have men and the world at her feet. Dizzy blondes and cute mutes went out with Sandra Dee; we flash our minds with our cleavages in the mating game. Or do we?

According to some disturbing new data, we may still be stalked by negative stereotypes, the myth that brains and allure don't mix. Sixty-eight percent of young women—in an achievement backlash—want to zone out mentally and keep house in the suburbs. Dr. Barbara Kerr believes the "underachievement and undercultivation of gifted women" have reached epidemic proportions. Afraid that IQ imperils romantic success, girls drop off academically from high school through college and lower their beams in love, relapsing into the antique strategies of "selective stupidity" and *e-z* listening. Pop how-tos fuel the dumbout. *The Rules* warns against behaving like another "smart girl," and *Secrets of Seduction for Women* ranks "trying to appear smart" number ten on the list of "classic turnoffs."

Times like these call for a higher authority, the mythic goddess of wisdom and sexual passion and her earthly counterparts. All seven of the scholar-sirens make mincemeat of the nerd propaganda. In societies equally, if not more, savante-phobic, they came out, spoke out, and used their brains to seduce, enthrall, and hold the grandees of their times. They shared much of course with other seductresses. They were big, conceited dames: wild, fun, free, alive, over the top, hot-sexed, androgynous, and adroit in love. Saboteurs of the status quo, they cast off feminine constraints and cut their lives to their own pattern, a prehistoric pattern. They were no strangers to hate campaigns and persecutions. They exploded the stereotypes.

As intellectuals, however, they put their own imprint on the seductress persona. If they lucked out in genes and good educations, they had to be tougher. They walked into the eye of male prejudice. Infighters from childhood, they bulldozed gender norms, gave conventional mothers no quarter, defected to supportive men, worked like demons, and aggressively tracked down and nabbed the best mentors.

They avoided smart women's biggest sand trap—the submergence of self into a Great Man—and stubbornly pursued their own agendas and self-fulfillment. Because they liked and wanted men, they put their minds to seduction, mastering the moves and rolling out their secret weapon, knowledge. They didn't tone it down or pipe down. On the other hand, they didn't come on like rhino trainers either. They strutted their brilliance with charm: wit, eloquence, and a thousand arts of enchantment.

In love they chose carefully, men in their corner who cherished and advanced them. They didn't lose their heads on the rapids, nor did they squash or dominate their partners. Relationships were equal, mutually inspirational. But when the music died and the inner goddess beckoned, they moved on. They tended to ramble, sample the goods, and chuck domestica.

Intellectually they were just as unorthodox and on the move. They went to town in their specialties and staked out revolutionary territory. Goddess-style, they took a holistic, comprehensive view of knowledge that included sex. In their work they sought a new and improved eros: gender equality, mind-body synthesis, female agency, sexual fulfillment, and sustained passion, with women—the natural mistresses of the field—at the helm. Practical instructions weren't above them. Although women blackballed and assailed them, they tipped them off on the realpolitik of seduction and clamored for feminine freedom and a happiness equal to their own.

Their composite mental and amorous enchantments made beauty, even when they had it, irrelevant. Their lives give the consummate lie to babe and ditz power, both macho scams designed to keep women in their place. The truth is, a woman with brains can pulverize men and drive them around the bend: to infidelity, opium overdoses, public tears, tantrums in hotel corridors, and plunges down staircases and mountain precipices.

Real men have always admitted the earth-toppling sex appeal of intelligent women. "A well-educated woman," said Stendhal, "is sure to inspire among the most distinguished men a consideration that verges on the fanatical." Literature teems with scholar-vamps, and a recent *Esquire* survey ranks "intelligence" the second most desired trait in women.

The reason for the libidinal pull of learning is rooted in prehistory, deep in the anlage of myth and courtship. "Both males and females," writes Timothy Taylor of the origins of sexual attraction, "may have found larger brains sexier."

For men, though, they carried a special charge. They replicated the mythic first goddess, the divine know-it-all and sexual energy of the cosmos. Her avatars throughout history, not surprisingly, have wiped up the mat with the competition, the mere beauty queens. It's chromosomal. Men can't escape. Like Inanna's lover, Dumuzi, they must bulge, "burgeon," and do woman's bidding when she steps from the "Boat of Heaven" with her *me*'s—the intellectual gifts of persuasion, judgment, psychological insight, computation, and philosophy—and robes herself in "allure," "the art of woman," and the "agate necklace of fertility."

CHAPTER SIX

Sorcières: *Siren-Artists*

Artistic experience lies so incredibly close to that of sex, to its pain and its ecstasy, that the two manifestations are indeed but different forms of one and the same yearning delight. —RAINER MARIA RILKE

[Seduction is] the female imaginary. —JEAN BAUDRILLARD

[In prehistory] women dominated man. She was a fascinating magician before whom his soul trembled. . . . From her sprang poetry, music, and all the arts.
                                                                —ÉDOUARD SCHURÉ

If it is chaste, it is not art. —PABLO PICASSO

*O*n a spring morning in 1827 the French artist Pierre Paul Prud'hon stepped back from his easel to check his latest painting, a soft-core Venus-and-Cupid allegory of the sort preferred by the Parisian haut monde. Behind him in the adjoining atelier worked his disciple the painter Constance Mayer, who'd served and adored him for twenty years. Just days before she'd staged a nasty scene. When he said he no longer loved her, she had not taken it with good grace. "I am ugly!" she'd shrieked hysterically. Now all was quiet in her studio, suspiciously so. When Prud'hon opened the door, he found Constance sprawled in a pool of blood, her neck slashed to the bone, with his razor in her hand.

The lives of female artists are full of such scenes. A successful art career by tradition wrecks a woman for love. The story of the great diva, dancer, poet, or painter laid low by romantic passion is one of the most enduring myths of Western culture. Novels, films, and biographies drub it into girls from grade school: Fly too high creatively, and you'll draw a just doom on your head; you'll wind up manless, miserable, two-timed, and driven to self-loss, madness, and suicide.

Dated as it sounds, this passé conceit still thrives. We hear endlessly of Maria Callas's and Sylvia Plath's calamitous unions with philandering brutes, of Mary Cassatt's lonely spinsterhood, of Camille Claudel's Rodin-induced insanity, of Alma Mahler's sacrifice of a great piano career for muse service to a string of tiresome geniuses. We're still haunted by the ancestral paternal voices warning of turf wars and dark reprisals: "Literature cannot be the business of a woman's life and it ought not to be"; "The woman who is an artist is merely ridiculous," a she-man, a "dog walking on his hinder legs," a wallflower, freak, and castrating bitch.

As might be guessed from the strength of male resistance, the opposite is true. The female artist is a natural love queen, one of the most potent seductresses on earth. Rather than at cross purposes, art and amour work synergistically, especially in women. The goddess, the first creatrix, knocked men out with her thaumaturgic magic.

Through the enchantments of music, song, dance, pictures, poetry, and theater, she took possession of her subjects and invested them with her holy eros. Her artist-priestesses were in the sacred sex trade, deploying their craft for aphrodisiacal ends—mystical union with the almighty life force. Hence the sexual charge of great artworks and the numerous erotic theories of aesthetic pleasure. Art, in brief, is too hot for women to handle; men cannot withstand a concentrated assault by an accomplished mistress of spells.

Some women have always known this. Less celebrated than the casualties, siren-artists exploited their legacy as sexual *sorcières* and scored in love *and* art. Rarely did they have youth, beauty, and deep cleavages to recommend them, but they ravished men through their creative diablerie. One musician lived with four adorers in a ménage à cinq; another danced her way from slavery to queendom; another assembled a seraglio of the best twentieth-century minds through her literary fascinations. All rose, with perfect synchrony, to the top of their professions. And they represent only a small sample; history and everyday life teem with *sorcières*.

It goes back, in all probability, to the cave where archaeologists believe Stone Age peoples worshiped the cosmic life principle in the form of a goddess. In these womblike sanctuaries they staged ecstatic rites in order to merge with the deity and appropriate her powers. Mimicking the creator, they made art. They filled caves with magical wall murals and talismanic statuettes and circle danced, drummed, and sang themselves into mystical transports. It was total theater—complete with animal masks, eerie lighting, and consciousness-altering drugs—in a sacrament of transfiguration. Through the rapturous medium of art, they were remade in the goddess's image and imbued with her generative spark and divine lust. Several scholars think women were at the "center of [this] magic," the shamans of artistic delirium, including poetry and "the stories that have come down to us as myth, legend and fairy tale."

Grace Hartigan, 1922–

Women, it's conjectured, were the original artists of the cave murals. If so, they have a direct descendant in the painter Grace Hartigan, one of the pioneer abstract expressionists and foremost American artists. Like the earliest shaman-creators, she paints with a sacral intent, vibrant "magic[al]" canvases designed to call down the almighty life force.

"I believe," she says, "I'm making life," by which she means eros in no uncertain terms. Her work is juicy, voluptuous, and prodigal, steaming with sexuality. Art and sex are as inseparable to her as they were for cave worshipers. "A powerful sexual woman is a powerful creator," she proclaims.

She knows whereof she speaks. Grace was one powerful seductress. Critic John Myers recalls that "men's nostrils seemed to flare" when she entered a room. Tall, big-boned, blond, and full-figured in the

Playboy mode, she was the sexual H-bomb of the fifties' avant-garde. In an era of feminine domestic subjection and Girl Scout purity, Grace commandeered men and ran with her libido. She seduced and subdued the whole macho tribe of abstract expressionists, who treated women like "cattle," according to Lee Krasner. "Macho?" Grace laughs. "They were pussycats."

Men were to Grace's art what women were to Modigliani's. They fired her jets. Throughout her distinguished artistic career, as she evolved with the protean versatility of another Picasso, lovers nurtured, encouraged, inspired, and promoted her. Even today at over eighty and sexually inactive by choice, she's fueled by men and eros. She shares her Baltimore loft with a young, supportive artist and his family, cultivates a following of male disciples, and says that "all the desire and passion are still inside."

The latest canvases in her packed studio are the most erotic and innovative to date–colossal Venuses with arms outflung in orgasmic ecstasy. But goddesses and *sorcières* have always filled her paintings. On the wall of her living room, a postmodern Aladdin's cave of kitsch, dolls, hanging dragons, and recherché antiques, hangs one of her earliest abstracts: *Secuda Esa Bruja,* mistranslated "The Witch Is Flying." It actually means "the witch is a shaker-upper."

Grace Hartigan was a shaker-upper and norm smasher from the day she was born. The eldest child in a middle-class New Jersey family, she bucked the tide throughout childhood and cultivated being "difficult and different." With a siren's instinctive dread of feminine enculturation, she repudiated her conventional mother and identified with her father, who told her she could be anything she wanted. She learned what she wanted in a Damascus epiphany. One day she saw a gypsy encampment in the neighborhood and found her calling: to run away with the gypsies in their satin skirts to a more colorful destiny.

It took awhile. After a lackluster high school career, she made one of the faux escapes so common to seductresses. At seventeen she married the first boy who read poetry to her and fled with him to California. When he left to serve in World War II, she returned home with a small son. Ironically she then achieved her true breakaway. Working as a draftsman in a war plant, she enrolled in an after-hours sketch class with artist Isaac Muse and discovered her vocation. He ignited her latent artistic abilities and introduced her to her body. "After sex with Ike," she recalls, "I was aching from head to foot. So *that's* what it's about!"

Three years later she left both Isaac and her husband and child for the heady Manhattan art scene, the revolutionary epicenter of abstract expressionism. She'd found her more colorful destiny. "Going to New York," she says, "was running off with the gypsies." She "lived like the men"—Jackson Pollock, Milton Avery, Philip Guston and company—and forged a distinctive, sock-it-to-me style of her own. She used allover composition, bold diagonal thrusts, hot acid colors, and street life bricolage with leap-off-the-canvas, signature bravura. The Kootz Gallery picked her up for its landmark exhibit "New Talent," and her career went into high gear.

So did her sex life. With the same unzipped authority she showed in art, she whisked up the men of her choice. She came on like a master *sorcière*, wandering nude through lovers' studios and alchemizing life into a "happening." A party thrower par excellence, she staged famous fetes such as the kite-making bash that ended in a wild carnival in Central Park amid shredded paper and splintered battens. She danced, caroused, and talked the talk nonstop—an art-speaking, Rilke-quoting proto–Bette Midler.

She crackled with sex, élan, and sass, and her packaging was pure hubba-hubba. Faithful to her gypsy proclivities, she dressed for flash appeal. She wore designer starewear, adorned with tulle-festooned hats and fancy fur coats. Once when she made one of her grand entrances at the Cedar Bar (the avant-garde hangout) in a satin-trimmed black mink, a local artist said she looked as if she had "the keys to Madrid in [her] pocket."

Clearly she had the men there. After a brief second marriage to a self-styled cowboy painter, she cleaned up romantically. She lived temporarily with the pinup boy of the avant-garde Alfred Leslie and reeled in other artists like photographer Walter Silver, sculptor Giorgio Spaventa, and painter Franz Kline. In all these liaisons the muse-creator dyad worked both ways. She and Franz critiqued each other's

work, Georgio sculpted her as *Walking Woman,* and Walter, who pho-
tographed her in matador drag, prompted one of Grace's most
renowned paintings, *The Persian Jacket.*

The same year *Life* magazine proclaimed her the "most celebrated
of the young American women painters," she took up with with
Bridgehampton gallery owner Robert Keene, who became husband
number three in 1959. Throughout the Keene courtship, however, the
flings continued. Besides trysts with Franz Kline, Grace had a torrid
affair with a swarthy nightclub baron and an intense "lavender marriage" with homosexual poet Frank O'Hara. For years the pair were inseparable and created together, writing and painting tributes back and
forth. But neither the O'Hara alliance nor the Bridgehampton marriage was destined to last. As soon as Grace encountered Winston
Price, she left her "meatloaf husband" and New York behind.

Winston, a brilliant Johns Hopkins epidemiologist, had fallen in
love with Grace through her paintings, and their meeting in 1960 was
a *coup de foudre.* Realizing that she'd found the "man of [her] life," she
cut all ties to her past (for which Frank never forgave her) and committed herself to a "total marriage."

Under Winston's adoring aegis in Baltimore, her work flourished.
He gave her the security, support, and perfect understanding of every
artist's dream. Although her work lost favor during the pop decades of
the sixties and seventies, it attained new levels of depth and daring.
She painted powerful female presences and experimented wildly: with
split-screen compositions, watercolor collages, stained canvases, wet-
into-wet technique, and jigsawed coloring book studies.

When Winston contracted terminal encephalitis in the seventies
and Grace's bearings slipped, she reached back to the mythic, lifesav-
ing origins of art. At her lowest ebb, she painted the transcendent *I Re-
member Lascaux,* a re-creation of the cave walls with a menagerie of
enchanted animals conjured into a state of triumphant, eternal repose.

Around the same time she embarked on her last affair—a seven-
year liaison with a "marvelous" Greek lover. Like all of Grace's
amours, passionate sex coexisted with creative reciprocity. While he
infused her paintings with new sensuality and Grecian themes, she
awoke his dormant artistic talent. "Known for bolstering the man's

ego," she fired his self-faith and transformed him into a sculptor of small wire birds. After Winston's death in 1981, she had two insignificant passades, then rechanneled her libidinous energies full spate into art. "It didn't suit her sexuality," she explains, not to be at the top of her game.

Over the next two decades she launched a concentrated artistic exploration of eros. These ranged from the sinister *Bacchus* (owned by Mick Jagger) and *Madonna Inn* to a portrait gallery of erotic heroines: vamps, Venuses, movie stars, and a "Manhattan" self-portrait. Even the recent goddesses, by her own admission, look like her. "When I envision a sexually powerful woman," she confesses, "it's myself."

Grace and Helen Frankenthaler, another pioneer abstract expressionist, once fantasized what they'd give up their art careers to become. Helen said a Rockette; Grace, a glamour puss, who finds a film god with his opera cape flung over the puddle when she steps out of a stretch limo.

Grace didn't have to choose. She got both: the life of a diamond-dazzle seductress and a major artist. She seemed to know instinctively that the two belonged together and paid no attention to the love vs. art propaganda. "Sure, I had that conditioning," she chortles in a smoky basso, "but you say, 'What are you talking about?' "

With Grace, you're talking about a *femme artiste* who "had it all" the traditional way, the prehistoric way, when painters were goddess avatars and conduits of divine eros. As one of her lovers put it when she showed him the door, "When I think of you, I think of life."

Not coincidentally, cave chambers filled with the most artwork were the most resonant; music rang through the dark caverns at the early religious rites. To the hypnotic rhythms of flutes, drums, whistles, rasps, and rattles made of clay and animal bones, preliterate man tranced himself into divine ecstasy, into mystical union with the Mother of All Being. He was possessed by her powers, holy sexuality included. This explains the deep libidinal pull of music still—the groin hit of Beethoven's *Kreutzer Sonata* or gutbucket blues and the erotic frenzies of rock concerts.

Instead of the first groupies, however, women may have been "the first musicians, and perhaps for some time the only ones." Certainly they made up the sacred orchestras of ancient Sumer. The sex goddess Inanna brought "the resounding musical instrument" to civilization, and her priestesses incarnated the goddess and conjured her cosmic eros with their drums, cymbals, harps, pipes, and sistrums at her ceremonies.

Violet Gordon Woodhouse, 1871–1948

In early-twentieth-century London a "little dark magician" reclaimed the prehistoric role of priestess-musician with spectacular results. Violet Gordon Woodhouse had a love life that Lewis Carroll might have imagined on Viagra. At the crest of Edwardian high prudery, this great musician lived openly with four men under the same roof. A bizarre, impish figure with no "features" or bustline and an Oz-inspired wardrobe of fishbowl earrings and feathered turbans, she fascinated her quartet of "superhusbands" into a lifelong ménage à cinq and never met a man or woman she couldn't seduce.

Little known today, she was considered one of "the greatest pianists of the world" and ranked in harpsichord and clavichord playing with Casals on the cello, Tertis on the violin, and Segovia on the guitar. The luminaries of her time, from Picasso to Bartók, idolized her, and even the queen made a pilgrimage to her home.

Long before women held career management seminars, Violet figured it out. Artists, regardless of gender, need freedom, praise, and wives. From infancy, she displayed an iron determination to get just that—no questions asked. Born the middle of seven children to the nouveau riche Gwynne family, she nudged her way past her brothers and sisters to the position of favorite.

Affectionately nicknamed Bobo, she learned to eke anything from her autocratic father through charm: exemption from compulsory sports on their Folkington estate and lessons with the resident governess. In classic siren fashion, she circumvented formal education and followed her bliss—in this case, music. An acknowledged prodigy by seven, she studied with the finest master teachers and set her sights on a concert career, an unthinkable ambition for a turn-of-the-century lady.

But, then, Violet was no ordinary lady. Plain as she was—with a small fist of a face, pinched lips, and dark circles under heavy-browed eyes—she knew how to get around men and get her way. At eighteen she chose the first of her backstage "wives," the shy, patrician Gordon Woodhouse, who fell so in love with her that he acceded to her incredible terms: liberty to pursue her career, carte blanche banking privileges, and no sex.

In a futuristic role reversal, Violet acquired the kind of spouse traditionally favored by male musicians, a servant-to-genius. After they married in 1895, Gordon changed his last name for her benefit (giving her the double surname Gordon Woodhouse), quit his job, managed the household, and put his fortune in the service of her talent and pleasure. Sexual dysfunction or cryptohomosexuality might explain his compliance, but he, like everyone, was bespelled by her.

People called her simply "the bewitching one." She had wit, vitality, sexual heat, a bowl-over style, and the charisma of genius. At her weekly musical salons she put the psychopomp of primal theater into her recitals. Costumed in lace-garlanded silk gowns, with her hair scrolled into butterfly chignons, she played with electrifying virtuosity and "gypsy rhythm in her wrists," entangling listeners in the "golden web" of her music.

One guest became so entangled that he never left. Bill Barrington, a Leslie Howard look-alike and heir to the tenth Lord Barrington, arrived on an invitation from his friend Gordon and after three days told his host he adored his wife. Gordon referred the question to Violet, who refused to be impeded by the petty bugbears of convention. The trio took off on a five-day "honeymoon" in a horse-drawn caravan through the New Forest and cemented their "civilized understanding" with the joint purchase of two houses, Southover Grange and a new base in London. Far from maintaining a low profile, Violet and Bill flaunted their passion. She sat on his knee in public, called him her "Fairy Prince," and semidiscreetly shared his bed.

At the horror of the thing, Gordon's mother disinherited him, but Violet had just begun. Over the next two years she added two (perhaps three) more lovers to her ménage. First came Max Labouchère, a wolfishly handsome lawyer of intellectual tastes and whipcrack repartee, who tried and failed to live without her. "God, how [he] loved" his "Tookes," he wrote, and soon moved to his own wing at Southover Grange.

At the same time, another resident, Adelina Ganz (daughter of a leading impresario), paid Violet court, perhaps successfully. Then Denis Tollemache, a young aristocratic cavalry officer, arrived on the scene, declared his passion, and took another room in the Woodhouse mansion. He'd heard her play as a teenager and never recovered.

Managing such an entourage demanded seductive skills of an advanced order. Violet reserved time alone with each devotee, distributed customized keepsakes, composed florid love notes, played off lovers, and feigned illnesses in emergencies.

At Southover she created an aesthetic Brigadoon that was difficult, if not impossible, to leave. No "humdrum constraints" existed in this charmed world of pastoral beauty and celestial music. Silent servants attended to every need, and inhabitants did as they pleased. In an atmosphere intensified by the collective desire for Violet, conversation attained a theatrical pitch that the hostess heightened with droll, ribald table talk. At night her men took turns reading aloud to their "little queen."

Violet "did what she wanted, how she wanted, with whom she wanted." Which included sex, possibly a great deal. With her "intensely warm-blooded nature," Rabelaisian tongue, and maverick sensibilities, she undoubtedly availed herself of her adorers. Bill of course was a regular, and Denis and Max both wrote of her embraces—Max, of her "chain" upon his "hum, hum, hum."

All this—the sex, adulation, private utopia, and freedom from domestica—provided the ideal ecosystem for her art. Her reputation as a pianist soared during the Southover years. The most exacting critics called her "one of the greatest living keyboard artists," Pablo Casals wrote her fan letters, and Ralph Vaughn Williams, who hated the harpsichord, wrote a folk fantasia for Violet under the spell of her artistry.

In 1904 Violet decided to focus exclusively on early instruments, and four years later she moved her ménage to more commodious accommodations, a romantic estate near Stratford-upon-Avon with a guest house for Denis called the Abode of Love.

During World War I this bell jar paradise temporarily shattered. Denis, Bill, and Max left for the front, and although Gordon stayed on and an infatuated female fan joined the fold, the spell broke. Gordon lost most of his assets, Max died in battle, Bill and Denis returned shell-shocked, and Violet had to go to work. If she'd remained on the concert circuit, she would be a household name today. She gained international fame and signed a three-year contract with Gramophone for the first-ever recordings of the harpsichord.

But in 1926 she inherited a fortune through an Agatha Christie-style twist of fate. The day before Gordon's aunts planned to cut him from the will, they were mysteriously murdered by the butler. Ignoring the scandal, Violet seized the spoils and retired from professional life. She bought a London mansion and a Gloucestershire estate that her men transformed into a "perfect setting" for their "live princess," with a connecting bedroom to Bill's and special wing for her Pekinese dogs. Gordon became a glorified male Martha Stewart, Bill attended to the gardens and grounds, and Denis squired her to London for the private concerts she continued to give.

Despite her retreat from the public arena, Violet's musical artistry grew in later years. She unearthed and mastered the difficult last works of Scarlatti, played for celebrities like the queen, and drew an even more impassioned following. As exotically caparisoned as ever—in Bo-Peep silk skirts, stacks of jangling bracelets, and violet-dyed hair— she worked the same erotic hoodoo. Part "czarina," part Tinker Bell, she mesmerized everyone she met with her quicksilver charm. Her music, though, continued to be her power draw.

An infatuated clavichord maker heard her play and said that "such a spell was cast on" him it was "as if one of the immortals had come to earth." Two women developed crushes and treated her "like a goddess." In her sixties Violet embarked on a love affair with a poet twenty years her junior. Sachie Sitwell not only loved and idolized her but appointed himself her muse. "You are the ONLY living master," he exhorted, and encouraged her to tackle and master the intricate Scarlatti oeuvre.

Violet spent her final years "surrounded by adulation." After Denis died, Bill and Gordon continued their ministrations to their "bewitching one" and perfumed her days with praise and presents. When she died, they made a shrine of her room, with her hairbrushes and bibelots laid out in perpetuity. Even in death they vied for first place in her favor, with Bill scheming (and losing) to have his name inscribed above Gordon's on Violet's tombstone.

The obituaries called her "one of the greatest musicians of our time." The *Times* wrote: "No one who ever heard her can ever forget her playing . . . legends have grown up about her." But she was forgotten, and the legends soured. If at all, she was remembered as that "witch," that "Dreadful Woman" with her "Women's Paradise" of harem boys. She trampled the taboos, lived outside the female artistic preserve, and bruised and bloodied patriarchal sensibilities.

She got her "paradise," though. The Sitwells put Violet's personal motto in the newspaper each year on the anniversary of her death: "Time will run back and fetch the age of gold." This was the mythic, prehistoric Grecian golden age, ruled by the great goddess and her suppliant male subjects. Violet simply had the "will to fetch." She switched on her inner seductress and harnessed the primordial sorcery of music to realize the most preposterous of feminist/artistic fantasies and live as she deserved, an "English Goddess of plenty."

When the earliest musicians raised their invocations to the almighty, celebrants stomped themselves into divine ecstasy in orgiastic circle dances. To lure the goddess in their midst and capture her regenerative magic, they staged elaborate fertility rites, miming coital motions and beaming up cosmic lust.

On one cave fresco a ring of nine women in caps and skirts dance around a naked man. Another depicts dancers in animal masks—creatures sacred to the goddess—enacting sexual intercourse a tergo, complete with erect penis and parted haunches. It was dirty dancing with a higher purpose. Sexual rapture promoted life and growth and transformed the dancer into a demigod imbued with holy eros.

The sex goddesses of antiquity, like Inanna, were "shining bright and dancing." Minoan priestesses whirled in delirious jeté turns (sometimes nude) and traced out serpentine figures to worship the goddess's divine sexual energy. Patriarchy later demonized these dancers as emblems of ungovernable lust, as bloodthirsty Salomes and diabolic Lamias. But as the original Lamia illustrates, they could do nothing to stop kinesthetic sorcery, with its power to send men into testosterone storm and three-sheets-to-the wind erotic transports.

Lamia, c. 300 B.C.

Lamia belonged to a species of hetaerae in ancient Greece known as the *auletrides,* virtuoso exotic dancers. Born a slave, Lamia possessed the brass knuckle will-to-thrive common to *sorcières.* While in bondage, she learned the Middle Eastern *aulos* (flute) and veil dances and persuaded her master to let her entertain at symposia parties. These performances were considered so sexually inflammatory that Plato banned the *aulos* from his ideal republic. In the heat of the show, men tore off their rings, threw them at dancers, and bid fortunes for their favors afterward.

Lamia wore a G-string and "coan vest" (a lacy cobweb over bare breasts) and piped and triple-stepped while pumping her pelvis "as if she were in the act." At the finale she auctioned herself to the highest bidder for the night.

As luck would have it, an Egyptian procurer caught her act, bailed her out of slavery, and delivered her to the bed of Ptolemy. For twenty years she held the position of official favorite. When she was enslaved a second time in a sea battle in 306 B.C., she made her captor, Demetrius of Macedon, a "slave to Lamia." Though ten years his senior, she bewitched him with her "remarkable talents," as both an *auletride* and accomplished conversationalist and bedmate.

"I do not fear your being satiated," she boasted in one of her letters. Nor was he; until she died, she ruled beside him as unofficial queen. Greek misogynists consequently branded her a she-demon and a bloodsucking man destroyer. The Athenian public, however, knew better. They deified her as Venus "Lamia" and raised a temple in her honor which she haunted, they said, for generations with her maddening flute music and undulating form divine.

Josephine Baker, 1906–1975

Two millennia later another hot-bodied dancer plugged into the primal magic of the earliest rites and boogied her way out of bondage. Josephine Baker started life trapped in a racist St. Louis ghetto and ended up enthroned as an international queen of song, dance, and seduction. One night on the Paris stage was all it took.

In 1925 the curtain rose on an all-black revue at the Théâtre de Champs-Élysées to a standard darkies on the bayou tableau. Then Josephine hurtled onstage, rump gyrating, legs flying in a rip-the-roof Charleston. At the end she reappeared and unleashed "the frenzy of African Eros." Naked except for a hot pink feather between her thighs, she dry-humped and slithered around her male partner and collapsed in a torrential orgasmic spasm. She brought down the house.

In one fell swoop, she catapulted Europe out of postwar rigor mortis into the Jazz Age and awoke a superstar. She was the "Ebony Venus," the "Creole goddess" who gave "all Paris a hard-on." Her cult lasted a lifetime and included the prerogative of every divine avatar: multiple men as muses, managers, adorers, fans, and transient lays.

Josephine never saw herself except as a creature of myth. Given the circumstances, it was pure megalomania. She was born out of wedlock into the dead-end squalor and poverty of a segregated East St. Louis slum. She wore newspapers for shoes, scavenged coal in railroad yards, hustled food, and suffered racist, sexual, and domestic abuse.

Yet when she went to live with a loving grandmother and heard fairy tales for the first time, she identified herself with a grandiose mélange of mythic characters: Santa Claus, Cinderella, "Prince Charming, *and* the Fairy Godmother." Had she known of Ishtar, who raised the dead with her seven-veil *danse lascive,* she'd have come nearer her supernatural counterpart.

Like all *sorcières,* Josephine's drive to make it was ruthless and single-minded. Neither seduction nor art is for choirgirls. She had no truck with "normal" socialization, raised hell in school, and stubbornly followed her lights. A demon for dance, she did a mean Messaround and Tack Annie and performed for pennies in her basement on orange crates lit by candles in tin cans. At thirteen she split for

Chestnut Valley, a twelve-block ragtime and red-light district, and supported herself waitressing and dancing on street corners with the Jones Family Band.

Jazz used to be spelled "jass," which meant "screwing." For Josephine, the original mack mama, the two went together from the start. Like the barrelhouse blues singers she idolized, she reclaimed the primal female role as an independent operator and sampler of men. By fifteen she'd already been married and divorced twice and had muscled her way onto the TOBA (tough on black asses) vaudeville circuit.

Nicknamed the Monkey, she was too skinny and dark for the prevailing high yeller beauty ideal. "I have no pretension to being pretty," Josephine once said. "I have pointed knees and the breasts of a seventeen-year-old boy . . . my face is ugly and my teeth stick out." The chorus girls taunted her: "God don't love ugly."

But with her kind of stage magic, she didn't need God's help. Refusing "to be eclipsed," she mugged, hammed, black-bottomed, and high-strutted like a "rooster flipping his tail." She won a part in the first Broadway all-black musical *Shuffle Along,* and went on to the Cotton Club, where Caroline Dudley nabbed her for the Revue Nègre in Paris.

At nineteen Josephine realized her most florid fairy-tale fantasies. The French, primed by the primitivist movement and Baudelaire's poems, adored her and saw her for what she was: a resurrection of the repressed sex goddess. The artist Paul Colin, also her lover, made her the poster girl of the twenties; Calder sculpted her; Picasso painted her; and Hemingway called her "the most sensational woman anybody ever saw." Women bobbed their hair à la Josephine, tanned their skin, and flexed their erotic muscle. She joined the Folies Bergère and danced her trademark fertility dance topless in a skirt of yellow phallic bananas to tumultuous acclaim.

With her name in lights, Josephine made the most of the aphrodisiacal charge of her celebrity and booty-shaking voodoo. She was a Masters and Johnson lab experiment fifty years before her time, living in tune with her V-8 anatomy. She slept with whoever made her "o's" "q": chorus boys, industry titans, and her secretary, Georges Simenon, later the author of five hundred books, and the only man to match her in sexual stamina and appetite.

According to lovers, it was "body to body the whole time" with
no sentimental software and Josephine in the lead, often upright and
dancing. Unlike the piteous Janis Joplin model of pop star promiscuity, however, the stag line of suitors was long. She accumulated dozens
of marriage proposals (Simenon included) and forty thousand love
letters in one year.

Josephine's ability to snag men's hearts sprang from more than
the primitive lure of the dancing goddess. She was seriously charming,
a velvet battering ram that could knock down any door and enter
laughing. Like every great siren, she combined an irresistible engag-
ingness with a personality as prismatic as an oil slick.

For her, the mix included a rare "gift for intimacy," down-home
candor, a fast mouth, a "delicious temper," and an effervescence that
just wouldn't quit. Plus she handled herself with seductive authority.
An "adorable" despot, she made it clear that she was one big woman.
With the superiority complex native to sirens and pathbreakers, she
thought she was a hotshot, a semidivinity anointed by destiny for
great things.

Even so, she needed a helping hand. As is often the case with *sorcières*, a man mentored her and boosted her up the ladder. Pepito, aka
Giuseppe Abatino, was a sleek self-created count, with a monocle, diamond rings, and a genius for spin. During their nine-year affair he
not only recharged Josephine's career through lucrative film and business deals but reshaped her image. Insistent that she grow artistically
and personally, he transformed her from *la belle sauvage* to "La
Bakaire," a soignée chanteuse and cosmopolite.

By 1930 her metamorphosis was complete. She threw the *sorcière*'s
delirium as before, but with a fire-and-ice curve. Singing French torch
songs as she vamped down spiral staircases in four-foot plumes, she
exuded the fascination of a "beast for sex" laced into the corset of a
"little lady."

She won Paris anew and lived as befitted her new persona: at a baronial villa, Le Beau-Chêne, with a snakeskin-upholstered Voisin
coupe in the drive. True to her divine pedigree, she strolled nude
through the gilt salons (once greeting George Balanchine at the door

in three strategic flowers) and populated the premises with a huge menagerie of "sacred" animals—monkeys, pigs, chickens, cats, parrots, and thirteen stray dogs.

Beneath the elegant packaging, Josephine also arrogated the goddess's privilege of "unrestrained free love . . . unbounded by human conventions." Despite Pepito's management of her image and career, he had no control over this sovereign sexpot. She test-drove every stallion in her path, from the Swedish crown prince on his swan-shaped bed to the architect Le Corbusier in a steamer stateroom bound for South America. Two lovelorn Hungarians resorted to violence, a draftsman stabbed himself, and a cavalry officer dueled Pepito.

After Pepito's death from cancer in 1935, Josephine tried her hand at marriage again. Her choice was the pick of the boulevards, a handsome blond money god and lady-killer, Jean Lion. But Josephine, like her nondomesticated ancestor Inanna, didn't take well to marital captivity. She absconded with Maurice Bataille (making love nine times one afternoon) and danced nude at a neighbor's dinner party. The union lasted fourteen months.

During World War II the polymorphic Josephine changed identities once more. A natural roadie and adventuress, she enlisted in the French resistance and traveled through Europe and Africa, infiltrating embassy parties as a singer and relaying coded information in invisible ink.

Although weakened by a life-threatening illness in Morocco, she opened a Red Cross club for black Americans and trekked across the desert to entertain the Free French forces. None of this crimped her amorous career. For five years she slept with the chief of counterintelligence who "worshipped her," and toyed with such Moroccan pashas as El Glaoui, the fabled king of the south.

After the war her mythomania went to her head. Not content merely to channel the goddess's life force, she sought to reinstate a mythical matriarchy. She acquired a consort, fourth husband Jo Bouillon, and set up command headquarters at a fifteenth-century castle in the Dordogne that flew her flag from the turrets.

She spent the rest of her life trying to keep Les Mirandes afloat.

Like a satire of matriarchal utopias, her female-ruled "Capital of World Brotherhood" ran on square wheels. Villagers bilked Josephine, servants robbed her blind, and estate management, even with Jo's aid, operated on a harum-scarum basis.

When her Great Mother dream culminated in a "rainbow tribe" of twelve adopted children, her minifiefdom went into arrears despite lucrative performances and tours across France and America. A splurge queen of excess, hubris, and "indiscreet extravagance," Josephine squandered 1.5 million dollars in ten years. By 1963 her marriage and matriarchal kingdom were finished, and her health and resources, on the skids.

But as often happens with self-mythologizers, she rose from the ashes and orchestrated a fairy-tale ending. In her sixties, she roared back—all flash, sequins, and hundred-proof pizzazz. As she traipsed through the lobby in a body stocking and face spangles for her 1973 Carnegie Hall opening, a bystander cracked: "I'd like to fuck her."

Although her sexual liaisons tapered off, she lost none of her allure. Robert Brady, a wealthy American artist and connoisseur of women, fell in love with her, and the two were unofficially "married" in a Cuernavaca church. The next year she died in her sleep in Paris with rave reviews heaped on her bed. Two days before, she'd mounted a one-woman show that recounted the miraculous story of her life, with thirty songs, twelve costume changes, and a smokin' Charleston.

Josephine received a sumptuous state funeral with a twenty-one-gun salute and the Légion d'Honneur and Médaille de la Résistance. But like other seductresses, she was a subversive who "broke all the rules" and accrued too much sexual power. She provided no humiliating love tragedies for public consumption and fooled few with her "jes' folks" self-parodies.

She was an artist who got away with it: got the men, the orgasms, the kudos, and the big career. For that she earned hostility from every quarter. Racist critics called her a jungle ape and "dingdong," and Hollywood filleted her as a tortured star in *The Josephine Baker Story*.

Yet Josephine was a mammoth *sorcière* with a "personality like thunder," heiress of the supreme African female deity, the double-sexed Mawu-Lisa. As in the Yoruban proverb, when she danced, she revealed the secret of the drum—cosmic eros—and shunted that power to earth. The Brazilians believed she was a goddess, and e. e. cummings said she was both "infrahuman and superhuman," an "unkillable something . . . beyond time."

Josephine always subscribed to her divinity and erected a statue of herself as the Virgin Mary at Les Mirandes. But she must have found a truer reflection of herself at her Temple of Love, where she swam nude in a pool surrounded by three marble incarnations of the sex goddess: Diana, Circe, and the "singing and dancing," "quick darting" Aphrodite.

Rhapsodic incantations accompanied the bacchanal of music and dancing in the cave temples. To the strains of primitive lyres and drums, shamans chanted the life-and-loin–quickening deity into being. Poetry and erotic rapture are inextricably entwined, joined at the groin. That's why great lines of poetry raise a "desirable gooseflesh" and why amorists always advised suitors to memorize poems as the "best weapon" in love. Women may have dominated this genre too in prehistory. The cosmic sex queen Inanna, goddess of "incantations" and "adorning speech," put a "rising cedar" in Dumuzi's pants with her lascivious verses, and priestesses wrote the aphrodisiacal *balbales* for the sacred marriage ceremony.

Cynthia the Golden, c. 25 B.C., and Maria de Ventadorn, c. 1165

In ancient Greece, hetaerae, by necessity, had to be adept "in composing and reciting . . . poetry." Even the nonartistic Romans had a soft spot for poetry. Although women weren't permitted to publish their verses, a siren with poetic gifts, such as Cynthia the Golden, could cut a wide erotic swath.

Cynthia not only gained literary fame with her epyllions and lyrics but captured Rome's finest, including the elegist Propertius, who enshrined her in his poetry. Far from a hearts-and-roses lady balladeer, she was a *puella dura* (tough dame), educated like a man and fond of fast chariots, blue hair dye, and torrid sex in the public thoroughfare.

During the Middle Ages—not a high tide for siren-poets—a renegade band of female troubadours briefly revived the breed. These privileged twelfth-century chatelaines, known as *trobairitz*, benefited from an oblique revival of goddess worship called courtly love in which suppliant men hymned the virtues of an idealized great lady. Most *trobairitz*, however, failed to sing their ordained part in the duet, the vulva-exalting song of Inanna, and composed heartbreak laments instead.

Maria de Ventadorn, "the most sought after lady ever," was an exception, a queenly soul who commanded that her lover should "do *her* bidding" in her tenson. But the oppressive medieval regime wore her down; her husband departed for a monastery and left her silenced and legally enslaved to her two brothers.

Louise Labé, 1522–1565

By the Renaissance women's lot had improved, and poetic *sorcières* made a comeback, especially in Venice among the cultivated Venetian courtesans. Farther north in Lyons, a thriving literary center and site of an ancient Roman temple to Venus, a poet-siren of a most unusual cast blazed into French history.

How unusual a sixteenth-century pageant makes plain. It was 1542, and the scene was a royal tourney in honor of Henri II and his siren-consort, Diane de Poitiers. Pennants snapped in the breeze, trumpets flourished, and armored knights vaulted into the arena, brandishing pikes, swords, and war axes.

One knight, with the motto *Belle à Soi* (Beautiful to Oneself), acquitted himself with such valor and broke so many lances that Diane and the king requested an interview. But when the knight lifted his visor, a young female face appeared—the blond, beautiful Louise Labé, better known as Captain Louise.

Even with her own violations of the feminine norm, Diane de Poitiers couldn't have imagined a seductress like Louise. Light-years ahead of her time, Louise Labé jumped the gender divide, charted her own amorous destiny, wrote dazzling poetry, and became "one of the most celebrated women of her time."

Her background ran true to form for *sorcières:* rebellion against an

antipathetic mother figure (a cruel stepmother), a compensatory intimacy with men, and an extraordinary education. Her father, a rich
merchant, provided his only daughter with distinguished tutors and
allowed her to share lessons in sports and classics with her three brothers. She developed proficiency in martial arts and dressed in a doublet
and velvet beret with a plumed feather.

At seventeen she found a lover and muse who awakened her poetic gifts and two years later made a match most calculated to foster
these gifts. With a *sorcière*'s determination to get what she needed creatively, Louise married a doting, wealthy older ropemaker. He gave
her freedom and financial security and helped her open a stylish salon
for Lyons "men of quality."

At these salons Louise wooed the select company with her conversation–to which one wrote an ode–and readings of her poetry and
chose the crème de la crème for lovers. Suitors courted her with poems and daring deeds and wept on her doorstep, in such numbers that
her man-killer reputation spread to Switzerland, where John Calvin
denounced *La Belle Cordière* (the beautiful ropemaker's wife) from the
pulpit as a whore and public menace.

In a contemporary engraving, she's more than beautiful. With
eyebrows arched high over Bette Davis eyes, a puckish nose, a plump
underlip, and an ironic half smile, her face radiates character and mischief. And she's dressed to kill, in a resplendent *finistrella* gown with a
French hood falling in heavy folds down her back.

But it was her poetry that drew men like postulants to her home.
Under the spell of her verses, her fans and lovers orchestrated their
publication and appended twenty-four eulogistic poems of their own
at the end. The inspiration, typically, was reciprocal. After this volume
appeared, Louise became famous, hailed throughout Europe as the
tenth muse and "France's greatest lyric poet."

Yet her collection was nothing if not subversive. Her twenty-three
sonnets, three elegies, and long "debate" all proclaimed female intellectual equality and erotic supremacy. These showoff poems deliberately employ the erotics of speech with intent to charm. Although
they assume a Petrarchan disguise of amorous lament, they're blatant
vehicles of self-parade and seduction.

While executing the equivalent of a triple axel on ice–feats of masculine and feminine rhyme played against intricate classical models–she hypes her sexual allure and power and rains down provocative invitations. "Kiss me. Again," she writes. "Four I'll return and hotter than fire."

In the "Debate of Folly and Love," she replaces a male god, "Love," with her own self-created sex goddess, "Folly," a swanky, obstreperous "Queen of Men," who knows "what it takes to be appealing" and has all humanity "under [her] control." Like another Inanna, she's the "sexual joy of the cosmos," "always laughing," dissolving inhibitions, and generating festivity. She teaches women how to seduce: to bolster male egos and at the same time to give them the business. She creates a tempest; she transforms vanilla love into the white lightning of passion. "You must be a sorceress," gripes Love, "a shameless woman!"

She's both: the divine wonder-worker redux and patriarchy's bad girl. She disrupts the status quo, lures women off the domestic preserve, pitches men into inappropriate arms, and decrees feminine sexual sovereignty. Men must "do or say" what women want. At the end, Jupiter pronounces Folly the winner and rules that she can lead Love, whom she's permanently blinded, wherever she wishes.

Like her priestess forebears, Louise summoned the sex goddess through the magical medium of poetry. Praised as she was as the Lyons Sappho, she couldn't have expected a free ride after such sedition. A husband cited her in a lawsuit for corrupting his wife's morals, chauvinists circulated scurrilous verses, and the ladies of Lyons cut and reviled her.

But the stouthearted Louise prevailed anyhow. Her indulgent husband left her wealthy enough to buy two vineyards, a country house, and a meadow, and she died nursed tenderly by a beau from the salon days. He erected a sculpture, we're told, over her tomb on her country estate. We can only imagine the statue he commissioned– *La Belle Condière* with a book of verses in one hand, a lance in the other, and Folly's calling card on the headstone: "I am a goddess. . . . I am the one who makes you great or who humbles you as I choose."

Louise de Vilmorin, 1902–1969

André Malraux called Louise de Vilmorin the twentieth-century Louise Labé, a "fair knight" and a poet of the same intricate and otherworldly brilliance. At seventeen, though, she seemed a far cry from "Captain Louise." Rather than mounted on a charger with a sixteen-foot lance, she lay on a rolling hospital bed, which she called Rosinante (after Don Quixote's horse), with tuberculosis of the hip, flicking a cigarette.

Louise de Vilmorin had a long, equine face, an overbite, a pallid complexion, and the tall, rawboned body of an adolescent boy. But at her feet sat six college boys transfixed by her voice. In a musical contralto she reeled out a zany story about an old couple who adopt a chair for a son, give it a trust fund, and advertise for a bride.

Laughter erupted. Then they all pitched in and competed with stories of their own. These young men—Louise's *société humoristique* and daily guests—also competed for her affections. As one later recalled, they all were in love with her. Preposterous though it sounds, Louise de Vilmorin was, perhaps even more than Louise Labé, an "empress of seduction," who enravished the most talented men of her time. "Laughter," she quipped, was "the scepter of [her] reign," but it was really her collective magic, woven of her verses, stories, and unearthly, iridescent personality.

Relatively unknown now, Louise was a French literary star fifty years ago: author of fourteen novels, three poetry volumes, and winner of the Monaco Prize and Légion d'Honneur. She made no secret of why she wrote. Sexual conquest "lights my lantern," she said; "that's what pushes me to write."

It had been so since infancy. Born into a festive, unconventional old French family in 1902, she received the genes, training, and spur to seduce from earliest childhood. Her mother was a celebrated seductress, and everyone in the large household of six children cultivated *le charme Vilmorin*. No rules and no banal restraints existed. Dinners were so uninhibited and witty that waiters were known to dash from the room in fits of laughter.

In common with many young sirens, Louise loathed her mother, a distant social lioness, and coquetted her way into her father's affections. In all her early photos she vamps for the camera with the fury-to-captivate of a child star on audition. When her father died in World War I, she transferred her charm offensive to her four older brothers, who petted and adored her.

Then, after TB interrupted her education, she acquired another indulgent male captive, her tutor, Abbé Mugnier. Using a progressive educational approach, the abbé permitted Louise to study only what interested her and encouraged her to write. He also fell completely "under her charm."

Louise almost married one of the suitors from her *société humoristique*, the writer Antoine de Saint Exupéry. For him, she was "poetry itself," the "only woman he ever loved," and the prototype of all the fey enchantresses in his fiction who lead men through a "magic door" into a "surreal world" and claim them for life.

But after a brief engagement Louise jilted him and married one of the power base husbands so often preferred by *sorcières*, a rich American sixteen years her senior. Henry Leigh-Hunt, though, couldn't compete with the charged Vilmorin climate of continual revelry and male admiration. After four dismal years in Las Vegas, Louise embarked on her first affair.

Over the next seven years in France she went through a quadrille of lovers, each with the initials A. M. The birth of three children did nothing to slow down this formidable manslayer. First came André Massénna, followed in quick succession by Sir Alexandre Mackenzie, Alexandre de Milo, Alexandre ("Sacha") de Manziarly, and André Malraux, distinguished men who loved her with "fire, fever, tenderness, and desperation" and who nourished her creatively.

Sacha, a brilliant lady-killer and *polisson* (down-and-dirty lover), set her career in motion. During their two-year liaison, he primed her confidence and encouraged her to write her first novel, *Sainte Unefois* (Onetime Saint). When editorial magnate André Malraux read it, he not only succumbed to the spell of her work and person but established her reputation with his book promotions. Her novel sold out, and fussy critics like Jean Cocteau hailed her as a "genius."

Caught up in the celebrity whirl, Louise reaped the erotic rewards of her literary diablerie. Divorcing her husband and discarding Malraux, she assembled a group of playmates, known as Louise's *bande*, and flipped through a card catalog of lovers including artist Jean Hugo and publisher Gaston Gallimard. She wrote another whimsical novella and on the brink of World War II married a man who might have walked out of a Grimm's fairy tale.

Pali Palffy, count of Presbourg, was the last of the Hungarian feudal overlords, a "devourer of women," who spoke six languages and lived in a castle at the foot of the Carpathian Mountains overlooking his domains. But only a few months into this fantastic marriage Louise's domestic phobia kicked in, and she fled to Budapest in the Presbourg Rolls-Royce.

There, ensconced as "Queen of the Danube Gulls," she wrote a novel and poetry for her club of admirers and as usual "burned up those who love[d] her . . . without so much as a backward glance at their ashes." Another Hungarian count, Tommy Esterházy, fell so "unimaginably in love" with her that he divorced his wife and persuaded Louise to follow suit and marry him.

However, by the time Tommy arrived in Paris after World War II for the wedding, Louise had already sighted bigger game. One of the world's greatest Lotharios, Sir Duff Cooper had just come to town as the new British ambassador, and Louise rose to the occasion. Unlike lesser seductresses, she didn't aim to please but to "madden, enthrall, [and] transport." She took a poetic tack toward a primal poetic goal, erotic intoxication.

When they met at an official function, she affected a look designed for maximum mystification: no makeup, ribbons knotted in a little-girl coiffure, and a Bavarian dirndl and shawl. Still unbeautiful in her forties, she had the curb appeal of a haunted carriage house on a storied estate.

Afterward Louise treated Duff to a "very Vilmorin evening," leading him through a maze of whimsical apartments to a candlelit children's playroom where "all transgressions were allowed." In full *sorcière* mode, Louise wrote poems on napkins, traded puns, and regaled the table with risqué stories. The next day Duff sent her a bouquet of lilacs and red roses. "You are a treasure," he wrote. "I want to be the miser."

For three years Louise lived with him and his wife, whom she called Bijou Blue and Bijou Rose, in an open ménage à trois at the Borghèse hôtel. An unofficial ambassadoress, she accompanied Duff to public functions and assembled a group of literati and bon vivants, the "Comus Bande," at embassy headquarters. She also trysted with old flame André Maurois on the side.

When the ménage broke up, Louise wrote her two best novels, *Julietta* and *Madame de,* both about *sorcières* who know "how to interest men," shake them up, and ensorcel them. *Madame de* became one of the most popular books by a woman in France and a cult film classic, due in part because the siren gets her comeuppance and dies of a broken heart, strangled in a skein of lies.

Louise, however, was very far from a comeuppance. Approaching fifty, she embarked on affairs with two young swells, twenty-six-year-old Roger Nimier and Orson Welles, to whom she famously said, "Darling, tonight I'll love you forever." With both she meted out strong doses of difficulty and caprice. "I have no faith in my fidelity," she taunted. Welles, a notorious womanizer, sent her fifty "my darling" telegrams from the set of *Othello* and installed himself so spousally in her home that she'd whisper to guests as she exited the room: "I'm going to fulfill my conjugal duty."

Her love life ran apace with her literary output through her fifties and sixties. She wrote five more novellas, a film script, and a translation of *Kiss Me Kate,* and threw herself into a torrid amour with a mystery lover in 1958, "XY," who inspired her only pornographic book, *Madame de V . . . Her Dark Thoughts.* Afterward this rogue-at-heart hit the road again, rebedding old lovers and picking up new ones in châteaus and resorts throughout Europe.

One conquest, Pierre Seghers, captivated by a candlelit poetry reading, begged her not to "play" with his heart. "I no longer know where I am," he wrote. Louise replied that he'd "nail[ed] her in the heart," but she played just the same. She continued on her sex-go-round and welcomed her first husband back when he returned in 1962, unable to forget her. Even her neglected children and grandchildren arrived to pay court.

Her fragile feminine "look" to the contrary, Louise, as female artists must, had an imperial ego and a tough hide. She considered herself a cross between Napoleon and Eleanor of Aquitaine. But old age and its assorted abrasions eroded her creativity at last, though she continued to bespell and subdue men.

She reunited with Malraux (now the minister of French culture) in the sixties and, sucked into his egotistic and diplomatic vortex, ceased writing. She amused guests, minted bon mots, and painted so competently that she had a show in New York City, yet she completed none of the novels she started.

She got, however, a death as poetically *exalté* as her fiction: laid out on her columned bed, draped in white silk, "surrounded by the household in tears." After he buried Louise at Verrières, Malraux remained there until he died, unable to tear himself away from the genius loci of the place and his "illness."

Her reputation, by contrast, has proved more forgettable. Except for *Madame de,* little remains in print, and her man-killer legend has faded like a pressed flower in an old book. There was nothing PC about her. Her apolitical, fantastical stories espouse no causes and tell no victim tales; her heroines knew and exercised their power.

For that and more competitive reasons, women abominated her. Anaïs Nin, once her tenant in Paris, savaged her as a narcissistic man-izer and scribbler of frivolous fairy tales. Louise returned the favor and cordially loathed most women, especially feminists, whom she called a "herd of vain she-asses."

Unlike Nin, however, Louise finessed both love and art, never abasing herself to male genius and producing a corpus of tightly crafted mythopoeic minimasterpieces. "She reigned in hauteur over the male sex," working in sync with her female birthright, artistic erotic magic.

"You are magical," said a lover, "real art"; "divine and fearsome," added Jean Cocteau. Louise always claimed her charm came from her "signature." She just didn't know what it was, the spiral logo of the first divinity she served, the myth-speaking, maze-making creatrix of poetry, delirium, and seduction.

The early religiosexual rites synthesized all the arts in a kind of ur-rock opera. Under the combined spell of music, song, dance, pictures, and poetry, celebrants lost themselves in ecstasy and merged with the source of All Living. They and the earth were charged with new life. From these sacred spectacles came comedy and tragedy, the one glorifying renewed sexual potency in orgiastic festivity; the other, the miracle of rebirth-in-death through the release of suffering into redemption.

The sex goddess Inanna controlled both genres. At the annual Sumerian marriage ceremony, the prototype of comedy, her priestess and the king copulated on the high altar to invoke the divine generative force, followed by a free-for-all of cross-dressing, sex, and carnival excess.

In the Lamentations, priestesses clawed their eyes and thighs and wailed *balags* to mourn the annual exile of Inanna's lover to the underworld, thus facilitating his predestined resurrection. Later the Dionysian rites subsumed these two forms in a riotous *komus,* with a procession of women bearing gigantic phalluses and a tragic "goat song" that bewailed the god's necessary dismemberment before his regeneration.

Theater, at base, was a drama about sex, an affirmation of the transcendent life instincts through collective rapture and illumination. And the original leading lady was the "sexual essence of creation," the great goddess. Not for nothing are stage stars enshrined as love goddesses, though few have taken advantage of it in private. Others weren't so dumb. Two in particular, comedienne Nell Gwyn and tragic diva Rachel, were world-class performers and seductresses, prima donnas who knew their heritage and what to do with it.

Nell Gwyn, 1650–1687

Nell Gwyn, Charles II's famous mistress, has long been canonized as a Protestant harlot-saint, guileless, blunt, softhearted, and faithful to the king until the bitter end. By tradition, an orange is placed on the altar of the Savoy Chapel each December in memory of her early days as an orange girl. But it's the wrong altar and the wrong halo. Nell was an avatar of the pagan sex goddess in her carnival guise, the lightning-crowned Inanna. She loosed the anarchic aphrodisiac of comedy, blasted men into festival orbit, and "unsettl[ed] all things."

Sentimentalists called her Little Pretty Nelly, a childish darling of Miss Muffet hug appeal. Nell Gwyn, however, had quills, sinew, and a thoroughly adult fix on life. She came up, as seductresses often do, the hard way and developed elbows at an early age. Soon after her birth, her father died in prison, and her alcoholic mother took over the management of a Covent Garden brothel.

Denied schooling, she spent her youth scavenging for ha'pennies in the fetid bowels of one of London's worst slums, Coal Yard Alley. At thirteen she went to work in Madame Ross's bawdy house, a cut-throat venue filled with tough, backstabbing "dunghill wenches." (More than three thousand prostitutes plied the streets in a city of a hundred thousand.) Her sister rescued her with a job as an orange girl in the King's Theatre, which Nell parlayed into a theatrical career through the pull of a rich lover.

A sharp-tongued street queen with fizz and attitude, she proved a born comic. She chose one of the best Shakespearean actors, Charles Hart, for a lover and coach and soon conquered London. An infatuated Samuel Pepys exclaimed that he'd never seen "so great performance of a comical part," and the leading dramatists wrote her into their plays. In each, she played variations on the same madcap siren— a cheeky prostitute, a tease in "gallant" drag, and a jilt who seduces her Don Juan counterpart by rolling on the floor with her legs splayed and crotch exposed. For the plague-ravaged British population, she represented hedonism and life renewal and was as in demand amorously as professionally. After a brief affair with Sir Charles Buckhurst, an aristocratic roisterer and wit, she caught the eye of the king.

The occasion was a performance of Dryden's *Tyrannic Love*, in which Nell, who'd killed herself for love, rose up on her bier as she was being carted off the stage. "I am the ghost of poor departed Nell," she recited, "I'll be civil; I am what I was,/ A little harmless devil." According to report, the smitten king "carried her off" that night. Not long after, she became a palace fixture, and a year later she left the theater to be a mistress to the man she always called Charles the Third.

Charles II, a cultivated, periwigged version of Hugh Hefner, loved and collected beautiful women, rotating among the voluptuous Barbara Villiers, "La Belle Stuart," and sundry blondes of passages. Nell stood out like an ugly stepsister in this company. Without a trace of prized china doll *joliesse,* she had unfashionably red hair, full "blub" cheeks, a small, slightly wattled chin, and a wide mouth with a protruding nether lip.

But she held her own among the beauty queens and jockeyed past them to first place in the king's affections. Though women came and went, including a long liaison with the French mantrap Louise de Kéroualle, Charles favored his "frisking comedian" above all. She grew dearer and more indispensable with time. By the end of his reign he confined his nights to her, toasted her health twice at dinner, and required his "constant diversion" so continually that courtiers accused Nell of "bewitching" him.

In a sense she had. When Charles lured her away from the theater onto his payroll, he allowed the imp of comedy, that most subversive *sorcière,* to infiltrate the royal premises. A one-woman show, Nell knew all the tricks of the trade. She aped cavaliers in male disguise, danced incomparable jigs, threw parties designed like theatrical spectacles, costumed and painted herself for display, and always amused.

She was an improv queen with a guttersnipe tongue and gift for springloaded repartee. She told his highness to "lock up his codpiece" when he pleaded poverty, ribbed him about his "French bitch," and refused to invite one of his ex's to his birthday party. "One whore at a time is enough for his majesty," she told him.

Charles, cramped by ceremony and wearied of state tedium, ate up this impudence and unbridled hilarity. With Nell, it wasn't just an act. Despite her horrific childhood, she was a merry jade, naturally ebullient and high-spirited. Whenever Charles strayed, she joked that he'd come back for her "fun and frolic." He also came back for other siren extras: her "frankly wanton" bedcraft, unusual cleanliness, maternal ministrations, and refreshing straight-on style.

As she rose in Charles's favor, Nell's income and status increased proportionally. She lived in high equipage in mansions at London and Windsor, drew a six-figure allowance, and saw both her sons ennobled. Like the prodigal spirit of Dionysian comedy itself, Nell squandered thousands at the gaming table and upholstered her homes with Neronian excess—private bowling alleys and handcrafted silver beds.

Contrary to legend, Nell didn't sleep alone while the king dabbled with playgirls. During the conflict with Holland, Nell wrote her dressmaker that "none of [her] lovers" had left for war. Too streetwise not to know which side her bread was buttered on, she didn't flaunt her infidelities, but she definitely enjoyed them. A "lovely" lieutenant, Stint Duncombe, "mount[ed] her well," and at least two others, a Dutch stud and a member of her "merry gang" of male drinking buddies, shared her bed.

Nor did she fit the camp follower image of a royal paramour. A free-souled law unto herself, she defied the king politically. She cultivated Whig friends (conspiring in the Monmouth plot to make Charles's oldest illegitimate son his heir) and took the protesters' side in the anti-Catholic riots. When the mob mistook her carriage for Louise de Kéroualle's, she stepped out with a hearty laugh. "Pray good people, be civil, I am the Protestant whore!"

At Charles's death four years later, his final thoughts were for Nell. "Let not poor Nelly starve," he said with his last breath. Thanks to his successor's generosity, she didn't starve, but she came downwind of a more lethal royal legacy. At thirty-seven she died of the pox Charles had given her.

The Reverend Thomas Tennison almost lost the bishopric for officiating at her funeral. Though whitewashed and venerated later, Nell drew vicious fire in her day. Too big for her britches, too insurgent, and sexually powerful, she was pilloried as "Puddle Nell" and the "hair[sic]-brained whore." Women, with the simon-says servility of the oppressed, keelhauled and cut her.

But Nell could take care of herself. An alley scrapper and tough infighter, she didn't give a fig for public opinion and made short work of the female sex. She enacted vicious caricatures of rivals, fed sweetmeats to an actress laced with jalap (a diarrhetic), and taunted the "French whore" to the brink of laudanum.

Like Inanna, "the sexual joy of the cosmos," Nell kicked ass. The two go together; without an attack gene and a goddess ego, art can't happen. An Oxford don of the time dedicated a book of classical deities to Nell and compared her to both Hercules the Mighty and Aphrodite. If he'd gone back farther, he'd have pegged her: the all-powerful deity of eros who reinvigorates the planet, commands carnival, heats the blood, and bewitches hearts with laughter.

Rachel Félix, 1821–1858

Men trembled and broke out in "ice cold shivers" at her performances, women fainted, and Charlotte Brontë "shuddered to the marrow of her bones." This was the *mysterium tremendum,* the bolt of awe and terror felt in the presence of the goddess. The semidivinity was Rachel Félix, known regally as Rachel, the greatest tragedienne of mid-nineteenth-century Europe.

A diva of "demonical powers," she returned to the archaic origins of tragedy and recovered women's holy office as shaman, the maker of divine delirium and agent of deliverance from death to life.

Tragedy carries a tremendous sexual thrust. And Rachel knew exactly how to handle that high-test primordial aphrodisiac. Unlike the normal run of lovelorn leading ladies, Rachel put the erotics of theater to full account and made out as brilliantly with men as at the box office.

Like Nell Gwyn, Rachel didn't look the part. She seemed closer to the poor little match girl than a "born empress" of drama and desire. A mite-size four feet eleven inches, she was flat-chested and rail-thin, with the bulging forehead of a beluga whale, close-set eyes, a pendulous lower lip, and a curved long nose. Her pedigree too lacked distinction. She was born on the road to itinerant Jewish peddlers somewhere en route from Switzerland to France. Soon afterward she fell off the old clothes cart unnoticed and was retrieved by a mongrel dog.

Nine years later she was miraculously rescued a second time. While she and her sister played the guitar and sang for handouts, the director of a Parisian music school wandered by and plucked them off the streets of Lyons. He enrolled them in the prestigious École de Musique Sacré, and the rest is history.

Once there, the savage little urchin kicked up a tempest and ignored lessons, preferring instead to mount tabletops and declaim French dramatic parts in a threadbare shawl. When the director caught her at it, he transferred her to a master teacher at the Théâtre Molière, who trained her in the classical repertoire.

She then moved to the Comédie Française, where she was taken on by the theatrical Svengali and queen-maker Joseph-Isidore Samson. "She's my discovery, my creation," he proclaimed, and tutored her gratis in his home for a year. In June 1838 she made her debut as Camille in Corneille's *Horace* and by fall was the toast of Paris, with ticket lines forming at midday and wrapping around the block.

She was nothing less than a "poetic revolution." She didn't rant or flail her arms in the approved stylized manner. Instead she prowled the stage with pantherine strides and built by slow degrees to a soul-shattering crescendo. At the play's climax she dissolved into a paroxysm of passion and shrieked "as if the earth had cracked at your feet." She resurrected the ur-priestesses of ancient tragedy, transforming the old victim heroines into spirit-possessed, ecstatic maenads.

A steely victrix, "driven to conquer or die," Rachel took command of her romantic life as masterfully as her stage career. In both she left nothing to chance. Just as she overrehearsed and planned her performances to the last detail, so she scoped out lovers, calculated her moves, and made sure her erotic destiny remained firmly in hand. Rather than a frigid schemer, however, she was a passion artist and man lover with a craving for novelty, rapture, and independence. "I am *free*," she insisted, "and mean to remain free. I will have renters, but not owners."

In common with other *sorcières*, she picked men who nurtured, inspired, and promoted her—an actor who devoted himself to her "genius," and the Parisian bigwig Dr. Louis Vernon, who made her his "new religion" and launched her in society. Rachel appeared at Vernon's levees and balls in chaste ingenue frocks on her father's arm. But beneath this lily maid disguise, she operated like a master siren on the make. While sleeping with Vernon, she seduced the nabobs he threw in her path. A marquis and famous lawyer visited regularly, and the celebrated poet Alfred de Musset courted his "Fan-Fan" with letters, poetry, and a play. Dukes and counts sought her hand, and at some point in 1840 she became briefly engaged.

An accomplished *charmeuse*—witty, piquant, spirited, and flirtatious—she consulted her pleasure. Or pleasures. Rachel had a low one-man threshold and liked her sexual menu varied, rich, plentiful, and highly spiced. Lovers called her a "mad Messalina" in bed who made them cry obscenities as she climaxed.

In 1841, with her theatrical career on a meteoric rise, she premiered in England, where Queen Victoria gave her a bracelet and pronounced her "a nice modest girl." But the "Jewish sorceress" behaved as immodestly, as extravagantly as ever, driving the British to mob hysteria with her rhapsodic performances and trifling with lords and stockpiling their presents.

When she returned home in glory, she dropped Dr. Vernon and sought men of her own caliber, a covey of lovers connected to her male counterpart, Napoleon. First she chose the gorgeous prince de Joinville, hero of the St. Helena expedition, then Count Alexandre Walewski, Napoleon's illegitimate son by a Polish countess. With a creator's homing instinct for wives, she found in Alexandre the perfect domestic support system for her genius. He loved her with dog-like devotion and provided a deluxe home on the rue Trudon custom fitted for her care.

Rachel, a flagrant self-adorer, emblazoned an *R* on every surface, and stenciled RACHEL on the wall of a gold and white salon surmounted by panels of the nine muses. A panorama of excess and pagan spectacle, the rooms featured white bearskins, Etruscan vases, lavish Persian hangings, and daggers and human bones on display tables. She opened a successful salon and blossomed creatively under this red carpet care. At the zenith of her career she branched out into new, high-risk territory. She tackled crone and comic parts and daringly sexualized her image by playing a lust-drunk Phèdre.

As her fame escalated, so did her male devotees. They formed a *cénacle Rachel,* and she availed herself of their sexual services on tour (in a carriage fitted out with a bed) and at home. An incurable polygamist and thrill junkie, Rachel couldn't be corralled into fidelity. "I love to be loved as I love when I love," she said. After Rachel and Alexandre had a son together, she disported so flagrantly with a noted journalist that the two split up.

Over the next decade she acquired two bracelets hung with rings from her lovers that were too heavy to be worn together. Yet throughout the philandering she remained—atypically for sirens—a steadfast, good mother. She bore a second child with Arthur Bertrand, son of Napoleon's steward, before moving on to men with still closer ties to Napoleon: Emperor Louis Napoleon and his cousin Prince Napoleon or Plon-Plon. As usual, she juggled lovers concurrently.

Once while the three traveled by train through England, Louis awoke to see his mistress in Plon-Plon's arms and diplomatically closed his eyes. Despite this brazen polyamorism, Rachel's ex's tended to remain on friendly terms with her throughout her life. She kept up a long correspondence with Dr. Vernon and stayed close to both Plon-Plon and Napoleon III, later tutoring the emperor on how to carry himself as a ruler.

By 1848 Rachel seemed impregnable. Deified as a "genius" and "goddess of love," onstage and in person, she moved from triumph to triumph. She wrung an unprecedented contract from the Comédie Française, performed grandstand recitations of "La Marseillaise," and reinvented herself as a romantic actress with brilliant results. She now played "*the* courtesan" in Victor Hugo's *Angelo,* the unscrupulous siren Lady Tartuffe, and other sexy supremas like Adrienne Lecoureur.

On a Russian tour the czar presented her with a solid gold crown and coffer of diamonds and rubies. Her power over men, if anything, increased. Influential lovers, such as publishing giant Michel Lévy and the Comédie Française director, did her bidding, and martyrs stalked and implored her. "Speak my queen," wrote one, "give me the word and I shall run as my hounds run when I whistle to them."

Yet one hound refused to heed her whistle: her health. By twenty-nine she had begun to cough blood, and she slowly succumbed to pulmonary tuberculosis. Disease, however, only threw her egoism and life lust into overdrive. "Watch me light a candle," she exalted, "instead of cursing the darkness." She pitched herself into a hectic round of love affairs and mounted an ill-fated barnstorm of America. Forced to compete with "Jocko, the Ape of Brazil" on Broadway, she played to half-full houses, collapsed onstage, and was carried home more dead than alive.

She died with the class of a high priestess. While a naval officer delivered marriage proposals at her feet, she contemplated eternity beneath the Egyptian pyramids. She passed her final hours in the gothic tower room of a Mediterranean villa facing a bas-relief of a grieving muse. She rouged her cheeks, sent back love letters encased in fruit baskets, and at the end cooled her feverish fingers in the jewels given to her by lovers and potentates. Just before she died, a photographer caught her in front of a statue of Cupid, her eyes averted from the camera toward the hereafter.

The future didn't reward her gaze. As Rachel Brownstein documents in her fascinating biography, Rachel didn't go down well with the Victorians. Alarmed by this "gypsy-like creature of lawless moods," this apotheosis of female sexual *über*power, they trashed and vilified her. Biographers pelted her with every known Jewish stereotype and called her a beast, monster, drunk, lesbian, and a "male talent."

Women were her loudest detractors. She defiled the sex, they carped, with her "sad selfishness" and "frightful skinniness." Two female writers of the day lit into her with particular venom. George Eliot compared her with Melusina, the fairy of the French legend who changes into a serpent once a week, and Charlotte Brontë likened her to both a snake and a demon that "shook with the passions of the pit."

They captured her exactly. Rachel was just that: a shamanistic entrancer, a demonic eruption from the deeps of history, and a serpentine embodiment of eternal life. Not your average Victorian church mouse.

But then everything about this tiny waif-woman was outsize and mythic. When she was going down for the count and knew she would die, she said confidently, "It's not so easy to bury people of my race and distinction." Perhaps in her fuddled state she confused herself with her stage heroines or perhaps she sensed her true significance, as a priestess of the resurrection rites and (what her votaries claimed) a "mouthpiece of the gods." Or more accurately as the goddess, the supreme spellbinder and erotic force of creation.

The women who hated these *sorcières* weren't just mustachioed Mrs. Grundys and village scolds; many, like George Eliot, Charlotte Brontë, and the ladies of Lyons and Restoration England, composed the female intellectual and social elite of their age. More than merely parroting the male party line, they had their reasons. Even the most successful women are subtly conditioned by gender stereotypes, the injunctions to modesty, silence, stasis, sacrifice, subservience, monogamy, and sexual purity.

Such self-constriction doesn't come cheap. And the merry artist-sirens gave the raspberry to the whole con. They refused to pay the price and got off scot-free, got all the marbles, men, and power. In a flash they invalidated women's lives and made the noble careers of muse-maids, art martyrs, stunted poets, and diva spinsters look like colossal wastes.

If women, however, could have seen past their broken noses, they'd have found a feminine identity beyond their fondest dreams. Female artists don't have to give up anything. Art and erotic power belong together by divine decree. Creativity contains aphrodisiacal plutonium, implanted there in the religiosexual rites of prehistory. The passions aroused by these ancient rites never disappear from the collective unconscious; women have only to tap the she-shaman to reignite them.

The *sorcières* can instruct us, too. Although fortunate in talent, teachers, and opportunities, they in large part, made their own luck. As artists they put their own stamp on the seductress persona. Their double job of nourishing their talents and making it against tough odds added shiv to their style. They took life by the throat, tore off the trodden paths, and picked mentors and men who sustained and nourished their gifts. With the artist's high "libidinal energy" and creative upkeep, they expropriated the male privilege of seraglios and support-wives, while giving as much inspiration as they got. Like all seductresses, they were originals but to the nth power, accentuating and flourishing their eccentricities. Criticism rolled off like water from a swan's back.

To the seductress's queen bee personality, they added creative punch and foxfire. Even more than other sirens, they were full-souled self-actualizers with the androgyny, élan, and goddess aura that made men compare them to deities. But as descendants of the priestesses of holy madness they threw wonder dust on the flames—artistic delirium—and were the lady galores of the seductress tribe, all excess, glitz, and italics.

In their seductive siegecraft, they led with their art. Their love potions, idiosyncratically brewed as they were, were laced with the belladonna of shamanistic magic. On top of the usual blandishments of ego inflation, maternal nurture, and intimacy, they laid on the voodoo of their artistic *spécialité*. They brought theatrical spectacle or dance, for example, to the bedroom; they spoke the cabalistic word spells of ancient ritual; they created erotic obstacle courses with the tools of their craft and raised the bar with the numinous self-sufficiency of their calling.

Few were beauty pageant material. Yet they becharmed themselves beautiful through the necromancy of their art. For them, clothes, makeup, ornament, and setting took on the religio-magical significance of dramatic rite. Their homes weren't designed to make men comfortable, but, like cave temples, to displace and transport. Their parties were strictly primitive—festivals of collective release and delirium.

Yeats said artists had to choose between life and art. Too smart for this ruse, *sorcières* fused both seamlessly. Their careers stoked their love lives and vice versa. They weren't waylaid by muse-artist, love-career dualisms but easily appropriated the and/both holism of the goddess. They were great artists and lived in excelsis, swathed in happiness and male devotion.

They may rile us for reasons beyond their gender blasphemies and enviable lives. They often trample values we hold sacred: home, motherhood, honesty, modesty, community spirit, to begin the list. But what can you expect from avatars of the divine wonder-worker? They're in the business of ecstasy and transformation. They dredge up the great goddess from the archaic depths of the psyche with their artistic diablerie and shake us to the roots of our being. They put us under their mythic spell, loosen our moorings, swell our loins, and lead us elsewhere—beyond self, safety, and civic responsibility.

No wonder patriarchy has been at such pains to punish *sorcières* and keep art out of female hands. Combined with women's other seductive charms, creative magic can blow men and culture off the map. Jean Baudrillard makes an absolute correlation between seduction and art; they're both, he says, works of "black magic" and mind-theft to another reality. This work, by rights, is a woman's, the original mage and creatrix, the deity's mistress of spells, who with her conjurer's trunk of brushes, words, musical instruments, masks, and dancing shoes can hijack men to seventh heaven, have her way with them, and "foil all systems of power."

CHAPTER SEVEN

Machtweiber: *Seductresses in Politics*

No people who place a woman over their public affairs prosper. —MUHAMMAD
THE PROPHET

Where a woman reigneth . . . there must needs Satan be president of the council. –
JOHN KNOX

*As noble-spirited and courageous men be ever more lovable and admirable than
others, so is the like true of illustrious, noble-hearted and courageous dames.*

—SEIGNEUR DE BRANTÔME

*Personal and institutional power has been wielded by women without their becom-
ing . . . anything less than women.* —WOLFGANG LEDERER

*C*atherine the Great lies nude in her royal bed as her favorite horse (with heart-shaped shoes) is lowered by block and tackle
onto her tumid loins. Cleopatra, after an all-night orgy with slave boys,
summons them the next day and poisons them with sweetmeats.
Butch-monarch Queen Christina charges into Versailles in filthy
breeches and puts the ladies to flight with her foul obscenities. We all
know the stories. No good comes of female political power. When
women rule, hormones run amok and men head for the hills. As John
Knox said four hundred years ago, nothing is viler, more sexually re-

pulsive than women who "bear rule, superiority, dominion or empire."
They're "repugnant to nature."

We're still under the pall of this pernicious myth. Women walk on
eggshells in public office, afraid of alienating male affections, being
too sexy, too dykey, unaware that female leadership is not only the
most natural but also the most seductive phenomenon on earth. Men
of course don't want us to know this, which explains the propaganda.
Catherine the Great and Cleopatra never stooped to horses or slave
boys, and Christina never renounced men for stormtrooper
machismo. (She had a long affair with a charming Italian cardinal.) All
three were magisterial rulers, and the first two, crack seductresses.

Their combined success is the heart of the trouble; *Machtweiber*
(siren-politicas) packed too much clout and were too disruptive of patriarchal domination. They resurrected an archetype beyond the
strength of man to resist—the Queen of Creation who fascinates and
overwhelms the libido against every precaution.

For aeons before the rise of modern civilization, mankind worshiped a mythic imperatrix who incarnated the erotic energy of existence and ruled the universe. Sex goddess and supreme governor, she
inspired men to adoration, awe, obedience, and holy hard-ons. She's
the way nature first intended it: a ruler-seductress with men and nations at her command.

Some women in Western history, undeterred by the thicket of
No Trespass signs, have stormed the halls of state and reclaimed their
ancient birthright. Exercising the divine right of queens, these
Machtweiber triumphed politically and romantically. Seduction has always been a mainstay of men in public life; it builds rapport, engi-
neers consent, and creates the charisma necessary to lead.

But women deliver a double whammy when they seduce in the
service of government. They echo the archaic fascinations of the
mythic Great Goddess. Their magnetic characters—wholeness, vitality,
grandeur, and color wheel multiplicity—elicit unconscious memories
of the divine All Woman; their management style, her Seductive Way.

By mixing sex and politics, *Machtweiber* potentiated their power
and magnified their sway and influence. They were glamorous, showy
commandas who shred every stereotype and render the old models of

female leadership obsolete. They give us political shimmy room. The staid, asexual chief of state persona is a real perversion of nature, a power drain to women and an offense to the divine scheme.

Machtweiber comprise three groups: the absolute monarchs who mirror the original goddess, the divine ordainers who sanctify male rule, and the revolutionary activists who reflect the modern demonization of the she-deity. Though all the following politicas key off from the master image of the Great Goddess, the autocrats came closest to filling her shoes.

More than life size, omnicapable, and grandiose, they deliberately exploited their mythic charge. In elaborate promotional campaigns, they impersonated the divinity and swathed themselves in archetypic panoply and cave rite spectacle. Patriarchy obstructed them at every turn and often cramped their personal sex lives. But they couldn't stop these heiresses of the ancient Queen of the Cosmos from doing it Her way—the holistic love-work way—and becoming some of the greatest monarchs of history.

Cleopatra, 70–69 B.C.–30 B.C.

In a culture that deified the royal family, Cleopatra was born a goddess, and not just any goddess but Aphrodite/Isis, the "most profoundly satisfying of all," heiress of the first divinity. She was also a shrewd publicist who leveraged her political career on her divine persona. With men and nations sucked up in her undertow, she could work her will as she wished on the ancient world.

Contrary to her siren-in-slinkwear reputation, Cleopatra was actually "one of the greatest politicians of all time." At the same time, she set the gold standard for seduction. An archfascinator, she conquered the twin titans of the age and put her charms to brilliant political and erotic account.

Hollywood got her all wrong. Short and zaftig, she resembled Elizabeth Taylor only in cup size. She looked more like a "before" plastic surgery profile: a low, beetling brow, large, hooked nose, prognathic jaw, and a wide, thin-lipped mouth. And her personality was anything but dumb starlet. She had brains, character, and edge. Born the third in succession to the Ptolemaic throne in 69 B.C., she learned the *enkuklios paideia* (origin of our encyclopedia) with the boys of the royal household, a polymathic curriculum of literature, rhetoric, philosophy, arithmetic, geometry, astronomy, medicine, drawing, singing, lyre playing, and horsemanship. A passionate scholar, Cleopatra excelled in science and language, mastering eight languages and becoming the first of the Greek Ptolemys to speak Egyptian. At ten she received her initiation into cutthroat politics. Her older sister, Berenice, dethroned their father, and Cleopatra fled with him to Rome, where they bribed and groveled their way through the hierarchy for three years. With Roman funds, they retook Egypt, wreaked carnage, and executed Berenice.

On her father's death in 51 B.C., Cleopatra was crowned Queen of Kings and coruler with her ten-year-old brother, Ptolemy XIII. She walked into a land mine. With her brother's party in the wings plotting to oust her, she faced a country on the brink of anarchy—rebelling nationalists, marauding bandits, bankruptcy, famine, and escalating dependence on Rome.

She proved more than equal to the task. As the "living law" she ingratiated herself with the native population through grandstand public appearances as Isis, then stabilized the economy, settled strife, established order, and checkmated Roman aggression. When her brother at last overthrew her, she counterattacked in a bold rearguard strike. She waited for Julius Caesar, the new strongman of the Roman Empire, to invade Alexandria to exploit the coup and smuggled herself into his presence in a rolled-up rug.

The fifty-two-year-old general was a jaded ladies' man, long accustomed to backstage groupies. But Cleopatra "spellbound" him "the moment he set eyes on her and she opened her mouth to speak." Captivated by her "playful temperament," "charm of her conversation," intelligence, and esprit, he made her his mistress that night and championed her cause.

He defeated her enemies in battle, installed her as sole ruler with another underage brother, and instead of annexing Egypt, a logical move, promised autonomy and returned the island of Cyprus. They celebrated their victory in a triumphal tour down the Nile in gods' costumes. Later Caesar summoned Cleopatra and their son, Caesarion, to Rome. It was more than a sexual diversion. He gave her a mansion on the Tiber, erected her golden statue in a temple to Venus Genetrix, and increasingly sought her counsel. He initiated legislation to marry her and implemented many of her ideas—calendar reform, library and canal design—and the theocratic Eastern concept of absolute rule that led to his assassination.

After his murder Cleopatra was a marked woman, mother of Caesar's only male heir and traitor to the revolutionary cause. But she saved her skin through adroit diplomacy. She escaped to Egypt, where she sat out the civil war by shrewdly appeasing both sides. Meanwhile she boosted the gross national product and consolidated her power. She commissioned public artworks that immortalized her divinity and ordered costumed processionals hymning her grandeur. "I am Isis, mistress of every land," sang priestesses. "I gave and ordained laws for men which no one is able to change."

When the tide turned against the conspirators, Cleopatra leveled her seductive forces at the new regime. Saturating the Near East with advance publicity, she sailed up the Cydnus River in a golden three-hundred-foot barge to meet Marc Antony, Octavian's coruler and commander of the eastern half of the empire. He was a handsome, muscled Hercules, a notorious womanizer with a crude, bluff barracks hall manner.

Cleopatra's grand opera entrance "completely overwhelmed" him. Dressed in the diaphanous robes of Isis/Aphrodite and enthroned on a silver poop, she drew into port with a crew of nubile nymphs swinging perfumed censers and playing musical instruments. Four nights of feasts, at her expense, followed. These were masterpieces of big top dazzle, banquets with light shows, jeweled place settings, extravagant menus, carpets of rose petals, and costly gifts. The philistine Antony went down like a sack of sand. Unhinged, unhorsed, he forgot to upbraid Cleopatra for inadequate support (his original plan) and followed her to Alexandria.

Over the next year she locked up her conquest. Playing to Antony's hedonistic sensuality, she introduced him to the *vie de luxe*— Oriental style. Eight dinners were prepared each night so that the food could be "served to perfection," gala fetes were mounted, and the "sophisticated erotic techniques of the East" deployed in the bedroom. Her turnout was pure goddess *abbondanza*. An expert in cosmetics (she wrote a treatise on the subject), she made up her plain face with hieratic glamour and wore see-through Sidonian silks adorned with Red Sea pearl earrings and artfully chased gold brooches. Heady perfumes suffused the palace—a monument to sybaritic enjoyment with vaulted gold and ebony ceilings and soft, embroidered couches.

This was a palace of revolving delights. Cleopatra provided a constant supply of novelties, from her jump-cut mood changes to impromptu expeditions through town in servants' disguises. She practiced a "thousand forms of flattery" on her roughneck lover, treating him "without the least reserve."

But she kept him up to the mark (not pleasure-drugged, as critics claim) and spurred him to conquest and glory. She also drove a hard bargain. In exchange for military aid in Parthia, she forced Antony to execute her enemies, including her sister Arsinoe, and give her parts of Asia Minor and Syria.

After Antony's return to Rome, political marriage to Octavian's sister, and three-year absence, Cleopatra made him pay for it. When he came back to Egypt still lovestruck, she enlisted him in her master plan to restore her empire to its original size. She made him fork over eastern provinces, legitimize their twins, and name Caesarion heir to the kingdom.

Envisioning a Roman-Egyptian dynasty, Cleopatra and Antony staged a sumptuous donations ceremony in which they sanctified their union, crowned their children, and filed through the streets in a triumphal procession as Isis and Dionysus reborn. In a final affront to Rome, Antony erected a statue of Cleopatra/Isis on the Acropolis and bathed her feet in public.

When the inevitable war with Octavian broke out, Cleopatra dispatched herself—unlike the canards—with exemplary military acumen. Even Antony's general praised "her capacity as a ruler" and strategic "intelligence." She fled the Battle of Actium by prearrangement and masterminded a comeback from the Red Sea that failed by a fluke. In the end she went out goddess style. Determined not to be paraded through Rome in chains, she died bedecked as Isis, poisoned by the sacred cobra, simultaneously outwitting Octavian and affirming her divinity and immortality.

Loathed by the Romans and feared by church fathers, she's been typecast as a vamp ever since, a "lascivious and insatiable" mantrap. Even a feminist scholar attacked her recently for her "sexual wiles," concluding that she failed because "she was forced into the same trap as every woman who uses sex to get her man."

But Cleopatra, the goddess-queen's deputy on earth, made sex the cornerstone of her politics, the better to rule, the better to love whom she liked. She might not have "failed" at all had it not been for Roman prejudice and superior might.

In fact she avoided the feminine "trap." She transcended gender roles, rose to the highest distinction as sovereign, and molded the destinies of the two greatest men of the world, all with eros and queenship working in perfect concert. Antony fell on his sword, content that he would meet her in the afterlife, his "most triumphant lady" and the "Queen Himself."

Elizabeth I, 1553–1603

The scene is engraved in stained glass in the British historical imagination: Elizabeth I dressed as an "Amazonian empress" addressing the troops on Tilbury Plain. "I know I have the body of a weak and feeble woman but I have the stomach of a king," she exhorts. "I myself will be your general, judge, and rewarder."

Elizabeth rivaled Cleopatra as a self-mythologizer. Brought to the throne when female rulers were thought "more than" "monsters," she threw dust in the eyes of her misogynistic adversaries by cunningly identifying herself with the goddess. To deflect male hostility, she pleaded feminine weakness and chose lesser deities for her imagos: Diana the moon goddess, Astraea, goddess of justice, and, as at Tilbury, an Amazonian queen. But the archaic Great Goddess was the true seat of her power.

On a personal level, it's true, sixteenth-century sexism condemned her to sublimated sexual gamesmanship and chaste flirtations. As queen, though, she was the mythic first imperatrix incarnate, governing through an inspired amalgam of sex and politics. She maneuvered England out of chaos and dissension into world-class leadership and at the same time made herself the love object of not only the nation but a battalion of hot-bodied cavaliers.

Elizabeth's childhood, like Cleopatra's, was a rough nursery. From infancy to her inauguration at twenty-five, she walked a political high wire without a safety net. Her father beheaded her mother when she was three, after which her own life as a possible claimant to the crown hung on the vagaries of warring factions at court. Every move was "fraught with danger and disaster." She lost her first lover to the block in a conspiracy over her accession, and she was sent to the Tower and very nearly killed several times by her half sister, Queen Mary.

Early on she learned the survival skills of a Machiavella: caution, circumspection, self-possession, deceit, patience, and the art of "answerless answers." She also developed a Mistress of the Universe mind and character. Given the Renaissance training of boys, she rode, danced, played musical instruments, and aced academics. She spoke six languages, mastered history, rhetoric, and moral philosophy, and had a gigabyte memory. Her sense of self was heaven-scaling. "God hath raised me high," she said; "my sex cannot diminish my prestige."

Foreshadowing her future goddess strategy, Elizabeth orchestrated her coronation to evoke a visitation from on high. Bonfires, bells, and choreographed pageants celebrated the arrival of the new Deborah, a semidivine national savior.

She engineered her appearance for iconic effect. Though not pretty—long-faced and hooknosed with narrow lips and an unruly head of red curls—she applied heavy maquillage and skin whiteners to give her face a masklike aura. Her costume trailed clouds of glory. Cut to the cleavage and festooned with "jewels," it was a billowing confection of gold and silver trimmed with ermine. Her rings contained "tiny portraits of herself." During the procession to Westminster Abbey, she "wonderfully ravished" the people through press-the-flesh declarations of love.

Once in office, she wheeled out the same seductive weaponry. Confronting unprecedented hostility to female sovereigns and a country in shambles—rampant debt, religious conflict, corruption, and no police or standing army—she "gained obedience without constraint" by drawing counselors, magnates, and Parliament into a web of quasi-erotic relationships. "Flirtation was her life blood." She handled business like a courtship dance. She scintillated, teased, flattered, prevaricated, and put men through hoops with her vacillations, contradictions, and haughty regality.

In the process she restored Britain to order and prosperity. She established a universally acceptable Protestant church, rejuvenated the economy, built up defense, and negotiated the withdrawal of the French from Scotland. During the Pax Britannia that followed, England's prestige at home and abroad soared: Industry and trade expanded, arts flourished, and the population boomed.

Elizabeth astutely safeguarded this reign of prosperity and her determination to be "governed by no one." She forestalled demands that she marry, a key bone of contention in her rule, through a lifelong anticipation waltz. Intent on preserving her divinely sanctioned hegemony, she averted male domination (legally enforced in sixteenth-century marriages) with promises and retractions for decades.

Reviving the old chivalric tradition, she positioned herself as the love queen of a romantic court idyll. Dressed in gem-encrusted, décolleté finery, she gave off *odeur de marjoram* at a time when few bathed. She put men at ease with her "mouth-filling oaths" and onslaught of comic palaver. Sometimes men laughed so much at her dinners they forgot to talk politics. She was an enchanting conversationalist, eloquent and sharp-tongued and versed in myriad subjects. As awhirl with élan as the life force herself, she enlivened every party and danced like a professional—difficult gaillards, full of cabrioles and heel-clicking leaps.

Although she took a thousand courtiers with her on her publicity tours through the kingdom, she had her favorites. First in her heart was Robert Dudley, a handsome cavalier who came within an ace of being prince-consort. Elizabeth's much-touted virginity may have been the centerpiece of her goddess campaign, but it may also have been a lie. She visited "Sweet Robin" day and night in his bedchambers and confessed to top-secret improprieties during one of her death scares. When Dudley, though, grew too importunate and trenched on her dominion, his days were over. "I will have here one mistress," she flared, "and no master."

Each of her subsequent favorites went the way of "Sweet Robin": intense courtships, heated ups and downs, and congés without marriage commitments. She played off her inamorati against one another and extracted their obedience in private and in affairs of state. Her treasure chests bulged with their jewels and love tokens. Christopher Hatton, her lord chancellor, endured a "hell's torment" of love in her service, torn between her "teasings, tiffs, [and] retributions" and sickbed visits and intimacies. He never married.

During the foreign threats to England in the second half of Elizabeth's reign, she manipulated suitors from abroad with similar political success. Through discreet alliances and covert amours, she foiled Roman Catholic plots to dethrone her and prompted her beau the earl of Essex to polish off the Spanish Army in Cádiz after the Armada victory. With divine sangfroid (goddesses include death in their totality), she coolly executed Essex when he conspired in treason, just as she'd beheaded her cousin Mary, Queen of Scots.

All the while her love affair with the British blazed higher; she became a "transcendental object of sexuality." Buccaneer-knights explored new worlds at her behest. To shine in her eyes, Sir Walter Ralegh voyaged twice to America and named the Virginia colony after his beloved Virgin Queen. By the time she died, she'd transformed herself into an idol, a totemic "Sun Queen" who personified the nation. "To have seen Elizabeth," said a visiting diplomat," is "to have seen England."

Because of her virginity spin, Elizabeth I has been treated less harshly than other absolutist *Machtweiber.* Sexually inactive, her power remains in bounds—a familiar Madonna–cum–Mary Poppins. Even so, she's taken her hits. Recent films caricature her as a boss lady on a bad hormone day or a clench-jawed modern careerist who tries, and fails, to have it all.

Elizabeth decidedly did not have it all. She lost out on the supersated sex she deserved. But she wasn't the mere "honorary man" some have claimed either. She actively traded on her gender, milking her affinities with the goddess queen of myth in order to "have her way as absolutely as her father did."

She actually improved on her father. Rather than terror and force, she got her way through the subtle beguilements of the sex divinity. With her numinous bewitchments, she made herself both the most beloved and able of English monarchs. The hardest-headed parliamentarians felt themselves under the sway of something supernatural. They said she was "absolute—that she had the power to release herself from any law, that she was a species of divinity."

Catherine the Great, 1729–1796

Russia has its own version of Elizabeth I on Tilbury Plain. In this patriotic freeze-frame Catherine the Great, uniformed as an imperial guardsman, caracoles on her stallion at the head of fourteen thousand troops. After dethroning her husband, Peter III, she addresses the multitude: We, "having God and justice on our side, have ascended the throne as Catherine II, autocrat of all the Russias."

Once again, with inspired promotional savvy, a female monarch invoked myth to solidify her authority. The difference was time and place. Eighteenth-century Russia, with its tradition of czarinas and folk veneration of the goddess, permitted Catherine her divine reward: absolute sovereignty and full expression of her superself, sex included. Making free with her mythic prerogatives, she put Russia on the map of modern history. She crowbarred the country out of the Dark Ages, reformed the government, expanded the empire, and led a renaissance in culture and the arts. Through it all, she ripped sexually. Until she died, an elite corps of honeymen loved her and filled her bed. Compared with John Kennedy or Louis XIV, Catherine was a sedate serial monogamist. No horses, revolving door hookups, and studs screened for jumbo johnsons. Only the *Machtweib*'s rightful due—reigning and having "so good a time" in the process.

Catherine knew few good times in the first half of her life. She endured ordeals, she said, that "would have driven ten other women mad." Completely non-Russian, she was born Sophia Augusta Fredericka to impoverished German nobility in 1729. Her home life

seethed with unhappiness. Her mother disliked her "unlovely" daughter, her father ignored her, and tutors had no use for her. She was an
insufferable square peg, they all complained, a smart aleck, rebel, and
tomboy. Then came four years in an iron body brace for a twisted
spine. But Sophie never grew taller than five feet or pretty. She had a
long nose, narrow bosom, and a chin so pointed her governess told
her to tuck it in to avoid hitting people.

Through a political toss-up, she found herself at fourteen affi-
anced to the heir to the Russian throne. She arrived in St. Petersburg
with three shabby dresses in a half-filled trunk, unaware of the *Walpur-
gisnacht* ahead. Her tyrannical mother-in-law, Empress Elisabeth, ha-
grode her, and her husband, the future Peter III, put her through a
Boschean hell. A freakish hyperkinetic creature, probably the product
of a chromosomal abnormality, Peter tortured rats and played soldiers
and could not consummate their marriage. He lapsed in and out of
madness, drank to excess, and beat her while the empress rained
curses on her for failing to produce an heir.

In this harsh school, however, Sophie developed a cast-iron ego.
She acquired starch, discipline, and indomitability and fashioned herself on an Olympian scale. While humoring Peter, she consumed the
great books, languages, and Russian history, Russianized her name to
Catherine, and cultivated the wise elders at court.

She also launched a multifront charm offensive. Retaining her
brio amid persecution, she laid herself out to amuse and "please." She
was the belle of the Thursday transvestite balls. In stylish male drag
Catherine worked the "sheer magic of personality" on courtiers and
assembled diplomats. Warm, gay, and funny, a jokemeister and animal mimic, she bragged that no man could be in her company "a
quarter of an hour . . . without feeling at ease."

After seven years of marital mayhem, Catherine took her charms
outside wedlock. Robustly sexed, she loved the "pleasures of the bed"
and handpicked top-shelf studs from the royal entourage. There was
the debonair Count Serge Saltykov, who fathered her first child; then
a gorgeous Polish count; and finally Gregory Orlov, the "giant with
the face of an angel."

Gregory, her lover for twelve years, engineered the coup that put

Catherine on the throne. Beginning with her coronation in 1762, Catherine played up her association with the Divine Female Authority of Russian legend. She called herself Little Mother, in reference to Baba Yaga, "Queen of the World," and she swept into Uspensky Cathedral to a fanfare of trumpets and crowned herself on the high altar.

Although an adherent of self-government in principle, she subscribed to absolute monarchy in practice. "Creation," she announced with divine grandeur, "has always appealed to me." For the next thirty-four years she devoted herself to a national makeover and accomplished it with such enticing artistry that the country accepted her totalitarian sway with scarcely a peep.

On her ministers and henchmen she practiced the same seductions she used on her beaux. An adept ego massager, she praised "in a loud voice," scolded "in a whisper," and courted consent through a barrage of erotic ploys: ornate dress, flash on the dance floor, gourmet banquets, amateur theatricals, and liberal doses of laughter and relaxed banter. Rather than direct confrontation and domination, she believed in making "men believe that they want to do what I tell them to do."

Through this eroticized MO, Catherine took Russia into a new age. A leader of vision, manifold industry, and sting-like-a-butterfly statecraft, she overhauled the administration, extended religious tolerance, expanded industry, and issued a number of humane edicts. She built hospitals and schools and ushered in a golden age of Russian architecture, art, theater, music, literature, medicine, and science.

With a nod toward feminine advancement, she founded the Smolny Institute for Young Ladies and placed Princess Dashkova at the head of the Academy of Sciences. Her court was the crown jewel of the hemisphere, filled with diamond-freighted nobles, and the masterworks of European art, furniture, and decor.

Internationally she got Russia off the mat. Both warrior and mother queen, she beefed up the navy and in seven wars prevailed over all three traditional enemies, Poland, Sweden, and Turkey. With goddess rapacity, Catherine knew the right side of a scimitar. She executed a popular czar pretender and set the stage for future foreign wars and the Bolshevik Revolution through the brutal suppression of slaves and peasants. Yet, all told, few rulers have earned "the great" more; Voltaire christened her "The Incomparable," "heir to the Caesars."

None of this power and might scared off men; it was a walloping aphrodisiac. After Catherine decommissioned Orlov (who died "broken hearted and mad"), she took nine more favorites, all prodigious cocksmen and ardent lovers. She loved them back—on her terms. Insisting on her right to "live according to [her] own pleasure, and in entire independence," she bedded and shed them to suit herself. She refused to let them shake her self-possession, with the possible exception of Gregory Potemkin, her "wolfbird" and "golden cock."

This colossus of a man and Catherine set each other on fire and may have married secretly. But they were too volcanic a couple to last and parted amicably after two years. She made him roving viceroy and overlord of the Black Sea territories, and he steered attractive lovers her way. Her last was her handsomest, a "devoted" guards officer—twenty-three to her sixty-one—who threw Potemkin to such fits of jealousy that he tried to oust him and reinstate himself.

On her deathbed Catherine demanded no mourners, "only stout souls and professional laughers." But she died the most grieved and beloved as well as the most powerful of Russian czars. Posterity, typically, has shortchanged her, Hollywood in particular. Marlene Dietrich and Elisabeth Berger reduce her to a vapid babe incapable of a coherent sentence; and Catherine Zeta-Jones, to a lonely boss lady without the love of a good man.

Catherine, however, wasn't typecastable. She was a multiple-choice character—female largeness personified, convinced that she was "exceptional" and "born to succeed." "Autocracy," she said of herself, "requires certain qualities." Half these qualities—the grit, stamina, and training—were acquired; the rest, goddess-given. As Voltaire put it, the secret of her reign was her dual ability to "charm *and* rule."

Originally Inanna, the Sumerian sex goddess, occupied the highest seat of heaven. On her seals she wears the insignia of her former glory—a tiered crown, a royal gown, and eagle wings spiked with maces—and she holds a staff of entwined serpents. She plants her foot on a lion, the emblem of kingship. But with the ascent of patriarchal domination, Inanna lost her absolute sovereignty.

Although still called the Queen of Heaven and Earth and Framer of All Decrees, she became the divine ordainer of male rule. At the sacred marriage ceremony, Inanna (played by a priestess) invested the king with the authority of office and infused him with divine eros, the cosmic life force, by copulating with him on the high altar. Without her imprimatur, he could not govern; without her wisdom and guidance, he could not keep the ship of state on course. Inanna's consort, Dumuzi, ran afoul the moment she left him alone and had to be chastened and educated to mature leadership through a descent to the underworld. Thereafter Inanna, the "Brave One" and "Honored Counselor," reigned by his side, the guarantor of the "right ordering of Sumerian society." And the source of her supernal statecraft was all in her *hi-li,* her holy sex appeal and ride-the-whirlwind sacred lust.

Theodora, A.D. 500–548

In one of the many legends told of her, Theodora once worked as a prostitute among the Amazons where she entertained a penniless stranger. He gave her all he had, a ring and a promise to marry her if he became emperor. Years later, of course, she handed the ring to Justinian and became the great sixth-century empress of Byzantium. The only true parts of the story are the emperor's lowly origins (his successful uncle summoned him to power from a "wild and desolate heath") and Theodora's early career in prostitution. She was a true child of Inanna, a *putain royale,* rambling rose, and anointer of kings.

From the time of Justinian's ascent to the throne, Theodora sanctified and guided his reign. Under her aegis the Byzantine Empire prospered for nineteen years, and it unraveled when she died in 548. She was the left ventricle of Justinian's rule, "one of the most influential women of any past era," and a ravishing seductress who beguiled Justinian into a permanent passion and his ministers and subjects into submission to their authority.

Theodora's background has all the ingredients of scandal sheet

copy. Though largely fabricated by enemies, her history still pullulates
with lurid sex and dark underworld dealings. The daughter of a poor
circus bear trainer and woman of easy virtue, she called the Hippo-
drome home—the racetrack/fairground of the city. After her father's
early death she and her sisters scraped by as gymnastic performers,
turning tricks on the side. Theodora's stunts shocked even the jaded
Byzantines. She danced nude, delivered obscene comic monologues,
and performed a specialty act in which trained geese picked barley
grains from her vulva. At postshow parties she reputedly took on
squads of men at marathon orgies and complained that her nipples
lacked orifices wide enough to permit intercourse.

But by the time she met Justinian, Theodora seems to have
mended her ways. After an amorous tour through the East, she'd returned to Constantinople a born-again Monophysite, a religion that
espoused the total divinity of Christ. According to tradition, Justinian
saw her through a window at a spinning wheel and "conceived an
overpowering passion for her." He was then forty, heir apparent to the
Eastern Roman Empire, and a devout, studious, "fascinating man." In
her early twenties Theodora was more than a picture of feminine
piety. Beautiful and fine-boned, with an "elegant figure," she had
black, flashing eyes set in a perfectly proportioned, heart-shaped face.
And she "knew how to put forth irresistible powers of fascination."
She percolated with sex appeal—wit, mischief, and off-color heat. Justinian called her his "sweetest charmer," raised her to patrician status,
and made her his wife. When he assumed the emperorship, she became Augusta and the unofficial coregent of the "most magnificent
the civilized world had yet known."

As Justinian's "Honored Counselor," Theodora parlayed her lessons in the seduction trade into political capital. Drawing on her theatrical training, she punched up the drama of office. She costumed
herself like a walking epiphany with thick cosmetics, cascading diadems, and gowns fringed with diamonds the size of walnuts. Her resplendent apartments and lay-'em-in-the-aisles banquets, aflow with the
rarest wines and delicacies, "dazzled and stupefied" visiting emissaries.

When she "wished to please," ministers and advisers were helpless
against her professional blandishments. She paired "consummate in-

telligence" with fetching affability. She praised, put men at ease, and kidded them if they grew too exigent. She improvised comic skits and once told a supplicant to rise off the floor, where he'd prostrated himself. "My dear sir," she said, "you've got a big hernia on your behind." Yet she played the grand empress to perfection. Haughty and imperious, she maintained her own court and entourage and brooked no disrespect. "Mistress Eagle," she let detractors know she meant business. She threw enemies in labyrinthine dungeons to rot and grow blind and ruthlessly pursued her own ambitions, some avaricious. She was all cosmic theater, a huge, variegated goddess-queen.

Although an able ruler in his own right, Justinian depended on Theodora's political judgment. He included her in his council, let her handle foreign dignitaries and correspondence, and consulted her on every important question. With a "feel for large affairs and the stamina to see them through," she had a sure sense of realpolitik. It was she who located the two trouble spots in the empire—rickety finances and religious division—and took measures to repair them.

At her instigation, Justinian passed the great reform of 535, which blew the whistle on embezzlers and sought religious harmony, one of the most divisive issues of the realm. Had Theodora's policy of toleration toward the Monophysites prevailed, the eastern provinces of Asia, Syria, and Egypt might have been appeased and the empire salvaged.

As Inanna's agent of sexual equality Theodora also instigated wide-sweeping reforms for women. Divorce laws were revised; pimps and rapists, punished by death; and actresses and prostitutes, granted legal protection. She founded a convent on the Bosphorus to shelter five hundred prostitutes.

Her courage saved Justinian's regime during the Nika revolt of 532. When a rebel mob torched the city and stormed the palace gates, Theodora barred the path of fleeing deserters. Like the mythic "Brave One," she called them to account. "If flight," she exhorted, "were the only means of safety, yet I should disdain to fly. Death is the condition of our birth, but they who have reigned should never survive the loss of dignity and dominion." "Flee," she taunted. "For my part, I adhere to the maxim of antiquity, that the throne is a glorious sepulcher."

Theodora died of cancer at fifty-one, devoutly religious and mourned by a desolated Justinian. Throughout their twenty-five years together he "loved her to distraction," with blind fidelity. Without her life spirit and political counsel he lost his will to rule and let the kingdom disintegrate under his listless gaze. Her death marked the decadence and the end of the Byzantine Empire.

Theodora has paid dearly for her unwonted preeminence. As heiress of the sex goddess with the snake-entwined staff of sovereignty she's been branded a "second Eve, a new Delilah" by nervous patriarchs. For centuries historians have preferred to see her going at it with gladiators rather than drafting laws and directing policy on a dais. But she, per the divine design, had both—queenship of the boudoir and "Queenship of the Throne Room." Even the piously Christian Justinian seemed to sense that. He made members of the Senate "fall down before her as if she was a goddess."

Eleanor of Aquitaine, 1122–1204

Throughout the Middle Ages troubadours celebrated the "sex symbol" of twelfth-century Europe; she "Draws the thoughts of all upon her/," they sang, "As sirens lure the witless mariners/Upon the reefs." The lady was Eleanor of Aquitaine, a formidable seductress, feudal magnate, and queen of two kings.

Instead of the reefs, however, she led both to greater kingcraft. She endowed her husbands with wealth and authority, directed their careers (not always to their liking), and governed astutely in their absence. Like her mythic counterpart Inanna, she equaled, even superseded her monarch-mates. Known as the "woman beyond compare," she shaped the manners and culture of her time and combined everything in tall tale proportions: looks, style, stature, statesmanship, and seductive power.

Eleanor came by her administrative-amorous flair through birth and upbringing. She was born in 1122 into a "noble race" of gifted rulers and swashbuckling lovers. Her grandfather introduced courtly love poetry to France and was twice excommunicated for abducting the fiery *"Dangereuse"* (Eleanor's grandmother) from her husband. Indifference to public opinion ran in her blood.

She was exceptional in other ways as well. Unlike most noblewomen—illiterate, incarcerated in castles, and treated like feudal pawns—Eleanor grew up in enlightened circumstances. She lived at the epicenter of the medieval cultural renaissance. Schooled in the New Learning and chivalry, with its *courtoisie* and woman worship (an ersatz revival of goddess cults), she developed an unusual "maturity of mind," "sprightliness," and sense of self-worth. After her mother's and brother's deaths, her father made her his boon companion and took her on progresses through his fiefdoms. On these diplomatic rounds she watched suzerainty in action and soaked up the heady atmosphere of the Provençal courts, teeming with artists, musicians, scholars, poets, and unruly vassals.

Eleanor's life took a momentous turn when she was fifteen. Her father died suddenly on a pilgrimage, and in one stroke she became heiress to the vast duchy of Aquitaine (roughly the southern third of France) and wife of the sixteen-year-old Louis VII. A culture shock awaited her. Accustomed to luxurious living and the oblations of amorous troubadours, she encountered a Paris still mired in the Dark Ages and an immature, monkish husband.

As she rolled into town with her retinue, Louis was smitten on sight. When merely the absence of deformity made a woman pretty, Eleanor was a major beauty: tall with blue eyes beneath high, arched brows, a straight Greek nose, a bowed mouth, and blond braids that fell to her waist.

She imposed her will on the king from the start. Flouting the hair shirt customs of the country, she enlivened the royal quarters with a posse of minstrels and merrymakers and filled her apartments with light, perfume, cushions, and color. Rondeaux and *pastourelles,* sung to zithers, wafted through the dark stone corridors of the palace.

Nothing like Eleanor's "devilish" dress had ever been seen on the Île de la Cité. St. Bernard himself mounted the pulpit to inveigh against her ornate jewelry and "garnished" gowns with their long trains of "rich materials." Her face paint was the mark of Satan; her daily baths were a crime against God; her undulating walk with her breasts "thrust forward" was a Jezebel's strut.

Eleanor's character, furthermore, dishonored Christian womanhood. She was capricious, insubordinate, nonmonogamous, and preemptory. She provided herself with a pet jongleur (an enamored Gascon poet), banished her disapproving mother-in-law to the provinces, and meddled in affairs of state. Most of Louis's first acts on the throne show her hand.

He invaded Toulon to please her, and when he burned a church by accident in the process, he joined the Second Crusade to expiate the crime. Unwilling to be backbenched with other wives, Eleanor left her two-year-old daughter at home and went with him. Like the divine "Whirlwind Warrior," she dubbed herself "lady of the golden boot" and galloped off to Jerusalem with a cavalcade of women dressed in armor and wielding battleaxes and spears.

En route she overstepped herself more than once. She reprimanded disobedient barons, cut sub-rosa deals with potentates, flirted with the suave Raymond of Antioch, and refused to accompany Louis when he botched the march on Jerusalem. At last, unable to bear his ineptitude any longer, she went over his head to Rome and wheedled a divorce from the pope. "Why do I renounce you?" Eleanor scolded her bereft husband, "Because of your fecklessness. You are not worth a rotten pear." With mythic panache, she dispatched the defective king off for repairs.

She also renounced Louis for another reason, a better opportunity. After their return from the Holy Land, Eleanor seduced "one of the most formidable princes of Europe" under Louis's nose. He was Henry, duke of Normandy, a stocky, high-mettled nineteen-year-old—heir to the northern chunk of France and England—and her husband's sworn enemy. Although ten years older than Henry, Eleanor had made herself the most desirable, "most talked-of woman of her day." The two had much in common: the same forceful personality, torrential ambition, political genius, and "robust sexual drive."

Her conquest was swift. During a state visit in 1153, she swooped on him in form-fitting brocade and monopolized him at dinner. Flourishing her learning, she flattered and amused him and deployed the "hungry falcon politics" she practiced on her vassals: "Dangle the prize before their eyes, but be sure to withdraw it before they taste it." She piled on the prizes—hunting parties, steamy tête-à-têtes, and frequent displays of her skills, tact, and charm—then challenged him to a game of chess. When he took her queen as planned, she riposted, "You have taken a queen at chess. Could you, I wonder, capture one in the game of life?"

He rose to the bait. Defying his father, he fought off her enemies and married her. As his "divine ordainer" Eleanor bequeathed him the Angevin Empire, an immense domain extending from Scotland to the Pyrenees. At first they were happy; their strong, high-volt natures clicked. But despite eight children and continued mutual attraction, they grew apart. Henry usurped her authority in Aquitaine and relegated her to administrative dogwork while he stirred up fresh skirmishes with warlords and womanized.

Eleanor, in keeping with her divine lineage, struck back. She acquired a lover, the famous troubadour Bernard de Ventadour, and inveigled Henry into permitting her to rule Aquitaine again. There she ran a magnificent court and inspired an efflorescence of culture and art. Poetry, music, and literature flourished, and under her direction, the art of courtly love (she'd carried Ovid's *Ars Amatoria* on the Crusades) was codified.

She also studied revenge. She aligned her sons and ex-husband in a three-pronged attack on Henry and would have won except for her children's blunders. When Henry captured her, she taunted him so insolently that he imprisoned her in Salisbury Castle for fifteen years.

He should have heeded her Inanna-style harangue. Henry never learned, and he died defeated by his sons at Villendry, a disheartened bitter "Old Eagle," whose last words were "Shame on a conquered king."

Eleanor, by contrast, left captivity a "sovereign in full sail" in 1189 and ruled England with distinction during her son Richard I's absence on the Crusades. She procured the lords' allegiance to Richard, enacted reforms, standardized weights and measures, built hospitals, and defended the coast of England against invaders.

She died at eighty-two with her flags flying. Besieged in a castle defending her lands, she told her attackers she'd be "damned in hell" before she'd surrender. She ended her days peacefully at the Abbey of Fontrevault, where she was a patron of an asylum for abused women.

If the church fathers impugned her during her lifetime, the establishment leagued her with the "very devil" afterward. She was the anti-Madonna, precisely the person women were forbidden to be—powerful in body, mind, sex, and politics. According to the smears, she murdered Henry's paramour, fomented patricidal havoc, and slept with sultans and slaves like a "common whore." Even relatively modern portrayals malign her. In *The Lion in Winter* she's a desiccated, bitter dumpee staring forlornly at her eye pouches in the mirror and upbraiding her husband's pretty mistress.

She's hard to fathom through the sexist fog machine. But seen aright, she's one of the top *Machtweiber* of the pack, a medieval power broker, a king maker and breaker, who queened it over an inhospitable age with class, valor, and supernal sex appeal.

Eva Perón, 1919–1952

Argentina in the first half of the twentieth century might as well have been the Middle Ages for women. Under South American machismo, they lived as subpersons—uneducated, disenfranchised, homebound, and divided into Madonnas and whores. The Evita anomaly still stumps scholars: how a demimonde adventuress could walk into the control room of the country, take over Juan Perón's administration, and become an "ideal of feminine power."

The answer was myth. The wily Evita scrambled the Madonna-whore signals and hit a deeper nerve, the submerged desire for the archaic, all-complete goddess. In her case she drew on an Inanna archetype, the sacred agent of male rule. Without Evita, Juan couldn't have cut it. Her political antennae and clever mythic strategy won him the presidency and secured their totalitarian control of Argentina for six years.

Like Theodora, Evita was born into the fille de joie guild. The fourth of five illegitimate children, she grew up on the squalid wastes of the Argentinian pampas, shunned and despised by local landowners. She escaped into tabloid fantasies of movie stardom and ran off to Buenos Aires at fifteen, some say with a tango singer. But she didn't find the white satin sheets and klieg lights of her dreams. Between the few walk-on parts she hustled in traveling plays, she lived on her back and knees, scrounging for pesos.

She wasn't even pretty; she had sallow skin and no *melones,* the first requisite for Latina sex appeal. But she stubbornly clawed her way through the male ranks, with a fixed eye on her goals and firm hand on the amorous reins. Men existed to serve her, period. After nine hardscrabble years, doors began to open. A movie magazine editor featured her in his pages, and finally a soap magnate gave her a role in a radio soap opera and made her a minor celebrity.

With name recognition and a sleek new pinup persona, Evita gained entrée into the power circles of the city. She became a fixture at government functions. At one of these, a benefit for earthquake victims, she met Vice-president Juan Perón, a popular hero of the masses and kingpin of the military junta that had taken over the state in 1943. In a piece of pure soap opera she snaked Juan away from Argentina's reigning sex goddess by sidling up to him and murmuring: "Thank you for existing; I will never leave your side."

Perón listened. He soon fell in love—insanely so by macho standards. Forgetting his manhood, he not only installed her in an adjoining apartment but invited her to his top-level meetings. A quick study in politics, she kept her ear to the ground and may have rescued his career during a countercoup in 1945. While Perón looked down the barrel of a gun in a jail cell, Evita rallied his populist supporters and staged the march of two hundred thousand on the capital that installed him as president.

Having consecrated his rule, Evita demanded her mythic perquisites. Juan did the unheard of: He married his mistress and gave her carte blanche as first lady. In the years that followed, she imposed her wishes on Argentina with the zeal of a chess master playing five games at once.

To smooth the way, she launched a full-dress seduction of the public. The tactic was double-barreled; the more the people loved her, the more her husband doted on her. He ended his compulsive womanizing and behaved like a "lovesick adolescent" in her presence until she died.

As soon as Evita moved into the presidential palace, the seductive machinery went into gear. The Casa Rosada was turned into a rococo movie palace of gilt, marble, and French antiques; and her ranch, filled with a menagerie of exotic animals. No courtesan queen ever made more of the erotic accessories of power—the limos, private planes, flunkies, and major jewels. And with the help of imagistas, she re-created herself as an iconic glamour goddess, haloed with a blond pouf and dressed in couturier splendor. "The poor," she said imperially, "like to see me beautiful; they don't want a badly dressed old hag."

Evita's cerebral seductions, though, were the heavy crowd pleasers. She took her script from soap opera. Touring the country in a series of *actos* (splashy public events), she addressed her "dear *descamisados*" from small-town balconies like a televangelist healer. In the purple prose of *radionovela*, she told them Juan was their "God." My heart "bleeds and cries and covers itself with roses," she harangued, "we cannot conceive of heaven without Perón." She chanted the words every man yearns to hear: "I am a fanatic for Perón! Viva Perón, viva Perón!"

By extension, she was their goddess, Venus, Cinderella, and the Virgin rolled into one. She dramatized herself so successfully as a semidivinity that she became a national *objet de culte*, Santa Evita. But true to her mythic ancestry, she was no saint. She had a sting in her tail, a "Lady Wildcat" temper and a touch of goosestep. She spiked her charm with *cojones* and sometimes swaggered around her apartment in Perón's military tunic.

Although without an official title, she took charge of the Ministry of Health and Labor and applied herself to the "right ordering of society." In a country where aristocrats owned 80 percent of the assets while 60 percent of the people lived in abject poverty, she worked to equalize the wealth. She decreed drastic reforms: a universal pension plan, general health care, and a gigantic building program of hospitals, schools, parks, and housing in Levittown-style complexes for the aged and poor.

To fund these projects, she ran the Eva Perón Foundation, a blatant extortion racket that siphoned off lottery profits and bilked the rich. In 1949 she obtained the vote for women and brought four million women to the polls for the first time. They elected six female senators and twenty-three deputies. "Women have the same duties as men," she pointed out, "and therefore should have the same rights." If Juan's army thugs hadn't threatened revolution, Evita would have been made vice-president, but she ensured that Perón's third wife would receive it automatically in 1971.

In any case, Evita was too sick to run by the election. Diagnosed with cervical cancer (likely contracted through Juan), she had less than a year to live. After her death at thirty-three, her cult swelled into a national mania, complete with miracle cures at her shrines and a macabre fixation on her mummified corpse and its supernatural properties.

Without her, Juan, like the mythic Dumuzi, guttered out. Lacking her divine imprimatur and guidance, he committed blunder after blunder until he was deposed and sent into exile in 1955. His will to live (and perhaps sanity) snapped. He picked another wife who resembled her and tried to instill Evita's soul in her through a reincarnation ceremony with a sorcerer. But the transplant failed; he remained a "vegetarian lion" without his "Chinita."

With time Evita has been downsized, like all *Machtweiber,* to manageable proportions, Disneyfied into a pop opera diva and dissed as a "Woman Behaving Badly" in an A&E special. Her image, dimmer by the day, merely suggests tales of shopaholic orgies, gold medal fellatio, and severed testicles in jars in her desk drawer.

Evita, admittedly, was an imperfect siren-politica—humorless, fascistic, undereducated, and possibly frigid. But her political accomplishments are nothing to sneeze at. She outwitted one of the sexist strongholds of the Western world, seized the position of strong-woman, told the aristocratic establishment to shove it, and gave Argentina a semblance of social justice.

She did this through self-mythologization with an old twist, transcending the binary goddesses and recalling the ancient synthetic deity of eros and earthly rule—another Inanna, "the divine ordainer," and power behind the throne. In the end it went to her head. Wasted with illness, she thought she might be a "supernatural being." That so

many believed her so long testifies to a buried psychic hunger for a
she-divinity at the helm, even in the heartland of machismo.

As male dominance gained ascendancy in the West, the goddess became less and less welcome in the throne room. No longer required to
validate the king's rule, she was booted downstairs and sent packing.
The powerful, autonomous female ideal did a 180; it now threatened
the social order and menaced the divine plan.

The jade was Lilith. Adam's first wife, who refused to lie beneath
him, she personified female sovereignty. When Adam rebuked her,
she flew off in disgust to the Red Sea and founded a kingdom more to
her taste. She ruled, fornicated day and night with a tribe of hot
demons, and devoted her life to terrorist raids on society with the object of reinstating her primacy.

For Hebrew mythmakers, Lilith epitomized the evil woman, the
unholy rebel who wanted to tear down the pillars of male privilege
and upend the sacred hierarchy of the universe. No good came of her.
Reversing the goddess's positive attributes, she brought death and
shape-shifted into hundreds of diabolic femmes fatales. Her names
are legion: the queen of Sheba, who quizzed Solomon with her rid-
dles and destroyed the Temple, and the whole society of female revolutionaries throughout Western history.

These hellcat *Machtweiber* mutinied against the establishment,
rabble-rousing and agitating like Lilith, "the original advocate of
women's rights." Though hounded by her bad press, they preserved
the sex goddess's affirmative character intact—overscale abilities,
wholeness, energy, and lovecraft. That two of the most prominent
were Americans should come as no surprise. With an entrenched double standard and boys' club tradition, many female leaders in the
United States worked outside the system as insurrectionaries and sisters of the "Sower of Discord."

Victoria Claflin Woodhull, 1838–1927

Victoria Woodhull had few friends in the ranks of nineteenth-century
feminism. The leading ladies of the movement drew back their skirts

in disgust; she was a "snake," an "impudent witch," and the "Mrs. Satan" of a popular cartoon, a bat-winged harpy peddling a broadsheet with the diabolic message "Be Saved by Free Love." As Henry James sneered, Victoria was "not respectable."

But Victoria's very lack of respectability, her wrong-side-of-the-tracks raciness and freedom from feminine socialization made her the most pioneering feminist of them all. While the blue-nosed suffragists dithered and compromised and chirruped of purity and uplift, Victoria cannonballed into the political arena with a full-scale revolutionary agenda.

More than the vote, she demanded total female emancipation: equal job opportunity, domestic freedom, federal support services, redistribution of wealth, and sexual liberation. She was ahead of both her time and ours. She argued that until we prevailed in the bedroom and recovered our pump-action orgasmic legacy, we lived in bondage to male authority—even if we could head Merrill Lynch and campaign for the Oval Office.

As the goddess's heiress Victoria had it both ways. She not only founded her own brokerage house and ran for president, two firsts for women, but was also a stellar seductress. Plying her amorous arts for pleasure and profit, she scaled other heights as well. Before her, no American woman had ever founded and run her own newspaper, addressed Congress, or practiced free love in public. All this she combined with frontline leadership in women's rights and a life of fabulous pluck and drama.

Just to have survived her youth required heroic mettle. The seventh of ten children, she was born into a brawling family of miscreants and social outcasts in a wooden shack on the fringes of Homer, Ohio. Her illiterate mother communed with spirits in the apple orchard, a talent she bequeathed to little Vicky, who began seeing angels and predicting the future in infancy. Against every law of probability, Vicky foresaw an elect destiny for herself.

Her father foresaw more concrete possibilities. Buck Claflin, a petty crook and lowlife con artist, farmed out Vicky and her sister Tennie as clairvoyants, a dollar a session. To heighten her prophecies, Buck whipped, starved, and abused Vicky (perhaps sexually) until she collapsed into a near-death coma.

The doctor who treated her, Canning Woodhull, promptly abducted and married her. She was fifteen, a scrawny, frail hayseed with a third-grade education and no resources except an "unshakable sense of her own worth" and a good preparation for seduction (with its basis in altered states of consciousness) and revolutionary politics.

All this potential, however, languished for years. Canning turned out to be a drunk, quack, philanderer, and wastrel. He subjected her to squalid boardinghouses and forced her to support him and their two children (one mentally defective) through acting and part-time prostitution. Finally the spirits directed her home, and she joined her family in a traveling medicine show as a psychic healer.

Now in her early twenties, she'd come through her assorted hells with survivor guile and armor-plated sex appeal. She practiced an early form of touch therapy that combined psychological counseling with escort service extras. Laying her hands on ailing clients, she mind-read their buried fears in a "deep, melodic voice" and made them feel they were "the center of the universe." Unfazed by the cultural flesh phobia, she believed she possessed "strong sexual powers" and should use them.

When the handsome Civil War veteran Colonel James Harvey Blood visited her for a consultation, she seduced him in five minutes. She'd filled out. She wore body-hugging black sheaths on her full curves and had the face of a Phidias Athena—chiseled features, plump mouth, and thick corona of auburn hair. As soon as he sat down, she fell into a deep trance, decreed their future union, and led him off to bed. They divorced their respective spouses, and he agreed to an open marriage in 1866.

Two years later Victoria got another command from the Beyond. Demosthenes's ghost ordered her to New York City, then the unruly capital of the postbellum greed grab. She and her sister Tennessee zeroed in on the seventy-six-year-old robber baron Cornelius Vanderbilt and captured him in a neat pincer movement; Tennessee took him on in bed, while Victoria channeled ancestors and stock tips in the séance parlor. He gave them their own brokerage firm, Woodhull Claflin & Company, which these "Queens of Finance" parlayed into a fortune. On Black Friday of the Great Gold Panic alone, they netted seven hundred thousand dollars.

Financially secure at last, Victoria turned to revolution. A reporter spotted her at the First National Suffrage Convention and pronounced her "The Coming Woman." He bet on the right horse. She started an incendiary, radical newspaper, *Woodhull & Claflin's Weekly* (the first to publish Karl Marx), and opened an avant-garde salon at her Murray Hill town house that teemed with raucous family members and such countercultural gurus as Stephen Pearl Andrews, a free lover, utopian, and spiritualist.

Andrews became her intellectual tutor and liege man; and General Benjamin Butler, a one-man steering committee. Over doughnuts and whiskey during their midnight trysts, she and Butler orchestrated her "Woodhull Memorial," which she delivered in person to the U.S. House of Representatives' Judiciary Committee.

Her ultimatum was a star legal turn. With Lilith's "smooth" eloquence, she argued that women, who were legally "persons," already had the vote by constitutional law. This was followed by a bigger bomb in 1872, when she formed the Equal Rights party and announced her candidacy for president. Before sold-out crowds across the country she demanded reforms that anticipated legislation by a generation: social security, national education, graduated income tax, antimonopoly laws, a global foreign policy, a league of nations, and, of course, universal suffrage. It was a Lilith platform—total social upheaval.

Her sex plank killed her. Feminists and small-town America gasped with horror as she perorated from the pulpit: "The very first necessity is freedom for women sexually." Defiling every sanctity of male privilege and feminine purity, she called for a single standard, orgasm parity, cultivation of erotic artistry, and women's "supreme authority in the domain of sex." If that led women outside the marital preserve, so be it. "Yes, I am a free lover!" she thundered, and lived up to her word. On a typical evening she told an escort at a rally that she "should dearly like to sleep with him" and ushered him home. Such pranks did not sit well with puritanical America. Supporters deserted and the campaign fizzled. Victoria was booed, blacklisted, and denied housing. When she retaliated by outing the hypocritical womanizer, Reverend Henry Ward Beecher (whom she bedded along with his cohort Theodore Tildon), she ended up in Ludlow Jail. There she received news of the 1872 election—the farewell to her presidential bid.

The scandal ruined her American prospects. Eventually she and her huge, dissolute family sailed for England to recoup their fortunes. Victoria divorced Blood (who roared that "the grandest woman in the world" had forsaken him) and recast herself for the British market. Wearing a sober black gown with a single red rose, she lectured on sex education.

She caught the eye of a wealthy banker, John Martin, who found her "more alive than anyone" and saw "miracles" in her presence. She cured him of an unspecified sexual problem and married him in 1883. From then until her death in 1927, she presided over their country estate like a *Masterpiece Theater* mistress of the manor.

On the surface, this seemed a retreat to Adam's Eden. But far from dominating her, Martin treated her with kid gloves and encouraged her radical activism. She published a leftist journal and advocated drastic social reforms, though in a diluted form. In 1892 she made a second bid for the U.S. presidency and shrugged off the loss with customary panache. "The truth is," she said, "I am too many years ahead of this age."

Perhaps for the first time, she understated. Victoria Woodhull adumbrated the twenty-first-century liberal agenda and envisioned the total empowerment of postmodern women. Just before she died, she stopped a gardener cleaning the walk. "Those weeds have the courage to grow in the path of man," she commanded. "Don't murder them."

She understood that to deflect the tide of injustice required more than due process and business as usual. Sometimes you had to be a rascal, a firebrand, a shapeshifter, and a *saboteuse*. "Woman," she said, is a "grand seductive force, a magazine of enticement and influence and power." She was her own proof positive: a "beautiful seductress" who rocked nineteenth-century America with a culturequake that still reverberates today.

Gloria Steinem, 1934–

Over Gloria Steinem's desk hangs a picture of Victoria Woodhull. The similarities between these two feminist icons are enough to suggest a

Woodhullian reincarnation trick. Both beautiful, smooth-tongued, and media wise, they shared the same louche backgrounds, disorderly childhoods, itinerant lifestyles, and four-star love lives.

They went head to head with the status quo, sowed discord, and led revolutions for social and domestic justice. But the amperage dropped in the channeling process. While Victoria identified with the goddess Nike, the Titan slayer, Gloria saw herself as Artemis, who "bonded with other women."

By solidifying female support, Gloria achieved greater practical gains than Victoria and transformed the social landscape of twentieth-century America. But she paid a price. To call off the dogs of feminine competition, she had to disguise the seductress, downplay her sex appeal, and discount the seductive arts in her program for women's liberation. She couldn't wave "GO FOR THE O'S" placards at Kenosha housewives; she couldn't flaunt her conquests and expect women's solidarity. As a result, she couldn't rise to Victoria's sweeping futuristic agenda. But she made a radical difference in our era and privately, at least, got it on—in Lilith style.

Just as Victoria Woodhull's upbringing fostered her development as a *Machtweib* revolutionary, so Gloria's equally unorthodox youth prepared her for the barricades and seduction. Her family was not your average Norman Rockwell household. One grandmother had been a hell-raising suffragist, and her mother worked as a journalist on the *Toledo Blade* when many women stayed at home.

After Gloria's birth in 1934 her mother quit her job and joined her father, Leo, in a peripatetic existence that involved summer months running a dance pavilion at a lake resort and the rest of the year, touring the country in an Airstream trailer. They lived on the move with creditors at their heels.

Of the two daughters, Gloria was her father's pet, fostering a lifelong devotion "to men as a sex." A jolly free spirit and hustler, Leo stamped his stationary "Originator" and bragged that he'd never worked for anyone. Thanks to this unconventional "carnival existence," Gloria spent her formative years without feminine indoctrination or formal schooling.

She was eleven when she entered school, but instead of education as usual, she led a bizarre double life. Her parents divorced in 1946, and for six years she shuttled between the classroom and a rat-infested Toledo shanty, where she nursed her mentally ill mother. Although forced to grow up too soon in grueling hardship, she escaped a worse fate: post–World War II socialization that decreed female niceness, chastity, conformity, and domestic servitude. Her mother, too deranged to mold her, simply told Gloria she'd been born under a "special star" and let her invent herself.

With a windfall profit from the sale of the back lot, Gloria was able to attend Smith College, then an incubator for smart wives of Ivy League scions. There too she broke the fifties mold. She wore jeans and net stockings instead of Peter Pan collars and pearls, and she savored premarital sex.

Hell-bent on "not [being] a victim," she positioned herself as a man chooser and *charmeuse*. In her senior year she became engaged to a "Mogul prince" of a man, a cultivated army flier who loved her brains and spikiness and supported her ambitions. But Gloria, unconditioned to the marital ideal, heard the key in the lock and broke the engagement.

Instead she spent two years in India on a grant. She organized women, helped the poor, and became a convert to Gandhian political thought. The Eisenhower America she returned to, however, did not roll out the welcome mat for reformists. So she freelanced in journalism for the next ten years, sharpening her verbal skills and waiting for the wind to change.

She also acquired a corps of power mentors, men who loved, aided, and rooted for her. Model pretty with showgirl legs and the stride of a dancer (the result of years of tap lessons in Toledo), she was, as one beau put it, a "knockout with a big brain." A-list New York City bachelors numbered among her lovers: Robert Benton, creator of *Bonnie and Clyde;* Tom Guinzberg, Viking Press heir; Herb Sargent, producer of *That Was the Week That Was;* Peter Falk; Mike Nichols; and others.

All had their choice of the most beautiful, accomplished women. But Gloria's charm cocktail was a potent brew. Benton said she gave him "a sense of himself" and inspired him to write through her ego nurture; Sargent praised her IQ and "natural" teaching abilities; the rest spoke of her relaxed indifference to "ordinary anxieties," her "funny," "bright" conversation.

By her own admission, she was strongly sexed, an "aerobics" expert in bed. Many tried to marry her, but with the goddess's polyamorism, she preferred serial minimarriages. One New Yorker says he could write a book about the number of "famous men who have wept on [his] shoulder" over her. She made men walk the tortuous path. Along with Ms. Goodfeel, she was the divine Lady Difficult—self-willed, opinionated, insubordinate, Mona Lisa mysterious, autonomous, and averse to commitment.

In 1968 her moment arrived. She entered activist politics and soon took the lead in the left-wing groundswell sweeping the country. She wrote exposés, stumped for McGovern, supported the grape pickers, and in a "blinding lightbulb" moment, discovered feminism and ran away with it.

Training her siren power on the body politic, she seduced to convert. Her calculated glamour and sex appeal demolished every man-hater-in-Birkenstocks stereotype and consolidated support from moderates and men. Decked out in black miniskirts and tinted aviator glasses hooked under long, streaked hair, she preached revolution in a phone sex contralto. The barbed sound bites were tossed off like flirtatious quips: "A woman needs a man like a fish needs a bicycle"; "If men could get pregnant abortion would be a sacrament."

As the ranks filled, she founded the Women's Action Alliance, the National Women's Political Caucus, and *MS.* (the first national magazine run by women), applying the seductive emollients of TLC and flattery to oil wheels and unify feminism.

Her love life meanwhile never missed a beat. Throughout the round-the-clock barnstorming, she surrounded herself with "lovable men who adored and were kind to her," especially African Americans such as Frank Thomas, former head of the Ford Foundation. No amount of self-denigration could conceal the evidence: She was too sexy, too successful with men. At last the sisterhood cried foul and assailed her with a barrage of sellout accusations.

Gloria's response was not Victoria Woodhull's. Instead of blowing them off, Gloria adopted a policy of appeasement. She pooh-poohed her charms and discredited seduction as a politically incorrect "primordial skill," an "alarmingly easy business." Anxious to placate angry rivals, she cut erotic empowerment (and a proactive plan to achieve it) out of the feminist agenda.

As one critic observed, she didn't "tell the truth." While continuing to burn up the track as a seductress, she sold American women on victim sexual politics and flower child openness and honesty. Unwittingly she eviscerated the movement. Bereft of its swerve and sex appeal, feminism withered on the vine. *MS.* became dull copy.

In 1989 the magazine foundered and became an adless, special-interest publication supported first by readers and later by a foundation. During these backlash years Gloria might have honorably retired to academe as a titled feminist figurehead. But she refused to pipe down on social issues and, with the goddess's protean plasticity, adopted a new persona.

After a bout with breast cancer in her fifties, she entered a period of intense self-analysis that radically altered and enlarged her perspective and resulted in three best-selling psychological how-tos. With deepened insight, she now argued that true liberation begins from a baseline of self-esteem and requires the active pursuit of psychic totality and growth.

By that criterion, she's a paragon of free womanhood. Since the early nineties she's been the principle of dynamic evolution in action. She moved from predictable lovers like Stan Pottinger, U.S. assistant attorney general for civil rights, to the wildly inappropriate business mogul Morton Zuckerman. Then, at sixty-six, she flip-flopped, reversed her ancient prejudice against matrimony, and married David Bale.

According to Hebraic legend, Lilith's rebellious raids will cease with the coming of the Messiah. And Bale is a New Age Messiah if there ever was one. Handsome and consciousness-raised, he's a successful entrepreneur who holds gender roles in contempt, espouses human and animal rights, and fell in love with Gloria's ideas before he met her.

Yet he hasn't stopped his wife's jihad on the established order. She's still in battle mode, mouthing off about equality and female entitlement and teaching "Revolution 101" to anyone who'll listen. Without the false front to maintain—the "what-me-sexy?" camouflage—Gloria has grown more radical and daring with time.

She may wind up the "pioneer dirty old lady" she once imagined, leading the lost postfeminist grandchildren to the frontier, the promised land of full empowerment in love, work, and political office. Anyway, she's praying. "Dear Goddess," she writes at the end of "Doing Sixty":

> I pray for the courage
> To walk naked
> At any age,
> To wear red and purple,
> To be unladylike,
> Inappropriate,
> Scandalous and incorrect
> To the very end.

Somewhere, in the brainwashed depths of the female psyche, we think we should be the precinct workers and backstage girls of male politicians. If we step out on our own and take the gavel, men won't love us anymore. As Jacqueline Kennedy put it, "There are two kinds of women; those who want power in the world and those who want power in bed."

This is the sort of bipolar fallacy that makes female leaders check their sex appeal at the statehouse door and yield the field to senate groupies and concupiscent chick interns. But that isn't the divine plan. *Machtweiber* are. They expose the false dichotomies—scare tactics to keep women from politics—and resurrect an archetype that predates the god-king, the prehistoric Mistress of the Universe, the first sex goddess.

These siren-politicas of course aren't typical. Most women who ruled in Western history were snookered by the phony dualities and lost out sexually or politically. But winners inspire and predict the future. They also instruct—often in unexpected ways.

Machtweiber throw out the child development bibles. Instead of the secure, supportive environments deemed essential for leaders, each, except Eleanor of Aquitaine, had a horrendous childhood, filled with neglect, cruelty, and violence.

Like other seductresses, they prevailed in spite of the "wrong" upbringing. Because of their combined grit and self-grandeur, they grew strong in adversity, acquiring autonomy and bulldog tenacity. They missed out on feminine education, avoiding the good-girl drill with its learned incapacity and inferiority.

No one told them they couldn't be big or have it all. They shot up nine feet tall, queen of creation size. They didn't know they were the return of the repressed. But their power and uncanny effect on the public stemmed from the archaic archetype.

Some, like Evita and the autocrats, instinctively played up the association and aureoled themselves with the symbols and images of divinity. The rest benefited on a more subliminal level. All styled their characters on the mythic paradigm: omnicompetence, male/female totality, gusto, and bigger-than-life swish and majesty.

They also evoked the she-deity in management style. Although *femmes fortes* of iron will and decided minds, they ruled via the Seductive Way, not brute force. They used the erotics of réclame like Aphrodite with her drumroll visitations to mortals.

Their public appearances were staged to harpoon hearts and strike fire in the loins. They wore glorious showstopper costumes accompanied by cosmetics, scents, and all the trappings of goddess worship— arts, cuisine, dance, music, pageantry, and break-it-down carnivalesque festivity. With their brains and eloquence, they charmed everyone in their service. Extracting consent without coercion, they sweet-talked people into their way of thinking. Lover-like, they teased, amused, vacillated, confounded, tormented, and ladled out praise and mother love. Old-time feminists used to commend straight-shooter authority on the job, but the greatest leaders (males included) are Teflon managers. They combine the fox and the lion, governing with a mix of guile, direct command, covert deal making, and the sly intoxicants of seduction—the shortest, though most circuitous, route to yes.

According to one school of thought, women make more pacific, competent leaders. In her comprehensive study of the subject, historian Betty Millan says that as a group they "excelled men." The *Machtweiber* in some ways bear her out. They're notable for their pragmatism, improvisational flexibility, long-range vision, self-promotional genius, administrative ability, and frequent humanitarian causes.

But they were no kinder, gentler matresfamilias. They did not govern like play school caregivers; they could be preemptory, high-handed, two-faced, self-serving, cruel, and bellicose. They had alpha woman egos, ferocious ambition, and ballsiness. They needed all the flint and devil they could muster in the societies they inhabited—none *Machtweib*-friendly. Some cultures, such as Elizabeth I's England, were less receptive than others and made a total goddess synthesis tough, if not impossible. The seductress isn't transhistorical, even if her archetype and art are.

Fortunately the climate is warming toward *Machtweiber*, in the United States and abroad. Yet politicas who want to take back their sexuality have their work cut out for them. As Gloria Steinem's recent feminist affray demonstrates, many women, through either secret envy or identification with the oppressor, have trouble embracing female leaders with flagrant sexual power. And male recidivists are still afoot. A sizable rear guard continues to crank out either/or agitprop and *Machtweiber* slurs, frightened that she-rulers with working libidos will castrate and subject them.

Both groups need to rest assured. All women rise on the skirts of the privileged, and men stand to profit, not lose, from female authority. Like Inanna, these eight leaders were the goddess's gift to their male consorts, fostering their talents and raising them to higher levels of maturity. Stateswomen, said the sixteenth-century Brantôme, are the best thing that can happen to a man. They're the answer, argues Robert Bly in his analysis of "The Maiden King," to the masculinity crisis today. Under the czarina's direction, the hero of the Russian fairy tale endures the training—in life and eros—necessary for true male adulthood and self-actualization.

Freud thought great leaders owed their force field to their subconscious appeal; they permitted people to express "forbidden impulses and secret wishes." If he'd included *Machtweiber* in his theory, he'd have found an explanation for those insoluble historical enigmas— Cleopatra and her walkover conquest of the ancient world; Evita and her subjugation of sexist Argentina; Gloria Steinem and her social revolution in America.

In every case their victories stem from a collective "secret wish" for the mythic Queen of Heaven who ran the ship of state on sexual horsepower and contained everything in the round of her Being: wholeness, rebirth, and intellectual, erotic, creative, spiritual, and political preeminence. It's our place in the divine plan, the command position. We were born to be "quings" (as one fourth grader called them), to set the world and men on fire.

CHAPTER EIGHT

Siren-Adventurers

A Woman should be good for everything at home, but abroad good for nothing.
—EURIPIDES

I hate a woman who gads about and neglects her home. —THEOGNIS

In order to explain what charm (vaghezza) is, you must know what it really is, for the word charm really means three things: first, movement from place to place.
—AGNOLO FIRENZUOLA

Life is a verb. —CHARLOTTE PERKINS GILMORE

*T*here are the good girls—baby-sitters named Cricket, wives with "Bloom Where You're Planted" on their mugs, and the moms of *Mister Rogers' Neighborhood.* Then there are the bad ones. They act up, leave home, mess around, and walk on the wild side. No mystery how men regard these two. The first they love and marry; the second, fuck, dump, and shuck. Small wonder tramps end up as they do, abandoned on the social ash heap, broken and alone.

The lives of the domestic renegades say it all. Isabella Eberhardt, the early-twentieth-century North African adventuress, came to the predictable end: orgiastic sex with Bedouins, hashish under the desert stars, desertion by her husband, and a sordid death (accidentally on purpose) in a flash flood. World War II spy and tennis celebrity Alice

Marble broke her heart over a Nazi sympathizer and never married. And the cat-prowling sex professionals, we know how they fared. Heartlessly screwed over and left for virtuous maids, they died of heartbreak, suicide, or consumption in fetid attics while their lovers waltzed off to wedded bliss.

Unfortunately for cultural moralists, it doesn't work this way. Never has. Not only do scores of adventurous home deserters prosper and end happily, but men have a weak spot for them. In contrast to the stereotype, they fall, fall hard, for ladies-on-the-loose, to the point of lifelong commitment and abject adoration. The whole good-bad girl propaganda is merely a male defense strike against these ultra-attractive rovers, an overt ploy to curtail runaway female sexual power. Gadders, no better or worse than other women, hold a treacherous allure, enough to topple the patriarchal order.

Their allure goes deep, a megaton aphrodisiac planted in the primitive recesses of the collective unconscious. Stationary angels-of-the-house held no charms for prehistoric man. The mythic first sex goddess was a divine dynamis, the "principle of life-energy," spinning with perpetual movement and activity. Her successors, from Neolithic Venuses to Aphrodite (*hodites* means "wanderer"), were all action goddesses, home deserters who rambled, explored, and philandered.

Inanna, the first recorded love deity, was a roving adventure queen who toured the firmament in quest of men and excitement and took money for her favors. She love-addled the cosmos. Undomesticated, polygamous, restless, and aggressive, she personified eros itself, the life force and flywheel of existence, and ruled the Sumerian pantheon. The gods "ben[t] and quiver[ed]" in her presence. From her sacred mountain, she commanded the universe, adorned in lapis lazuli, a lion beneath her foot, her wings spread for flight and adventure.

Early womankind, it seems, took its cue from Inanna. As recent studies demonstrate, our female ancestors showed no innate preference for home, stasis, and monogamy but were "promiscuous appetitive roving diplomats," avidly carousing and glutting their inordinate orgasmic demands. This worked to women's evolutionary advantage. Through comparison shopping and plural partners, they gained tangible benefits: more and better sperm, social leverage, and increased resources.

With time, dominant males usurped this female advantage. Anxious to ensure paternity and feminine submission, they tethered women at home and denied them freedom of motion. For safekeeping, they imposed infibulation, sequestration, and purdah and enforced Madonna-whore thought control—virtuous inmates versus vicious escapees. Zero tolerance for the disobedient.

Some women nevertheless escaped. They shot the bolt, soared into the wild blue, and recouped their ancient erotic birthright and sovereignty. Inanna's avatars, they each, while sharing a constellation of qualities, typified one of the goddess's three adventuress personas: *wasi'at,* the one who roams about; *labbatu,* the fierce lioness; and *karkid,* the prostitute. They torpedoed the clichés; life treated them well. It was wide screen, packed with color, drama, steadfast love, and best of fates in the final reel.

When she cruised the highways and byways, the unhousebroken Inanna sang a theme song: "As I go out, as I go out/I go around heaven and earth." Freed of domestic freight, this divine runaround scouted the territory in quest of novelty, action, and romantic escapades. While Sumerian wives veiled themselves in subservience to husbands and were hurled into the river if they strayed from home, Inanna was a law unto herself, exempt from patriarchal rule.

Eventually of course it caught up with her; by 1500 B.C., she had lost her mythic supremacy and suffered the same fate as earthly *wasi'ats.* Hebrew theologians regarded her as the archenemy of male hegemony and demonized her as the Whore of Babylon. Wandering the land on a ten-horned beast and fornicating pell-mell, she epitomized the antitype of the good Jewish housewife, a wicked Dinah who stepped abroad and brought damnation upon herself and Israel.

Agnès Sorel, 1422–1450

To medieval lawgivers, *vagatio* (movement beyond home) was the mother of all female sin, and Dinah, the cautionary exemplum. Virtuous women stayed inside, under the custody of men, rooted to the spinning wheel, dressed in hopsack, and haloed in humility, chastity, and silence. The scarlet wretches who left their posts and rambled were "arsonists of sacred places" on a free fall to hell.

One of these evil sisters journeyed in 1438 across the war-torn Loire Valley, beleaguered by real arsonists and *écorcheurs* (flayers), the most brutal cutthroats in Europe. The sixteen-year-old Agnès Sorel miraculously survived the trip and lived to achieve a greater miracle: the position of official mistress to a king (the first in French history) and unprecedented riches, power, and influence.

As Charles VII's *maîtresse en titre* she prompted the military defeat of Britain and inspired a national cultural and economic renaissance. The virginal Joan of Arc received the credit and laurels, but the nefarious adventuress Agnès Sorel actually saved France.

At the height of her prosperity, Agnès built an altar to Mary Magdalene, the medieval model of female freedom and self-ownership and bête noire of the church fathers. Agnès's patron saint served her well. Orphaned in early childhood, she was adopted by a beneficent aunt in Touraine who preferred her to her own daughter. Rather than remain there, immured in maidenly virtue, Agnès set out to seek her fortune as a companion to Isabelle of Lorraine, two hundred miles away.

At this lively, sophisticated court with its continual round of fetes, she found an avant-garde culture in which women were revered and expected to shine and master the "grand gesture." Dress and deportment were competitive. Ladies wore fur-trimmed, decorated gowns, cinched at the waist by pearl- and gem-studded clasps, and vied for the spotlight in conversation, grace, and style.

Agnès soon eclipsed them all. "Her speech," said a courtier, "was so far beyond other women that she was regarded as a prodigy." With her "laughing moods" and "gentlest spirit in the world," she was also regarded as a *ravisseuse*. And she looked like a stained glass Madonna.

When most women were swag-bellied, pockmarked, and seamed with premature aging, Agnès possessed the kind of beauty seen once in a century. Full breasted and svelte, she had a carved-in-ivory face, with heavy-lidded bedroom eyes, a Cupid's bow mouth, and a pointed chin that protruded gently at the tip. Masses of thick chestnut hair, shot through with golden highlights, spilled over her temples and cascaded down her back.

When Charles VII first saw her on a state visit, he stood "abashed and amazed." At the time he was no great shakes either physically or governmentally. After letting Joan of Arc's offensive fizzle out, he trifled with paramours and base companions while the British lorded it over Normandy and Aquitaine. He suffered fits of "weak nerves" and showed it. Bald, with hooded eyes and fat lips bracketed by deep creases, he hid his scarecrow physique in voluminous robes when courtiers wore codpieces and tunics.

Agnès, though, saw possibilities in this unprepossessing "pauper king." In the best courtly love tradition, she snapped him out of his swoon and ignited his latent intellectual, military, and managerial gifts. According to legend, she made the salvation of France the price of her favors. She forbade him to touch her "beneath the chin" unless he shaped up. She told him an astrologer had promised her a "valiant and courageous" king; obviously that man wore the crown of England. At that Charles burst into tears and promised to reform.

He did. As soon as she became his mistress in 1444, he publicly acknowledged her at court and, defying the ordinances against "women's words" and "advice," made her his chief counselor. At her insistence, he sacked his dissolute sidekicks, resumed the war against the English, and assembled a loyal team of competent "men of arms and kind companions."

These Agnès handpicked for him. Her friend, capitalist entrepreneur Jacques Coeur, salvaged the economy. As treasurer steward he stabilized the currency, reformed taxation, and revived commerce and industry, ushering in a period of unprecedented prosperity.

Two other brilliant recruits—Pierre de Breze, "the eagle of all the world," and the scholarly Adonis Étienne Chevalier—both fell in love with her. With Étienne, Agnès may have had (true to her free-range character) a secret affair; he carved an amorous quotation with her initials on his wall, commissioned her portrait, carried her insignia on his shield, and spent his life "obsessed by the Lady of Beauty."

Agnès created the same obsession in Charles; "he could not bear to have her away from him for an instant." But she was often away. During their seventeen years together, Agnès traveled incessantly among the many châteaus he gave her, from Beauté sur Marne to Chinon to Vernon in Normandy. The *vagatio* stereotype crumbled in her wake. She dispensed charity on her estates and loved her four children and many pets tenderly. Jean Fouquet painted her as the Madonna.

The church was not persuaded. When Charles first brought her to Paris, she headed the procession on horseback like a graven idol. Bedizened in the gaudiest wares from Jacques Coeur's Eastern trade, she floated through the streets in a red velvet gown, jeweled poulaines (pointed shoes over a foot long), and a high-peaked miter trailing an azure veil to the ground.

Her face bore the mark of "Lucifer"–thick white paint, rouge, shaved eyebrows, and a hairline plucked back to the crown of her head. The clergy published broadsides calling her the "Beast of the Apocalypse," and the Bishop des Ursins threatened the king in person.

None of which deterred Agnès. Emboldened by the attacks, she laid it on. Wafting rare oriental perfumes, she appeared at court feasts in riotous luxury: long trains, ropes of emerald and gold necklaces, and tight silk dresses with peekaboo lacing that exposed her whole left breast. Secure in her power, influence, and position, she "felt invulnerable."

Foolishly so. She didn't reckon on the resistance to such undue female power and freedom. Charles's eldest son, Louis, the "universal spider," hired a Lothario to seduce her and, failing in that, slapped her in the face and rounded up a group of nobles who banished her to Loches, her castle on the Loire.

Vengeful women also hovered on the sidelines, poised to strike. Her first cousin and "sister" tried to seduce Charles the moment Agnès invited her to Loches and turned her back. With competitive rapacity, Antoinette ambushed him in hallways and cried on his shoulder but got nowhere until after Agnès's death.

Antoinette didn't have to wait long. With her customary wanderlust and thirst for action, Agnès set off in 1450 to join Charles, as usual, on the battlefield. Conditions couldn't have been worse. The hundred-mile route was war-ravaged and dangerous, and Agnès was in the last stages of pregnancy. She gave birth on arrival and died a few days later of dysentery and other complications from the trip. Baffling the

Madonna-whore typecast to the end, she read aloud from her breviary and behaved with celestial piety in her final hours. Charles buried her like a saint at Loches in a stately sarcophagus with two angels at her head and two lambs at her feet.

Afterward he knew no peace. Inconsolable and unmoored, he relapsed into his old debauchery and toyed first with Antoinette, then with a revolving seraglio of young playthings. In a pathologic inversion of his mistress's roving spirit, he spent the remaining ten years of his life moving restlessly from château to château "consumed with sorrow and anger."

Predictably, historians have found her less memorable, writing her off as a no-count royal courtesan. Self-willed enchantresses who violate propriety and women's place still ruffle feathers. It's easier for posterity to eulogize the unproblematic, asexual St. Joan than deal with the complex, dissident Agnès, who directed a king and held "heroes and sages" "in her chains." Worse, one who struck off her *own* chains. Agnès's favorite pet was a greyhound that refused to follow the pack and obeyed "neither whistle nor call." And for decades French soldiers marched into battle chanting, "We've got to move! Agnès ordered it!"

Jane Digby, 1807–1881

When seventeen-year-old Jane Digby wafted into St. James's Palace for her debut in a demure white gown, Regency England took her to their heart. With her pastel beauty—blond ringlets, cameo features, violet eyes—and her "pleasing modesty," she incarnated the Romantic ideal of 1824. She became the iconic heroine of the age, Wordsworth's "Phantom of delight" given form and substance, a maiden bathed in "angelic light," born for the "household."

Except she wasn't. Appearances to the contrary, Jane Digby was born for adventure and the repudiation of every genteel female virtue. A Romantic of the perfervid Byronic school, she led a life of pure costume melodrama. As polite society watched aghast, she divorced three husbands, migrated from bed to titled bed, lived with an outlaw "Mountain King," and married a Bedouin sheikh in her late forties.

She ended her days as "Queen of the Banditti" on the Syrian desert, leading raids on charging stallions and spellbinding men until her seventies.

How she went wrong confounded the best minds. Born to noble parents—the illustrious Digbys—she was raised according to the most orthodox pattern for young ladies. She was taught the sanctity of "confinement to the bounds of home" and the proper graces and arts that accompanied it: needlework, flower arranging, pious offices, and sedate gentility. But the demonic child behaved like a changeling. She refused to sit at her tatting, escaped outdoors for rough-and-tumble games with her male cousins, and eavesdropped on their lessons.

She went bad early and ran off with a band of itinerant Gypsies. Her charm, though, always saved her from punishment. Her parents could not bear to reprimand their "golden-haired mischief maker," with the result that the mischief increased and multiplied.

By her teens she was a confirmed high-estrogen scamp. Although she took well to the debutante drill of dance, piano, and voice lessons, she couldn't be broken to harness sexually. She wrote florid love po-ems to a lady-killer cousin, attracted beaux from Bath to Dorset, and once eloped with her groom, leading her frenzied father on a horse chase over three counties.

Her modest maid performance at her debut presentation back-fired. Overidentifying with the part, Jane followed the aristocratic script and married the highest bidder, a starchy lord who might have come from central casting. In less than a year she learned why Edward Law, Lord Ellenborough, had been called Horrid Law at Eton. Rarely at home, he clubbed with his buddies by night and frolicked with his mistress by day, leaving her picture on the bureau for Jane to discover.

Vengeance followed fast. Dressed in décolleté gowns that exposed her nipples, Jane trolled the party circuit and worked swiftly—first an affair with her cousin (with a child whom she palmed off as Edward's); next her father's librarian; then, penultimately, Prince Felix Schwarzen-berg. She and this mesmeric Bohemian prince locked eyes across the ballroom, waltzed to "*Ah quel plaisir d'être en voyage*" (Ah, what a pleas-ure to be traveling), and plunged headlong into one of the most talked-about amours in London. Pedestrians on Harley Street watched Felix lace up her stays through open blinds, and the entire reading public devoured the *Times* after Edward found out and staged a divorce trial, replete with salacious evidence and lurid testimonials.

Mid-trial Jane slipped off to France by packet boat—pregnant, disgraced, and barred forever from polite society. For several stormy years she and her lover circulated among the Parisian demimonde. She had two children (one of whom died following the death of her English son), and Felix played the man-about-town, often in the company of diplomatic widows. Eventually she had enough and dumped the prince, deaf to his pleas that he loved her "better and longer" than any other woman. "Waiting," she retorted, "was never my forte."

She packed up and wended her way to Munich, the pleasure capital of Europe and mecca for adventuresses. King Ludwig I, a handsome womanizer, was ever on the watch for fascinators. When he saw Jane at an open-air café, he pounced; he declared her his soul mate, placed her portrait in the "Gallery of Beauties," and snared her into a six-year "deep intimacy." Throughout the affair Jane fielded dozens of marriage proposals from German nobles and officers and slept where she pleased. One of these transient bedmates, Baron Karl Theodore von Venningen Üllner, made such a row that she broke down and married him when she became pregnant. He installed her in his glamorous schloss and poured a fortune into her happiness. But Jane had a housing problem. Despite a deluxe house and garden renovation and new baby, she started going AWOL to parties in Munich.

At a ball there, she met Spiridion Theotoky, a Greek count built like Mr. Universe togged out in a white tutu and gold-encrusted red velvet vest. She pleaded "nerves" to Karl and, from a nearby spa, sped out each night on her stallion for trysts with Spiro. When the lovers tried to elope, her husband apprehended them, shot his rival, and took him back to the schloss to die. Under Jane's ministrations, Spiro made a full recovery, and they fled again, ignoring Karl's pleas for a ménage à trois.

Jane then divorced Karl, for whom there was never "another woman," and married a third time. She moved to Spiro's baronial seat on Corfu and Hellenized herself. She converted to Greek Orthodoxy, swam in the Aegean, and threw syrtaki-dancing parties where guests smashed gold-monogrammed china on the tiles. She had a son, the only child she ever cared about, and seemed to have geared down. But all that changed when her husband was posted to Athens. King Otto fell in love with her, Spiro retaliated with casual affairs, her son died, and once more she lit out.

After leaving the count, Jane toured the Mediterranean and drowned her sorrows in the beaux who came her way—two so serious one died in a duel and the other committed suicide. On her return to Athens in 1852 she found a frisson worthy of her attention. General Xristodolous Hadji-Petros, leader of a tribe of mercenary bandits, looked as though he had walked off the set of *Abduction from the Seraglio*. A huge mustachioed ruffian in a tasseled beret, pleated skirt, and cinch belt loaded with weapons, he bore Jane off to the Lamian mountains.

With the self-fluidity of the "one who roams," Jane changed her persona to suit the occasion. She exchanged her Parisian wardrobe for Albanian shifts, slept in caves, and galloped over ravines with his hard-drinking banditti. She gave Xristo a mansion with a bedroom built like a "throne-room," but the setting went to his head, and she discovered him flagrante with her maid.

At this juncture Jane's real adventures began. Still beautiful at forty-five and the "incarnation of vitality and health," she ditched Xristo and set sail for Damascus. Speaking perfect Turkish and costumed in green satin riding habits, she hired Bedouins for long treks through the desert and took them to her tent by night.

One became the great love of her life. Medjuel el Mezrab, a tribal prince twenty years her junior, combined the looks of Rudolph Valentino with the manners and cultivation of a "polished Englishman." During a brutal twenty-four-hour camel ride across the Syrian desert, he grew so taken with Jane's charm, courage, and explorer zest that he asked her to marry him.

With characteristic impetuosity, Jane agreed—on condition that he divorce his wife and live monogamously. When she married Medjuel in a Muslim ceremony in 1855, she was written out of the rolls of humanity. Her family disowned her and turned her picture to the wall; she had wed a black man. But for once Jane had landed on her feet. Medjuel answered her most romantic heartsongs and resolved her claustrophobia and nineteenth-century gender bind. As his wife Jane had the best of all worlds—male warrior status, nomadic domesticity, and femaleness cranked up to high.

Dressing in the height of Arabian seductiveness, she wore transparent gauze on her face, a blue caftan festooned with jewelry, and a veil that fell from a coronet of gold coins to her feet. With her eyes lined with kohl and her hair dyed black and arranged in two ankle-length braids, she passed for "a woman of thirty" instead of fifty-one.

On her wedding night she amazed her husband with her prowess. In his culture that meant something. Much was required of both sexes. Medjuel, a renowned cocksman, a *Nak. kaz al-ga'ad,* had to master the nuances of thirty-eight kinds of vagina, imaginative foreplay, and the thrust work to induce multiple female orgasms. Jane, by the same token, was expected to do her part. She must kiss in a hundred ways, clasp the penis with her vulva, and execute the up-and-down swinging motions of the hips called *hez,* "moving [her] bottom like a riddle."

Their shared sexpertise, strong chemistry, and passion for action and adventure made for a happy union, which lasted twenty-five years. Medjuel showered her with gifts and devotion, and she built him a Baghdad mansion worthy of a caliph: voluptuous gardens and fountains, exotic menageries, and a sumptuous roof for postprandial lounging. Diplomats and scholars throughout Europe made it their headquarters and regarded Jane as an authority in the area. She was "out and out," said Middle Eastern expert Sir Richard Burton, "the cleverest woman" he had ever met.

But Jane and Medjuel rarely remained long in Baghdad. Impatient with "cooped up town life," they spent at least half a year on the "wide and boundless desert." Heeding the call of her "roving blood," she hunted antelopes and wolves, charged into tribal battles, and mock-raced Medjuel on their thoroughbred horses and camels. "Oh," Jane exclaimed amid these escapades, "how I *love* such excitement." A sheikh awarded her the sword of a famous Saracen warrior for her bravery.

Throughout old age Jane lost none of her thrill fever and magisterial swerve. After watching a Bedouin sword dance, she said, "If I chose, I could surpass them all in fire and agility." Men (including the Brazilian emperor) still adored her, and Medjuel, except for one indiscretion in the desert, remained faithful to the end. She loved him like "an impetuous girl of seventeen," and he returned her devotion threefold, making ardent love to her and pampering her until she died, at seventy-four. At her funeral he bolted from the cortege and galloped back to the grave site on her favorite mare just as the coffin was lowered into the earth. He never remarried.

Jane inspired a total of eight novels. The most famous, Balzac's *Lily of the Valley*, portrays her as Lady Arabella, a fiery siren-adventurer who lures the hero from his frail, servile "lily." At the end he repents of his folly and returns to the love of the asexual house slave. Arabella, he fumes, was far too much a "mistress of [herself]"; she recognized "no laws" and had to be "always moving."

Jane's contemporaries couldn't have put it better. She was a "notorious and profligate" rogue whose name became "a byword for scandalous behavior for generations." But like Balzac's minx Arabella, Jane scorned "bourgeois notions" and public censure. All that mattered was life on the edge, Medjuel beside her, "one foot in the stirrup," and the limitless horizon before her. "This was freedom! This was life!"

Lola Montez, 1821–1861

If Jane Digby had remained Lady Ellenborough, she would have been in the audience at Her Majesty's Theatre. It was the gala event of 1843, a command performance of *The Barber of Seville* with a much-heralded entr'acte by a Spanish noblewoman. When the first act ended, ladies eagerly raised their lorgnettes, then dropped them in stunned disbelief. They saw no genteel señora in a black mantilla, but a dark spitfire in a short multicolored skirt that showed off her shapely calves—a forbidden sight in Victorian England.

Still more shocking was her dance. To the violent chattering of castanets, she undulated across the stage, thrashed her skirts, stamped her feet, and, at the crescendo, chased an imaginary spider up her thigh. When she came out for her bows, catcalls erupted over the din:

"Betty James! Fraud! Fraud!" Then she was gone. Maria Dolores de Porris y Montez flashed off the stage into the wings, her first and last appearance at Her Majesty's Theatre.

The impostor was Lola Montez, aka Eliza James, the "man-killing spectacle" of Europe and, bar none, the greatest seductress of the nineteenth century. Unburdened by Jane Digby's all-for-love Romanticism and forced to earn her way, she had the bedrock self-sovereignty and embattled drive necessary for the big leagues.

An "insatiable *amoureuse*," wanderer, and hellion, she went through men like cordwood, afraid of only one thing, domestic captivity. "I am a free independent being," she declared, "subject to my whims and sensations alone." Yet few women of any age have ever been loved so deliriously. A king abdicated for her, and the cream of Europe discarded wives, careers, and earthly prospects for a place in "Lola's harem."

Fluidity, Lola's ruling principle, governed her sense of identity like everything else. Along the way she acquired as many personas as the goddess Inanna. Her childhood altered with each telling. In one story, she was born in Spain to a grandee or famous matador; in another, to British aristocrats who lost her to a caravan of Gypsies.

The real story was less colorful. She was born out of wedlock in a dreary Limerick flat to a fourteen-year-old girl, herself illegitimate. Months later her parents married and took little Eliza with them to India with her father's regiment. He died on the journey, and in less than a year her mother remarried Lieutenant Patrick Craigie and settled in Bengal.

There Eliza was abandoned to the care of indulgent ayahs who yielded to her every whim and gave her free run of the post. Wild, willful, and fearless, she roamed the jungle barefooted, swam nude in snake-infested pools, and chewed betel until her mouth turned red. By six she'd become the child from hell, petted by the regiment and so dreaded by her mother that she was sent to her stepgrandparents in Scotland to be domesticated.

The project failed. Impervious to the most brutal Calvinist coercions, she persisted in perversity and bolted naked through the streets of town when they locked her in the house. Teachers decried her "indomitable self-will," and the Aldridge Academy for Ladies proclaimed her the "chief agitator against adult authority." Her mother arrived unprepared. After a ten-year absence she paid a surprise visit in 1837 to announce Eliza's engagement to a sixty-year-old judge in India. Her daughter didn't think so. As soon as she heard the news, she smashed the tea service to the floor, ripped up her trousseau, and snaked her mother's traveling companion and eloped with him.

Eliza soon learned to repent of her folly. Shut up with the boorish Thomas James in an airless stateroom to India, she realized she'd exchanged one form of imprisonment for another. The moment they arrived at his remote garrison in the Himalayas, she plotted her jailbreak. Armed with an "instinctive zest for flirtation" and dumbfounding beauty, she ignored marital military protocol and descended alone on the regimental balls. Two years and several conquests later, she absconded to England. On board she hooked a rich cavalry officer and lured him to her cabin, where passengers observed their nude gambols through the half-open door.

With a little help from the officer, she hit London on all cylinders. A famous painter said it was worth the trip just to look at her. She had the eyes of a pre-Raphaelite sorceress—blue, black-lashed, and arched with flaring brows—and breasts "that made madmen" everywhere. Her dramatic looks and temperament seemed tailor-made for the theater, and she shrewdly targeted flamenco, still an unknown art form in Europe. She spent a year in Cádiz and returned as an aristocratic Spanish widow speaking heavily accented English. Incredibly, no one recognized her. Perhaps they never would have if Thomas James hadn't resurfaced before her 1843 debut and blown her cover with a noisy divorce suit.

As it was, she had to flee to the Continent, where her imposture went over without a hitch. She toured the capitals of Europe, taking her racy road show from triumph to triumph. Men clapped "until their hands were bloody." But she gave them a poor return for their devotion. She made terrible scenes. She decapitated Prince Heinrich LXXII's prize flowers and strung them around his horses; she gatecrashed a celebration for the czar; she horsewhipped the police; and she ignited a revolutionary riot in Warsaw when she mooned a corrupt government official. Law enforcement squads stood helpless; she cried foul, drew daggers, and broke the furniture.

Amid this scorched-earth tour she paused for a brief sexual divertimento with Franz Liszt. Curious about the vaunted charms of this heartthrob composer, she presented herself at his stage door. Instantly captivated, he said that "all other women pale[d]" beside her and pronounced himself "completely satisf[ied]" in bed. He wrote a sonata in her honor and took her along on stag parties where she puffed cheroots and entertained his friends with her "merry unaffected" badinage and ribald stories. But the "lightless satellite" role was not for Lola.

A few months down the road she departed for Paris, the international roost for fortune-seeking, hedonistic birds of passage. She immediately fell in with the roistering bohemians and nouveau riche free spenders and almost married among them. Just before the wedding, however, her fiancé, a self-made newspaper millionaire, died in a duel, a misfortune she attributed to her absence from the scene. A crack shot, she was a fabled habituée of the Lepage Shooting Gallery.

With her fiancé's legacy, Lola recuperated with a pleasure tour through Europe, towing behind her more lovers, said observers, than legs of a "centipede." When she reached Munich, she went straight for the main attraction.

Elbowing past palace guards, she stormed Ludwig I's private apartments and assailed him with rapid-fire Spanish and provocative poses. The sixty-year-old king, beset with civic unrest and sexual insecurities, was ripe for the picking. Stupefied, he asked if her breasts were real, to which Lola responded by slashing open the front of her bodice with a pair of scissors. The next day Ludwig told his cabinet he was "bewitched," "in the grip of passion like never before."

Lola proceeded to prosper as never before. For sixteen months she played the set-piece king's mistress. She stroked his ego (comparing him with Lorenzo the Magnificent), coddled him through illnesses, serenaded him in a voice of "liquid sweetness," and humored his sexual whims. At his request she gave him flannel swatches secreted in her vulva, let him suck her unwashed toes, and talked dirty. She wanted him to "*besar* [fuck] her with great gusto and pleasure"; she said her "*cuno* belonged to him."

But her *cuno* belonged to Lola alone. When not in Ludwig's service (and true sex occurred only twice), she entertained a private *Lolianer,* or Lola's harem, at her palatial mansion on the Barestrasse. A group of university students founded a fraternity in her honor, slept with her on a rotating basis, and bore her up the crystal staircase on their bare shoulders. Warned about these high jinks by his irate counselors, Ludwig turned a deaf ear until it was too late.

When he made Lola countess of Lansfeld, the lid blew. The university closed, three cabinets resigned, and a rioting mob descended on the home of "Her Whorish Majesty," crying for blood. Lola strode out on her balcony and toasted them with champagne, then beat a quick retreat to Switzerland. In her absence Ludwig fell apart. Shattered and deranged without her, he honored his vow, "my kingdom for Lola," abdicated, and spent the rest of his life languishing in backwater spas for exiled aristocrats.

Lola's life meanwhile went on as before—*accelerando con molto.* There was a seraglio of "corsairs" on Lake Geneva, a quickie marriage/divorce to a young British blade, and a grand tour through America with her flamenco revue. The country, with its Barnum and Bailey tastes and raw, frontier energy, couldn't have been better suited for Lola's risqué showmanship, and she succeeded beyond her wildest expectations. Accompanied by the usual tumult, she wound up her victory march in California and felt so at home among the transient population of mavericks and floaters that she put down temporary stakes.

She made another quick-stop marriage to a newspaper editor and moved to the Sierra foothills, where she hitched a grizzly bear to a tree in her yard and reinvented herself as a combination Jane Addams and Calamity Jane. Between charitable forays through the country, she swapped off-color stories with cowboys in saloons and thundered across the hills on wild stallions.

All went well until a handsome actor strolled through town. She purloined him from his wife and led him off on a tumultuous barnstorm of Australia. The trip home, however, altered her life forever. During one of their violent spats the actor jumped to his death at sea, after which Lola decided to reform. Blaming herself, she sold her jewels and became a staid–for her–"queen of the lecture room."

To packed houses she lectured on her storied life and the secrets of seduction. In love, she preached, women could "play as well" as men, if not better. They just needed to develop "the quills of a porcupine," stop good-girl servility, and learn the erotic arts. Apart from the obvious physical ones (which she minutely itemized), these included brains, vitality, lovecraft, and "charming" conversation. Look at the experts, she counseled, seductresses like Agnès Sorel and Catherine the Great, who wielded "a power *stronger* than *strength*." Such paragons deserved the same treatment as men, she argued, and freedom from home and the ties that bind.

After her triumphal career on the podium, Lola retired to Ninetieth Street in Manhattan, where she feuded with judges and allegedly ran an orgiastic free love commune. But true to her contention that she was both "better than a devil" and "worse than an angel," she converted to Christianity and died prematurely at thirty-nine with an enamored Episcopal priest by her side.

In 1998, a small claque of modern *Lolianer* gathered around her grave at Greenwood Cemetery to dedicate a new headstone. Asked, "Why Lola?" one replied that she was "the first who really did women's lib." Yet feminists have consistently frozen her out. She was forbidden to speak at a Boston girls' school during her own time and cut from Judy Chicago's *Dinner Party* of notable women in the 1970s.

As to be expected, the male establishment joined the assault, calling her an "unspeakable female" and a power-hungry impostor who "appropriated male privilege" as late as 1996. The film industry delivered the unkindest cut of all. For her crimes against *vagatio* and masculine repose, Max Ophüls enslaves her to a sadistic circus ringmaster in *Lola Montez* and locks her in a cage.

Lola, however, was a lockpick from way back, inured to arrest warrants and attack. She knew no man would be penalized for leaving home, laying the world, and singing a hymn to freedom. She may have even known she had the authority of myth behind her and the future of feminism before her. Move like the "goddess," she told women, with a "flying step," and "live before [you] die."

* * *

When a woman steps out of the house for adventure, she opens the floodgates, loosing every kind of female vice on society: insubordination, self-will, promiscuity, and that trait so dreaded by men, aggression. "Anger," writes Susan Brownmiller, is "unattractive," the ultimate sexual turnoff. Not in male love poetry, erotica, or ancient myth. Sex goddesses of antiquity were fierce, bellicose power queens. Just as the "war instinct and eroticism" share the same neural circuitry in the libido, so these mythic love deities were pumped by rage, violence, and bloodshed. It was part of their "joyful, voracious appetite for life," their life-death totality, and plenum of being.

From the earliest times lions symbolized this aggressive aspect of the erotic divinity (as seen in the 18,000 B.C. Chapel of the Lioness in *Les Trois Frères*) and persisted into the cult of Inanna. She plants a foot on a lion on her seal, and her name was *labbatu*, Lady Lioness. Unfettered from home and free to indulge her wildness, Inanna mauled foes with the same gusto she gave to sex. "Manly" and courageous, she prowled the roads with weapons and "Holy Woman's rage," fought "hand-to-hand," and crushed the "one she loath[ed]." The ancient Greeks recycled Inanna into a mythical race of Amazons—nomadic warrior women with raging sexual appetites who lived on horseback, ransacked civilization, repudiated housework, and refused to marry.

Hortense Mancini, 1646–1699

Seventeenth-century Europe had its own "Queen of the Amazons" to contend with, the "mad, mad" "Vagabond Duchess" Hortense Mancini. Rich, privileged, refractory, and as free with firearms as she was with men, Hortense lived a life that might have been dreamed up by a gothic romancer on Benzedrine. Pursued for twenty years by a demented husband and his armed posses, she dashed from melodrama to melodrama, conquering every heart in her path, male and female. She was a macha Hotspur, a drifter with attitude unleashed in a "softer sex" culture that enshrined feminine sweetness, chastity, stasis, and subordination and gave miscreants no quarter.

Hortense's first impression on the world, ironically, was seraphic. When Cardinal Mazarin, the de facto French ruler during Louis XIV's

minority, summoned his niece to Versailles at age eight with her four
sisters, he pronounced her an "angel." He was wrong. "Her mother's
darling," Hortense was a handful: spoiled, undisciplined, and in-
tractable to feminine socialization.

She ran riot through the palace, laughed too loud, refused to
obey, and flirted with everyone in pants, including Louis's brother
Philippe, who declared he "could not live without her." Bundling her
off to a convent failed (the nuns returned her in tears), as did the services of a stern governess. But the cardinal was no wiser and gave
Hortense his entire fortune, the greatest in Europe, provided that her
husband, the legal heir, change his name to Mazarin.

Despite the catch clause, titled suitors clamored for her hand:
Charles, the future king of England; Prince Pedro of Portugal; Charles
Emmanuel II of Savoy; and others. Her assets included more than
wealth and high spirits; her beauty "surpassed all imagination." In
striking contrast to the "white and golden" belle ideal, she was dark
and full-bodied in the Italian style, with a Roman nose, sultry pout, jet
black eyes, and masses of raven hair that tumbled down her back in a
riot of corkscrew curls. She had her pick.

But in a deathbed lapse of sanity Cardinal Mazarin chose for her
and selected an aristocratic rotter and sycophant of no charms whatever. A tall spindleshanks, Armand Charles, marquis de la Meilleraye,
lacked animation, education, and wit and harbored a streak of madness. But the cardinal, drooling dementia notwithstanding, had spoken, and the wedding took place in February 1661.

In five years Armand reduced Hortense to the "unhappiest
woman" on earth. His mind snapped and spiraled into a paranoia that
revealed the whole rationale behind female sequestration. Panicked at
the possibility of Hortense's roving libido, he barricaded her at home,
denied her male guests, and forbade her to kiss their children, of
whom she had four in quick succession. At one point, the sex-crazed
marquis lopped off all the genitals in the cardinal's priceless art collection.

Women had two recourses for marital abuse in those days—prayer
and laudanum. Except Hortense. Traducing every sacred and secular
marital law, she declared war on her husband. She escaped his house

arrest five times, twice fled from convent prisons, and sued him for a separation. Exhausted by her demands, Louis XIV finally gave in and let her live independently until her case came to court.

Hortense saw her opportunity. Dressed in male disguise, she slipped out of Paris with a lover and merry band of followers and headed to Italy. An Alpine layover resulted in a liaison with her lover's equerry and another pregnancy. But she scorched into Rome unperturbed, "dancing and running about" and flirting with all the men. Scandalized relatives foolishly packed her off to a convent. She broke out as usual and sped to France for a furious round of adventures and hairbreadth escapes.

Louis XIV's demand that she desist and settle abroad only provoked worse audacities. She mounted a madcap campaign to rescue her unhappily married sister that involved an armed standoff in the forest, a sea chase with her brother-in-law's warships, and shipwreck on the coast of Marseilles. After a cascade of parallel dramas, always with Armand's armies at her heels, Hortense and her sister fetched up in Savoy, under the protection of Charles Emmanuel II, her old suitor.

A swashbuckling monarch who understood her, Charles gave her liberty, luxury, a château, and "all the privileges and none of the responsibilities of a petty sovereign." For three years Hortense flourished, strapping on her "whirlwind warrior" sandals and running with her archaic passions. She hunted the woods in men's trousers, paraded through the streets bathed in hares' blood, swam in all seasons, and hitched up her skirts and danced with peasants.

Indoors she did what a sex deity does best; she seduced her secretary, César Vichard (author of *Dom Carlo*, source of the Verdi opera), and studied philosophy and history with him between bouts of lovemaking. Though no intellectual, Hortense had a mind and mouth on her. While in Savoy, she tossed off her memoirs, which sold briskly in four languages. "I have found at last," she said at the end, "that quiet which I had sought so long in vain."

Self-knowledge was not her long suit. After Charles died and his wife ousted her, Hortense was back on the adventure trail, accompanied by twenty men (including her secretary lover) and talking of "nothing but violins and hunting parties." Hounded every step by Armand's forces, she arrived in London penniless and caked with mud to cheering crowds. Her old beau Charles II soon joined them. He called her the "finest woman he had ever seen in his life," installed her in a "Little Palace" conveniently across the park, and settled a handsome pension on her.

For a while she held first place in the royal seraglio. At the opening of Parliament she appeared by the king's side "raised high above the other ladies." He said he'd rather talk to her than anyone else and gave her the world: an exotic menagerie, a fleet of gold-livered servants, *grandes toilettes* from Paris, and the best chef and cellar in London.

But typically, Hortense's hormones got the better of her. Unable to keep her hands to herself, she dallied with courtiers on the side, among them the prince of Monaco. The king looked the other way and only once stopped her pension, but his ardor cooled.

Not all of her infidelities were sexual. Her most celebrated was an *amitié amoureuse* with the sixty-year-old seigneur de Saint-Évremond. This famous French philosopher in exile fell hopelessly in love with Hortense and tagged behind her for the rest of her life as her personal tutor, factotum, and poet laureate. "Everything about her," he raved, "turned to love; she was a miracle of beauty, miracle of love."

Under his guidance, she acquired a "newfound reputation for wit and intelligence" and opened a stylish, if unconventional, salon. Highbrow debates and readings were carried on amid revelrous festivity: games of ombre and trente-et-quarante, arias sung by a "Golden Soprano," and Hortense's furlanos, danced to Gypsy guitars.

Her erotic explorations often took her beyond the cavalier population. Like the double-gendered sex goddess, Hortense also had lesbian affairs, then openly tolerated. She joined X-rated "horse races" at exclusive ladies' nights and became so embroiled with the countess of Sussex that her husband had to abduct her from Hortense's clutches. Other female admirers included the author Aphra Behn, who dedicated a novel to her and called herself her "entire slave." "Each sex," said Saint-Évremond admiringly, "provided its lovers for Hortense."

Charles II's death in 1684 cut Hortense's financial supply lines, leaving her at the mercy of her husband, who still pursued her with deranged fury. Future kings, however, continued her pension, though in smaller and smaller amounts. She downsized her lifestyle but remained as extravagant as ever in spirit and libido. At thirty-seven she hurled herself into a grand passion with a heroic Swedish general and almost lost her mind when an infatuated rival killed him in a duel.

Afterward her mad run at life grew into a desperate quest for escape. She incurred gambling debts and slid into other excesses. Her militant fiber and colossal selfhood, however, spared her the usual thrill addict's burnout. "Never have I been in better health, never more beautiful," she boasted in middle age, but she collapsed in a coma at fifty-four and never recovered, except to rebuff a priest on her deathbed.

Her picaresque saga didn't end there. Once her insane husband got his hands on her remains, he refused to part with them and lugged them around France on a yearlong pilgrimage. Every time the cortege approached, peasants poured out with the sick and dying to touch the bier of the mysterious saint. Many miracle cures were reported.

To have seen herself regarded as a saint would have given Hortense a good laugh. She'd always been Satan in skirts to the status quo. The court poet, Lord Rochester, compared her to Messalina, and coffeehouse wits said she copulated with stallions and valets and soused the whole city with her "cunt gravy."

But Hortense, like the sex goddess, was beyond Madonna-whore polarities; she snarled the categories. She might have deserted her children, cheated at cards, and committed a hundred other offenses, but she was a force of nature, "raw libidinous energy," a boundary-busting *labbatu*, whom men could not help but adore. "She comes, she comes!" chanted pub crawlers of her. "Resign the day—/She must reign, and you obey."

Beryl Markham, 1902–1986

Beryl Markham looks so leonine on her book jacket photo that we expect her biography to be titled *Lady Lioness*. It might well have been. This *über*siren, called simply "the creature" for her primitive erotic power, was the direct offspring of the goddess who "rides out on seven great lions" and roves the planet for men, excitement, and prizes.

Although passed over for more manageable action heroines, she was one of the greatest adventurers of modern times. Her exploits as a bush pilot and horse trainer set records, and her historic east-west solo flight across the Atlantic surpassed Amelia Earhart's. In seduction, she scored just as impressively; lovers succumbed to her spell as if they were "under the influence of some swami."

Raised wild in the African bush, Beryl received an early initiation into female erotic magic. When she was four, her Kipsigis nurse tied a cowrie shell on a leather thong around her wrist—symbol of vulva power. The charm worked. Throughout her childhood she was known as the girl with the "powerful *dawa* [charisma]."

No meddling parents or schoolmasters interfered with the exercise of this force. Her mother, having eloped with another Kenya settler in 1905, had long gone, and her laissez-faire father let nature take its course. Given free rein on the horse farm at the edge of the Njoro wilderness, she roamed the Mau forests with a tribal boy her age and learned what he did: how to hunt, wrestle, hurl spears, bear pain, avenge wrongs, and acquit herself with courage and cunning.

On several occasions her father made halfhearted attempts to civilize her and trucked in governesses for the purpose. But each time the enfant terrible ran them off. The first discovered a black mamba snake in her bed, and another discovered what happened when she tried to thwart Beryl. When the governess locked her in a hut, Beryl battered down the door with a forty-pound elephant tusk and disappeared into the bush for three days.

Where her feet went, her libido followed. On nights of the full moon she and her tribal boyfriend ventured deep into the forests to watch the Kikuyus perform their mating dances. At these all-night ceremonies dancers in black and white monkey hides and colored feathers gyrated in a circle to determine "who stayed the longest and leapt the highest." Sex, she learned early, had nothing to do with sin and monogamy. The name of the game was stamina, pelvic virtuosity, and the quantity and quality of partners.

Five semesters at a Nairobi boarding school proved futile. She

terrorized the staff, once carrying a matron bodily out of the classroom and biking off through the gates to the Athi Plains. And her
dawa created its own tourbillion. "It was impossible," recalled one
classmate, "to keep track of the number of small boys who wanted to
marry her."

Once back at the Njoro farm, she reverted to her old untram-
meled existence. Sleeping in a mud rondavel on monkey skins, she
came and went as she wished, and haunted the stables, where she acquired enough expertise to become "head boy" of eighty Thoroughbreds. On her horse Pegasus, she traveled to gymkhanas and race days
throughout the county and made off with all the prizes. The local Masais called her "She who cannot fall off a horse."

She was equally unseatable in affairs of the heart. Released from
guilt trips, inhibitions, and ideological freight, she took sex neat—at
her pleasure, on her own terms. Hardly the preferred "lie still and
think of England" approach for proper Edwardian maids. Beryl's marriage at sixteen therefore turned out predictably. When Jock Purvis, a
landholder twice her age, disappointed (premature ejaculations and
drunken scenes), she cruised the colony for lovers and accrued so
many that her husband hammered "rows and rows" of nails for each
of her infidelities.

After two years she left him and careered around Kenya, taking up
horse training and cavorting with the Happy Valley set. Without
money or backers, she cracked the all-male preserve of the racetrack
and cadged favors until she won the first woman's trainer's license in
Africa. Through demonic dawn to dusk toil, she brought in a string of
victories and became the country's top trainer.

On the party scene she played to win as well. With her blond
marcelled bob, red-lacquered nails, and high-boned beauty, she radiated a Garboesque glamour and "dressed like Solomon in all his
glory." She was one of the star swingers of the Muthaiga Club revels,
dancing, drinking, and mate swapping the nights away. The men "surrounded her as surely as bees to a honeycomb" and nagged her with
marriage proposals.

When her divorce came through, she finally succumbed to pres-
sure and married Mansfield Markham. This dashing, rich aristocrat, a

titled Mr. Darcy, did everything superhumanly possible to keep her down on the farm. After a shoot-the-moon buying spree in Paris, he gave her a blue-ribbon horse farm and fleet of finest Thoroughbreds.

But she strayed anyway. She led safaris and got so involved with Prince Henry, duke of Gloucester that the queen mother intervened and bribed her off with a lifetime annuity. A baby born at this time was probably Henry's, but Mansfield gamely accepted the boy as his own and raised him in England while Beryl restarted her life in Africa.

Free again at last, she discovered the ultimate form of female gadding, flight. She found the "world without walls," the open frontier, and the rip of speed, danger, and altitude she craved. In 1933 she became the first Kenya-trained pilot to gain a commercial license and launched a daredevil business. Piloting a crude biplane over uncharted flatlands where one mishap meant certain death, she spotted game for safaris with a Luger and vial of poison at her feet.

Even more glamorous with a new nose bob and a Parisian makeover, she was the femme fatale of the Rift Valley. Her "delicious sense of humor," combined with a "one of the boys" *sans gene*, had a bewitching effect on big-game hunters and her flying buddies. Then there was the off-the-meter bedcraft. Those who experienced it said she provided "the most startling and erotic sex of their lives." During a two-month period she juggled twelve lovers simultaneously, without any contretemps, a feat attributable to her ability to make each partner feel as though *he* were "the one who interested her."

Among this cavalcade of inamorati, she nearly captured the one man who might have kept her interest. Denys Finch Hatton, Kenya's premier Casanova, was Beryl's male counterpart—a high-T adventurer, rolling stone, and free spirit. He discarded his effete deskbound lover, Isak Dinesen, and romanced Beryl on long devil-may-care flights through Africa, filled with song, laughter, poetry tutorials, and torrid sex. His freak death at takeoff on a trip they'd planned together (which she canceled at the last minute) left her shattered for years.

Perhaps it explains her own brush with death soon after. One Christmas she found herself at the coffee plantation of Kenya's resident sadist, John Carberry, who defied her to make the "water jump," the infamous westward flight across the Atlantic. The feat was considered suicidal; more than thirty pilots had already failed in the attempt, and five women died. But Beryl picked up the gauntlet. On September 4, 1936, she taxied down the runway against 50 mph headwinds, without radio capacity and with only two fuel tanks. Battling fatigue, gales, and several hair-raising spinouts, she crash-landed twenty-one hours later in Nova Scotia. This made her the first person to fly east to west nonstop, a more daring stunt than Lindbergh's or Earhart's.

Her achievement, though, was soon forgotten. After a brief turn in the spotlight—a New York City motorcade and radio show with Milton Berle—she returned to a chilly reception in England. Perceived as a déclassé home deserter, she could find no sponsors for further flights and spent the next ten years eddying around America.

She migrated by instinct to Hollywood, the asylum of choice for glamorous escapees and soldiers of fortune. She worked as a consultant on *Safari* with Douglas Fairbanks, Jr., beach-partied with stars, and married a sometime ghostwriter and professional charmer named Raoul Schumacher. By now she should have learned. Except for a book they wrote together, *West with the Night*, about her African adventures, the marriage played out like the other two.

Restive in captivity, Beryl soon grazed the territory for "dashing young men" and bedded them without apology or concealment. When Raoul caught her red-handed with his best friend, they officially separated, though he remained "absolutely besotted" with her and broke down mentally when she left. During her final months in America, Beryl flew reconnaissance missions for the war effort and gallivanted with Burl Ives, Sir Charles Mendl, and a doctor half her age.

At forty-seven she backtrailed to Kenya and undertook the second-greatest challenge of her life. When another siren-adventurer might have kicked back and dusted her trophies, Beryl returned to horse racing after a thirty-year absence, without connections or start-up funds. In only two seasons she reestablished herself as the leading trainer. Her horses won the St. Leger four times; the East Africa Derby, five; and the prestigious Kenya Triple Crown—victories so astounding that track habitués accused her of using voodoo, a "Beryl Bloom," brewed with African magic.

The voodoo didn't stop with horses. Men couldn't resist her. Her farm manager, Jürgen Thrane, idolized her, and her jockey, Buster Parnell, said he loved her "like a lover." In her fifties she looked decades younger and held court at her posh cottage "like the Queen of Sheba." "She was a knockout," recalled Parnell; "there wasn't a woman in Nairobi could hold a candle to her. It was almost," he added, "as though she had a hundred watt bulb in her head and the rest of us had only seventy-five."

The next ten years put her radiance and "fantastic ego" to the test. All her horses fell ill of a mysterious disease, and after a demoralizing venture in South Africa, she returned to Kenya broke, down on her luck, and old. But the *dawa* still blazed. Approaching seventy, she reconquered the track (twenty-three winners in 1972) and crackled with swish and fight. When thieves robbed and beat her, she tongue-lashed them in Swahili; when revolutionaries raked her car with gunfire, she swanned into the Muthaiga Club with blood streaming from a nick in her neck.

Men continued to swarm. A fortyish bachelor whom she called "Fweddy dahling" visited her for overnights three times a week, and George Gutekunst, who filmed her documentary in 1983, fawned over her. "I ADORE YOU," he wrote in one of his letters, "take care of yourself until I can . . . see and kiss you again." But take care of herself she did not. Living dangerously to the last, she drove her battered Mercedes through town like a bat out of hell and died in 1986 five months after falling from the top tier of the racing stadium.

Powerful seductresses who desert home, play with the boys, sport-fuck, and win too many prizes are profoundly disturbing. Hence the canonization of the sexless, safely married Amelia Earhart and the denigration of Beryl Markham. She broke the feminine contract and torched the double standard, unpardonable offenses to traditionalists of both sexes.

Women especially loathed her and vice versa. "I certainly have nothing to do with women . . . EVER," she snapped. One bit her finger to the bone, and her modern female biographers inflict her with neuroses and an unhappy life.

Beryl disagreed. She claimed she'd had "as good a lot of yesterdays as anyone might want": "dangers and pleasures," movement, and "horizons." Her idea of hell was the contented feminine norm—marital bondage. Her most terrifying nightmare wasn't death in the icy Atlantic or an elephant charge, but being eaten alive by an army of siafu ants, "minute, numberless, and inexorable," devoured inch by inch by the dull domestic grind. As her enemies charged, she was a "tramp," one of Inanna's lionhearted prowlers, sex questers, and saboteurs of the established order.

Members of this underground sorority recognize each other, and in 1983 Martha Gellhorn, the macha war reporter and seductress, drove sixteen miles through the bush to visit her. When she arrived, she found the eighty-one-year-old Beryl in tight Pucci pants, entertaining two rapt young men. Martha clicked instantly. This woman, she wrote, was not "your run-of-the-mill Circe. Imagine Circe casting a spell on Ulysses so she could go along on the journey, learn navigation, see the world. . . . It was easy to entrance the whole lot, that being her nature, and she knew what she wanted: knowledge and adventure."

"Prostitute" in Arabic means "She who goes out." It all originated with Inanna, the prototypic *kar-kid* "who roams about." When this wayward goddess sallied forth, she decked herself in whorewear, toured the taverns, took her pick, and got paid for it. One of Inanna's main personas was "Hierodule of Heaven," or Holy Harlot, and her priestesses were sex professionals. Prostitution in ancient Sumer was a sacred, not a profane, business. The prehistoric worship of the female sexual principle still endured, and the marriage ceremony marked the most hallowed event of the year.

At this supreme rite Inanna's priestess copulated with the king, thereby investing him and the populace with *hi-li*, the eros and creative spark of all being. In thanks, he placed gift offerings on her altar, a practice continued at later shrines where worshipers left money on the laps of sacred prostitutes.

Judeo-Christianity came down hard on these erotic high priestesses with their transcendent powers and condemned them to hell and the dregs of society. But archetypes aren't so simple to dislodge. The "divine hierodule and seducer" won't be banished to the underworld; she crops up all over Western history, eluding the law and staking out her ancient claim to male adulation and munificence.

The Hetaerae of Ancient Greece

One of the most elite cadres of sex professionals, paradoxically, surfaced in the sexist stronghold of the ancient world. Terrified of the maelstrom of sexual passion, Athenian civilization confined women to home, stripped them of rights, and put them under the jurisdiction of fathers and husbands.

Only one group escaped: prostitutes. These ran the gamut from the one-obol *dicteriades* who stood naked in the doorways of public brothels to the regal hetaerae who owned their destinies and lived in state. Independent, educated, and footloose, hetaerae mingled equally with men, chose their lovers, and enjoyed the status of modern movie idols. They were Aphrodite's chosen people, mysteriously suffused with beatitude and liberated from the lot of mortal women. Renowned for their brains, they wisely traded on this numinous effect to enhance their prestige and ensure their freedom. Like their mythic counterparts, they were a race of rovers, love pirates, and sensationalists.

Rhodophis, c. 600 B.C.

The fabulous Rhodophis began as most did, in dire adversity. A slave at the royal court of Samos, she weaseled a passage to Egypt as a ladies' maid and seduced a Greek tourist, who sold his inheritance to marry her. But marriage bore an uncomfortable resemblance to Samos. She jumped ship and meandered through Egypt until she reached Naucratis, "a good place for beautiful prostitutes," where she earned such sums she built a pyramid "to render her name immortal." According to legend, she haunted her pyramid for eternity, appearing nude to wayfarers and luring them into endless treks through the desert.

Phyrne, c. 350 B.C.

A generation later Phyrne capitalized more deliberately on her goddess aura. A raw recruit who arrived in Athens at thirteen from the
harsh caper fields, she found herself outgunned. The agora teemed
with gorgeous hetaerae accoutered in blond wigs, chandelier earrings,
heavy cosmetics, and transparent purple chitons. The girl, however,
devised a shrewd counterstrategy. Instead of competing with these
birds of paradise, she niche marketed herself as a luxury model,
shrouded in divine mystery.

She swathed her perfect body in an opaque *deplos,* wore no
makeup or wig, made love in the dark, and charged exorbitant fees,
adjusted to her tastes. Once a year she staged a sacred striptease. At the
annual Festival of Poseidon she walked naked from the holy temple
through the crowds to the shore and reenacted Aphrodite's birth from
the sea.

As she grew into a national attraction, a superstar commanding a
"king's ransom" for a single night, poets and painters enshrined her as
the goddess made flesh. Her lover, Praxiteles, used her for his Cnidian
Aphrodite, the first sculpture to depict the love deity both nude and
"full of joy and pleasure." As immodest as her mythic model, Phyrne
invited Praxiteles to copulate with her beneath the statue, which had
made her "worthy to stand among the gods."

That was precisely what the city fathers feared—female sexual
power run wild in the pantheon and all hell to pay. They charged her
with blasphemy and would have executed her if her lawyer hadn't
saved her with an eleventh-hour reprieve. When the case seemed lost,
he tore off Phyrne's *deplos* and exposed her breast to the judge and
jury. Filled with the "holy awe of the divinity," they voted to release
her as a "prophetess and priestess of Aphrodite."

Granted divine immunity, Phyrne lived to enjoy a happy and
prosperous old age. With her immense fortune, she offered (though
rebuffed by the town worthies) to rebuild Thebes after Alexander the
Great destroyed it. She died, according to report, with her forehead
resting on the marble foot of the statue of Eros.

This was the only time "rest" was ever applied to her. An avatar of the "mobile" "active" Aphrodite, Phyrne coursed through the courtesan ranks, outran her captors, and attained Olympian autonomy and liberty. Worse than her harlotry, worse than her strip show, this was the unpardonable crime: "mobility," the rank violation of female quiescence and containment. "Phyrne had talents for mankind," sniped the poet Alexander Pope, "open she was, and unconfined,/Like some free port of trade."

The Grand Horizontals

Mid-nineteenth-century France marked another nadir of feminine enfeeblement and home quarantine. Bruised and bloodied in the capitalist marketplace, men required balm in Gilead, a sainted housekeeper who devoted her life to male succor and domestic peace. She was quiet, timid, and submissive and epitomized immobility—even in bed. If she were loveworthy, she lacked "sexual feeling of any kind" and lay "motionless [during sex] . . . as passive and inanimate as a flower." Frigid was fashionable; the style setter of the age, Empress Eugénie, proudly flaunted her *froideur.*

But just as female claustration in Greece coexisted with (and subversively promoted) hetaerae, so this cult of the domestic nun brought with it the Grand Horizontals. These hell-fired courtesans, mirror opposites of angelic *femmes au foyer,* held undisputed sway over Paris for almost twenty years and behaved like a tribe of female Neros, glutting themselves on pleasure, hemorrhaging money, turning marquis into sex slaves, and princes into frogs.

Motion was their middle name. They lived on parade, public spectacles in constant transit from one hot spot to another. Each afternoon at five they rolled through the Champs-Élysées in their custom carriages, while the mob gawked from the sidelines. Ostrich feathers bobbed from their cartwheel hats, priceless lace trailed from their ruffled gowns, and mascara and rouge lay thick on their haughty faces.

Tabloids recorded their adventures in avid detail: their masked balls, dinners of peacock galantine, and preposterous stunts. Blanche d'Antigy bathed in two hundred bottles of Montebello water, Mademoiselle Maximum lit her cigarettes with bank notes, and La Barucci dropped her dress when she was introduced to the duke of Wales. "I showed him the best I had," she cracked, "and it was free." Like the hetaerae, the Grand Horizontals were fleet of mind and tongue, with black belts in the arts of fascination. "A love affair is like a war," said the redoubtable Mogador; "tactics help you win it."

Cora Pearl, 1835–1886

Of these arrogant love commandas, one outrivaled the rest in hype and glamour: the "Queen of Outrage," Cora Pearl. She dyed her dogs to match her gowns, wore nothing to a costume party, dueled a rival in the Bois de Boulogne, caned a Russian count, and pitched Prince Napoleon's vanload of orchids on the floor and danced a hornpipe on them. Parisians repeated her mots and drank a cocktail called the Tears of Cora. She devastated men. Every New Year's they lined up at her door and presented her with gift offerings like a high priestess. One prince said he'd "try to pilfer the sun if that would satisfy a whim of hers."

Her story followed the classic rape-to-riches plot of nineteenth-century courtesans, driven by a rage for personal freedom. From earliest childhood she was a breakout artist and insurgent. Born Eliza Emma Crouch in Plymouth to an indigent music teacher and his wife, she had the extraordinary luck to be sent to a French convent by a charitable grandmother after her father deserted the family.

But the scrappy girl blew it. Dead set against virtuous femininity, she bucked the program and sowed pandemonium with her tomboy pranks and insurrections. Once back in England, she had to take one of the semistarvation jobs reserved for unskilled girls, assistant to a milliner.

On her way home from work one day, a prominent diamond merchant offered to buy her a sweet, then drugged and raped her. Effectively "ruined" for the marriage market and faced with a lifetime of twopenny grunt labor, Eliza split for Paris with a dance hall proprietor for a life of sin.

Paris in 1855 was sex city central, one big "brothel and gambling hall," with as many as a hundred thousand prostitutes competing tooth and nail for a place in the elite *garde*. Only 1 percent made it, and Eliza's chances seemed slim. For starters, "she was plain." She had a round, freckled "clown's" face, with small, piglet eyes, a large mouth, and unfashionably red hair.

Like Phyrne, though, Eliza knew how to spin her product. An audacious self-publicist, she rechristened herself Cora Pearl and invented a head-turning style that put her assets on display. She wore second-skin gowns with bustles (the first in Paris) that showed off her curves to perfection—a wasp waist with breasts so round and high-sprung she had them molded and cast into a golden goblet. Adopting a "new look every evening," she popularized wigs and pioneered modern makeup. She dyed her eyelashes and used bright lipstick, silver face powder, and "slap," a foundation borrowed from London dolly-mops.

Cora's personality was no less original. A coarse vulgarian with a "sewer of a mouth," she released men from their devil's bargain with the angel of the house. In her company they knew the corset-loosening ecstasy of "barriers broken down," "organic relief," and "the ease of existence!"

She gave transvestite balls, waltzed with her pet pig, and once wagered a group of men she could serve them a dish they'd be unable to cut. After raising the bets to astronomical sums, she hired waiters to carry her out nude on a silver platter, sprinkled with parsley. Insanely extravagant, she inverted the house saints' parsimony and bought out the store. In memory of her rapist, she stockpiled diamonds and paved her shoes with them in her one stage appearance, giving the ones that rolled away to the dressers.

Such prodigality did not come cheap. But Cora could afford it. Around her neck she wore a "chain of gold" hung with the coats of arms of her twelve biggest providers. Her first link, the duc de Rivoli, funneled a small fortune into her for six years. He supplied her with stables, servants, chefs, closets of gowns, and a vast mansion, where she sat fifteen to dinner each night and served violet garnishes to the tune of fifteen hundred francs.

Bounty, however, of whatever proportions couldn't buy her quiescence or fidelity. She tooled around town on a velocipede (precursor of the bicycle) in male drag and availed herself of a toothsome side dish, her lover's nephew Prince Achille. She and the prince bounded off on hunting trips and wanton weekends together, stirring up duels, dramas, and scrapes with bad checks. When the duc found out, Cora struck first. As soon as "a liaison was finished it was finished," she insisted, and "she herself would terminate it."

Wealthy replacements quickly picked up the slack. The names include the face cards of the Second Empire: William, Prince of Orange, the Turkish emir, Gustave Doré, the duc de Mornay, and the emperor's brother Prince Napoleon, who kept her in luxury for ten years. Dozens of lesser lights danced around her as well, inundating her with presents. One sent her a box of candy, each wrapped in a thousand-franc note; another, a silver horse crammed with gold and jewels. In eight weeks an Irish scion squandered his entire inheritance on her.

Amid the gifts and adulation Cora kept her cool. Disciplined against the perils of "uncontrollable passion," she played off her lovers against each other and led them in crazy eights. Men, she believed, preferred the "chase" to "the kill," and she obliged them with obstacle courses of the dizziest detours and roughest terrain. That is, until her fatal miscalculation in 1871.

One of her lovers, a young restaurant heir, lacked the stomach for her extreme love sports. When she gave him his congé, he stalked out, seized a loaded gun, and barged into Cora's drawing room. He fired wildly in her direction, then turned the barrel on himself and collapsed in a bloody heap on the floor. Although he recovered and became a pillar of bourgeois society, Cora was condemned as his murderess, driven from Paris, and hounded throughout Europe.

Demonized, blacklisted, and ostracized, she drifted aimlessly for several bleak years. She lost her whole fortune—some to the roulette wheel—and called herself "Cora minus the Pearls." But her luck turned in middle age. Her old admirers joined forces and set her up in genteel comfort, with a full-time maid and good Parisian address. Her "merry disposition" never deserted her. Physically and mentally active, she wrote her memoirs and studied an early version of Esperanto which she called Corapuk. She died of intestinal cancer at fifty-one "without fear of the other side" and "confident of forgiveness."

Her confidence in worldly forgiveness was misplaced. By the time of her death in 1886 the Grand Horizontals, blamed for all the French fin-de-siècle moral, financial, and military woes, had gone out of favor. Her memoirs didn't sell. But, then, she'd never "cared a fig for public opinion." She laughed at the concierges who turned her from hotels and the women who iced her. As a result, she shunned female organizations, the early feminists in particular.

Cora, though, "was a movement on her own," with the emphasis on movement. Panicked by domestic incarceration, she fled the nineteenth-century "temple of the hearth" and set up her own temple, where she lived at liberty and collected her reward. She claimed she'd known "no other happiness" than "independence." But she did.

When most women were imprisoned in parlors or sweatshops, she knew the thrill of adulation, goods, services, action, and the band striking up the waltz for one of her *transvesti* balls. "Let us live and enjoy life," she used to say—a motto no Second Empire "lady" ever stitched on her petit point stool.

La Belle Otero, 1868–1965

"Spell sex," said Maurice Chevalier, "with capital letters when you talk about Otero. She was the most dangerous woman of her time." The last of the Grand Horizontals, La Belle Otero led out the age of the great courtesans with a bombs-away fireworks finale. Known as the Suicide Siren, she drove eight men to their deaths and provided the best show in town for twenty-five years. Tangoing around the world like a "lusty, uncontrolled panther in heat," she conquered five kings and countless plutocrats and made and lost more money than almost any courtesan in history.

Her appearance was just as superlative as her exploits. Besides her sultry Carmencita face, she had a body to make men faint—runway legs and voom-voom measurements of thirty-eight, twenty-one, thirty-six. Her breasts, which wags said "preceded her by a quarter of an hour" when she entered a room, inspired the Cannes Carlton to name its twin domes *les boîtes à lait* [milk bottles] *d'Otero*. Even Colette waxed poetic; they looked like "elongated lemons," she said, "firm, and up-turned at the tips."

Otero attributed her sensational endowments to heredity: a lovely Gypsy mother and Greek aristocratic father, who died in a duel defending his wife's honor. Honor in fact was her mother's least virtue. The village *puta*, she had seven children by an array of men in a forlorn mountain town in northern Spain. Carolina Otero Iglesias, her second, grew up unsupervised, unschooled, and neglected in desolate poverty.

At eleven she was abducted by the shoemaker, held captive, and raped until her pelvis broke. Thus began her obsession with her "*liberté.*" A year later she ran away from home and lived by her wits and body until she met a dancer named Paco. He taught the fourteen-year-old how to dance, and for the next seven years he pimped and hustled jobs for her as they crisscrossed Spain on the cabaret circuit.

By chance one night she landed a gig at a waterfront bar in Marseilles. An American impresario, Ernest Jurgens, dropped in, watched her dance, fell "madly hopelessly in love," and recruited her for his dance hall in New York City. Never mind his wife and three children at home. He took her to Paris for lessons and costumes, renamed her Caroline de Otero, and launched her as an Andalusian aristocrat and the "International Queen of Dance."

His gamble paid off. On opening night Otero swiveled out in a plunge-back white satin gown and brought down the house with her eye rolls and lascivious gyrations to flamenco guitars. Flowers rained down on the stage, *olé*'s filled the press, and the haut monde packed the theater night after night. Soon Jurgens found himself at the end of a long stag line of wealthy suitors.

One of the first words Otero learned in English was "Tiffany's." Merchant princes like William Vanderbilt whisked her off to glamorous locales and wooed her with matched pearls, heirloom diamonds, and emerald bracelets. Desperate to stay in the running, Ernest embezzled the show's receipts and fled abroad to beat the rap; there he went from bad to worse and finally killed himself.

Caroline, on the other hand, thrived. Flush with cash, jewels, men, and theatrical success in America, she booked a European tour and vanquished the magnificos of the Continent. While Vanderbilt and others continued their largesse, she plundered the hearts and bank accounts of titled swells from Paris to Moscow. One young Russian prince sent her a million rubles wrapped in a scrawled note, "Ruin me but do not leave me."

Leaving, however, was Caroline's signature. A fly-by lover, an "austere and merciless" sex goddess, she told Colette that a man became yours not the moment you spread your legs, but "the moment you twist his wrist." This treatment was often too fortissimo for the fainthearted. Her drama coach's son drowned himself in the Seine, an art student threw himself under a coach, two noblemen blew their brains out, two more leaped from windows, and a schoolteacher hanged himself from the tree in the Bois de Boulogne where he'd first seen her.

The trail of bodies notwithstanding, men followed her, she said, "like flies" and paid her "whatever she want[ed]." Her tour of Russia was a long looting expedition. Gorged with riches, she fought off royal satyrs. At the castle of one overheated duke, she jumped from the bedroom in her peignoir into the snow and sledded off with her rescuer for a three-day sex marathon. As a St. Petersburg farewell she entertained guardsmen with a tabletop temple dance, swirling around the candelabrum and snuffing out candles with her fingers. "The flames," she exclaimed, "do not consume Otero."

Nor did they. When she wrapped up her show in Paris, she hit the glory sweeps. One night she found a gingerbread loaf in her dressing room tied to a string (the traditional method of propositioning dancers) with an attached rope of pearls and the single name Albert.

The new conquest was Albert, Prince of Monaco, a jillionaire playboy with deep pockets and sexual problems only Caroline could cure. He set off a regal stampede. For her thirtieth birthday, five monarch-lovers (Prince Albert, King Leopold of Belgium, Prince Nicholas I of Montenegro, Grand Duke Nikolai Nikolaevich, and Edward, Prince of Wales) chipped in and threw her a gala surprise party at Maxim's.

Among them, they kept Caroline in Babylonian opulence. Caparisoned in head-to-toe emeralds, rubies, and diamonds, she looked "like a precious idol decked with gifts of the faithful." Her gowns were designer extravaganzas cut within an ace of her nipples, embellished with gold net sleeves, chiffon overskirts, and tight satin-embroidered belts. Newspapers breathlessly reported the minutiae of her wardrobe, equipage, and outrageous mansion. She bowled down the Bois in a gilt barouche driven by black mules and owned an angel-frescoed bedroom like the Sistine Chapel, with a carved bed in the center festooned in blue silk damask.

But no matter how gilded, it was still a cage. "I wasn't meant," gibed Otero, "to be domesticated." With Paris as her pied-à-terre, she spent most of the year on the road with her flamenco show, expanding her repertoire to include pantomime and *Carmen* vignettes and tripping out on novelty. Like the "advancing, assertive" Aphrodite, she actively solicited her pleasures and propositioned men and women, including Maurice Chevalier.

Her pulse ran high. After work she downed massive mounds of corn and chorizo, stripped to her chemise, and danced until dawn with "perspiration running down her thighs." This quest for extra-life led her into dangerous territory, the casino, where she grew increasingly caught up in a cliff edge flirtation with ruin.

A fire-breathing sensationalist, she was a notorious troublemonger and short fuse. She sued everybody who miffed her, flung urine at an impudent waiter, slugged a tiresome woman in a hotel lobby, and stomped out of the opera when an escort looked at another woman. "When one has the honor of being with La Belle Otero," she exploded, "no one else exists."

Yet beneath the Latin *furia*, Otero had a level head. She retired at the top of her game at forty. Still in possession of her sex appeal, still murder with men, she held enough liquid assets to set herself up in style. Although besieged with marriage proposals, she couldn't bear the prospect of being "monotonously matron," bought a fourteen-room mansion near Nice, and freelanced as the spirit moved her.

She weekended with a Peruvian grandee, traveled to Madrid to help the young Alfonso XII "relax," and received a few army officers. For routine sex, she slept for ten years with Aristide Briand, a statesman with a libido fully equal to Otero's, who made love eight times a night. But no man, even one so remarkably endowed, could compete with Monte Carlo next door, and finally Caroline lost everything–the jewels, a villa, and a Pacific island–in the fever of play.

Reduced circumstances, however, couldn't graze her self-grandeur. At sixty she promenaded up and down the rue d'Anglais in sumptuous furs like a grand duchess. Men continued to find her the incarnation of "unadulterated" sex and made pilgrimages to her Nice apartment, where she amused them with war stories and one-liners.

"The king of Monaco," she reminisced, "wouldn't give anyone the sweat off his balls." She wrote a highly colored version of her life and made a stink when a movie about her came out in the fifties with an actress who "wasn't nearly as beautiful as [she]." Supported by monthly checks from a mysterious benefactor, this "sensual, soulless creature" grew religious and died at ninety-six preparing a rabbit stew.

Although vilified by respectable society, Otero bollixed the stereotype. She was snubbed as a "degenerate," ejected from theaters, accused of nymphomania, and attacked in the face by a matron with a bottle of vitriol. But she didn't fit the satanic mold.

She felt real affection, albeit polygamously, for her lovers, and mentored many women, including Colette and a guttersnipe whom she trained and married to a lord. Presciently she saw the positive uses of her trade for feminine empowerment. She once said if she won the jackpot at Monte Carlo, she'd endow a university for prostitutes. "Think of the variety of courses," she quipped, "the possibilities are infinite."

She was only half kidding. If she'd wished, this whizbang seductress could have wised up and rescued her contemporaries–dutiful wives embalmed in feminine "virtues," dead-bolted at home, and bullied and two-timed by their lords and masters. She might have something to teach modern women as well. One who visited her in 1938 thought so but couldn't put her finger on her secret. Otero was "impossible" to grasp; she had "the quality of a goddess," she said, but was "earthy at the same time." Had she known the right goddess, it would have been easy–the earthy *kar-kid*, queen of the cosmos, wanderer, adventuress, and the "ultimate femme fatale."

Siren-Adventurers: The Decline

With the twentieth century the great siren-adventurers dwindled away. They lost their goddess swank, style, machisma, and rule. The "terrible maneater" Mata Hari, for instance, was really a pathetic pretender, eaten alive by every man in her path. Neither a spy nor a seductress, she performed tacky pseudo-oriental stripteases, slept with faceless soldiers for peanuts, and concocted her secret agent yarn to get attention and improve business. Everything went smash. Her true love jilted her, and she accommodated the French search for an anti-maternal scapegoat with a string of suicidal blunders.

By mid-century the Betty Crockerization of women had almost extinguished the race. Herded into suburbs and terrorized into domestica, the adventuress tried and failed to crossbreed with June Allyson.

The reputed courtesan queen of the age, Pamela Harriman, was an admitted "backroom girl," a supermenial to important men who wiped their feet on her. Riches and respectability came at the price of domestic subjection, vicarious achievement, and the bread of humiliation. And she didn't even "particularly enjoy going to bed with men."

Her contemporary, the World War II spy-seductress Aline de Romanones, was made of sterner stuff. Known as Tiger, she cast off domestic trammels for a life of high "adventure" in the OSS. She careened around the Costa Brava in breakneck car chases, killed a man with a Beretta .25, and played a tough hand in love with matadors and Eurotomcats. But she too caved to the feminine mystique when a Spanish lord bought her off with titles and jewels and incarcerated her in the zenana of corseted Hispanic high society.

Not until the new millennium did women finally break the *vagatio* chokehold and reclaim the siren-adventuress. Before that, seductresses went one way, and action divas the other, with neither operating at full sexual potential. Persuaded of the incompatibility between sex appeal and adventure, macha lionesses downsexed and/or blew their love lives. Drag race champion Shirley Muldowney lost her heart to a cheating scoundrel, and Air Force bomber pilot Kelly Flinn became the doormat mascot for the nineties, sleeping with barflies because she wanted "to be loved" and whimpering that "she had no idea how to protect [her]self" when her boyfriend betrayed her and ruined her career.

The sex professionals lost altitude too. Assimilated into the system and assailed by amateur competition, they succumbed to drugs, airheadism, titty bars, and trophy wifedom. The cream of Hollywood, escort empress Heidi Fleiss, did jail time on felony charges, compliments of an informer lover with a Svengali "hold on her." Higher-end courtesans traded their strut and independence for tycoon husbands. Modeling themselves on society matrons, they struggled through elocution and etiquette lessons, toned down, girdled up, and learned to navigate narcoleptic lunches in gated compounds.

Siren-Adventurers: The Revival

All that has changed. Now the "one who roams about" is off and running. Babes with black belts are box-office gold and centerfold athletes rack up men with the medals. Free spirits everywhere are bringing their libidos with them into the action zone—into sports, "gotta sing gotta go" rock bands, exploration, and high-risk jobs. The coast is clear as never before for women with the need to move and a *horreur du domicile*. We have independence, mobility, economic parity, and the social license to rove.

Yet many remain stuck in neutral, mired in fear and defunct ideologies. As the "Surrendered Wife" and nesters' movements illustrate, a huge contingent has rushed back to the domestic corral, panicked over abandonment, divorce, and loneliness. They're under the delusion, instilled in women for millennia, that the spoils go to the good shut-ins. They're terrified their inner wild woman will lead them over the brink into the howling void of male rejection and radical isolation. As Leslie Blanch warns, travel "begins when love leaves off."

Of course some women will always prefer home port to the high seas. But siren-adventurers provide hope for the bold and restless. Not only is there life beyond the picket fence; it can be life with a capital *L:* adventure, knowledge, self-actualization, space to stretch, and the erotic jackpot.

With a few seductive smarts, she-rovers can get and keep all the men and marriage proposals they want. Loneliness isn't the price of liberty, nor is iniquity. One cultural critic warns that "the beginning of a woman-adventure is always 'going to be bad.' " But badness has nothing to do with it; action vamps cross the moral wires just as they cross the threshold of the future.

Admittedly they were the bad-attitude sistas of their day. With even greater racket than other seductresses, they staged break-the-china revolts against feminine norms and repressive custom. Endowed with colossal egos and vitality (sometimes owing to early "spoiling"), they came through adversity with flying colors. Hardship only toughened them up and honed their fighting edge. Since lax caregivers failed to inculcate gender roles or respect for rules, they broke from the starting gate unimpeded. Heroines-in-space, they were free to heed their hormones, invent themselves to taste, flex their feminine advantage, and blaze their own trails—with or without helpful mentors.

Whatever path they took, they instinctively followed the Seductive Way. As the most primal exemplars of the breed, they fired up seduction to archaic pitch. They dramatized the heart's core of the erotic arts, the defeat of stasis and ennui. Since antiquity, this has been the goal of the *ars amatoria:* not simply to incite passion (the easy part) but to keep it alive and in motion, to maintain the dynamic rapture of the early magico-sexual rites. These least civilized of seductresses cut through the cultural frills to the chase, leading men through a time warp to the first cave ceremonies.

They were exhibitionist priestesses of gaud and nudity, with temple-to-eros settings, full of animals, gilt, and *volupté.* Wired to move, they specialized in the kinesthetic voodoo of the shamans—hot-limbed sensuality on horseback, on promenade, and on the dance floor. As befitted deputies of the sensation seeker goddess, they ramped it up in the bedroom with go-getter lust and polished skills.

In their psychological lovecraft, they aimed square at the subpsyche, the deep memory well of sexual myth where goddesses laid men out with terrorjoy. They occasionally dispensed mother balm, but exclamation points were their chief business: the strong wine of praise,

conversational dazzle, peak exploits, and the euphoria of loosened
stays—unbound license and carnival.

Their labyrinths should have carried a health advisory. And the
suitors who survived them found no pillowed breast at the end. These
feisty, proud love queens required men on their toes, awestruck and
anxious to please. If they enrapt and transfigured lovers with holy
eros, they exacted a price, the steepest of all seductresses—kings' ran-
soms, duels, even insanity and death. None of which guaranteed a
thing. Siren-adventurers, like the "whirlwind" Inanna, couldn't be
contained; they were fizzing dynamos of change, mystery, and contradiction, with heavyweight, clear-the-tracks goddess identities.

Because they burned down the house of matrimony and worked
so much mischief on male libidos, they drew the special wrath of the
established order. They were the terroristas of sirens. They broke the
oldest taboo, sequestration, and unleashed the repressed sex deity of
roving lust and rolling conquests on society. Both men and women
(their special nemesis) went for blood. They stigmatized them as
heartless whores, ostracized and persecuted them, and wrote them out
of history books.

To be sure, they weren't paragons. In their itch for excitement and
velocity, they erred into excess: temper tantrums, gunslinging, gambling, vain posturing, and biographical fabrications. They usually
made a hash of motherhood and female friendships. But they weren't
mean bitches either.

As morally mixed as the housewife next door, they had moments
of piety, generosity, and kindness and didn't always destroy men. In
many cases they spurred them to action and achievement, and when
they found their true loves, heroes of their own venturesome caliber,
they rewarded them with loyalty and the goddess-mate of every man's
dreams, the one who never bores.

"Progress," said one of the second-wave feminists of the 1980s "depends on adventure." Perhaps more than any seductress group, siren-
adventurers presage and plot the future. Generations ahead of their
time, they invaded the masculine preserves of action and exploration
and took their sexual power with them. They dissolved the categories.
They proved that men were right. When the mate-guard bars come

down, women run roughshod over everything: labels, limits, and hierarchies.

The twenty-first-century postfeminists have caught up with the adventuresses. They've hit the go button, entered the male domain, discovered their tongues, minds, and hot genitals, and swept away boundaries and good/bad girl distinctions. They want identities and genders as fluid as Lola's and Hortense Mancini's; they want free-form erotic relationships and new home lives, with elbowroom and sabbaticals. They want—maybe more than men—to gad. The action queens were there first and know the territory. They have the courage, tools, bulletproof egos, and erotic Baedekers we need for full empowerment on the frontier.

"Everybody is an explorer," says a well-known adventurer. How, he asks, can "you live your life looking at a door and not go open it"? Maybe we can't; maybe like Inanna and our nearest primate cousins, we were born to lark and ramble and philander.

Yet most women for most of civilized history had no choice. The outlaw who broke the latch and bolted knew the same thrill of the opened door as men—only more so. The stakes were higher, the risks greater, and she had no cheering section.

But once she spread her wings, she soared. She recovered her mythic birthright as Queen of the Mountain, the almighty sex goddess who sings the "unencumbered song," as she cruises the cosmos for loot, kicks, and love slaves. This is the sacred rambler, lioness, and whore, whom no power can cuff and corral.

Whenever society thinks they've got her padlocked, she is out on the loose again. She's everywhere, even deep in macho country. She's the "little girl who lives on the hill" of the R & B classic who "rustles and tussles like Buffalo Bill," storms a rock star's seraglio, and throws her mojo on the master. The women flee and Bo Diddley cries, oh, how he cries, for mercy.

CHAPTER NINE

Goddess-Trippin': Into the Future

Women all want to be sirens but don't know their trade. —FEDERICO FELLINI

What destroyed them [women] all? Nothing but ignorant loving/ They were unversed in the art: love requires art to survive. —OVID

'Tis Woman that seduces all mankind. —JOHN GAY

The Master of the Universe has bestowed upon them [women] the empire of seduction; all men, weak or strong, are subjected to the weakness for the love of women.
—SHEIKH NEFZAWI

*A*t first glance the seductress seems a vanishing species. Caricatured, debased, and trivialized, she's dwindled into a Eurotart, gold digger, fellatrix, groupie, cupcake, and ho. She's lost her swerve and sovereignty. Cultural commentators say her glory days are over: Our age is simply "incapable of generating the great myths or figures of seduction." Men, they argue, have numbed out on sexual hype and erotic glut. Swamped by a surplus of party girls and easy pieces, they're inured to love queens. One blond babe is as good as another, easily exchanged for a newer, sleeker model next year. "Nobody," writes columnist Maureen Dowd, "really believes in romance any more."

Many should-be seductresses, it's true, have gone belly up. Sex goddess Jennifer Lopez admits she's an "idiot when she falls in love" and abased herself to a gangsta-rapper boyfriend like a "subordinate." Another glamorous self-made multimillionaire, Leslie Friedman, sank a fortune and three bitter years into an ignominious campaign for a husband. She bought décolleté designer dresses, stalked charity benefits, bribed colleagues, and talked "like a bimbo"—all for seventy-three dates without a bite.

Other high achievers, beyond such base ploys, aren't faring much better. Memoirs, novels, and sitcoms recount their abject maneuvers and serial humiliations at the hands of crude bruisers and slick Lotharios. The younger generation of college coeds is worse off still, subjected to a "brutal" hookup scene that reduces them to interchangeable sex toys and fraternity roadkill. Small wonder so many female leaders abdicate romantically (à la Hillary Clinton), and critics pronounce the death of the seductress in modern times.

The New Seductress

But a seductress comeback is afoot, both imaginatively and literally. Nancy Friday foreshadowed her return in *Women in Love* when she discovered that a significant sampling of women fantasized about "The Great Seductress." Now power vamps are everywhere: fiction, films, comic books, Internet, and television.

Sexy commandas pilot complex warships through intergalactic space in sci-fi pulps; wondersirens, like *Xena: Warrior Princess,* seduce and clobber recreants on prime TV; brassy manizers of the old Barbara Stanwyck mold inundate feature films; and full-blown seductresses, such as Sabina in *The Unbearable Lightness of Being,* wreak heartbreak in serious literature. Marvel Comics publishes a guide to its gallery of luscious sheroes, and Everquest logs on dozens of women each night who play virtual seductresses in its popular computer game.

Life is catching up with fantasy. In every category, curl-of-the-wave women are recovering their seductive birthright. They're taking their sexual power with them to the top, to boardrooms, playing fields, and concert halls. France, of all retro places, has produced a swanky cadre of "thinking [men's] Kim Basingers," cabinet officials who sail into top-level conferences with "a retinue of meek male attendants in their wake." American businesswomen are not far behind. A study finds that most have recouped the seductive arts of dress, réclame, rapport, and wit and frankly use their sexuality "to persuade, win favor, and gain power."

Gone too is yesterday's girl-jock in do-rags and baggy sweats. Triathletes flaunt designer haircuts, Olympians pose nude in *Rolling Stone* and cart boyfriends around, and boxer Laila Ali, Muhammad's daughter, packs as much punch outside as inside the ring. Married to her uxorious trainer, she pairs an unbroken boxing record with knockout sex appeal, appearing in a recent sports magazine as an Afrofemme Rita Hayworth: propped on a bed in a red sheath, one hand on a cocked hip, with attitude, in-yo-face sensuality, and drop-dead curves.

Siren pioneers also populate the arts. *Sorcières* again, they're throwing the old black magic of music, song, dance, poetry, theater, and pictures and putting men at their mercy. Pianist Helen Mercier spellbound Bernard Arnault, head of the LVMH fashion empire, at one of her concerts. He hunted her down, married her, and has remained transfixed, calling her "beautiful and fantastic" ten years and three children later.

Pop music divas have channeled the sex goddess too. Bold, brash, and bedizened like rhinestone Sheenas of the Jungle, these hip-hop sistas refer to themselves as "Lady Devastator" and "Miss Thang" and rip it down with divine attitude. They're sex empresses—no mistake—who turn men into housecats and demand queen bee treatment. If a guy can't give her "twenty-one orgasms," raps Lil' Kim, then bye-bye. "You can't stop a chick from ballin'."

In the visual arts there's another siren morph in progress. Female artists have scrapped their grungewear and one-of-the-boys affect for "seductress" makeovers. A mascot of this movement, the British bombshell Cecily Brown paints nine-foot canvases that throb with raw, assertive, gynocentric sexuality—hot pink and red whirlpools of erect penises, yonis, and explosive female orgasms. A sultry, whole-hog voluptuary, she wears designer boots and mascara and makes a killing on the man market. In a throwback to the days of the suicide sirens, one lover cut his throat and leaped (nonfatally) from her second-story window in February 2000.

Belles laides and Silver Foxes likewise are dialing up their allure and sexual clout. With the surge in weight gain and multiculturalism and the inevitable ennui caused by beauty inflation, "nonbeauties" have started to claim their place in the sun.

Larger women have their own fashion magazine, *Mode,* and for the first time a queen-size actress, Camryn Manheim, plays a heroine with a love interest on prime TV. Runways, fashion spreads, and television commercials teem with a mosaic of physical types: wide-bodied, beak-nosed, and every ethnic variation on earth. As trend spotter Faith Popcorn observes, "character," not looks, "will count" in the future. The Barbra Streisand/Bette Midler effect, so anomalous in the last century, is going mainstream.

The same holds true for senior sirens. As age is revised steadily upward, seductresses clock in older and older. Cher, with her entourage of paladins, refuses to pack up her toys and go home, and Elizabeth Taylor will not quit. This veteran of eight marriages and seventeen-plus romances, alleycats with the same lech-hearted zest of a decade ago and dates not one but four beaux. *Charmeuses* like ninety-three-year-old Kitty Carlisle Hart, with an adoring suitor and booked social calendar, are plotting the curve of the future, pushing the siren frontier to whatever year we choose.

The New Seductress: The Blocks

With the new millennium, we're poised for takeoff. We've got an open freeway, pacesetters at the fore, and a twin-turbo engine in our chassis. So why are we fumbling with the keys and locked in the garage? Most of us haven't been as lucky as the neoseductresses. Through centuries of conditioning, we've been palsied by a swarm of sexual fears and bad habits.

Until we can purge them, we can't peel out. First, we've gone soft in love, debilitated by millennia of enforced passivity and learned incapacity. We harbor an unnatural dread of erotic initiative and would rather suffer slow death with Saturday reruns than risk gaffes, rejections, and mistakes with serious consequences. But you have to play to win, to put it out there. And armed with lovesmarts, we can hedge our risks, spread our bets, and break the bank.

Along with erotic inertia, we're hounded by rivalry qualms. Afraid of opening the sluices of female competition, we downsex and damp our fires. If we snake all the guys, the girls will claw us to ribbons and cast us into social nowheresville.

Actual sirens, though, belie these social exile terrors. Although no favorite of women en masse, seductresses made friends at their own high watermark, shared a freemasonry among themselves, aided young protégées, and shrugged off feminine hostility. They didn't need the ladies' club; they had one of their own, a secret order of the goddess sorority.

Another spoke in our wheel is the fear of male emasculation and revenge. We're scared we'll deliver the deathblow to an already enfeebled masculine ego with our unbounded sexual power. It'll be a hollow victory if we win the battle and lose the war and wind up with a pack of spineless schlubs and vindictive malcontents.

Men, as we've seen, are already the weaker sex in sex, prey to a thousand performance bugbears. Now, however, they're in the throes of a massive crisis of confidence and gender identity. Because of feminist inroads and upheavals in the workplace, they're in a parlous state, shorn of their pride and ancient prerogatives. With women's increased erotic independence and rising expectations, they are especially nervous in the bedroom, the traditional proving ground of manhood. Studies show them more erotically vulnerable than women in general, more romantic and more attached to home, hearth, and mate. They place "all their emotional eggs in the basket of the woman [they] love."

Beneath the macho facade, they're shaking in their jackboots. Love doctors admonish women to treat these men-in-crisis with kid gloves, with fifties-style lickspittle and submissive feints. But paradoxically these servile tactics only reinforce men's chauvinistic defensive strategies and perpetuate the problem.

Only the seductress can repair the shredded male psyche and set

men on course again. As a reincarnation of man's first, sacred love object, she fulfills men's deepest heart songs and restores the primal,
mythic bases of masculine identity. By releasing our sex goddesses, we
release men too. "Set me free," Dumuzi implores the divine Inanna,
and she delivers him to true manhood. She incites him to gallantry
through her courtship demands, fuels his confidence through her sexpertise and praises, and sensitizes him through an annual maturity
journey each year to the underworld. She raises him from shepherd to
king, from macho pseudohero to real hero.

Coincidentally, several gender theorists have proposed the Dumuzi model as a solution to the current impasse. The older lunar heroes, they argue, with their expansive, holistic, pacific, and relational
masculinity can rescue men from the narrow, brutal virility inherited
from the violent solar gods. Some, like Robert Bly, envision a perfected female counterpart for this redeemed man: a seductress, a Kali
sex goddess and "Golden Woman."

But we can't retrieve this "Golden Woman" until we finish the job
and jettison some toxic cultural baggage along with our fears. As the
seductresses have shown us, we have to slough off female socialization. We've been carefully indoctrinated in erotic disempowerment—
raised wrong, maleducated, and media poisoned.

From earliest infancy girls are trained to conform, obey, keep
house, sit pretty, and blend in. The entertainment industry and standard education reinforce the process with Strawberry Shortcake heroines and sex-appropriate games, toys, and classroom protocol. Their
spirits and libidos are subtly shrink-wrapped for domestic consumption.

By adolescence the socialization is complete. As Carol Gilligan,
Mary Pipher, and others document, teenagers lose whatever strut they
possessed and cave into a contaminated mass culture. They learn to
snag guys the MTV way, through beauty, slutwear, group think, eager-
to-please passivity, and sexual compliance. With demolished self-
concepts, impoverished personalities, and degraded kneepad skills,
they're setups for romantic disaster. Many never learn to get their hus-
tle on and drift into a midlife limbo of the discarded and desperately
alone.

The New Seductive Way

Once we've delivered ourselves from these cultural bogies and detoxed our psyches, we can begin to recoup our craft. Since every era requires its own erotic menu (disinhibition, for example, in repressed Victorian times), we'll need to fine-tune the love arts for the twenty-first century. The basic blueprint of course never changes. Engraved deep in the erotic memory of the race, the Seductive Way maps the sexual drama and subliminally, ineluctably determines how we arouse, heighten, and retain desire. But we have to retrofit it for modern purposes, adjust the *ars amatoria* to serve our special needs and preferences.

Physical Arts

In our hyperreal world of surfaces and spin, we've gone hog-wild over physical inducements to love. We learn eye locks for love eternal, twist ourselves into tantric tortoises, and furiously tone up, make up, and dress up. But the material onslaught has backfired. Our senses have been anesthetized through overkill. And sex itself has grown banal in the tell-all, show-all carnival of frankness. What's required now is erotic shock treatment, a way to kick up sensuous turn-ons again.

Amid the media cavalcade of Stepford Barbies and the deluge of mass-marketed, assembly-line sexual stimulants—name-brand body oils, bras, and romantic ballads—we've been lost in the crowd. Since the whole point of the "ritual theater of sex" is a one in a million impact, we've got to get exceptional and quirky again. Break from the pack. Stamp all our bodily lures, as the seductresses did, with signature me-ness, and hand-tooled extravaganza.

In bed, for example, we need to haul back and heed the cry of our own hot buttons and anatomy. We've listened too long to experts who tell us how our equipment works, how we're programmed for a lower sex drive, monogamy, affection, commitment, a rich provider, and a one-shot orgasm based on the male model.

Unfettered women, like the steamy seductresses, show us our natural, goddess-given heritage—female hypersexuality, rock slide multi-orgasms, and a disposition to philander, often simultaneously with comely studs. Lacking our clutched self-consciousness, the great sex queens laid it down the old way, the Inanna way: Mae West with her muscleman marathons and thousand and one climaxes and La Belle Otero with her eight-a-nighters.

We've been terrorized into underperformance. Instead of a female Viagra (an oxymoron if there ever was one), we should tune out the advice fascists and befriend our inner she-savage. Sociologists suggest that the increase in cyberromance and vicarious sex will create a "touch hunger" in this century, a desire for the real, unscripted thing. The seductress will be there with her adorers, riding buck and sating her sacred hypersexuality.

Dance and gesture can be juiced up too. Although we attend swing, funk, and aerobics classes in record numbers, we're enslaved by regimented, follow-the-leader routines. Or the reverse. We scorn lessons and spastically let it all hang out. Seductresses, by contrast, trained seriously, then copped their own moves.

Kinesthetic shamans, they put steam in their walk, surrendered to the beat, and reinvoked the archaic priestesses who writhed, jived, and pumped their pelvises to summon the Divine Feminine and torch male souls. Modern Afrosirens are on to this: They learn to "roll their body good" as a major "part of the public performance in attracting a partner." It's a promise of sexual skill, a show of *self,* and the goddess's calling card.

We've not made the most of music either. Awash in sonic stimulation night and day, we're flooded by so many formulaic love songs that our aural receptors have dulled. Sensitizing them again may necessitate drastic measures—self-designed sound tracks or live ones. Seductresses routinely played instruments and snake-charmed suitors with bravura songs and melody, right down to Edith Piaf fifty years ago.

Renaissance courtesans excelled on the lute and viol, and the unmusical Isabella Stewart Gardner practiced scales each day for a euphonious speaking voice. An unplugged musical moment, spoken, sung, or played, delivers a direct hit to the libido and induces the divine delirium of the first sexual rituals.

As for our settings, they'd be pronounced impossible–bland and standardized–by the great *sorcières* of interior design. Intimidated by style czars, we've been herded into copycat, genteel, color-coordinated milieus. We're decorator-dependent, afraid to strike out and design off-beat, seductive rooms of our own such as Minette Helvétius's blue salon athrong with cats in satin coats or Louise de Vilmorin's mind-altering maze of alcoves full of odd tchotchkes, a stag's head named Fifi, and a stray refrigerator.

When seductresses dined, they didn't turn to Martha Stewart. No more by the book about food than anything else, they played fast and loose with recipes and produced dramatic, outré menus of their own: southern soul food mixed with haute cuisine in Wallis Simpson's case; an exotic pea, lemon, and sherry puree in Ninon de Lenclos's.

Nor did they indulge to excess. Contrary to Messalina-at-the-orgy stereotypes, the *grandes amoureuses* ate and drank (if at all) in moderation. Cruise and resort advertisements promote a pigout version of romantic dining, Neronian portions and entire bottles of champagne, more designed for Pickwickian syndrome than a hot tussle on a hotel floor. If we want to reap the full sensual return from cuisine, we'll have to season it up with surprise-me flare and dine again for seduction rather than satiety or displaced lust.

On the fashion front, we're closer to divine dress than we've been in decades. We're glamming up, piling it on, and personalizing our appearance through a thousand style options. Specialists computer-image our "look" and custom-design our hair color, cosmetics, and wardrobe. Glitz is in: sequined nail extensions, silver slip dresses, diamond Rolexes, and fun furs.

But despite the goddess dazzle, we've turned down the applause meter. We've fluffed ourselves up by formula and Seventh Avenue diktat and find ourselves replicated like a hall of mirrors at every club and opening. Although the industry peddles the notion of personal self-expression and éclat, clothes are merchandised for "niche conformity"–prefab and predictable. The peel ethos has boomeranged too. Who looks twice at a troupe of coeds in thong bikinis and triangle tops?

Seductresses often faced similar overexposure problems, especially in the high-flash, anything goes cultures of the Second Empire and classical Greece. But they learned to dress with knock-'em-dead originality. During the heyday of harlot regalia in ancient Greece, for example, when courtesans wore see-through bright tunics, pancake makeup, and festoons of jewelry, only Phyrne stopped traffic. Men lined up four deep in the agora each morning to watch her walk past, swathed from head to toe in a dark opaque robe, without ornaments or face paint.

In scent, though, we've finally got it right. After a brief infatuation with body odors, we're back to goddess basics. Like Inanna and her priestesses, we saturate ourselves in perfumes (even custom-mixed) and suffuse our environs with candles, incense, and aphrodisiacal oils when we set our love snares.

Psychological Arts

But we've OD'd on physical enticements, the least potent and most elementary in the Seductive Way. Except for a tweak in the direction of novelty, drama, and individuality, they've had enough play. While we've been crunching at the gym and buying lingerie, our erotic imaginations have been on vacation, enfeebled by the false promises of a slick consumer culture.

As every seductress knows, the mind is where the action is—the stratospheric passions and soul-singeing enchantments. The ancient Greek seductress and erotic master teacher Aspasia took it for granted that her students were already versed in sexual positions, song, dance, poetry recital, and "the use of oil, cosmetics, and aphrodisiacal drinks and foods." Her entire *ta erotika* (seductive system) focused on cerebral charms: character development, mind-body integration, and the psychology of the hunt, which included craft, wit, "honest praise," and "words of enchantment and magic."

Words today may be our least utilized erotic resource. Everywhere linguists and cultural critics deplore the current low ebb in female conversational skills. Women, trained as listeners and peacemakers, have lost the art of *bel parlare*, of "fascinating speech." We have trouble telling jokes, clam up in male company, and mouth facile femme-speak like dolls with pullcords. We ratify, concur, question, conciliate, perform the interactional shitwork, and talk about "tedious subject matter." We've cut out our tongues on the false premise that "knowledge is power and the lack of it charmingly feminine."

By muzzling ourselves, we've spiked our best guns. Every seductress worth her stag line had the gift of gab and a trove of quips, quotes, opinions, facts, anecdotes, and sexy zingers. The plainest sirens in the pantheon—the skeletal Catherine Sedley and the prognathic, hooknosed Cleopatra—became fabled enchantresses through their verbal wizardry alone. "As a bull's horns are bound with ropes," say the amorists, "so are men's hearts with pleasant words." The chute gates are open, the Brahmas loose in the rodeo ring, awaiting "ladies of words of power."

Another erotic skill to dust off and put back in circulation is festivity. In spite of unparalleled prosperity and post–9/11 solidarity, we're mired in gloom. We're a fun-challenged civilization, chronically worried and low-spirited, seeking frantic relief in canned entertainment, mood-altering drugs, and joyless anarchic binges.

The sex goddess by definition commands celebration. Her divine élan requires that mankind frolic, unbend, and ecstatically rejoice at her altar. The seductress therefore incarnates joie de vivre and acts as the iconic Mistress of Revels.

She uncorks the champagne and strikes up the band; she throws private theatricals with potatoes for tickets like Pauline Viardot and serenades the city by gondola like Veronica Franco. Some party mavens are born, not made. But as in the Renaissance, we can learn "how to be festive," we can study celebration like cuisine or tai chi; check your Prozac at the door.

After festivity comes the labyrinth. In our overmediated age of relationship coaches and conflict management, we've settled into a flannel nightgown version of romantic love—comfy, familiar, easy-as-Sunday-morning. We're not cutting the mustard; we're cutting Z's, counseling, cuddling, and pair-bonding ourselves into erotic narcolepsy. Passion needs wake-up calls. It needs vital tension and tourbillion to survive: difficulty, challenge, nips of pain, and a journey through the deity's whorled and tortuous erotic maze.

Lola Montez would be a couples' therapy nightmare today. With her, men shot the rapids—one minute, pitched to paradise; the next, plunged into an inferno of white water. She played rough. She sent lovers sachets from her vagina and ravished them in bed, then emptied their coffers, threw their possessions out the window, and took them to task with guns and knives. But passion she knew. By far the greatest seductress of the nineteenth century, she was adored to madness by the cognoscenti and never discarded or forgotten.

Philosopher Jean Baudrillard complains that we're living in a "culture of premature ejaculation" through "too much security." Seductresses don't trade in that culture. As avatars of "Our Lady of the Labyrinth," they're delay queens who specialize in the longest route home, via corkscrew turns, false doors, dangerous drops, and vanishing perspectives. It's the archetypic love map, etched for eternity in the male brain, forever beckoning. The call to adventure is the real love call.

If seductresses stirred men up and put them through labyrinthine paces, they also massaged them. Accomplished smoothies, they clairvoyantly intuited their lovers' needs and wounds and salved them with ego strokes and TLC. They had Ph.D.'s in people skills—another lost twenty-first-century art. Desocialized by cyberspace, television, the demise of manners, and feminism's anticharm legacy, we've forgotten the winning ways of the enchantresses.

According to Daniel Goleman, we've spiraled into terminal social ineptitude, unable to interpret others' emotions or address them adequately. A staggering ten million suffer from social anxiety disorder and lack the necessary know-how to navigate a dinner date without a sex depressant like Paxil.

Sirens weren't born with an extra gene for politesse; they acquired it through observation, practice, and help from wise elders. Françoise de Maintenon, for instance, was such a klutz when she first entered society that she cowered speechless in the corner of her husband's drawing room.

But she apprenticed herself to the grand swami of couth Ninon de Lenclos and developed into the suavest operator at Versailles. "Beauty without grace," quipped the sage Ninon, "is a hook without bait."

With savoir-faire sweetening our postmillennial brains, glamour, and shiv, we're baited, as they say in fishing, for the honey hole.

Ultimately, though, the biggest draw on the market will be strong, self-complete supremas. With the spread of conformity and image-driven superficiality, the allure of an individuated woman in full possession of herself and her powers will prove irresistible. We were born for plentitude and inner fulfillment. Abraham Maslow thought self-actualization an innate drive. Nature intended us to grow, burgeon, and maximize our individual potential, to be world-class achievers like Lou Andreas-Salomé, Émilie du Châtelet, and Catherine the Great.

Nature also intended us to win the best men this way. "Whenever a woman has captivated a man with a lifelong fascination," writes erotic philosopher Ellen Key, "the secret has been that he never exhausted her; that she 'has not been one, but a thousand.' "

As heiresses of the first omninatured deity, seductresses are replete and contain multitudes: male/female dualities, contradictions, protean identities, and myriad dimensions. Like the self-glorifying divinities, they have giant, unladylike egos and vaunt their charms without apologies. (Who says a little saving grandiosity isn't good for women?)

They're also Inanna the "lioness." Whether blessed with iconoclastic backgrounds or cursed with hardship, they muscle their way to the top, seizing the right mentors and lovers and kicking obstacles to the curb. They're the "goddess unbound by social order," norm smashers who live by a different law, the divine right of sex queens.

All this may be old news for today's sirens. More entitled, confident, educated, mobile, and sexually liberated than previous generations, they've moved beyond yesterday's constricting fears and complexes. Intuitively they've mastered psychological arts and rejiggered the mix for postmodern susceptibilities.

It's instinctive. The Seductive Way is our ancestral inheritance, implanted in the collective unconscious, to be accessed and repossessed. The wisdom will find us out. "Seduction," predicts Baudrillard, "is destiny." The seductress may have petered out at the fin de millénium, but she's roaring back.

The Future: Seduction and the Seductress

Futurists forecast a whole new sexual order on the horizon, a swing of the cosmic pendulum. They foresee a culture-wide period of "feminization," in which sex and reproduction are separated; women's characters, more self-integrated and androgynous; and "global equality," even female "primacy," is institutionalized. Society, they prophesy, will be forced to "accede to what women en masse want to do."

It's just a question of what we want to do. Although the stage is set and the cast assembled for a seductress revival, most women haven't heeded the call. Conflicted and browbeaten, they're marking time, afraid of change. Yet we've come to a crossroads. The "plague years" have bottomed out. With the promises of the sexual revolution in tatters and female sexual pride on life support, we've been pushed, willy-nilly, to a breaking point, to action.

Male Resistance

As in the past, it may not be all smooth sailing. Seduction riles and dismantles patriarchal domination. Since Phyrne and Aspasia first came downwind of Greek patriarchal vengeance, enchantresses have been sand in the social machinery, ostracized, vilified, and persecuted.

America, with its puritanical, masculinist heritage, has been especially hard on freewheeling *charmeuses*. In Salem they were burned as witches; in Hollywood, pulped and recycled as noir hellcats or sick hoochies. A hundred years ago Henry Adams warned that the powers that be would never tolerate an "American Venus."

Some guys out there want to make sure it never does. Bruised and battered by the gender revolution, these macho diehards are not going to take this lying down. They've unleashed backlash campaigns (of the kind chronicled by Susan Faludi), pseudo-Darwinian defenses of male sexual superiority, and a slew of defensive shenanigans: commitment phobia, date rapes, and dominance games.

So we may have to brace for resistance. A beleaguered male minority isn't about to cheer our parade. But the seductresses, no strangers to sniper fire, can show us how to deal. Premier operators, they circumvented the flak, ignoring criticism and disporting above the machinations of half men with heroes of their own rank. When it came to the pass, they put on Inanna's armor—her "mighty love clothes," and "fiendish wings"—and hid scorpions under their beds. But, then, love has never been a game for cowards.

Male Support

Most men, though, are all too ready for the seductress. They're tired of copping tough guy postures and shouldering the globe like Atlas. Their sensibilities are tuned up for outsize, magisterial love goddesses. At base men have never lost their prehistoric preference for the great goddess, the mistress of the universe and plenum of being. Evolutionary psychologist Geoffrey F. Miller believes they've always preferred magnificas over mere lookers with low waist-to-hip ratios.

Recently *Esquire* celebrated "dangerous" sex queens who take charge, pulsate with "chthonic forces," and pitch men into "fatal ecstasy." *Talk* ran a similar tribute to men's "private goddess"—the "butch and femme," "potent and tenacious" action heroine.

Psychologist John Munder Ross thinks alpha women of this mold attract men today because they permit an opportunity for male heroism and a genuine display of *cojones*. What "the lover" most craves, he writes, is to "pay homage to Aphrodite." The root meaning of "hero" is "to serve." Men yearn, as the Mexican film *Esmeralda Comes by Night* dramatizes, for their predestined place in the cosmic scheme of things: at the feet of the Almighty Feminine.

Esmeralda, the heroine of this movie, based on a novel by Elena Poniatowska, is an Inanna redux. A health professional of independent means, she's a lusty life force and rambling rose who's married to five men simultaneously. Unfazed by moral convention, she rotates merrily among husbands until she's arrested at the altar on the verge of acquiring number six.

In the trial that follows she seduces everyone, including the chief prosecuting officer. While the court deliberates, her husbands and placard-waving protesters descend on the prison and demand her release. Freed by popular acclaim, she's feted at the end by all her lovers and spouses.

Each dances with her in turn to a slow salsa, "Lady Traveler Who Goes by Sky and Sea," after which her poet-husband recites a fulsome encomium. "You are a dream!" he exclaims. As the film fades out, rain sweeps over the parched town and the prosecuting officer picks up an umbrella and dances in the downpour like Gene Kelly.

As in the ancient mythic drama, the sex goddess reanimates the arid earth. Her male votaries celebrate their renewed virility and carouse in sacred ecstasy. That the film comes from the heartland of machismo suggests the crushing modern burden of hypermasculinity and the accompanying fantasy of release. None of which means that men welcome polygamous "Lady Travelers" for their wives. But Esmeralda embodies an atavistic wish for women nearer the first divinity: autonomous, self-contained, polymorphous, prepotent, adventurous, fascinating, and so hypersexed she needs five men—at least. As her husband's poem underscores, she is a "dream."

But in dreams begin responsibilities, a directive to speed the day. Full erotic empowerment, the last feminist frontier, is there for the taking. Like Esmeralda, we can walk away with all the chips, success at work and love and the men of our choice. We can recover our divine sexual primacy—orgasmic megapleasure, va-va-voom charisma, and our role as arbiter in the mating game. With our lovecraft, we can twist a man's heart like a pretzel. And we don't have to compromise our brains, abilities, and principles. The higher we climb, the greater the sex appeal.

Not that sexual sovereignty will solve all our problems. It won't banish conflicts, incompatibilities, wailing children, shattered careers, and betrayals of the flesh and spirit. It doesn't guarantee faithful lovers or happy ever after. But it helps our chances and torches up our lives so that they're more vital, interesting, integrated—and sexier. We're ready for this. A third sexual revolution, if we wish, is on the horizon. The pieces are in place: a crack operating manual, inspirational heroines, talismanic stories, and perfect timing.

"Revolution," by definition, means "new things," *res novae.* A seductress uprising, for a change, won't desolate and ravage the old order. It benefits both sexes. The 2050 temptress will also be something new, a goddess-trippin' siren with technocharms we can only imagine.

Yet in essence nothing about her will be really new. Her core identity and Seductive Way will be as they were forty thousand years ago when they were fused into the human libido, when the Divine Feminine catwalked through the cosmos and laid down the law in love: women on top, on the move, aureoled in satiety, and trailed by squadrons of lunar heroes—happy at last—in her labyrinthine toils.

NOTES

PREFACE

p. *xi* **Across the culture** . . . : Linda Grant, *Sexing the Millennium* (New York: Grove Press, 1994), 6.

xi **The population of** . . . : Quoted in Candace Bushnell, Ariel Levy, "The Blonde Who's Had More Fun," *New York* (February 11, 2002), 48. "The number of never married American women more than tripled over the past two decades," Sarah Bernard, "Success and the Single Girl," *New York* (April 26, 1999), 34.

xi **We say we're** . . . : Susan Quilliam, *Women on Sex* (New York: Barricade Books, 1994), 2, and Marcelle Karp and Debbie Stoller, eds., *Bust Guide to the New Girl Order* (New York: Penguin, 1999), front pages.

xi **"No one disputes** . . .": Gina Kolata, *New York Times*, June 21, 1998, 3, and Daphne Merkin, "The Marriage Mystique," *New Yorker* (August 3, 1998), 74.

xiii **Whether consciously or** . . . : Ovid, *The Art of Love*, trans. Rolfe Humphries (Bloomington: Indiana University Press, 1957), Book 3, 155.

xiv **Lola Montez lectured** . . . : Sixteen of the sixty or so *charmeuses* in this book shared their seductive wisdom, either directly in nonfiction guides or indirectly in fiction and poetry, and focused on psychological siegecraft. See the work of Cleopatra, Aspasia, Louise Labé, Veronica Franco, Émilie du Châtelet, Ninon de Lenclos, Germaine de Staël, George Sand, Lou Andreas-Salomé, Martha Gellhorn, Louise de Vilmorin, Lola Montez, Victoria Woodhull Claflin, Frank Leslie, Mae West, and Colette.

xiv **It's no coincidence** . . . : Rollo May, *Love and Will* (New York: Dell, 1969), 146.

xiv **"Venus favors the** . . .": Ovid, *Art of Love*, Book 1, 124.

xiv **They'd impress on** . . . : Guy de Maupassant, *Bel-Ami*, trans. Douglas Parmee (New York: Penguin Books, 1975), 317.

xv **Second-wave feminists** . . . : Germaine Greer, *The Madwoman's Underclothes* (New York: Atlantic Monthly Press, 1986), 152–68, and Simone de Beauvoir, *The Second Sex*, trans. H. M. Parshley (New York: Bantam, 1952), 645.

xv **"Seduction," notes philosopher** . . . : Jean Baudrillard, *Seduction*, trans. Brian Singer (New York: St. Martin's Press, 1990), 8.

xvi **Nancy Friday said . . .** : Nancy Friday, *Women on Top: How Real Life Has Changed Women's Sexual Fantasies* (New York: Pocket Books, 1991), 64.

CHAPTER I: SEDUCTRESS: THE WOMEN AND THE ART

2 **They strike terror . . .** : Men, when it comes to the sexually autonomous woman, are prey to a witch's brew of terrors. They're afraid, first, of her biological superiority. Sexually insatiable, the progenitor of life, she holds the trump cards, seeming to incarnate nature itself. As the personification of nature she contains the destructive, anarchic currents of sexuality—impulses to violence, cruelty, mayhem, and emotional chaos. She also embodies sexual mystery. To encounter women in the erogenous zone is to trespass upon that irrational no-man's-land, meet the enigmatic sphinx, and confront the riddle.

A loss of power perhaps frightens men most of all. Despite their sexual strut and bravado, they are "inescapably at [women's] mercy" in the bedroom. Inadequacy threatens a man at every boudoir threshold, and when he leaves it, after witnessing a woman's orgasmic inexhaustibility, he faces another rejection anxiety: cuckoldry. Then another one looms: a horror of engulfment, of being sucked into women's sexual valence, of losing selfhood and consciousness and drowning. At a primitive level, men are terrified that women will devour, imprison, and annihilate them, draw them to the ocean floor like Lorelei and wrap them in seaweed.

Men dread the thought of castration as well. Because women lack penises, men subconsciously fear retaliation in kind. Men employ a wide assortment of counterphobic strategies, such as Madonna cults and grandiose claims about male sexuality, but they really *are* the weaker sex in eros, beset with apprehensions and insecurities, especially in the case of those unsure of their manhood. Wolfgang Lederer, M.D., *The Fear of Women* (New York: Grune & Stratton, 1968), 220. For more on this male sexual fear of women, see Camille Paglia, *Sexual Personae* (New York: Vintage, 1990), passim; Karen Horney, M.D., "The Dread of Women," *Feminine Psychology*, ed. Harold Kelman, M.D. (New York: Norton, 1967), 133–46; Sigmund Freud, *Sexuality and the Psychology of Love*, intro. Philip Rieff (New York: Collier, 1963); Karl Stern, *The Flight from Women* (New York: Paragon House, 1965); H. R. Hays, *The Dangerous Sex: The Myth of Feminine Evil* (New York: Putnam's, 1964); and Carl Jung, "Man and Woman," *The Feminine Image in Literature*, ed. Barbara Warren (Rochelle Park, N.J.: Hayden, 1973), 250–60.

3 **Thirty to 50 percent . . .** : Samuel S. Janus, M.D., and Cynthia L. Janus, M.D., *The Janus Report on Sexual Behavior* (New York: John Wiley, 1993), 27 and 162. They claim that despite the increase in sexual activity, only 15 percent always have orgasms during lovemaking, 18. See also Susan Quilliam, *Women on Sex* (New York: Barricade Books, 1994), 221. Double the number of women as men today have problems with sexual pleasure: "There are 50 million women with sexual dysfunction—an inability to experience sexual pleasure or to achieve orgasm." Myron Murdock, M.D., quoted in Mary Ann Marshall, "A Dose of Desire," *Mademoiselle* (November 1998), 90.

In another study, 50 to 60 percent reach orgasm always or most of the time. Cited in *Modern Maturity* (September–October, 1999), 57. The *New York Times*, May

17, 1998, reports that women are gravitating to Viagra because it can take them as long as one and a half hours to climax. A landmark study in the *Journal of the American Medical Association* 281 (February 10, 1999), 537–44, found that 43 percent of women (contrasted with 31 percent of men) "aren't interested in sex, fail to lubricate, can't reach orgasm, or experience pain." Cited in Stephen Rae, "RX: Desire," *Modern Maturity* (March–April 2001), 89. Gynecologist Dr. Jennie Freiman confirmed the high prevalence of anorgasmic dysfunction among her successful, educated clientele in New York City.

3 **"Seduction," says philosopher** . . . : Baudrillard, *Seduction*, 7.

3 **Unless "subverted by** . . .**":** Mary Batten, *Sexual Strategies: How Females Chose Their Mates* (New York: Putnam's, 1992), 97.

3 **Sexier by a** . . . : The half-male, half-female Tireseas of Greek myth was struck blind by the angry father god Zeus because he said that women got ten times more pleasure in sex than men. The myth, despite the legends of a lower female sex drive, has recently been scientifically validated.

The clitoris has eight thousand nerve fibers, twice the number of the penis. Women's climaxes last twice as long as men's, yield stronger spasms (because of more vasocongestion and larger surface area), and become increasingly intense with repetition.

If continuously stimulated, they can achieve up to fifty an hour–the number limited only by muscle fatigue–throughout their reproductive lives and beyond. Dr. Mary Jane Sherfey believes that women's souped-up sexuality predisposed them early on to polyandry and cat-prowling peregrinations beyond the home that prompted the male crackdown still in evidence today.

See Mary Jane Sherfey, M.D., *The Nature and Evolution of Female Sexuality* (New York: Vintage, 1966); William H. Masters and Virginia E. Johnson, *Human Sexual Response* (New York: Bantam, 1966); Sarah Blaffer Hrdy, *The Woman That Never Evolved* (Cambridge, Mass.: Harvard University Press, 1981); Natalie Angier, *Woman: An Intimate Geography* (New York: Houghton Mifflin, 1999); and Helen Fisher, *The First Sex* (New York: Random House, 1999), 208–10. Throughout human history, almost every culture, until quite recently, has recognized women's hypersexuality and insatiability.

4 **As the construction** . . . : "The primordial image," says Erich Neumann, is "the self-portrait of the instinct," and governs erotic behavior like a "magnetic field." He adds: "Male sexuality is influenced by the archetypal figure of the Feminine which is active in the unconscious." *The Great Mother*, trans. Ralph Manheim (Princeton: Princeton University Press, 1963), 6 and 97.

Also see Joseph Campbell: "There can be no doubt that in the very earliest ages of human history the magical force and wonder of the female was [*sic*] no less a marvel than the universe itself; and this gave to woman a prodigious power. . . ." Campbell agrees with many other students of myth that this powerful female archetype is rooted deep in the male subpsyche. Quoted in Jamake Highwater, *Myth and Sexuality* (New York: Meridan, 1991), 36–37.

4 **In one Neolithic** . . . : See fig. 6.6, Timothy Taylor, *The Prehistory of Sex* (New York: Bantam, 1996), 160.

5 **We hear the** . . . : Quoted in Havelock Ellis, *Studies in the Psychology of Sex* (New York: Random House, 1906), vol. 1, 138 and 136.

5 **Many seductresses of course** . . . : April Fitzlyon, *The Price of Genius: A Life of Pauline Viardot* (London: John Calder, 1979), 70.

5 **"Hit on a . . ."**: Jeremy Johnson, "Dating the Elderly," *Abercrombie and Fitch* (Spring 2001), 62.

6 **Feminists as diverse** . . . : See de Beauvoir, *The Second Sex*, who says that the temptress, by definition, "denies her brain," 645. Susan Brownmiller continues this line of thought: "Knowledge is power and the lack of it is charmingly feminine; between the bluestocking and the dumb broad, there is no doubt who lies closer to a natural feminine state," *Femininity* (New York: Fawcett Columbine, 1984), 110. Germaine Greer copped out of the whole game because she was "sick of belying [her] own intelligence." *The Female Eunuch* (New York: Bantam Books, 1970), 58.

7 **Great leaders, claim** . . . : The article that advances this view is considered canonical in studies of human sexuality: David Givens, "The Nonverbal Basis of Attraction," *Psychiatry* 41 (November 1978), 346–59.

7 **With classic calumny** . . . : Quoted in Robert Browning, *Justinian and Theodora* (New York: Praeger, 1971), 259, and quoted in Sabrina Mervin and Carol Prunhuber, *Women Around the World and Through the Ages* (Wilmington, Del.: Atomium, 1990), 197. Charles Diehl, *Byzantine Empresses* (New York: Alfred A. Knopf, 1963), 48.

7 **The *Machtweiber* (German** . . .: See Virginia Allen, who defines the *Machtweib* as a "woman of power," a "devastatingly beautiful, seductive" femme fatale who aspires to wealth, power, and Imperial favor." Goethe's Countess Adelheid and Lady Macbeth are two examples of these seductresses of political ambition and power. *The Femme Fatale: Erotic Icon* (Troy, N.Y.: Whitston Publishing, 1983), 16.

8 **Biobehaviorist Richard Wright** . . . : Quoted and discussed in Angier, *Woman: An Intimate Geography*, 343–45.

8 **Intelligent women everywhere** . . . : Ingrid Bengis, *Combat in the Erogenous Zone* (New York: Bantam, 1972), 42. This notion, propagated by the second-wave feminists of the seventies and eighties, sounds passé now, but it was the unanimous, party line. "To admit the necessity of seduction," they believed, was "to admit that one [had] not the strength to command." Sally Kempton, *Esquire* (October 1979), 254 and 472.

9 **"It takes a . . ."**: Quoted in Edgar H. Cohen, *Mademoiselle Libertine: A Portrait of Ninon de Lenclos* (Boston: Houghton Mifflin, 1970), 92.

9 **The art of** . . . : Paul Friedrich, *The Meaning of Aphrodite* (Chicago: University of Chicago Press, 1978), 144. Although the art of love has been debased in recent decades into sexual cookbooks and flirtation manuals, it has a respected history. Havelock Ellis says it dates back at least as far as "the ancient Greek erotic writings" by women that have been lost. "Art of Love," *Studies in the Psychology of Sex*, vol. 2, 507–75. Summarizing the art, Ellis says it recognized that love was not "a mere animal instinct or a mere pledged duty, but . . . a complex, humane, and refined relationship which demanded cultivation," 514.

Among the key texts are Ovid, *Art of Love;* Andreas Capellanus, *The Art of Courtly Love*, ed. Frederick W. Locke and trans. John Jay Parry (New York: Frederick Ungar, 1957); Montaigne, "That Our Desire Is Increased by Difficulty," and

"On Some Verses of Virgil," *The Complete Essays of Montaigne*, trans. Donald M. Frame, vols. 2 and 3, 1585–88 (Garden City, N.Y.: Anchor, 1960), 57–122; Robert Burton, *The Anatomy of Melancholy*, ed. Floyd Dell and Paul Jordan-Smith (New York: Tudor, 1927), 611–866; Stendhal, *Love*, trans. Gilvert and Suzanne Sale (Harmondswood, U.K.: Penguin, 1957); and Honoré de Balzac, *The Physiology of Marriage*, ed. J. Walker McSpadden (Philadelphia: Avil, 1901).

See also Bertrand Russell, *Marriage and Morals* (New York: Bantam, 1929); José Ortega y Gasset, *On Love*, trans. Toby Talbot (New York: NAL, 1957); Ellen Key, *Love and Ethics* (New York: B. W. Huebsch, 1911); André Maurois, "The Art of Loving," *The Art of Living*, trans. James Whitall (Bombay: D. P. Tapaporevala, 1940); Theodor Henrik van de Velde, M.D., *Ideal Marriage: Its Physiology and Technique* (Westport, Conn.: Greenwood, 1965) and Theodor Reik, *Psychology of Sex Relations* (New York: Farrar & Rinehart, 1945).

More recently, Ethel Person and Helen Fisher have written brilliantly in this tradition. See *Dreams of Love and Fateful Encounters* (New York: Penguin, 1988) and *Anatomy of Love: The Mysteries of Mating, Marriage, and Why We Stray* (New York: Fawcett Columbine, 1992). Though less focused and comprehensive, Diane Ackerman's *Natural History of Love* belongs to the genre (New York: Random House, 1994).

9 **They want to see . . . :** Love's first quality, said Stendhal, is "impact," a blowout where men see stars, and feel the divine power to their boots. Stendhal, *Love*, 250.

9 **But seductresses and . . . :** Fashion has been the bête noire of feminists. "Serious women," they proclaim, "have a difficult time with clothes," and accuse the fashion industry of inflicting mutilization, subservience, commodification, and caricatured femininity. Brownmiller, *Femininity*, 110.

10 **Many plain sirens . . . :** Bernard Rudofsky, *The Unfashionable Human Body* (Garden City, N.Y.: Anchor, 1974), 62.

10 **"He who is . . .":** Quoted in Baudrillard, *Seduction*, 90.

11 **"Every woman," say . . . :** Maurois, "The Art of Loving," 26.

11 **The house of . . . :** See Gaston Bachelard, *The Poetics of Space*, trans. Maria Jolas (Boston: Beacon, 1964), 3.

11 **Music is depth . . . :** See F. Gonzalez-Crussi, *The Five Senses* (New York: Vintage, 1989), 37. "The power of music over the human mind," he writes, "cannot be overestimated." For a more complete account, see Robert Jourdain, *Music, the Brain and Ecstasy* (New York: Avon, 1997).

11 **After Ivan Turgenev . . . :** Quoted in Fitzlyon, *Price of Genius*, 150.

12 **From the *Kama Sutra* . . . :** Ovid, *Art of Love*, Book 3, 163.

12 **"'Twas surely the . . .":** Thomas Fuller, quoted in Burton Stevenson, *The Home Book of Quotations* (New York: Dodd, Mead, 1956), 362.

12 **As study after . . . :** For this see Shere Hite, *The Hite Report on Male Sexuality* (New York: Ballantine, 1981), which finds that men yearn for multiorgasmic women and feel angry with anorgasmic ones, 616–73. Other studies confirm this: Anthony Pietropinto and Jacqueline Simenauer, *Beyond the Male Myth* (New York: NAL, 1977), 33–34, and Willard Gaylin, M.D., who writes, "The more orgasms he provokes in a woman, the greater his power." *The Male Ego* (New York: Viking, 1992), 132.

Poet William Blake put it best two hundred years ago: "What is it in women that men require?/ The lineaments of satisfied desire." Theodor Reik speculates that this stems from male performance anxiety, an unconscious identification with the other, and the contagious effects of sexual excitement. *Psychology of Sex Relations*, 237–39.

13 **"Plow my vulva . . ."**: Quoted in Diane Wolkstein and Samuel Noah Kramer, *Inanna Queen of Heaven and Earth* (New York: Harper & Row, 1983), 37, 48, and 39.

13 **Feminists used to . . .** : Eva Figes, quoted in Irene Franck and David Brownstone, *The Women's Desk Reference* (New York: Viking, 1993), 665.

13 **It's a "continuous . . ."**: Ellis, *Psychology of Sex Relations*, vol. 2, 547.

13 **Archaeologist Timothy Taylor . . .** : Taylor, *Prehistory of Sex*, 7.

13 **Cerebral lures consequently . . .** : William Shakespeare, *A Midsummer Night's Dream*, ed. Madeleine Doran (Baltimore: Penguin, 1959), act 5, scene 1, line 8, 98.

14 **Philosopher Jean Baudrillard . . .** : Baudrillard, *Seduction*, 46.

14 **Love goes brackish . . .** : Michael R. Liebowitz explains this natural entropy of passion in terms of the ramp effect. Just as a drug that becomes less and less effective with use, so romantic love tapers off as we become more tolerant to it. "Tolerance," writes Liebowitz, "is the real problem in romantic relationship, because it leads to people getting bored with each other. The problem becomes worse the longer a relationship lasts, unless one of two things happen. The first is that with time they become more attached and comfortable with each other, and willing to sacrifice excitement for security. The second is that we find ways to put some novelty and change into our love life." Liebowitz thinks only option two is viable in vital partnerships. See *The Chemistry of Love* (New York: Berkley Books, 1983), 131.

14 **Love philosophers belabor . . .** : Burton, *Anatomy of Melancholy*, 833; Montaigne, "On Some Verses of Virgil," *Complete Essays*, vol. 3, 104; Stendhal, *Love*, 58; Montaigne, "That Our Desire Is Increased by Difficulty," *Complete Essays*, vol. 2, 320.

14 **The first sex . . .** : Lawrence Durrell, *Justine* (New York: Penguin, 1957), 105. Pain and eros are more closely related than we like to admit. Havelock Ellis devotes a section of his magisterial *Psychology of Sex* to the relationship, and some thinkers define eroticism as an "alliance of pleasure and pain." Burdach, quoted in Ellis, 67.

Courtly love actually made suffering a precondition for love; Andreas Capellanus, who formulated an *amour courtois* code in the twelfth century encapsulated it: "That love is suffering is easy to see." *Art of Courtly Love*, 2. Fear, anger, humiliation, doubt, disappointment, and anxiety, then, may not be inimical to love (as hug gurus would have us believe), but dark, primal strands in the fabric of eros.

"Primitively," argues Robert Briffault, "sexual feelings are associated not with tenderness but with delight in the infliction of pain . . . With both sexes, sexual attraction is pre-eminently sadistic, and is gratified by pain." *The Mothers*, intro. Gordon Rattray Taylor (New York: Grosset & Dunlap, (1927), 1963), 39.

Two studies bear this out. In the first, men were more attracted to a woman who denigrated them; in the second, more attracted after a frightening passage across a high, shaky bridge. See Liebowitz, *Chemistry of Love*, 125 and 27. Apparently we like our passions highly spiced, with a "sting and a smart" in them. Montaigne, "On Some Verses of Virgil," *Complete Essays*, vol. 3, 72.

14 **Anxiety is the . . .** : André Gide, *The Immoralist*, trans. Richard Howard (New York: Vintage, 1970), 113.

15 **Psychologist Theodor Reik** . . . : See Reik, *Psychology of Sex Relations*, 38, 85–89, and passim. Love, he writes, "is related to feelings of satisfied vanity, of fulfilled pride, and realized ambition," 4.

16 **After first applauding** . . . : Quoted in Wolkstein and Kramer, *Inanna*, 12.

16 **The queen of** . . . : Miriam Robbins Dexter, *Whence the Goddesses: A Source Book* (New York: Teachers College Press, 1990), 16, and Anne Baring and Jules Cashford, *The Myth of the Goddess* (London: Arkana, 1991), 265.

16 **Primitives believed in** . . . : See Taylor, *Prehistory of Sex*, 48–49, and Helen Fisher, *Anatomy of Love* (New York: Fawcett Columbine, 1992), 27.

16 **Ever since Scheherazade's** . . . : Proverbs 6, verse 24.

16 **In ancient Greece** . . . : Friedrich, *Meaning of Aphrodite*, 143.

16 **Renaissance courtesans studied** . . . : Quoted in Seigneur de Brantôme, *Lives of Fair and Gallant Ladies*, trans. A. R. Allinson (New York: Liveright, 1933), 166.

16 **Before the recent** . . . : Ibid., 164. Other famous aphorisms to this effect include "As bull's horns are bound with ropes, so are men's hearts with pleasant words"; "fluency of speech will incline to love." Burton, *Anatomy of Melancholy*, 700, and Capellanus, *Art of Courtly Love*, 6.

16 **Contrary to the** . . . : Most books on female comedy stress its turnoff for men. See Linda Martin and Kerry Segrave, *Women in Comedy* (Secaucus, N.J.: Citadel Press); Nancy A. Walker, *A Very Serious Thing* (Minneapolis: University of Minnesota Press, 1988); and Regina Barreca, *They Used to Call Me Snow White . . . but I Drifted* (New York: Penguin, 1991).

16 **"What is more . . ."**: Baudrillard, *Seduction*, 102.

17 **As Jean-Paul Sartre** . . . : Jean-Paul Sartre, *Being and Nothingness*, trans. Hazel E. Barnes (New York: Washington Square Press, 1966), 456. James Alter recently expanded on this idea. "To speak with clarity, brevity and wit," he writes, "is like holding a lightning rod. We are drawn to people who know things and are able to express them." "Once upon a Time, Literature. Now What?," *New York Times*, September 13, 1999, E1.

17 **The goddess Inanna** . . . : Quoted in Wolkstein and Kramer, *Inanna*, 24.

17 **Love guides since** . . . : Baldesar Castiglione, *The Book of the Courtier*, trans. Charles S. Singleton (Garden City, N.Y.: Anchor Books, 1959), 212, and Ellis, *Psychology of Sex*, vol. 2, 22.

17 **In Shere Hite's** . . . : Hite, *Hite Report on Male Sexuality*, 339.

18 **The lure of** . . . : Mircea Eliade, quoted in June Singer, *Androgyny: Toward a New Theory of Sexuality* (Garden City, N.Y.: Anchor Books, 1977), 19.

18 **"The indistinctness of . . ."**: Baudrillard, *Seduction*, 12.

18 **Venetian courtesans wore** . . . : Lynne Lawner, *Lives of the Courtesans* (New York: Rizzoli, 1987), 20. See boxed quotation, "A Courtesan Dressed as a Man," accompanied by a letter from Pietro Aretino, 23.

18 **As a French** . . . : La Bruyère, quoted in Thérèse Louis Latour, *Princesses, Ladies and Adventuresses of the Reign of Louis XIV* (London: Kegan Paul, Trench, Trabner, 1924), 63.

18 **Ninon de Lenclos, the** . . . : Quoted in Cohen, *Mademoiselle Libertine*, 118, and in Ishbel Ross, *The Uncrowned Queen: Life of Lola Montez* (New York: Harper & Row, 1972), 310.

18 **This aliveness, if** . . . : Mircea Eliade, *The Sacred and Profane*, trans. Willard R. Trask (New York: Harper & Row, 1959), 97.

18 **Sirens have been . . . :** There's a long tradition of the seductress's mental imbalance. Sometimes the seductress is a complete lunatic, like Lucy Westenra of *Dracula* or a full-blown schizophrenic like Oliver W. Holmes's snake woman in *Elsie Venner.* Usually, however, she displays garden-variety psychic disorders: narcissism, sadism, nymphomania, manic depression, exhibitionism, emotional frigidity, and sundry neuroses. A random selection of heroines from such works as *Antony and Cleopatra,* "Dolores," *Nana, Lulu, Justine, Miss Julie, Damage,* and *Disclosure* could fill a psychiatric clinic.

Feminists Elizabeth Janeway, Jean Baker Miller, and Dr. Avodah Offit all argue that the seductress is a sick soul, a "histrionic" personality, a psychically annihilated wreck, and a messed-up neurotic. See Elizabeth Janeway, "Who Is Sylvia? On the Loss of Sexual Paradigms," *Women: Sex and Sexuality,* ed. Catherine Stimpson and Ethel Spector Person (Chicago: University of Chicago Press, 1980), 4–20. Also see Miller, *Toward a New Psychology of Women* (Boston: Beacon Press, 1976) and Offit, *The Sexual Self* (New York: Congdon & Weed, 1977).

18 **They gave off . . . :** Rollo May, "Introduction," *Existence: A New Dimension in Psychiatry and Psychology,* ed. Rollo May, Ernest Angel, and Henri Ellenberger (New York: Touchstone, 1958), 31. For definitions of mental health that go beyond Freud's union of love and work, see Abraham H. Maslow's famous definition of self-actualization, *Toward a Psychology of Being* (New York: Van Nostrand Reinhold, 1968); Carl R. Rogers, *On Becoming a Person* (Boston: Houghton Mifflin, 1961); and Roberto Assagioli, M.D., *Psychosynthesis* (New York: Viking, 1965).

18 **Great swaggering queen . . . :** Baring and Cashford, *Myth of the Goddess,* 39.

19 **"Clothed with the . . .":** Ibid., 176.

19 **It needs vital . . . :** Angier brilliantly discusses this blend of "sedation" and "elation." *Woman: An Intimate Geography,* 318.

19 **Too muchness was . . . :** Neumann, *Great Mother,* 5.

19 **"She is famine . . .":** Quoted in Kate and Douglas Batting, *Sex Appeal: The Art and Science of Sexual Attraction* (New York: St. Martin's Press, 1996), 17.

19 **The sex goddess . . . :** Wolkstein and Kramer, *Inanna,* 41.

20 **She's been villainized . . . :** Neumann, *Great Mother,* 172.

20 **Athena, Jupiter's stooge . . . :** Women may be women's worst enemies when it comes to sexual power. As Dolly Parton, the bombshell of *Nine to Five,* says, women treat her "like the bastard at a family reunion." Women blackball enchantresses, distrust, shun, and excoriate them. For a survey of the numerous attacks on the seductress, see de Beauvoir, *Second Sex,* who labels seductresses infantile dissemblers engaged in the "pure will to please," 645; also 178, 340, 512, and passim.

Two other powerful arguments against the siren figure are Jane Gallop's and Mary Ann Doane's objections that despite her superficial appearance of strength, she carries male "epistemological baggage" and achieves only "problematic successes." Mary Ann Doane, *Femmes Fatales* (New York and London: Routledge, 1991), 3, and Jane Gallop, "French Theory and the Seduction of Feminism," in *Men in Feminism,* ed. Alice Jardine and Paul Smith (New York and London: Routledge, 1987), 114. Psychiatrist Avodah K. Offit believes that the temptress is a quasi-neurotic whose distinguishing traits are her "insatiable and dramatic quest for attention, great demands on others' resources, and an emotional intensity out of all proportion to the stimulus." *Sexual Self,* 50.

Among the many more objections to this woman are Brownmiller, *Femininity;* Madonna Kolbenschlag, *Kiss Sleeping Beauty Goodbye* (New York: Bantam, 1979); Miller, *Toward a New Psychology of Women;* Carol Cassell, *Swept Away* (New York: Bantam, 1984); Janeway, "Who Is Sylvia?," 4–20; and Mary Daly, *Gyn/Ecology: The Metaethics of Radical Feminism* (Boston: Beacon, (1978), 1990).

21 **They're stronger than . . . :** Baudrillard, *Seduction,* 8.

21 **Women from business . . . :** bell hooks, quoted in Tad Friend, "Lock Up Your Sons–The 21st Century Woman Is in the Building," *Esquire* (February 1994), 56.

21 **In her *Bitch* . . . :** Elizabeth Wurtzel, *Bitch: In Praise of Difficult Women* (New York: Doubleday, 1998), 30.

21 **Summarizing the current . . . :** "Courtney Love," Interview, *Rolling Stone* (November 13, 1997), 166 and 164.

21 **It frees women . . . :** Men persuaded us as part of the sixties' sexual liberation bargain to drop our traditional defenses. In the past a woman used intricate feints, deceits, and courtship dances to win leverage in a rigged game. She drove up her value with crafty abstentions and laid out elaborate snares. But with shrewd prescience, the macho wing of the sexual revolution conned us into authenticity, a dubious concept peddled by existentialists.

We agreed to honesty, openness, and yeses while they conceded nothing. Betty Friedan marketed their scam with wide-eyed gullibility. "Inauthenticity was bred into women by weakness," she preached, unaware of the necessary dissimulation that defines all social relations. *The Second Stage* (New York: Summit Books, 1981), 56. See Erving Goffman, *The Presentation of Self in Everyday Life* (Garden City, N.Y.: Anchor Books, 1959) and John Lahr's excellent summation of the issue in his review of *The Misanthrope, New Yorker* (May 8, 1995), 95–96.

Without artifice, society would collapse; personality, which comes from the Latin *persona,* means "mask." Especially in the realm of sexuality, disingenuousness may be an important survival strategy. Evolutionary psychologists say it thrives in both sexes and observe that "we may teach our children that honesty is the best policy, but natural selection favors the skillful lie. In the context of courtship, a successful deceit carries a protective advantage." Batten, *Sexual Strategies,* 98.

22 **"Venus favors the . . .":** Ovid, *Art of Love,* Book 1, 124.

22 **Pollsters find epidemic . . . :** Quilliam, *Women on Sex,* 31 and 18. Books like *Women and Self-Esteem* lead women's studies' reading lists, and Gloria Steinem's *Revolution from Within* (Boston: Little, Brown, 1992) finds a plague of low sense of self among American women. She observes that wherever she "traveled [she] saw women who were smart, courageous, or valuable, who didn't think they were smart, courageous, or valuable," 3.

In one study of college seniors, twice as many women as men rate themselves below average sexually; none say they're above average. Ellyn Kaschak, *Engendered Lives: A New Psychology of Women's Experience* (New York: Basic Books, 1992), 162, and Janus and Janus, *Janus Report,* 93.

22 **Georg Simmel observed . . . :** Georg Simmel, "Flirtation," *Georg Simmel: On Women, Sexuality, and Love,* ed. Guy Oakes (New Haven: Yale University Press [1911], 1984), 141.

22 **His feminist contemporary . . . :** See Ellen Key, *Love and Ethics* and Robert T. Michael et al., *Sex in America* (Boston: Little, Brown, 1994), 130.

23 **Activists say that . . . :** Amber Hollibaugh, "Desire for the Future: Radical

Hope in Passion and Pleasure," *Pleasure and Danger: Exploring Female Sexuality*, ed. Carole S. Vance (Boston: Routledge, 1984), 407.

23 **We're naturally magnetized . . .** : Ernest Becker, *The Denial of Death* (New York: Free Press, 1973), 135, and Sartre, *Being and Nothingness*, 454–55.

23 **But the sexy . . .** : Patricia Seller, "Women, Sex and Power," *Fortune* (August 5, 1996), 46.

24 **Robert Graves believed . . .** : Quoted in Elizabeth Gould Davis, *The First Sex* (New York: Putnam's, 1971), 72.

CHAPTER 2: THE SEDUCTRESS ARCHETYPE

26 **They "take hold . . ."**: Neumann, *Great Mother*, 8.

26 **Some scholars contend . . .** : This is one of the most heated, acrimonious issues in archaeological and women's studies today. Charlotte Allen summarizes the dispute in "The Scholars and the Goddess," *Atlantic Monthly* (January 2001), 18–22. Important voices arguing against either a goddess religion or prehistorical matriarchy are Cynthia Eller, *The Myth of Matriarchal Prehistory* (Boston: Beacon, 2000); Philip G. Davis, *Goddess Unmasked: The Rise of Neopagan Feminist Spirituality* (Dallas: Spence Publishing, 1998); Ian Hodder, "The Past as Passion and Play: Catalhoyuk as a Site of Conflict in the Construction of Multiple Pasts," *Archaeology Under Fire: Politics, Nationalism, and Heritage in the Eastern Mediterranean and Middle East*, ed. Lynn Meskell (London: Routledge, 1998); and Lynn Meskell, "Goddesses, Gimbutas, and 'New Age' Archaeology," *Antiquity* 69 (1995), 74–86.

Major spokespeople for the other side include Marija Gimbutas, *The Gods and Goddesses of Old Europe* (Berkeley and Los Angeles: University of California Press, 1982); Riane Eisler, *The Chalice and the Blade: Our History, Our Future* (San Francisco: Harper & Row, 1987); Riane Eisler, *Sacred Pleasure: Sex, Myth, and the Politics of the Body: New Paths to Power and Love* (San Francisco: HarperSanFrancisco, 1995); Elinor W. Gadon, *The Once and Future Goddess* (San Francisco: HarperSanFrancisco, 1989); Buffie Johnson, *Lady of the Beasts: The Goddess and Her Sacred Animals* (Rochester, Vt.: Inner Traditions International, 1994); Judith Yarnall, *Transformations of Circe: The History of an Enchantress* (Urbana and Chicago: University of Illinois Press, 1994), Jean Markale, *The Great Goddess*, trans. Jody Gladding (Rochester, Vt.: Inner Traditions International, 1999); and Gerda Lerner, *The Creation of Patriarchy* (New York: Oxford University Press, 1986), 141–60.

One of the most cautious prehistorians, Margaret Ehrenberg, ultimately concedes that the Venus figurines "strongly suggest a common meaning and linked social or religious tradition throughout Europe," *Women in Prehistory* (Norman and London: University of Oklahoma Press, 1989), 72.

27 **Historian Richard Rudgley . . .** : Richard Rudgley, *The Lost Civilizations of the Stone Age* (New York: Touchstone, 1999), 199.

27 **Most mythologic systems . . .** : For a discussion of this, see Joseph Campbell, *The Masks of the God: Primitive Mythology* (New York: Penguin, 1959), 315; Shahrukh Husain, *The Goddess* (London: Duncan Baird, 1997), 42–72; and Davis, *First Sex*, 15–85 and passim.

27 **This ur-divinity, by . . .** : Neumann, *Great Mother*, 18.

27 **Her double D breasts . . .** : Quoted in Rudgley, *Lost Civilizations*, 198.

27 **To our ancestors . . .** : Scholar Paul Friedrich believes the synthesis of maternity and sexuality makes women too powerful sexually; ergo it has been suppressed in patriarchy. See chapter 9, "Sex/Sensuousness and Maternity/ Motherliness," *Meaning of Aphrodite*, 181–91.

27 **Another queen-size goddess . . .** : Joseph Campbell, quoted in Gadon, *Once and Future Goddess*, 14.

28 **To the Ice Age . . .** : Many believe lunar notations led to the achievements of astronomy, mathematics, writing, and agriculture and taught *Homo sapiens* to think abstractly. For a discussion of this, see Baring and Cashford, *Myth of the Goddess*, 20–21.

28 **With her, "there . . ."**: Gimbutas, *Language of the Goddess*, 321.

28 **Though better known . . .** : Campbell, *Masks of the God*, 313.

28 **From the scenarios . . .** : Taylor, *Prehistory of Sex*, 133.

29 **Which meant they . . .** : François Boucher, *20,000 Years of Fashion* (New York: Harry N. Abrams, 1965), 23.

29 **Stone Age women . . .** : See ibid., 26–30, for more detail on this. Also see Rudgley's description of the elaborate beaded costumes of Paleolithic man, *Lost Civilizations*, 190, and E. O. James, who describes two Stone Age frescoes of women dancing in caps, skirts, and "wide skirts of crinoline type," on an Alpera rock shelter. *From Cave to Cathedral* (London: Thames & Hudson, 1965), 31.

29 **They were in . . .** : Norman Rush, *Mating* (New York: Vintage, 1991), 199.

29 **Underscoring the archaic . . .** : On the presence of pain in passion, see the work of Robert J. Stoller, M.D., *Sexual Excitement: The Dynamics of Erotic Life* (New York: Touchstone, 1979) and *Observing the Erotic Imagination* (New Haven: Yale University Press, 1985). Amorists eloquent on this topic include: Capellanus, *Art of Courtly Love*, 2, 26–27, 54; and Stendhal, *Love*, 47, 211, 250, and 257. "There is a delicious pleasure," Stendhal writes, "in clasping in your arms a woman who has caused you much suffering," 211. See also Denis de Rougemont, *Love in the Western World*, trans. Montgomery Belgion (New York: Harper & Row, 1956), 243; Maurois, "The Art of Loving," 15; Balzac, *Physiology of Marriage*, 41; Van de Velde, *Ideal Marriage*, 19–20, and 110; Person, *Dreams of Love*, 65 and 74; and penultimately, Ellis, "Love and Pain," *Psychology of Sex*, vol. 1, 66–188.

29 **As eros evolved . . .** : Hermann Kern, *Through the Labyrinth* (New York: Prestel, 2000), 30.

30 **"Sex," in essence . . .** : Paglia, *Sexual Personae*, 91.

30 **When the hero . . .** : Philip Roth, *Sabbath's Theater* (Boston: Houghton Mifflin, 1995), 5.

30 **One of her . . .** : Baring and Cashford, *Myth of the Goddess*, 264.

30 **But she's a . . .** : Ibid., 109. This recapitulation may be due to a land bridge that once connected Crete to Old Europe.

30 **It was a . . .** : Gimbutas, *Language of the Goddess*, 121.

30 **At the deepest . . .** : Neumann, *Great Mother*, 18.

31 **But the "glorification . . ."**: Jacquetta Hawkes, *Dawn of the Gods* (New York: Random House, 1968), 131.

31 **Art, for the . . .** : Quoted ibid., 73.

32 **Just as the . . .** : Ibid., 137.

32 **Through cultic magic . . .** : Baring and Cashford, *Myth of the Goddess*, 66.

32 **To the hypnotic . . .** : Karl Kerenyi, *Goddesses of the Sun and Moon*, trans. Murray Stein (Dallas: Spring Publications, 1979), 49.

33 **As before, pain . . .** : See Rodney Castleden who, countering the hearts-and-flowers view of the Cretans, comments on the "disturbing" Minoan obsession with the "shedding of blood," and discusses the possibility of human sacrifice. *Minoans: Life in Bronze Age Crete* (London: Routledge, 1990), 169. Montaigne, "On Some Verses of Virgil," *Complete Essays*, 3 and 72.

34 **Above her shines . . .** : Barbara G. Walker, *The Woman's Dictionary of Symbols and Sacred Objects* (San Francisco: HarperSanFrancisco, 1988), 370.

34 **Like them, she . . .** : Betty De Shong Meador, *Inanna: Lady of the Largest Heart* (Austin: University of Texas Press, 2000), 12 and 91.

34 **She is known . . .** : Tikva Frymer-Kensky, *In the Wake of the Goddess* (New York: Free Press, 1992), 29.

35 **Perpetuating the twin-sexed . . .** : Meador, *Inanna*, 162.

35 **After she crowned . . .** : Wolkstein and Kramer, *Inanna*, 12.

35 **Then she set . . .** : Meador, *Inanna*, 159 and 161.

35 **She bragged to . . .** : Quoted in Baring and Cashford, *Myth of the Goddess*, 214 and 37.

35 **She was the deity . . .** : Wolkstein and Kramer, *Inanna*, 6 and 24.

36 **During her ordeal . . .** : Ibid., 60.

36 **She seized the . . .** : Meador, *Inanna*, 114–15.

36 **She was the quintessential . . .** : Beverly Moon, "Inanna: The Star Who Became Queen," *Goddesses Who Rule*, ed. Elisabeth Benard and Beverly Moon (New York: Oxford University Press, 2000), 77.

36 **Earthly wisdom became . . .** : Wolkstein and Kramer, *Inanna*, 15.

36 **Included in the package . . .** : Ibid., 15 and 48.

37 **Her hair—a huge turn-on . . .** : Samuel Noah Kramer, *History Begins at Sumer* (Philadelphia: University of Pennsylvania Press, 1981), 18.

37 **Once within the high altar . . .** : Wolkstein and Kramer, *Inanna*, 38 and 39.

37 **Possessed by their goddess . . .** : Frymer-Kensky, *Wake of the Goddess*, 48.

38 **They limited her . . .** : Friedrich, *Meaning of Aphrodite*, 62.

39 **She was a walking . . .** : Ibid., 94.

39 **She inspired art . . .** : Rufus C. Camphausen, *The Encyclopedia of Erotic Wisdom* (Rochester, Vt.: Inner Traditions International, 1991), 14.

39 **Attended by bees . . .** : Homer, "Hymn to Aphrodite," *The Homeric Hymns*, trans. Charles Boer (Chicago: Swallow Press, 1970), 75. See Friedrich's interesting discussion of this combined sexual and maternal aspect in Aphrodite in chapter 9, *Meaning of Aphrodite*. He points out that the union of these two qualities confers too much power on women and has therefore been suppressed throughout later history, 181–91.

39 **Despite the loss . . .** : Homer, "Hymn to Aphrodite," 81, and Bruce S. Thornton, *Eros: The Myth of Ancient Greek Sexuality* (Boulder, Colo.: Westview Press, 1997), 51.

39 **Like her prehistoric . . .** : Kerenyi, "Aphrodite," *Goddesses of Sun and Moon*, 59.

39 **With divine variability . . .** : Quoted in Thornton, *Eros*, 52.

40 **Although the Greeks . . .** : Ibid., 50.

40 **Sculptors subjected her . . .** : Quoted in Will Durant, *The Life of Greece* (New York: Simon & Schuster, 1939), 313. Neither the prehistoric cultures nor the

Cretans nor the Sumerians and Babylonians invested their sex goddesses with symmetrical proportions and rosebud lips. Their deities instead flaunted exaggerated primary sex characteristics, and even the Minoan Snake Goddess looked numinous, glamorous, and formidable rather than aesthetically pleasing.

As Freud and others have pointed out, beauty is an Apollonian defense mechanism against women's fearful sexual powers. See Friedrich, *Meaning of Aphrodite,* 88, and Sigmund Freud, *Civilization and Its Discontents,* trans. Joan Riviere (Garden City, N.Y.: Doubleday, 1930), 25, in which he calls beauty "aim-inhibited sexuality." Rita Freedman also analyzes this: "Beauty safely conceals women's frightening dimensions." *Beauty Bound* (Lexington, Mass.: Lexington Books, 1986), 61, as does Camille Paglia at length in *Sexual Personae.* "Beauty is an Apollonian freeze-frame," she explains, that "halts and condenses the flux and indeterminacy of nature," by which she means woman's "billowy body," which reflects the "surging sea of chthonian nature," 30 and 32.

Pinups belong in the realm of adolescent male sexuality, a way of fending off sexual terrors. On this, see Pietropinto and Simenauer, *Beyond the Male Myth,* 344–45; Lederer, *Fear of Women,* 256; and Willard Gaylin, *The Male Ego,* which analyzes male beauty junkies and their insecurity and assorted pathologies at some length, 173–78.

40 **There was "no . . .":** Homer, "The Hymn to Aphrodite," 72, and Hans Licht, *Sexual Life in Ancient Greece* (London: Abbey Library, 1932), 204.

40 **Warriors dropped their . . . :** Homer, "Third Hymn to Aphrodite," *Homeric Hymns,* 84.

40 **When Hera wanted . . . :** *Iliad,* Book XIV, 262.

40 **This "complex, learned . . .":** Friedrich, *Meaning of Aphrodite,* 144.

40 **Finally, there were the virtuoso . . . :** Ibid.

41 **She had the Graces . . . :** Homer, *Homeric Hymns,* 75.

41 **Her necklaces, brooches . . . :** See the meaning of her goldenness in Friedrich, *Meaning of Aphrodite,* 78–79. "The Hymn to Aphrodite," 75.

41 **Aphrodite, the "weaver . . .":** Quoted in Thornton, *Eros,* 61.

41 **Filled with "sweet longing" . . . :** Homer, "The Hymn to Aphrodite," 77–78.

42 **This likely duplicated . . . :** These dildo fetes are pictured on numerous Greek vases. For more on this topic, see Eva C. Keuls, *The Reign of the Phallus: Sexual Politics in Ancient Greece* (New York: Harper & Row, 1985), 82–86.

42 **After the procession . . . :** Opium was associated with Aphrodite and sacred to her; this suggests that it was featured in her ecstatic rites as it was on Crete. See Camphausen, *Encyclopedia of Erotic Wisdom,* 14.

42 **Other festivals ran . . . :** Note the feast at Argos, where priestesses worked themselves into such frenzies that "hysteria" became associated with their unhinged mental states, and the Hybristika, the Feast of Wantonness, when men wore veils and sometimes castrated themselves in their transports, running through the streets with their severed genitals and throwing them at women in exchange for feminine clothes. See Lederer, *Fear of Women,* 144–45. At the festival of Aphrodite Anosia flagellation took place. For more on this festival, see Licht, *Sexual Life in Ancient Greece,* 130, and for other similarly extravagant rites, see Burgo Partridge, *A History of Orgies* (New York: Bonanza Books, 1960), 19–22.

42 **Aphrodite was not the marble . . . :** This refers to Phidias's statue

Aphrodite of the Eleans. The tortoise signified: "The woman should stay home and keep quiet," Thornton, *Eros*, 172.

42 **She was an "awesome . . .":** Quoted ibid., 150 and 62.

43 **Whether we use . . . :** Homer, "The Third Hymn to Aphrodite," 85.

43 **"Why should I . . .":** Raphael Patai, *The Hebrew Goddess* (New York: Ktav Publishing, 1967), 210.

44 **Entwined with her . . . :** Ibid., 219.

44 **With protean wizardry . . . :** Ibid., 239.

45 **Aphrodite's seductive eloquence . . . :** Ibid., 222.

45 **She enticed victims . . . :** Ibid., 230.

46 **Monster of depravity . . . :** Ibid., 214.

47 **Nor have they lost . . . :** William Shakespeare, *Antony and Cleopatra*, ed. Maynard Mack (Baltimore: Penguin, 1960), act II, scene ii, line 237, and quoted, Hermann Kern, *Through the Labyrinth* (New York: Prestel, 2000), 30.

47 **They prefer the most . . . :** Stephen Nachmanovitch, *Free Play* (Los Angeles: Jeremy P. Tarcher, 1990), 106.

47 **One of the uses . . . :** Neumann, *Great Mother*, 6.

48 **The seductress deities . . . :** Buffie Johnson links Aphrodite's goldenness to her celestial character and celebrates her birth goddess connections, while archaeologist Marija Gimbutas reads prehistoric vulva drawings as tributes to motherhood without considering the possibility of a sexual subtext. Johnson, *Lady of the Beasts* (Rochester, Vt.: Inner Traditions International, 1994), 74, and Gimbutas, *The Language of the Goddess* (San Francisco: HarperSan Francisco, 1991), 105.

48 **Feminist critic Mary . . . :** Mary Ann Doane, "Film and Masquerade: Theorizing the Female Spectator," *Issues in Feminist Film Criticism*, ed. Patricia Erens (Bloomington: Indiana University Press, 1990), 48.

48 **As the hapless . . . :** Sophie Parkin, *Dear Goddess* (London: Headline, 2000), 173.

CHAPTER 3: *BELLES LAIDES:* HOMELY SIRENS

49 **On that final . . . :** Edith Wharton, *Age of Innocence* (New York: Collier, 1920), 333.

50 **As Nancy Etcoff and . . . :** Una Stannard, "The Mask of Beauty," in *Women in Sexist Society*, ed. Vivian Gornick and Barbara K. Moran (New York: NAL, 1971), 195. See also Nancy Etcoff, *Survival of the Prettiest* (New York: Anchor Books, 1999).

50 **They unsettle all . . . :** William Gass, "Throw the Emptiness out of Your Arms: Rilke's Doctrine of Nonpossessive Love," *The Philosophy of Erotic Love*, ed. Robert C. Solomon and Kathleen M. Higgins (Lawrence: University Press of Kansas, 1991), 452.

50 **But as prehistorians . . . :** Georges Bataille, *Eroticism: Death and Sensuality*, trans. Mary Dalwood (San Francisco: City Lights Books, 1962), 31.

50 **Anthropologist H. R. Hays . . . :** H. R. Hays, *In the Beginnings: Early Man and His Gods* (New York: Putnam's, 1963), 36.

51 **If evolution decreed . . . :** Neumann, *Great Mother*, 96 and 110.

51 **Nor has this primordial . . . :** Robert Graves, for example, resurrected this Neolithic deity as the goddess ideal of his *White Goddess*, the "woman with a hooked nose" who can transform herself into serpents, owls, and other beasts and make men's "eyes water," and hair "stand on end." *The White Goddess* (New York: Farrar, Straus and Giroux, 1948), 24.

51 **The "Serpent of . . .":** Bernard Berenson, quoted in Isabel Ross, *Charmen and Cranks* (New York: Harper & Row, 1965), 155.

51 **Dressed in skintight . . . :** Louise Hall Tharp, *Mrs. Jack* (Boston: Little, Brown, 1965), 109.

51 **Then at the climax . . . :** Quoted in Douglass Shand-Tucci, *The Art of Scandal: The Life and Times of Isabella Stewart Gardner* (New York: HarperCollins, 1997), 213.

51 **The psychologist William James . . . :** Ibid., 213.

52 **She was, as . . . :** Quoted ibid., 23.

52 **In an age . . . :** D. G. Brinton, M.D., and Geo. H. Napheys, M.D., *Personal Beauty* (Bedford, Mass: Applewood Books, 1994 [1869]), 10.

52 **Yet this homely . . . :** Quoted in Tharp, *Mrs. Jack*, 28.

52 **"She throws out . . .":** Quoted ibid., 109.

52 **"I may not . . .":** F. Marion Crawford, *To Leeward* (Boston: Houghton Mifflin and Co., 1883), 54.

52 **Her father's favorite . . . :** Tharp, *Mrs. Jack*, 8.

52 **But he underestimated . . . :** Crawford, *To Leeward*, 111.

53 **More heinously, she . . . :** Tharp, *Mrs. Jack*, 126.

53 **She arrived at cotillions . . . :** Quoted ibid., 110.

53 **The man was . . . :** Shand-Tucci, *Art of Scandal*, 44.

53 **At their daily . . . :** Quoted in Tharp, *Mrs. Jack*, 139.

54 **Frank said his . . . :** Quoted ibid., 83, and Crawford, *To Leeward*, 103.

54 **America's first "lady . . .":** Nelson Landsdale, "Mrs. Gardner and Her Palace," *The American Heritage New Illustrated History of the United States*, vol. 2, *The Gilded Age*, ed. Robert G. Athearn (New York: Dell, 1963), 981, and Shand-Tucci, *Art of Scandal*, 211.

54 **"Battered, depleted, [and] . . .":** Quoted in Tharp, *Mrs. Jack*, 272.

55 **But she was still . . . :** Crawford, *To Leeward*, 53.

55 **On her travels . . . :** Tharp, *Mrs. Jack*, 90.

55 **An observer remembered . . . :** Quoted ibid., 322.

55 **One wrote her . . . :** Quoted ibid., 220.

55 **Time did not . . . :** Crawford, *To Leeward*, 349.

55 **She profaned the . . . :** Emily Thornwell, *The Lady's Guide to Perfect Gentility* (New York: Derby & Jackson, 1860), 75.

55 **She wore the . . . :** Women, as to be expected, cut her socially and vivisected her character, but she disdained to notice. Once when a grande dame left her out of her daughter's wedding, Belle attended anyway, bearing rubies for the bride.

55 **She traced her ancestry . . . :** Quoted in Tharp, *Mrs. Jack*, 322.

55 **Bernard Berenson called . . . :** Quoted ibid., 220.

55 **This misunderstood "ugly . . .":** Jane Harrison, *Prolegomena to the Study of Greek Religion* (New York: Meridian Books, 1955), 187 and 195.

56 **As a local paper . . . :** Quoted in Tharp, *Mrs. Jack*, 109.

56 **"The weapons at . . .":** Antonia Fraser, *The Weaker Vessel* (New York: Vintage Books, 1984), 399.

56 **To a man . . . :** Quoted ibid., 407.

57 **The only daughter** . . . : V. DeSola Pinto, *Sir Charles Sedley* (London: Constable, 1927), 137.

57 **Having inherited her** . . . : Quoted ibid, 133, and quoted in Fraser, *Weaker Vessel*, 400.

57 **One of his slurs** . . . : Quoted in Pinto, *Sedley*, 135.

58 **Casting the curative** . . . : See Harvey Mindess, who with an increasing number of theorists, beginning with Norman Cousins, subscribes to the therapeutic value of laughter and comedy. *Laughter and Liberation* (Los Angeles: Nash Publishing, 1971).

58 **"We [James's mistresses] . . ."** : Sedley quoted in Pinto, *Sedley*, 138.

58 **Characteristically, she needled** . . . : Quoted ibid., 140.

58 **Because of the "favor"** . . . : Ibid., 206.

58 **Rail thin, her** . . . : Quoted ibid., 156.

59 **Again, though, her "wit** . . .": Quoted ibid., 136.

59 **She promptly captured** . . . : Quoted ibid., 216, fn. 3.

59 **Appropriating the swan** . . . : Neumann, *Great Mother*, 43.

59 **When she dispatched** . . . : Quoted in Fraser, *Weaker Vessel*, 307.

59 **Rigged out in** . . . : Quoted ibid., 407.

59 **When he asked** . . . : Quoted ibid., 408.

59 **Derided as the** . . . : Ibid., 2, and see Olwen Hufton, "Constructing Woman," *The Prospect Before Her* (New York: Vintage, 1995), 28–61.

59 **She swanned around** . . . : Pinto, *Sedley*, 3.

60 **"What strange mysterious** . . .": Charles Sackville, earl of Dorset, "A Faithful Catalogue," *The Poems of Charles Sackville, Sixth Earl of Dorset*, ed. Brice Harris (New York and London: Garland Publishing, 1979), line 38, 138.

60 **She was just as bizarre** . . . : Quoted in Greg King, *The Duchess of Windsor: The Uncommon Life of Wallis Simpson* (New York: Citadel Press, 1999), 420 and 124.

60 **Nicknamed Minnehaha, she** . . . : Charles Higham, *The Duchess of Windsor: The Secret Life* (New York: McGraw-Hill, 1988), 40.

61 **Vivacious and quick-witted** . . . : Quoted in Ralph G. Martin, *The Woman He Loved* (New York: NAL, 1973), 50.

61 **Beginning in grade school** . . . : Quoted ibid., 29.

61 **Although the "least pretty"** . . . : Higham, *Duchess of Windsor*, 16.

61 **When she "came out"** . . . : Quoted in King, *Duchess of Windsor*, 35.

61 **Harsh-featured and plain** . . . : Quoted ibid., 35.

61 **As their union unraveled** . . . : Quoted ibid., 431.

62 **At her celebrated dinners** . . . : Higham, *Duchess of Windsor*, 213.

62 **The moment he met** . . . : Quoted in Martin, *Woman He Loved*, 87.

62 **After that she became** . . . : Ibid., 138.

63 **"Home," he always** . . . : Quoted ibid., 172.

63 **After David's abdication** . . . : Quoted in King, *Duchess of Windsor*, 239.

63 **With age, the** . . . : Buffie Johnson, *Lady of the Beasts* (Rochester, Vt.: Inner Traditions International, 1994), 47.

63 **Yet despite all** . . . : Higham, *Duchess of Windsor*, 383.

63 **He showered her** . . . : Charles J. V. Murphy and J. Bryan III, *The Windsor Story* (New York: Dell, 1979), 109.

63 **With typical seductress** . . . : Higham, *Duchess of Windsor*, 387.

63 **"It would take** . . .": Quoted ibid., 394.

63 **Like the bad wife . . .** : Gimbutas, *Language of the Goddess,* 192.

63 **"She got him . . ."**: Quoted in Murphy and Bryan, *Windsor Story,* 113.

64 **Truer to the owl goddess's . . .** : Georgina Masson, *Courtesans of the Italian Renaissance* (New York: St. Martin's, 1975), 88 and 118.

64 **"Overly tall," Tullia . . .** : Quoted in Lynne Lawner, *Lives of the Courtesans: Portraits of the Renaissance* (New York: Rizzoli, 1987), 72.

64 **Beauties of the . . .** : See the Renaissance writer Agnolo Firenzuola on these requirements, which he illustrates with numerous geometrical drawings. About the correct alignment of eyes, nose, and mouth he writes: "And there is as much distance from the tip of the chin to the top of the upper lip as from the top of the nose to the hairline, which is the end of the forehead. And there is as much distance from the top of the upper lip to the beginning of the nose as from the inner corner of the eye to the middle of the bridge of the nose. The base of the nose must be as wide as it is long," etc. Firenzuola, *On the Beauty of Women,* trans. Konrad Eisenbichler and Jacqueline Murray (Philadelphia: University of Pennsylvania Press, 1992 [1541]), 25.

64 **Tullia was born . . .** : Ethel Colburn Mayne, *Enchanters of Men* (New York: Putnam's, 1925), 82.

64 **Her mother, herself . . .** : Ibid., 83.

64 **She proved an infant . . .** : Quoted ibid., 83.

64 **With shrewd perspicacity . . .** : Masson, *Courtesans of the Italian Renaissance,* 86.

65 **When pile-it-on excess . . .** : Mayne, *Enchanters of Men,* 83.

65 **Sparkling with "devilish" . . .** : Quoted in Lawner, *Lives of the Courtesans,* 73 and 72.

65 **Although she lavished . . .** : Quoted in Masson, *Courtesans of the Italian Renaissance,* 107 and 106.

65 **She made all her clients . . .** : Ibid., 96.

65 **The maximum difficulty . . .** : Quoted in Mayne, *Enchanters of Men,* 88.

65 **"She knows everything, . . ."** : Quoted in Masson, *Courtesans of the Italian Renaissance,* 102.

65 **None of his "other mistresses" . . .** : Ibid., 94.

65 **Almost a hundred thousand . . .** : Quoted ibid., 94.

66 **When a local dramatist . . .** : Quoted ibid., 95.

66 **"Let's leave out . . ."**: Quoted ibid., 101.

66 **She saturated the city . . .** : Quoted ibid., 102.

66 **Muzio regarded her . . .** : Quoted ibid., 106.

66 **Once more the "Queen . . ."**: Mayne, *Enchanters of Men,* 86.

67 **"You are young . . ."** : Quoted in Masson, *Courtesans of the Italian Renaissance,* 113.

67 **Tullia, "more queenly . . ."**: Mayne, *Enchanters of Men,* 85.

67 **"Monster, miracle, sibyl!" . . .** : Quoted in Masson, *Courtesans of the Italian Renaissance,* 94.

67 **"Fierce and hawk-like," . . .** : Quoted in Joanna Richardson, *The Courtesans: The Demi-Monde in Nineteenth-Century France* (Cleveland and New York: World Publishing, 1967), 96.

67 **But she exercised . . .** : Ibid., 84.

67 **Just as her critics . . .** : Rupert Christiansen, *Paris Babylon: The Story of the Paris Commune* (New York: Viking, 1994), 116.

67 "Ugly, elegant, and remote" . . . : Judith Yarnell, *Transformations of Circe* (Urbana and Chicago: University of Illinois Press, 1994), 29.

67 Yet this eerie . . . : Harrison, *Prolegomena*, 168.

68 While the she-vulture . . . : The theme of death-point sexuality and the perverse attraction to self-destruction and disintegration has been well studied. The two seminal works are Denis de Rougemont, *Love in the Western World*, trans. Montgomery Belgion (New York: Harper & Row, 1956) and Bataille, *Eroticism: Death and Sensuality*.

68 "All of my wishes" . . . : Quoted in Richardson, *Courtesans*, 98.

68 Thanks to her three-year . . . : Ibid., 82.

69 "I am not badly . . .": *The Goncourt Journals*, trans. Lewis Galantiere (New York: Greenwood Press, 1968), 164.

69 "You go back . . .": Quoted in Richardson, *Courtesans*, 85.

69 To win Count . . . : Quoted ibid., 96.

69 When no respectable . . . : Quoted ibid., 92.

69 She wore *bouchons* . . . : *Goncourt Journals*, 243.

69 Transfixed by her . . . : Quoted in Richardson, *Courtesans*, 85.

69 When La Paiva accepted . . . : Quoted ibid., 86.

69 A hawk-eyed businesswoman . . . : Quoted ibid., 91.

70 She bought a sixteenth . . . : Quoted ibid., 90.

70 At this ornate shrine . . . : Quoted ibid., 93.

70 Though entirely unschooled . . . : Quoted ibid., 87.

70 He eventually married . . . : Quoted ibid., 96.

70 Hissed in the street . . . : Quoted ibid.

70 With her primal erotic . . . : Quoted ibid.

71 Dumas *fils*, though . . . : Quoted ibid.

71 These were "man-seizing" . . . : Harrison, *Prolegomena*, 198 and 166.

71 They sang the song . . . : Storms and shipwreck were a central metaphor for ancient Greeks of the soul-uprooting, deranging, and destructive power of sexuality. See Thornton, *Eros*, 35–37. Death by drowning is a common image also of "man's fear of being overwhelmed by female sexuality or for loss of identity and self-control in sexual intercourse." Patrick Bade, *Femme Fatale* (New York: Mayflower Books, 1929), 8.

71 By the same token . . . : Harrison, *Prolegomena*, 178.

71 She fetched up . . . : Margaret Crosland, *Piaf* (New York: Fromm International Publishing, 1985), 79.

71 No man in fact . . . : Ibid., 100.

72 Throngs of "young guys" . . . : Simone Berteaut, *Piaf* (New York: Harper & Row, 1969), 29.

72 "I'm ugly," she . . . : Quoted ibid., 139 and 236.

72 In both work and love . . . : Ibid., 183.

72 First she panned . . . : Ibid., 217.

73 She stroked her . . . : Jean Cocteau, intro., Edith Piaf, *The Wheel of Fortune*, trans. Peter Trewartha and Andrée Masoin de Vinton (New York: Chilton Books, 1958), 15, and Crosland, *Piaf*, 92 and 15.

73 Edith's departure left . . . : Quoted in Eugen Weber, review, Yves Montand et al., *You See I Haven't Forgotten*, trans. Jeremy Leggatt (New York: Alfred A. Knopf, 1992), *New York Times Book Review*, November 15, 1992, 31.

73 **Contrary to the . . . :** Quoted in Crosland, *Piaf,* 85.

73 **Her landlord during . . . :** Quoted ibid., 76, and Berteaut, *Piaf,* 104–05.

73 **A lover of . . . :** Quoted in Crosland, *Piaf,* 115.

73 **Eddie, who left . . . :** Quoted ibid., 106.

74 **"She made me . . .":** Quoted in Berteaut, *Piaf,* 358.

74 **She'd have laughed . . . :** Crosland, *Piaf,* 192.

74 **"I had a . . .":** Piaf, *Wheel of Fortune,* 62.

74 **"A woman who . . .":** Quoted in Berteaut, *Piaf,* 131.

74 **Early in her career . . . :** Quoted ibid., 82.

74 **As her half sister . . . :** Ibid., 176.

75 **From the topmost bleacher . . . :** Fitzlyon, *Price of Genius,* 162.

75 **Everyone who saw Pauline . . . :** Quoted ibid., 42 and 70, and Avrahm Yarmolinsky, *Turgenev: The Man, His Art and His Age* (New York: Orion Press, 1959), 86.

75 **For forty years . . . :** Fitzlyon, *Price of Genius,* 187.

75 **The ugly duckling . . . :** Rupert Christiansen, *Prima Donna: A History* (New York: Penguin Books, 1984), 77.

76 **Nicknamed the Ant . . . :** Fitzlyon, *Price of Genius,* 25.

76 **In a period of fascistic . . . :** Ibid., 42. See Rupert Christiansen on the intolerance for plainness on the Paris stage and ruthless ranking of actresses on the basis of pulchritude in *Paris Babylon.* "Few societies," he writes, "have so completely reduced women to sex objects as the Second Empire did," 92.

76 **Then she sang . . . :** Fitzlyon, *Price of Genius,* 28.

76 **It was a voice . . . :** Quoted ibid., 43.

76 **Critics compared it . . . :** Quoted ibid., 50 and 52.

76 **Like Dante's siren-ogre . . . :** Quoted in V. S. Pritchett, *The Gentle Barbarian: The Work and Life of Turgenev* (New York: Ecco Press, 1977), 36.

76 **She enchanted men . . . :** Quoted in Fitzlyon, *Price of Genius,* 49.

76 **He praised her . . . :** Quoted ibid., 60.

76 **Louis Viardot, a theater . . . :** Quoted ibid., 47, and ibid., 85.

77 **One of the most ardent . . . :** Quoted ibid., 94.

77 **For him, it was . . . :** Ibid., 165.

77 **He was six feet . . . :** Quoted ibid., 161.

77 **He treated her . . . :** Ibid., 451.

77 **She had a personality . . . :** Quoted ibid., 67.

77 **She told her St. Petersburg . . . :** Quoted ibid., 183–84.

77 **One huffy Russian . . . :** Quoted ibid., 431.

78 **"Laugh," he beseeched . . . :** Quoted ibid., 223.

78 **"Ah," she said, "I too . . .":** Quoted in Fitzlyon, *Price of Genius,* 281.

78 **The latter endured . . . :** Quoted in Fitzlyon, *Price of Genius,* 350 and 353.

78 **He dreamed of . . . :** Ibid., 417.

78 **"There have always . . .":** Quoted ibid., 312.

78 **"One of the greatest . . .":** Ibid., 246.

78 **"She is perfect" . . . :** Quoted ibid., 460.

78 **She died in 1910 . . . :** Ibid., 464.

79 **Objectively she resembled . . . :** Gautier poem quoted ibid., 12.

79 **When Turgenev drew . . . :** Quoted ibid., 448.

79 **"Transformation," say folklorists** . . . : Pierre Brunel, ed., *Companion to Literary Myths, Heroes, and Archetypes*, trans. Wendy Allatson et al. (New York: Routledge, 1992), 1430.

79 **They belie the** . . . : See Erik Erikson, who maintains "we feel beautiful according to how we've been loved. A child who is loved becomes more beautiful." *Journal of American Psychological Association*, 10 (1962), 451–74. Nancy Friday summarizes this axiom of self-esteem in "The Mutual Gaze and the Crying Storm," *Power of Beauty*, (New York: HarperCollins, 1996), 24–33.

79 **They knew—who better?** . . . : Shakespeare, *A Midsummer Night's Dream*, act I, scene i, line 8, 98.

79 **For that reason** . . . : Havelock Ellis expands on this idea that beauty of clothing, for example, operates as substitute for beauty of body in every society, *Psychology of Sex*, vol. 1, 158.

80 **When they talked** . . . : Robert R. Provine, *Laughter: A Scientific Investigation* (New York: Viking, 2000), 2.

80 **Symmetry, as George** . . . : George Santayana, *The Sense of Beauty* (New York: Dover, 1955 [1896]), 59 and 61.

80 **Belles laides knew** . . . : See Mario Praz, *The Romantic Agony*, trans. Angus Davidson (New York: Oxford University Press, 1970), 27, 25–94, and 199–300, and Wolfgang Kayser, *The Grotesque in Art and Literature*, trans. Ulrich Weisstein (New York: McGraw-Hill, 1963), 184 and passim. For a mathematical explanation of this mode of beauty, see Frank Close, *The Meaning of Asymmetry* (Oxford: Clarendon Press, 2001). The Zen proverb "True beauty is a deliberate, partial breaking of symmetry" approaches this aesthetic view.

80 **A belle laide "wins** . . .**":** George Sand, *Consuelo: A Romance of Venice* (New York: Da Capo Press, 1979), 7. Sand actually modeled her "ugly" seductress in this book on Pauline Viardot.

81 **"Prettiness suggests nothing"** . . . : George Moore, *Confessions of a Young Man* (New York: Capricorn Books, 1959), 83, and George Bernard Shaw, *Man and Superman* (Baltimore: Penguin Books, 1903), 207.

81 **A whole subgenre** . . . : This is a major, though neglected theme, in both film and literature. Movies include *The Truth About Cats and Dogs, Funny Girl,* and *The Mirror Has Two Faces*. Novels abound with *belles laides*. Some of the better-known homely sirens are Baroness Munster of Henry James's *The Europeans*, the bespectacled Hebe of Mary Wesley's *Harnessing Peacocks*, fat Drenka of Philip Roth's *Sabbath's Theater*, steatopygic Nora of Glenn Savan's *White Palace*, "ugly" Marian Halcombe of Wilkie Collins's *The Woman in White*, and the plain, fascinating Penelope of William Dean Howells's *The Rise of Silas Lapham*.

81 **In Marcel Proust's** . . . : Quoted in Carolyn Heilbrun, *Toward a Recognition of Androgyny* (New York: Norton, 1964), 79.

81 **Living dolls are** . . . : See Pietropinto and Simenauer, *Beyond the Male Myth*. They call the fixation on beauty a "throwback to adolescent masturbatory fantasy." The pretty "Dream Girl they believe is a teenage fantasy," 344 and 355. John Munder Ross in *What Men Want* (Cambridge, Mass.: Harvard University Press, 1994) analyzes the adolescents' tendency to objectify women and overvalue their beauty at some length. He connects this to their immature ego development and "the fear of seduction and engulfment of ultimately painful overstimulation by a woman," 190.

"Beauty safely conceals woman's frightening dimensions," writes Rita Freedman in *Beauty Bound*, a theme taken further by Camille Paglia, who sees it as a
male defense against woman's terrifying connection to the blood, flux, and de-
structiveness of nature, 61, and *Sexual Personae*. Freud always held that beauty was
"aim-inhibited sexuality," and linked scopophilic perversions to fear of female sexuality. *Civilization and Its Discontents*, 25, and *Three Essays on the Theory of Sexuality*,
trans. James Stachey (New York: Basic Books, 1962).
    For the standard studies of male sexual fears and the accompanying defense
mechanisms, see Lederer *The Fear of Women;* Hays, *The Dangerous Sex: The Myth of
Feminine Evil;* Horney, "The Dread of Women," 133–46; and Stern, *Flight from
Women*. Laura Mulvey elaborates on Freud's ideas of beauty as aim-inhibited sexuality and a scopophilic perversion in "Visual Pleasure and Narrative Cinema,"
Feminisms: An Anthology of Literary Theory and Criticism, ed. Robyn R. Warhol and
Diane Price Herndl (New Brunswick, N.J.: Rutgers University Press, 1991), 432–42.
    81 **While plastic surgery** . . . : Jane Brody reported in 1988 that "65 percent of
women do not like their bodies"; in 2000 a *People* poll found 80 percent women
"felt insecure about their looks." *New York Times*, October 20, 1988, B14, and "How
Do I Look," *People* (September 4, 2000), 114.
    82 **"Divinity within," he** . . . : Quoted in "Beauty," *Encyclopedia of Sexual Be-
havior*, ed. Albert Ellis and Albert Ararbanel (New York: Hawthorne Books, 1961),
vol. 1, 216.
    82 **Naomi Wolfe wrote** . . . : Wolfe, *The Beauty Myth* (New York: William
Morrow, 1991), 61.
    82 **But Zsa-Zsa Gabor** . . . : Quoted in Freedman, *Beauty Bound*, 64.

CHAPTER 4: SILVER FOXES

    84 **"I own," wrote** . . . : Quoted in Sydney George Fisher, *The True Benjamin
Franklin* (Philadelphia: J. P. Lippincott, 1899), 329.
    84 **Ancient Greek chroniclers** . . . : Brantome, *Lives of Fair and Gallant
Ladies*, 227.
    84 **The aged Jane Digby** . . . : Quoted in Tharp, *Mrs. Jack*, 322.
    84 **As the French** . . . : Brantôme, *Fair and Gallant Ladies*, 232.
    85 **As a recent survey** . . . : And that's a generous figure. Other studies show
a much lower rate of sexual satisfaction in the general female population, ranging
from 30 to 15 percent. Susan Crain Bakos, "From Lib to Libido," *Modern Maturity*
(September–October 1999), 57.
    85 **Prepatriarchal societies invested** . . . : Barbara G. Walker, *The Crone:
Women of Age, Wisdom, and Power* (San Francisco: Harper & Row, 1985), 24. See
Shahrukh Husain, on the subject of the elder deity's sexual voracity: "The crone
retains a powerful appetite for sex and like Hecate, Circe, and the Cailleach Beur,
copulates with young men by deception, coercion, or *sheer charisma*" (italics mine).
Goddess, 111.
    86 **Around her the** . . . : Bernard Fays, Franklin, *Apostle of Modern Times*
(Boston: Little, Brown, 1929), 461.
    86 **She "didn't know it"** . . . : Ibid., 459.
    86 **Statesmen, philosophers, historians** . . . : Willis Steell, *Benjamin Franklin
of Paris 1776–1785* (New York: Minton, Balch, 1928), 69.

86 "**Gaiety**" **resounded until . . . :** Jules Bertaut, "Madame Helvétius," *Égéries du xviiie siècle* (Paris: Librairie Plon, 1928), 166.

86 **A rabid advocate . . . :** Quoted in Judith Curtis, "Françoise d'Issembourg d'Happoncourt de Graffigny (1695–1758), *French Women Writers: A Bio-Biblio Sourcebook*, ed. Eva Martin Sartori and Dorothy W. Zimmerman (New York: Greenwood Press, 1991), 210.

87 **As "cunning and . . .":** Bertaut, "Madame Helvétius," 137.

87 **Christened the "light . . .":** Amelia Gere Mason, *The Women of the French Salons* (New York: Century, 1891), 188.

87 **Every morning his valet . . . :** Mademoiselle Gaussin once turned down six hundred livres for her favors with a flick of the hand at Helvétius. "Sir," she said to the disappointed suitor, "look like this man and I will give *you* twelve hundred Louis!" Quoted in Bertaut, "Madame Helvétius," 148.

87 **Proclaiming her his . . . :** Quoted ibid., 149.

88 **Her most serious . . . :** Quoted ibid., 158.

88 **Reconstituting her salon . . . :** Ibid., 166.

88 **The best minds, . . . :** Quoted in Fisher, *True Benjamin Franklin*, 329.

88 **In a backyard . . . :** Steell, *Franklin of Paris*, 76.

88 **Almost a male . . . :** His letter on the subject recommends "old women to young ones" because of their brains, conversation, and "disposition to please," quoted in Fisher, *True Franklin*, 127.

88 **Yet after seven weeks . . . :** Quoted in Carl Van Doren, *Benjamin Franklin* (New York, Viking, 1938), 651.

89 **Nearly every day . . . :** Steel, *Franklin of Paris*, 77.

89 **Minette shrieked with . . . :** Ibid., 70.

89 **"Let us *avenge* . . .":** Quoted in Van Doren, *Franklin*, 652.

89 **When he was at last . . . :** Quoted ibid., 653. A recent play about their relationship, *Balloon*, by Karen Sunde, portrays Minette as Benjamin Franklin's prompt and silent serviceable muse. But she was his equal in character, conversation, and charisma, even though she "spelled like a scrubwoman." Fays, *Franklin*, 459.

89 **After Franklin left . . . :** Chamfort, born illegitimate and educated in charity institutions, rose to become a member of the French Academy and intimate of Louis XVI and the nobility. Later he became secretary of the Jacobin Club during the Revolution but killed himself when he ran afoul of Marat and Robespierre and was threatened with imprisonment. Collections of his work include *Pensées, Maxims et anecdotes,* and *Oeuvres complètes.*

89 **As the nation hurtled . . . :** Quoted in Bertaut, "Madame Helvétius," 176.

89 **As "light and lively" . . . :** Ibid., 167 and 181.

90 **Franklin's drinking song, . . . :** Quoted in Carl Van Doren, *Benjamin Franklin's Autobiographical Writings* (New York: Viking, 1945), 477.

90 **Also, of course . . . :** Terrified of their "grand" motherly influence on children, eighteenth-century clerics tried to banish the aged from the nursery.

90 **Through the adroit . . . :** Brantôme, *Fair and Gallant Ladies,* 214.

90 **They gamboled in . . . :** Jehanne d'Orliac, *The Moon Mistress,* trans. F. M. Atkinson (Philadelphia: J. B. Lippincott, 1930), 272.

91 **But Catherine preferred . . . :** Her motto was "Odiate et aspetate." Quoted ibid., 267.

91 **Her father's favorite . . . :** Ibid., 29.

91 **Her teacher was** . . . : Ibid., 41.

91 **They learned classical** . . . : Ibid., 40. For the sort of narrow education girls of this period received, see Hufton, *The Prospect Before Her,* 28–61 and passim.

91 **Women had to** . . . : Castiglione, *Book of the Courtier,* 211.

92 **His jealous mistress** . . . : Quoted in d'Orliac, *Moon Mistress,* 68.

92 **Although sycophants called** . . . : Quoted in Armel de Wismes, *The Great Royal Favorites* (Nantes: Artaud Freres, n.d.), 15.

93 **Even Henri admitted** . . . : Quoted in Mark Strage, *Women of Power: The Life and Times of Catherine de'Medici* (New York: Harcourt Brace Jovanovich, 1976), 68.

93 **He taxed the churches** . . . : Quoted ibid., 61.

93 **He wore Diane's** . . . : Quoted in Grace Hart Seely, *Diane the Huntress: The Life and Times of Diane de Poitiers* (New York: D. Appleton-Century, 1936), 162.

93 **She "ruleth the** . . .": Quoted in Strage, *Women of Power,* 67.

93 **The "Dissimulation Queen"** . . . : Quoted in d'Orliac, *Moon Mistress,* 267.

94 **When Diane recovered** . . . : Quoted ibid., 215.

94 **Faithful to her credo** . . . : d'Orliac, 211 and Helen Weston Henderson, *The Enchantress* (Boston: Houghton Mifflin, 1928), 155.

94 **According to rumor** . . . : Supposedly Henri handed him a box of candy. "Hallo," Henri sniped, "every body must live." Quoted in William W. Sanger, *The History of Prostitution* (New York: Eugenics Publishing, 1939), 112.

94 **Brantôme, who saw** . . . : Brantôme, *Fair and Gallant Ladies,* 230, and quoted in Seely, *Diane the Huntress,* 234.

94 **Her elder enticements** . . . : d'Orliac, *Moon Mistress,* 22.

95 **With the ascendance** . . . : See Marina Warner, *Alone of All Her Sex: The Myth and Cult of the Virgin Mary* (New York: Vintage, 1983), 190 and 177–91.

96 **"Nothing," said this** . . . : Quoted in Edgar H. Cohen, *Mademoiselle Libertine: A Portrait of Ninon de Lanclos* (Boston: Houghton Mifflin, 1970), 188.

96 **Lovelocks spilled to** . . . : Quoted in Maud Cruttwell, *Madame de Maintenon* (London: J. M. Dent, 1930), 39.

96 **"It was a fight," she** . . . : Quoted ibid., 285.

96 **"You are as** . . .": Quoted in Charlotte Haldane, *Madame de Maintenon* (London: Constable, 1970), 27.

96 **Louis at first** . . . : Quoted ibid., 77.

97 **Childhood wounds still** . . . : Louis XIV's traumatic childhood fits a classic psychiatric profile. Unsatisfied by any of his wet nurses as a ravenous baby, he behaved in perfect accordance with Melanie Klein's theory. He split the breast— i.e., all women—into polarized opposites, the good and the bad. His puritanical mother and their overintimacy only exacerbated the split and his attachment to feminine purity. He also suffered from a secret sense of inferiority because of his spotty, neglected education and the accumulated scars from his tenth year during the Fronde, when he lived on the lam, in fear of his life.

97 **"She knows how** . . .": Quoted in Haldane, *Madame de Maintenon,* 78.

97 **Nicknamed the Thaw** . . . : Quoted in Cruttwell, *Madame de Maintenon,* 76 and 382; Haldane, *Madame de Maintenon,* 165; and quoted in Vincent Cronin, *Louis XIV,* (London, Harville, 1964), 232.

97 **She called him** . . . : Quoted in Haldane, *Madame de Maintenon,* 79.

97 **By 1680 the** . . . : Quoted in Cruttwell, *Madame de Maintenon,* 113.

97 **Françoise now passed . . . :** Quoted in Nancy Mitford, *The Sun King* (New York: Penguin, 1966), 45.

97 **As with so many senior . . . :** Quoted in Cronin, *Louis XIV,* 343.

97 **"However much you . . .":** Quoted ibid., 301.

97–8 **She put up with . . . :** Quoted in Cruttwell, *Madame de Maintenon,* 93.

98 **But her reign . . . :** Quoted ibid., 234.

98 **She outlived Louis . . . :** Quoted ibid., 203.

98 **She died at . . . :** Quoted in Cohen, *Mademoiselle Libertine,* 194.

98 **She always credited . . . :** Quoted in Cruttwell, *Madame de Maintenon,* 369.

99 **The misogynistic Greeks . . . :** See Athenaeus, for examples of this vituperative view of old women, *The Deipnosophists,* Books XIII–XIV, trans. C. B. Gulick (Cambridge, Mass.: Harvard University Press, 1937), passim. Also see Simone de Beauvoir's summary in *The Coming of Age,* trans. Patrick O'Brian (New York: Warner, 1972), 146–84.

99 **Of the twelve senior . . . :** Friedrich, *Meaning of Aphrodite,* 143. Learned speech was considered suprapotent by the Greeks. Virtuous women consequently were permitted to say "as little as possible." Quoted in Susan Groag Bell, *Women from the Greeks to the French Revolution* (Stanford, Calif.: Stanford University Press, 1973), 25. The culture was vociferous against female literacy and conversational skill. Two examples are Menander's "A man who teaches a woman to write . . . is providing poison to an asp" and Xenophon's "Is there anyone with whom you hold fewer discussions than your wife?" Quoted in Mary R. Lefkowitz and Maureen B. Fant, *Women's Life in Greece and Rome* (Baltimore: Johns Hopkins University Press, 1982), 31, and Bell, *Women from the Greeks,* 27.

99 **Gnathaena and Glycera . . . :** Athenaeus, *Deiphosophists,* 149.

99 **Until she died . . . :** Ibid., 149.

99 **She visited George . . . :** Quoted in Curtis Cate, *George Sand: A Biography* (Boston: Houghton Mifflin, 1975), xxi.

100 **Surrounding the "priestess" . . . :** Quoted in Joseph Barry, *Infamous Woman: The Life of George Sand* (Garden City, N.Y.: Doubleday, 1977), 316, 317, and 318.

100 **A "female Don Juan" . . . :** Quoted ibid., 101.

100 **"Old women," she . . . :** Quoted in Belinda Jack, *George Sand: A Woman's Life Writ Large* (New York: Alfred A. Knopf, 2000), 313.

100 **By the third year . . . :** Quoted in Barry, *Infamous Woman,* 84.

100 **Her first novel, . . . :** Cate, *George Sand,* 198.

101 **Although praised for . . . :** Quoted ibid., 602.

101 **Never beautiful–even . . . :** Quoted in Dan Hofstadter, *The Love Affair as a Work of Art* (New York: Farrar, Straus and Giroux, 1996), 140.

101 **With an "odalisque's . . .":** Quoted ibid., 120.

101 **While he caressed . . . :** Quoted ibid., 132.

101 **When she threw . . . :** Quoted in Barry, *Infamous Woman,* 191.

101 **Under cover of . . . :** André Maurois, *Lelia: The Life of George Sand,* trans. Gerard Hopkins (New York: Penguin, 1953), 290.

101 **"This complicated being . . .":** Quoted in Barry, *Infamous Woman,* 209.

101 **"Is she indeed . . .":** Quoted ibid., 241.

101 **Afterward she slid . . . :** Quoted ibid., 244.

101 **In addition to . . . :** Felizia Seyd, *Romantic Rebel: The Life and Times of George Sand* (New York: Viking, 1940), 156.

102 **"There are some . . .":** Quoted in Barry, *Infamous Woman,* 273.

102 **She went on . . . :** Maurois, *Lelia,* 540

102 **Like Morgan le Fay, . . . :** Quoted in Barry, *Infamous Woman,* 351. In her view, she aged backward. "It is quite wrong to think of old age as a downward slope," she wrote. "On the contrary, one climbs higher and higher with the advancing years and that too with surprising strides." Quoted in Maurois, *Lelia,* 542.

102 **"To preserve my . . .":** Quoted in Hofstadter, *Love Affair,* 143.

102 **Alexandre Manceau sweetened . . . :** Quoted in Cate, *George Sand,* 622.

102 **"I have laughed . . . :** Quoted in Barry, *Infamous Woman,* 338.

102 **"Brainwork," she said . . . :** Quoted in Maurois, *Lelia,* 542.

102 **Still "not exclusively . . . :** Barry, *Infamous Woman,* 166.

102 **After Manceau's death . . . :** Quoted ibid., 345.

102 **Her final words . . . :** Quoted ibid., 381.

102 **Although women never . . . :** Quoted ibid., 226. Like so many seductresses, George Sand never got on with other women. Her own daughter despised her, village housewives execrated her, and her best friend, Lizst's mistress, directed a crazed vendetta against her. Simone de Beauvoir assails her for her lack of solidarity with other women, and some female biographers, such as Renee Winegarten, gloat over her tragic unhappiness. In return George had a low opinion of her sex. Although she abhorred their enslaved position, she refused to support the feminist revolutionaries, arguing that women had been rendered too dependent to act responsibly. See "She Had It All," *New York Review of Books* (October 11, 1979), 11, and Renee Winegarten, *The Double Life of George Sand, Woman and Writer* (New York: Basic Books, 1979).

102–3 **"To know how . . .":** Quoted in Barry, *Infamous Woman,* 376.

103 **With age, George . . . :** Quoted ibid., xiv.

103 **Crowned with supraconfidence . . . :** Quoted in Donna Dickerson, *George Sand* (New York: Berg Publishers, 1988), 165.

103 **For a century . . . :** Quoted in Barry, *Infamous Woman,* 268, and quoted in Seyd, *Romantic Rebel,* 33.

103 **As Sainte-Beuve told . . . :** Quoted in Hofstadter, *Love Affair,* 157.

103 **Colette, the celebrated . . . :** Quoted in Lois W. Banner, *In Full Flower: Aging Women, Power and Sexuality* (New York: Alfred A. Knopf, 1992), 23, and Colette, *Ripening Seed,* trans. Roger Senhouse (New York: Penguin, 1959 [1923]), 71.

103 **After squandering her . . . :** Colette, *Ripening Seed,* 71.

103 **Ensuring that her . . . :** Margaret Crosland, *Colette: The Difficulty of Loving* (New York: Dell, 1973), 45.

104 **The entire time . . . :** Judith Thurman, *Secrets of the Flesh* (New York: Alfred A. Knopf, 1999), 296.

104 **Seated beside him . . . :** Quoted ibid., 336.

104 **She "saved" him . . . :** Ibid., 356.

104 **To Colette, the . . . :** Colette, *Julie de Carneilhan,* trans. Roger Senhouse (New York: Farrar, Straus and Giroux, 1952), 164.

104 **But she had something . . . :** Husain, *Goddess,* 135, and Yarnall, *Transformations of Circe,* 10.

105 **When she was elected** . . . : Robert Phelps, *Belles Saisons: A Colette Scrapbook* (New York: Farrar, Straus and Giroux, 1978), 248.

105 **This "impudent woman"** . . . : Quoted in George Eells and Stanley Musgrove, *Mae West* (New York: William Morrow, 1982), 148.

105 **The crone goddess** . . . : Husain, *Goddess*, III.

105 **She roamed the night** . . . : Ibid., A sampling of these divine she-leches includes the Empusae, Mormolyceia, and Lamiae of Greek mythology, the Irish Morrigan, the Baltic raganas, and such fairy-tale descendants as Desart Fairy of "The Yellow Dwarf." All lured youths to their beds by turning themselves into beautiful young women.

105 **But Mae West** . . . : *"Playboy* Interview: Mae West," *Playboy* (January 1971), 74.

105 **She seemed endowed** . . . : Quoted in Richard Meryman, "Mae West: A Cherished, Bemusing Masterpiece of Self-Preservation," *Life* (April 18, 1969), 69.

106 **A Bavarian corset** . . . : This was turn-of-the-century working-class Brooklyn, where girls miss-prissed and walked the purity chalk line; one slip and the plunge into "female depravity" began. Ronald G. Walters, *Primers for Prudery: Sexual Advice to Victorian America* (Englewood Cliffs, N.J.: Prentice-Hall, 1974), 69.

106 **Terrified, as seductresses** . . . : She discoursed on these preferences often. "I never wanted motherhood," she said, "because you have to think about the child and I only had time for me. Just the way I didn't want no husband because he'd of interfered with my hobby and my career." Or again: "I never wanted children . . . motherhood's a career in itself." Quoted in Eells and Musgrove, *Mae West*, 14, and *Playboy*, 80. The homemaker-phobic Mae also loathed domestica. "I was never the cottage-apron type," she told *Playboy*, 80.

106 **"There's nobody in . . ."**: *Playboy*, 80.

106 **Sex, the story** . . . : Quoted in Lillian Schlissel, intro., *Three Plays by Mae West: Sex, The Drag, and The Pleasure Queen* (New York: Routledge, 1997), 10. DE-PRAVED, NASTY, VICIOUS! screamed headlines. Quoted in Eells and Musgrove, *Mae West*, 98.

106 **While Mae was** . . . : *Playboy*, 74.

107 **Convinced that a "thrill . . ."**: *Go West Young Man*, Paramount, directed by Henry Hathaway, 1936.

107 **A matinee idol** . . . : Quoted in Eells and Musgrove, *Mae West*, 76.

107 **Rich, famous, and** . . . : Mae West, *Goodness Had Nothing to Do with It* (New York: Avon, 1959), 50.

107 **"Let 'um *wonder*"** . . . : Quoted in *Playboy*, 76, and West, *Goodness*, 219.

108 **On the verge** . . . : Eells and Musgrove, *Mae West*, 56, and *Playboy*, 74.

108 **Thirty-three, blue-eyed, and** . . . : Quoted in Eells and Musgrove, *Mae West*, 293.

108 **At "seventy-sex," her** . . . : *Playboy*, 74.

108 **She rewrote the** . . . : Quoted in Eells and Musgrove, *Mae West*, 295.

108 **She died at** . . . : Quoted in *Playboy*, 78.

108 **Unlike Marilyn, Mae** . . . : "The Strong Woman: What Was Mae West Really Fighting For," *New Yorker* (November 11, 1996), 105.

109 **"I was the first . . ."**: Quoted in Emily Wortis Leider, *Becoming Mae West* (New York: Farrar, Straus and Giroux, 1997), 339, and West, *Goodness*, 213.

109 **One critic associated . . . :** Quoted in Eells and Musgrove, *Mae West,* 128.

109 **"I'm the woman's . . .":** Quoted in *Life,* 62C; *Playboy,* 73 and 78.

109 **Or as her *Diamond Lil . . . :*** Mae West, *Diamond Lil* (New York: Dell, 1932), book jacket.

109 **Wealth, she loved . . . :** West, *Goodness,* 221.

109 **"No loadstone so . . .":** Burton, *Anatomy of Melancholy,* 624.

110 **When women her age . . . :** Quoted in Madeleine B. Stern, *Purple Passage: The Life of Mrs. Frank Leslie* (Norman: University of Oklahoma Press, 1953), 79.

110 **Only older women, . . . :** Mrs. Frank Leslie, *Are Men Gay Deceivers?* (Chicago: Neely, 1893), 227.

110 **At the apex . . . :** Quoted ibid., 114.

110 **No modest matron . . . :** Ibid., 3.

110 **In a crackpot scheme . . . :** Ibid., 13.

110 **Her mother forced . . . :** Quoted ibid., 7.

111 **The mistress was . . . :** Quoted in Ross, *Uncrowned Queen,* 202.

111 **She rechristened Miriam . . . :** Stern, *Purple Passion,* 23.

111 **Her "beauty," wrote Frank . . . :** Quoted ibid., 38.

112 **The Leslies opened . . . :** Quoted ibid., 73.

112 **She wore the . . . :** Quoted ibid., 74.

112 **He died in . . . :** Quoted ibid., 98.

113 **The astonished business . . . :** Quoted ibid., 105, 122, and 106.

113 **The "belle," she wrote . . . :** Leslie, *Are Men Gay Deceivers?,* 31 and 231.

113 **But she refused . . . :** Quoted in Stern, *Purple Passion,* 119.

113 **She was fifty-five, . . . :** Leslie, *Are Men Gay Deceivers?,* 178, and Key, *Love and Ethics,* 81.

113 **"He was of no use" . . . :** Quoted in Stern, *Purple Passion,* 160 and 162.

113 **With a Scarlett O'Hara . . . :** Leslie, *Are Men Gay Deceivers?,* 111, and Stern, *Purple Passion,* 108.

114 **To better reflect . . . :** Quoted in Stern, *Purple Passion,* 109.

114 **The same "habit . . .":** Leslie, *A Social Mirage* (London and New York: F. Tennyson Neely, 1899), 306.

114 **Go for the clout . . . :** Ibid., 17 and 87.

114 **"The fascinating woman" . . . :** Leslie, *Are Men Gay Deceivers?,* 111 and 232.

114 **Frank Leslie's carpets . . . :** Quoted in Stern, *Purple Passion,* 125.

115 **We're witnessing, reports . . . :** Ben Brantley, "Strutting Past the Ingenues: Women of Experience Grab the British Spotlight," *New York Times,* August 16, 2000, E4.

115 **Surrealist artist Beatrice Wood . . . :** Quoted in Roberta Wood, "Beatrice Wood, 105, Potter and Mama of Dada, Is Dead," *New York Times,* March 14, 1998, A15.

115 **"Honey," said Lena Horne . . . :** Quoted in Joan Rivers, *Don't Count the Candles: Just Keep the Flame Alive* (New York: HarperCollins, 1999), 113.

115 **Because of poor . . . :** Rita M. Ransohoff, Ph.D., *Venus After Forty* (Far Hills, N.J.: New Horizon Press, 1987), xv.

115 **A woman's chances . . . :** Cited in Betty Friedan, *The Fountain of Age* (New York: Simon & Schuster, 1993), 261, and Sara Rimer, "For Aged Dating Game Is Numbers Game," *New York Times,* December 23, 1998, A1.

115 **The rest, though . . . :** Colette Dowling, *Red Hot Mamas* (New York: Bantam, 1996), 19. Many wise elders counsel women to hang it up. Internalizing the patriarchal battleax stereotypes, they adjure seniors to celebrate cronehood and retreat from the field. Betty Friedan recommends handling the sexual "blackout" through communes and "enlightened" polygamy, and Germaine Greer and Carolyn Heilbrun advise flat-out resignation. Let nature take its course, they argue, be done with diets, cosmetics, and coquetry, and "leave romance to the young." Heilbrun charges, "Sex after sixty cannot be the object of any undertaking." Friedan, *Fountain of Age*, 258. Carolyn Heilbrun, *The Last Gift of Time: Life Beyond Sixty* (New York: Ballantine, 1997), 112 and 113. Greer celebrates the "emancipation from the duty of sexual attraction" and the consolations of proud singlehood in *The Change: Women Aging and Menopause* (New York: Fawcett Columbine, 1991), 41 and passim.

116 **Jean-Paul Sartre called . . .** : Sartre, *Being and Nothingness*, 455.

117 **"May the gods," . . .** : Ovid, *Art of Love*, Book 1, VIII, line 113, 29.

118 **Above the entrance . . .** : Quoted in Roger S. and Laura H. Loomis, eds., *Medieval Romances* (New York: Random House, 1957), 387, and Barbara G. Walker, *The Women's Encyclopedia of Myths and Secrets* (San Francisco: HarperCollins, 1983), 674.

CHAPTER 5: SCHOLAR-SIRENS

120 **"Men hate intellectual . . ."**: Alfred Lord Tennyson, "The Princess," Part II, line 442, quoted in Stevenson, ed., *Home Book of Quotations*, 2193.

120 **For that reason . . .** : Such a goddess was the divine sage as well as the sexual energy of the universe. Primitive peoples envisioned her as the moon, which contained her wise blood, and in fact, "moon" and "mind" share the same root, the Indo-European *manas*. Walker, *Women's Encyclopedia*, 670. "In ancient societies," notes scholar Miriam Dexter, "the dumb but beautiful image was not an ideal." Miriam Robbins Dexter, *Whence the Goddess* (New York: Teachers College, 1990), 22.

121 **Being smarter than . . .** : Ellen Winner, quoted in Howard Gardner, *Extraordinary Minds* (New York: Basic Books, 1997), 41.

121 **Veronica Franco, a brilliant . . .** : Masson, *Courtesans of the Italian Renaissance*, 155.

121 **Her forte was . . .** : Wolkstein and Kramer, *Inanna*, 17. Aphrodite's attendant was Peitho (persuasion), and the Scandinavian sex goddess Freya's other name was Saga or Sayer. Walker, *Women's Encyclopedia*, 325.

121 **"Rhetoric in all . . ."**: Leonardo Bruni, quoted in Margaret L. King, "Book-lined Cells: Women and Humanism in the Early Italian Renaissance," *Beyond Their Sex: Learned Women of the European Past*, ed. Patricia Labalme (New York: New York University Press, 1984), 77.

121 **Those who rebelled . . .** : During the Renaissance, Italy produced a galaxy of vocal female intellectuals—translators, orators, and writers—but they sacrificed sex and personal fulfillment. Of the ten major humanist scholars of the quattrocento, three remained single and all but one withdrew in silence after marriage. The rule was *Maritar o monacar* (Marry or take the veil). King, "Book-lined Cells," 131.

121 **These renegade birds . . .** : Margaret F. Rosenthal, *The Honest Courtesan* (Chicago: University of Chicago Press, 1992), 73.

122 **Determined to "educate . . .":** Ibid., 87.
122 **A maestra of . . . :** Masson, *Courtesans of the Italian Renaissance,* 164.
122 **She bragged that . . . :** Ibid., 157 and 158.
123 **An "expensive mouthful" . . . :** Ibid., 153.
123 **She's the one in charge . . . :** Quoted in Rosenthal, *Honest Courtesan,* 227.
123 **I'd not give . . . :** Quoted in Lawner, *Lives of the Courtesans,* 56.
124 **In such a utopia . . . :** Rosenthal, *Honest Courtesan,* 253.
124 **"Of all the world's . . ." :** Quoted ibid., 133.
124 **Her devotees called . . . :** Quoted ibid., 95 and Baring and Cashford, *Myth of the Goddess,* 265.
125 **The imperious Louis . . . :** Quoted in Cohen, *Mademoiselle Libertine,* 246.
125 **Like Inanna's alter ego . . . :** Wolkstein and Kramer, *Inanna,* 15.
125 **The tastemaker of . . . :** Voltaire quoted in Cohen, *Mademoiselle Libertine,* 301.
125 **The most distinguished men . . . :** Ninon quoted ibid., 74.
125 **They also bowed . . . :** Ibid., 49.
125 **Such a power . . . :** See Hufton, *Prospect Before Her,* 3–62 and passim.
125 **When the curé . . . :** Ninon quoted in Cohen, *Mademoiselle Libertine,* 26.
126 **Rather than the traditional . . . :** Quoted in Emile Magne, *Ninon de Lenclos,* trans. Gertrude Scott Stevenson (New York: Henry Holt, 1948), 12.
126 **Her most besotted . . . :** Segrais quoted in Cohen, *Mademoiselle Libertine,* 57.
126 **Unlike the priggish . . . :** Ninon quoted ibid., 38. Soren Kierkegaard expressed a similar sentiment: "A man who could not seduce men cannot save them either." Quoted in W. H. Auden and Louis Kronenberger, *The Viking Book of Aphorisms* (New York: Viking, 1962), 249.
126 **Her "enchanting" conversation . . . :** Quoted in Cohen, *Mademoiselle Libertine,* 269.
126 ***Toute le monde . . . :*** Ninon quoted ibid., 246.
127 **Your conversation is . . . :** Chapelle quoted ibid., 134.
127 **A live wire . . . :** Ninon quoted ibid., 118.
127 **No less uninhibited . . . :** Saint-Évremond quoted ibid., 119.
127 **She reportedly brought . . . :** Ibid., 74–75, and Ninon quoted ibid., 174.
127 **"Love with passion . . .":** Ninon quoted ibid., 174.
127 **She was, penultimately . . . :** Tallement quoted in Cohen, *Mademoiselle Libertine,* 39.
128 **The man was . . . :** Quoted ibid., 136.
128 **Physically magnetized by . . . :** Quoted ibid., 140–41.
129 **She reserved a . . . :** Saint-Évremond, quoted ibid., 202.
129 **Shunned all her life . . . :** Ibid., 255.
129 **They were tyrannized . . . :** Quoted in Magne, *Ninon de Lenclos,* 234.
129 **"A woman who . . .":** Ninon quoted in Cohen, *Mademoiselle Libertine,* 174.
129 **One suggested that . . . :** Quoted ibid., 295.
130 **"Her mind was . . .":** Quoted in Rudolph Binion, *Frau Lou: Nietzsche's Wayward Disciple* (Princeton: Princeton University Press, 1968), 32.
130 **But it was a mind . . . :** Wolkstein and Kramer, *Inanna,* 18. Today it's called personal intelligence, a heightened understanding of others and oneself. See Gardner, *Extraordinary Minds,* 36, and *Frames of Minds: The Theory of Multiple Intelligences* (New York: Basic Books, 1983), 237–76.

130 **One of our deepest . . . :** For a sampling of views on this, see Person, *Dreams of Love and Fateful Encounters,* 58–62, 82, and passim; Alice Miller, *The Drama of the Gifted Child,* trans. Ruth Ward (New York: Basic Books, 1981), 15; Ortega y Gasset, *On Love,* 36–39 and 136–7; Robert Solomon, *About Love* (New York: Simon & Schuster, 1989), 189–99; and Maurois, "The Art of Loving," 22–30. Paul Valéry says it succinctly: "Love is directed toward what lies hidden in its object." *Lovers' Quotation Book,* ed. Helen Handley (New York: Penguin, 1987), 25.

130 **Lou Andreas-Salomé, the . . . :** Lisa Appignanesi and John Forrester, *Freud's Women* (New York: Basic Books, 1992), 241.

130 **The god-men of . . . :** Quoted in Angela Livingstone, *Salomé: Her Life and Work* (Mount Kisco, N.Y.: MoyerBell, 1984), 169.

130 **Her titanic ego . . . :** Stanley A. Leavy, intro., *The Freud Journal of Lou Andreas-Salomé,* trans. Stanley A. Leavy (London: Hogarth Press and Institute of Psycho-Analysis, 1965), 25.

131 **When she found school . . . :** Quoted in H. F. Peters, *My Sister, My Spouse: A Biography of Lou Andreas-Salomé* (New York: Norton, 1962), 31.

131 **After her studies . . . :** Quoted ibid., 66.

132 **From the moment . . . :** Anaïs Nin, intro., ibid., 8.

132 **Lou's clairvoyant grasp . . . :** Quoted in Appignanesi and Forrester, *Freud's Women,* 247.

132 **With the fury . . . :** Quoted in Peters, *My Sister,* 132.

132 **He called her . . . :** Quoted ibid., 153, and quoted in Livingstone, *Salomé,* 40.

132 **One regular said . . . :** Quoted in Peters, *My Sister,* 154.

132 **Although she invited . . . :** Quoted in Livingstone, *Salomé,* 61.

133 **They don't "need . . .":** Quoted ibid., 137.

133 **During her mid-thirties . . . :** *Fenitschka* quoted ibid., 208.

133 **Any number of . . . :** Quoted in Peters, *My Sister,* 196.

133 **He changed his name . . . :** Quoted in Livingstone, *Salomé* 104.

133 **Their life together . . . :** Ibid., 110.

133 **For Rainer she . . . :** Quoted in Peters, *My Sister,* 215; Livingstone, *Salomé,* 104; Binion, *Frau Lou,* 215; and Livingstone, *Salomé,* 101.

134 **Despite Zemek's popularity . . . :** Peters, *My Sister,* 267.

134 **She not only . . . :** Mary-Kay Wilmers, intro., Lou Andreas-Salomé, *The Freud Journal,* trans. Stanley A. Leavy (London: Quartet Books, 1964), xi.

134 **Victor Tausk, a tall . . . :** Quoted in Peters, *My Sister,* 279.

134 **She'd bewitched him, . . . :** Quoted ibid., 270.

134 **"The reception of . . .":** Quoted ibid., 263.

134 **Expanding on her . . . :** Quoted in Livingstone, *Salomé,* 144.

134 **Through intercourse, she wrote . . . :** Under Hendrik Gillot Lou studied extensively "rites and rituals" of primitive societies. Peters, *My Sister,* 53.

135 **Some "geniuses" of . . . :** Andreas-Salomé, *Freud Journal,* 149, and quoted in Livingstone, *Salomé,* 144.

135 **"Yes, I am . . .":** Quoted ibid., 213.

135 **She didn't exaggerate . . . :** Andreas-Salomé, *Freud Journal,* 118.

135 **Others—Freud, Rilke, . . . :** Andreas-Salomé, *Freud Journal,* 26 and quoted in Peters, *My Sister,* 13.

135 **At the same time . . . :** Freud quoted in Appignanesi and Forrester,

Freud's Women, 241; Lesley Chamberlain, "Rilke's Muse, and Freud's?," *Times Literary Supplement* (October 20, 2000), 36; and Livingstone, *Salomé,* 166.

135 **"The Fairy godmother . . ."**: Quoted in Appignanesi and Forrester, *Freud's Women,* 267.

135 **But this gift . . .** : Wolkstein and Kramer, *Inanna,* 16.

135 **Inanna's deputy, the sexy . . .** : Quoted in Frymer-Kensky, *Wake of the Goddess,* 40.

135 **Although usually considered . . .** : For a detailed discussion of this, see Walker, *The Crone.* The Goddess, she writes, "was regarded as the sole origin of orderly, logical thought. Out of her intellectual gifts to women arose such disciplines as mathematics (originally meaning 'mother-wisdom'), calendars (originally 'lunar' or 'menstrual'), [and] systems of measurement," 7.

136 **"A genius in . . ."**: Samuel Edwards, *The Divine Mistress* (New York: David McKay, 1970), 241.

136 **"The wench," said . . .** : Quoted ibid., 9.

136 **"The most brilliant . . ."** : Quoted ibid., 232 and Nancy Mitford, *Voltaire in Love* (New York: E.P. Dutton, 1957), 14.

136 **"No great lord . . ."**: Ibid., 11.

136 **They took bets . . .** : Quoted ibid., 221.

137 **With one, she feigned . . .** : Quoted ibid., 24.

137 **This national hero . . .** : Ibid., 31.

137 **"Fascinated by her . . ."**: Ibid., 41.

138 **The high-tension sexual . . .** : See Ira O. Wade, *Voltaire and Madame du Chatelet: An Essay on the Intellectual Activity at Cirey* (Princeton: Princeton University Press, 1941) for a discussion of their mutual influence on each other and his lengthy analysis of Emilie's probable authorship of *Examen de la Genèse,* 45–89.

138 **The academic establishment . . .** : Quoted in Edwards, *Divine Mistress,* 181 and book jacket.

139 **They should, she advised . . .** : Quoted ibid., 92 and 224.

139 **She oversaw his diet . . .** : Ibid., 186.

139 **But he was content . . .** : Quoted ibid., 129.

139 **"I have lost . . ."**: Quoted ibid., 268.

139 **They sniggered at her . . .** : Quoted ibid., 157.

139 **"The light of . . ."**: Quoted ibid., 1 and 2.

140 **She was also known . . .** : Quoted in Carl Rollyson, *Nothing Ever Happens to the Brave: The Story of Martha Gellhorn* (New York: St. Martin's, 1990), 25 and 41.

140 **Later, at Bryn Mawr . . .** : Ibid., 32.

140 **She dangled a . . .** : Quoted ibid., 29.

140 **Uninhibited, sensuous, fun-loving . . .** : Quoted ibid., 24.

141 **He shared Martha's . . .** : Martha Gellhorn, quoted in Rick Lyman, "Martha Gellhorn, Daring Writer, Dies at 89," *New York Times,* February 17, 1998, B11.

141 **They married in . . .** : Quoted in Victoria Glendinning, "The Real Thing," *Vogue* (April 1988), 398.

141 **Her record of . . .** : Rollyson, *Martha Gellhorn,* 82.

141 **She wore a black . . .** : Quoted ibid., 90.

141 **Invading the no-woman's-zone . . .** : Ibid., 108.

141 **They used each . . .** : See Martha's "discerning and engaging" portrait of

Hemingway on their trip to China together and his play *The Fifth Column,* in which he portrays her as Dorothy, a woman with her flair and the "loveliest damn body in the world." But there the similarity ended. Unlike her passive, somnambulistic stage persona, Martha was a tiger. Quoted in Bernice Kert, *The Hemingway Women* (New York: Norton, 1983), 355, and quoted in Jeffrey Meyers, *Hemingway: A Biography* (New York: Harper & Row, 1985), 317.

141 **"He would be . . ."** : Quoted in Meyers, *Hemingway,* 350.

142 **Her powerful pieces . . .** : Rollyson, *Martha Gellhorn,* 108.

142 **During the postwar . . .** : Quoted in Lyman, "Martha Gellhorn," B11.

142 **A "female flying . . ."**: Quoted in Rollyson, *Martha Gellhorn,* 247.

143 **Traditional "soft and . . ."**: Martha Gellhorn, "A Promising Career," *The Novellas of Martha Gellhorn* (New York: Vintage Books, 1991), 331.

143 **These swanky sexpots . . .** : Gellhorn, "Till Death Do Us Part," *Novellas,* 303, and *His Own Man* (New York: Simon & Schuster, 1961), 67 and 73.

143 **Increasingly anti-American . . .** : Quoted in Rollyson, *Martha Gellhorn,* 318.

143 **Hemingway's cronies thought . . .** : Quoted ibid., 182. The three-volume *Notable American Women* devotes a page to her mother, the St. Louis suffragist and civic leader, but omits Martha. Ironically, she was an ardent feminist, referring to American women of the fifties as "Arab females." Quoted in Rollyson, *Martha Gellhorn,* 272.

143 **More "ambitious than . . ."**: Quoted ibid., 236.

143 **With the goddess's . . .** : Quoted in Lyman, "Martha Gellhorn," B11.

143 **As the deity's . . .** : Frymer-Kensky, *Wake of the Goddess,* 48. Hemingway griped that he felt like one more addition to her "collection" of men. Quoted in Rollyson, *Martha Gellhorn,* 202.

143 **She once said . . .** : Quoted in Lyman, "Martha Gellhorn," B11.

144 **Despite male claims . . .** : Neumann, *Great Mother,* 296.

144 **Hence the sexual . . .** : Guy Sirello, "Beauty and Sex," *The Philosophy of Sex,* ed. Alan Soble (Savage, Md.: Rowan & Littlefield, 1991), 21.

144 **As a result, academics . . .** : Madeleine M. Henry, *Prisoner of History: Aspasia of Miletus and Her Biographical Tradition* (New York: Oxford University Press, 1995), 17.

144 **At the very least . . .** : Paul Werner, *Life in Greece in Ancient Times,* trans. David Macrae (Geneva: Minerva, 1978–81), 53.

145 **Added to these . . .** : Henry, *Prisoner of History,* 17.

145 **Plutarch says that . . .** : Quoted in C. Hayward, *Dictionary of Courtesans* (New Hyde Park, N.Y.: University Books, 1962), 32.

145 **Attracted, according to report . . .** : Plutarch, "Pericles," *The Rise and Fall of Athens,* trans. Ian Scott-Kilvert (New York: Penguin, 1960), 190.

145 **He became so . . .** : Henry, *Prisoner of History,* 13.

145 **Without his encouragement . . .** : Ibid., 3.

145 **Socrates, one of . . .** : Quoted in Werner, *Life in Greece,* 32.

145 **A canny performance . . .** : See Henry, *Prisoner of History,* 38, for a discussion of the subtleties and complexities of this performance.

146 **The seducer, she . . .** : Ibid., 47.

146 **This was volatile . . .** : Lugo Basserman, *The Oldest Profession,* trans. James Cleugh (New York: Dorset Press, 1967), 15.

146 **Playwrights assailed her . . . :** Aristophanes quoted in Henry, *Prisoner of History*, 28.

146 **PC scholars condemn . . . :** Ibid., 6.

146 **Judy Chicago accordingly . . . :** Judy Chicago, *The Dinner Party* (Garden City, N.Y.: Anchor, 1979), 122.

146 **And she comes . . . :** Wolkstein and Kramer, *Inanna*, 26 and 15.

146 **In early nineteenth-century . . . :** J. Christopher Herold, *Mistress to an Age* (New York: Time-Life Books, 1958), 469.

146 **For most of . . . :** Quoted ibid., 558. Wayne Andrews, *Germaine: A Portrait of Madame de Staël* (London: Victor Gollancz, 1964), 209.

147 **This vamped-up opera . . . :** See de Staël's essay on Aspasia in the *Biographie universelle*, 1811–57, discussed in Gretchen Besser, *Germaine de Staël Revisited* (New York: Twayne, 1994), 113–14.

147 **"A dictionary of . . .":** B. d'Andlau, *Madame de Staël*, trans. Georges Solovieff (Coppet: n.p., 1975), 32.

147 **She molded public . . . :** Besser, *Germaine de Staël*, 144.

147 **Heavyweights from Goethe . . . :** Quoted in Vivian Folkenflik, *An Extraordinary Woman: Selected Writings of Germaine de Staël* (New York: Columbia University Press, 1987), 5.

147 **She suddenly metamorphosed, . . . :** Quoted in Dan Hofstadter, *The Love Affair as a Work of Art* (New York: Farrar, Straus and Giroux, 1996), 23.

147 **Her huge black . . . :** Quoted in d'Andlau, *Germaine de Staël*, 50, 25, and 61.

148 **"Of all the men . . .":** Quoted in Herold, *Mistress to an Age*, 56.

148 **"No one could . . .":** Ibid., 64.

148 **"The most brilliant . . .":** Ibid., 85.

148 **She flattered, teased . . . :** Quoted in Andrews, *Germaine*, 150.

148 **When he fled . . . :** Quoted ibid., 104.

148 **During the Terror . . . :** Herold, *Germaine*, 344.

149 **By the time Germaine . . . :** Hofstadter, *Love Affair*, 8.

149 **"Her mind dazzled . . .":** D'Andlau, *Germaine de Staël*, 39, and quoted in Hofstadter, *Love Affair*, 23–24.

149 **Still, over the ensuing . . . :** Quoted in Andrews, *Germaine*, 169.

149 **He moaned, "No one . . .":** Quoted ibid., 101.

149 **During their roller-coaster . . . :** Quoted in d'Andlau, *Germaine de Staël*, 50.

149 **Criticism should be . . . :** Quoted in Vivian Folkenflik, *Extraordinary Woman*, 13, and Herold, *Mistress to an Age*, 243.

150 **As a philosopher . . . :** Herold, *Mistress to an Age*, 233, and see Germaine's self-assessments in *Corinne*, Folkenflik, *Extraordinary Woman*, 254, and her Cleopatra biography, Besser, *Germaine de Staël*, 114–15.

150 **Included this time . . . :** Herold, *Mistress to an Age*, 504, and quoted in Andrews, *Germaine*, 190.

150 **Her death stunned . . . :** Quoted in Herold, *Mistress to an Age*, 580.

150 **Her male detractors . . . :** Quoted ibid., 223, and Besser, *Germaine de Staël*, 139.

150 **"Monsieur," she told . . . :** Quoted in Andrews, *Germaine*, 131.

151 **In Corinne's climactic . . . :** Walker, *Women's Encyclopedia*, 201.

151 **These truths, like . . . :** Wolkstein and Kramer, *Inanna*, 16.

151 **But Germaine emerged . . . :** According to tradition, Germaine never achieved true happiness. But scholar Vivian Folkenflik vigorously refutes this, citing Germaine's own life assessment in her final book, *Ten Years of Exile.* "Mme. de Staël gives us enough in passing to let us know that she has made her life in exile a full one: the pleasure of knowing someone who will lend you his house when you are exiled from Paris, the delights of intimate conversation with long-term friends and complicated flirtatious games no one else can play; the enterprising determination of a woman in her midforties to investigate her property in America; the enjoyment of playing and hearing music, and the genuine curiosity about Indian rarities, encountered by chance. If she takes some satisfaction in this, we may be able to share it with her. Necessarily on the periphery, she had succeeded in making herself a life elsewhere," 36.

151 **She transcended her . . . :** Quoted in Folkenflik, *Extraordinary Woman,* 27 and 19, and d'Andlau, *Madame de Staël,* 25. Germaine defined happiness at one point as "the union of all contrary things" and elaborated further: It's "hope without fear, activity without anxiety, glory without calumny . . . the good side of all conditions, talents, and pleasures, without their accompanying evils," 18.

151 **"One must adore . . .":** Quoted in Herold, *Mistress to an Age,* 460 and 234.

151 **Sixty-eight percent of . . . :** In this study, women said they'd rather "raise babies, make dinner parties, and dress up" than have careers. Quoted in Erica Jong, "Are We Having Fun Yet?," *Talk* (October 2000), 136.

151 **Dr. Barbara Kerr believes . . . :** Barbara Kerr, *Smart Women,* rev. ed. (Scottsdale: Arizona State University, 1994), 239; see 219–42 for her findings. For more support for her conclusions, see Marie Richmond-Abbott, *Masculine and Feminine* (New York: McGraw-Hill, 1992), 134–40, and Person, *Dreams of Love,* 283 and passim.

151 **Afraid that IQ . . . :** Dale Spender, *Women of Ideas and What Men Have Done to Them* (London and Boston: Routledge & Kegan Paul, 1982), 19.

151 **The Rules warns . . . :** Ellen Fein and Sherrie Schneider, *The Rules* (New York: Warner, 1995), 34, and Brenda Venus, *Secrets of Seduction for Women* (New York: Dutton, 1996), 77. Also see Brigitte Nioche, *What Turns Him On* (New York: NAL, 1989), 39; Helen Gurley Brown, *Having It All* (New York: Simon & Schuster, 1982), 208; Georgette Mosbacher, *Feminine Force* (New York: Simon & Schuster, 1982), 127–37; Tracey Cabot, *How to Make a Man Fall in Love with You* (New York: St. Martin's, 1984), 46, 125, to begin the list.

Arlene Dahl's classic retroadvice is all too pervasive: "The successful female never lets her competence compete with her femininity. . . . Never upstage a man. Don't top his jokes. . . . Never launch loudly into your own opinions on the subject." Quoted in Harriet G. Lerner, *The Dance of Deception* (New York: HarperCollins, 1993), 49.

153 **"A well-educated woman" . . . :** Stendhal, *Love,* 186. Ovid thought women should learn two great languages well, as a bare minimum, and Robert Burton insisted that "the lineaments of the mind are far fairer than those of the body, incomparably beyond them." *Anatomy of Melancholy,* 631. Moderns such as Bertrand Russell and André Maurois make the same point, and the postmodern Jean Baudrillard sees seduction as a mind game for the intellectual elite.

Frymer-Kensky points out that "desire for learning is a lust," 158, and Cathleen Schine observes in the novel *Rameau's Niece* (New York: Plume, 1993) that "the desire to know is desire," 117. Freud believed ideas were "acts of love," and recently Bruce Weber wrote in the *New York Times* of the necessity of intellectuality in love relationships. "Learning is desirable," he said, "not least because it enriches the emotions." Quoted in Norman O. Brown, *Life Against Death* (Middletown, Conn.: Wesleyan University Press, 1959), 69, and *New York Times,* May 24, 2000, E1.

153 **Literature teems with . . . :** Literature, which sounds the depths of love, has long featured smart seductresses. Aphra Behn's femme fatale in *The Fair Jilt* speaks several languages, reads voraciously, and speaks with a "great deal of wit." Two of Jane Austen's smart sirens outshine their romantic rivals, and the enchantress Lyndall of *The Story of an African Farm* devours books and men with equal relish. Then there is Edgar Allan Poe's prototypic scholar-vamp Ligea; George Meredith's rapier-witted *Diana of the Crossroads;* and Madeleine Forestier of Guy de Maupassant's *Bel-Ami,* whose fascinations, whose "lively intelligence and shrewdness" carry her to the command center of Parisian politics. *The Fair Jilt or the Amours of Prince Tarquin and Miranda* (London: Routledge, 1913), 87, and *Bel-Ami,* trans. Douglas Parmee (New York: Penguin, 1975), 234; and "The Desire Survey," *Esquire* (February 2001), 78.

152 **"Both males and . . .":** Taylor, *Prehistory of Sex,* 49.

153 **Like Inanna's lover . . . :** Wolkstein and Kramer, *Inanna,* 24, 26, and 33.

CHAPTER 6: *SORCIÈRES:* SIREN-ARTISTS

156 **We're still haunted . . . :** Robert Southey's letter to Charlotte Brontë, quoted in Joan Coulianos, ed., *By a Woman Writt* (Baltimore: Penguin, 1973), xv; G. M. Hopkins, quoted in Sandra M. Gilbert and Susan Gubar, *The Madwoman in the Attic* (New Haven: Yale University Press, 1984), 3. Renoir, quoted in Linda Nachlin, "Why Have There Been No Great Women Artists," *Women, Creativity, and the Arts,* ed. Diane Apostolos-Cappadona and Linda Ebersole (New York: Continuum, 1995), 62. Samuel Johnson, quoted in John Bartlett, *Familiar Quotations* (Boston: Little, Brown, 1941), 234. More recently William Gass commented that literary women "lack that blood congested genital drive which energizes every great style." Gilbert and Gubar, *Madwoman in the Attic,* 9.

156 **Hence the sexual . . . :** Most psychoanalytically oriented philosophers trace art back to its sexual roots. For an overview, see Klaus Laemmel, "Sex and the Arts," *The Sexual Experience,* ed. Benjamin J. Sadock, M.D.; Harold I. Kaplan, M.D., and Alfred Freedman, M.D. (Baltimore: Williams and Wilkins, 1976), 527–65.

Prominent exponents of this view include Camille Paglia, *Sexual Personae;* Herbert Marcuse, *Eros and Civilization* (New York: Vintage, 1962); Norman O. Brown, *Life Against Death;* and Jean Baudrillard, *Seduction.*

See also Liam Hudson and Bernadin Jacot, who connect aesthetic and sexual rapture: "There exists a mechanism which enables us to fall under the spell of a work of art in just the way that we fall under the spell of a person. In the presence of the person by whom we are besotted, as in the presence of works of art, . . . our defenses collapse." *The Way Men Think* (New Haven, Yale University Press, 1991), 147.

157 **It was total theater . . . :** For scholarly reconstructions of these archaic rites, including drug use, see Richard Rudgley, *The Alchemy of Culture* (London: British Museum Press, 1993), E. O. James, *Seasonal Feasts and Festivals* (New York: Barnes & Noble, 1961); Curt Sachs, *World History of the Dance,* trans. Bessie Schonberg (New York: Norton, 1937); Neumann, *The Great Mother;* and Riane Eisler, *Sacred Pleasure* (San Francisco: HarperSanFrancisco, 1995).

157 **Several scholars think . . .** : Neumann, *The Great Mother,* 296, and Baring and Cashford, *Myth of the Goddess,* 21.

157 **Women, it's conjectured . . .** : Women may well have executed the famous cave painting of horses and hunting scenes. Their handprints supposedly surround the Altamira murals that fill a low-ceilinged women's quarter. Violetta Miguela asserts: "[C]ave art is a genuinely women's art." Quoted in Davis, *First Sex,* 45. Davis cites as evidence the female "delicacy of line; their feeling of compassion for the hunted beasts; [and] the caricaturish depictions of the hunters—certainly not flattering to the male of the human species," 45.

One Lascaux drawing bears an unmistakable feminine touch, a picture of a prostrate stick man with a hard-on beside a monstrous bison, the goddess's avatar. In a comic wink at men's utter sexual helplessness before the Feminine Principle, a bird's head pops up below the scene like Groucho Marx's duck.

Underneath a richly fretted Çatal Hüyük shrine, female artists were buried with their palettes in hand, the paints still fresh. Another student of cave art, Grace Hartigan, also believes women were responsible, quipping that they were making grocery lists. Phone conversation, January 2000.

One theorist, Le Roy McDermott, professor of art at Missouri State University, concludes, after studying the Venus figurines, that they were sculpted by women since the distortions suggest a woman looking down at herself. See the discussion in Husain, *Goddess,* 11.

157 **Like the earliest shaman-creators . . .** : Quoted in Robert Saltonstall Mattison, *Grace Hartigan: A Painter's World* (New York: Hudson Hills Press, 1990), 79.

157 **"I believe," she . . .** : Quoted ibid., 100.

157 **"A powerful sexual . . ."**: Interview, March 15, 1999.

157 **Critic John Myers . . .** : John Bernard Myers, *Tracking the Marvelous: A Life in the New York Art World* (New York: Random House, 1981), 127.

158 **She seduced and subdued . . .** : Quoted in Whitney Chadwick, *Women, Art, and Society* (London: Thames and Hudson, 1996), 326.

158 **"Macho?" Grace laughs . . .** : Telephone interview, May 23, 1999.

158 **She shares her . . .** : Quoted in Mattison, *Grace Hartigan,* 136.

158 **It actually means . . .** : I'm indebted to professor Carlos Johnson for this insight.

158 **The eldest child . . .** : Cindy Nemser, *Art Talk: Conversations with Twelve Women Artists* (New York: Charles Scribner's, 1975), 152.

159 **"After sex with . . ."** : Interview, March 15, 1999.

159 **"Going to New York" . . .** : Ibid.

159 **She "lived like . . ."**: Nemser, *Art Talk,* 152.

159 **Once when she . . .** : Interview, March 15, 1999.

160 **The same year** *Life . . . :* "Women Artists in Ascendance," *Life* (May 13, 1957), 74.

160 **For years the pair . . .** : Frank wrote a number of poems to Grace, a line of which is engraved on his tombstone: "Grace/to be born and live as variously as possible." Grace in turn painted Frank in two major works and collaborated with him on a series of painting-poems.

160 **As soon as Grace** . . . : Interview, March 15, 1999.

160 **Realizing that she'd** . . . : Quoted in Mattison, *Grace Hartigan,* 54. Quoted in Brad Gooch, *City Poet: The Life and Times of Frank O'Hara* (New York: Alfred A. Knopf, 1993), 359.

160 **Around the same time** . . . : Interview, March 15, 1999.

160 **"Known for bolstering . . ."** : Ibid.

161 **"It didn't suit . . ."** : Ibid.

161 **"When I envision . . .":** Ibid.

161 **"Sure, I had . . .":** Ibid.

161 **"When I think . . .":** Ibid.

161 **Not coincidentally, cave** . . . : See Robert Jourdain, who explains how archaeologists concluded the presence of music at the early ceremonies via the resonance within the artistic epicenters of caves. *Music, the Brain and Ecstasy* (New York: Avon, 1997), 305. Also see Rudgley's comprehensive account of Stone Age music in "The Song of the Stalactites," *Lost Civilization of the Stone Age,* 201–08.

161 **Instead of the first** . . . : Sophie Drinker, *Music and Women* (New York: Feminist Press at CUNY, 1995 [1948]), 63.

162 **The sex goddess** . . . : Wolkstein and Kramer, *Inanna,* 17.

162 **In early-twentieth-century** . . . : Quoted in Jessica Douglas-Home, *Violet: The Life and Loves of Violet Gordon Woodhouse* (London: Haverill Press, 1996), 319.

162 **A bizarre, impish** . . . : Quoted ibid., 24 and 106.

162 **Little known today** . . . : Quoted ibid., 75.

163 **People called her** . . . : Quoted ibid., 117.

163 **Costumed in lace-garlanded** . . . : Osbert Sitwell, *Noble Essences* (Boston: Little, Brown, 1950), 287, and quoted in Douglas-Home, *Violet,* 306.

163 **The trio took** . . . : Douglas-Home, *Violet,* 53.

163 **She sat on** . . . : Ibid., 57.

164 **"God how he . . .":** Quoted, Ibid., 164.

164 **At the same time** . . . : A number of prominent lesbians, such as Ethel Smyth and Radclyffe Hall, courted Violet, and she might have reciprocated their affections, perhaps physically. This is in keeping with the widespread bisexuality and androgynous propensities of seductresses. In a photograph of Violet with her amorous triad, Adelina sits confidently on the left, her arm cocked in a jaunty akimbo.

164 **No "humdrum constraints"** . . . : Douglas-Home, *Violet,* 92.

164 **At night her** . . . : Quoted ibid., 116.

164 **Violet "did what . . .":** Ibid., 92.

164 **With her "intensely . . .":** Sitwell, *Noble Essences,* 281.

164 **Bill of course** . . . : Quoted in Douglas-Home, *Violet,* 119.

164 **The most exacting** . . . : Quoted ibid., 74.

165 **She gained international** . . . : These can still be heard on *Great Virtuosi of the Harpsichord,* vol. 3, Pavillion Records Ltd. The grainy and overmiked recordings, however, give only the faintest idea of the éclat of her playing.

165 **She bought a** . . . : Sitwell, *Noble Essences,* 283, and quoted in Douglas-Home, *Violet,* 94.

165 **Part "czarina," part** . . . : Quoted in Douglas-Home, *Violet,* 267.

165 **An infatuated clavichord** . . . : Quoted ibid., 242–43.

165 **Two women developed . . .** : Ibid., 227.
165 **"You are the . . ."**: Quoted ibid., 285.
165 **Violet spent her . . .** : Ibid., 299.
166 **The obituaries called . . .** : Quoted ibid., 306.
166 **If at all . . .** : Quoted ibid., 175 and 103.
166 **The Sitwells put . . .** : Quoted ibid., 311.
166 **She switched on . . .** : Sitwell, *Noble Essences*, 283. Robert Jourdain points out that finely wrought music with its Piranesi towers of tease-and-anticipation and swooping resolutions creates the same ecstasy of successful lovemaking. Unlike other female musicians of the time, such as Amy Beach, Violet frankly put this primordial aphrodisiacal charge in music to her own uses.
166 **Sexual rapture promoted . . .** : "Sensual desire and religious emotion," say anthropologists, are "indissolubly bound," and the first humans "danced out their religion." Neumann, *Great Mother*, 293, and E. O. James, *From Cave to Cathedral*, 18.
166 **The sex goddesses . . .** : Wolkstein and Kramer, *Inanna*, 41.
167 **Lamia wore a . . .** : Quoted in Nickie Roberts, *Whores in History* (London: HarperCollins, 1992), 30.
167 **When she was . . .** : Plutarch, "Demetrius," *Lives of the Noble Greeks and Romans*, 1088.
167 **Though ten years . . .** : Basserman, *Oldest Profession*, 227.
167 **"I do not fear . . ."**: Quoted in Hayward, *Dictionary of Courtesans*, 11.
168 **At the end . . .** : Phyllis Rose, *Jazz Cleopatra: Josephine Baker in Her Time* (New York: Doubleday, 1989), 31.
168 **She was the Ebony . . .** : Quoted in Lynn Haney, *Naked at the Feast: A Biography of Josephine Baker* (New York: Dodd, Mead, 1981), 101, and quoted in Jean-Claude Baker and Chris Chase, *Josephine: The Hungry Heart* (New York: Random House, 1993), 3.
168 **Yet when she . . .** : Quoted in Rose, *Jazz Cleopatra*, 14.
169 **Like the barrelhouse . . .** : See Angela Y. Davis's discussion of the strong, sexually pioneering blues singers and their tradition of female autonomy, promiscuity, and erotic pride. They sang, "I ain't gonna marry, ain't gonna settle down"; "I'm a good woman and I can get plenty of men"; "I'm a young woman and ain't done runnin' round." *Blues Legacies and Black Feminism* (New York: Vintage, 1998), 17 and passim.
169 **"I have no . . ."**: Quoted in Rose, *Jazz Cleopatra*, 140.
169 **The chorus girls . . .** : Quoted in Baker and Chase, *Josephine*, 57.
169 **Refusing "to be . . ."**: Quoted in Haney, *Naked at the Feast*, 28.
169 **The artist Paul Colin . . .** : Quoted ibid., 104.
170 **According to lovers, . . .** : Quoted ibid., 87.
170 **For her, the mix . . .** : Rose, *Jazz Cleopatra*, 263, and Baker and Chase, *Josephine*, 243.
170 **An "adorable" despot . . .** : Haney, *Naked at the Feast*, 180.
170 **Singing French torch songs . . .** : Quoted ibid., 87 and 165.
171 **Beneath the elegant . . .** : Frymer-Kensky, *Wake of the Goddesses*, 48. Here Frymer-Kensky is speaking of the nonproper "divine" "embodiment of sexual attraction and lust," *Inanna*, 47.

171 **For five years . . .** : Quoted in Haney, *Naked at the Feast,* 220.
172 **A splurge queen . . .** : Friedrich Nietzsche, *Birth of Tragedy,* trans. Francis Golffing (New York: Anchor, 1956), 35.
172 **As she traipsed . . .** : Quoted in Haney, *Naked at the Feast,* 308.
172 **But like other seductresses . . .** : Ibid., 69.
172 **Racist critics called . . .** : Quoted ibid., 246.
172 **Yet Josephine was . . .** : Quoted ibid., 278.
173 **The Brazilians believed . . .** : Quoted ibid., 99.
173 **But she must have found . . .** : Friedrich, *Meaning of Aphrodite,* 58 and 144.
173 **That's why great lines . . .** : See Norman O. Brown, "Poetry, the creative act, the act of life, the archetypal sexual act. Sexuality is poetry," quoted in Gilbert and Garber, *Madwoman in the Attic,* 13. Emily Dickinson and Montaigne, "On Some Verses of Virgil," *Complete Essays of Montaigne,* vol. 3, 66.
173 **Women may have . . .** : Neumann, *Great Mother,* 296. Also see Norma Lorre Goodrich, *Priestesses* (New York: HarperPerennial, 1989), 1–11, and Davis, *First Sex* and Drinker, *Music and Women,* 68–69.
173 **The cosmic sex . . .** : Wolkstein and Kramer, *Inanna,* 16, 17, and 37.
173 **In ancient Greece . . .** : Friedrich, *Meaning of Aphrodite,* 144.
174 **Maria de Ventadorn, (c. 1165):** Meg Bogin, *The Women Troubadours* (New York: Paddington, 1976), 168 and 101.
174 **Light-years ahead . . .** : Dorothy O'Connor, *Louise Labé, sa vie et son oeuvre* (Paris: Presses françaises, 1926), 86.
175 **After this volume . . .** : Kenneth Varty, "The Life and Legend of Louise Labé," *Nottingham Medieval Studies* 3 (1959), 108.
176 **"Kiss me. Again . . ."**: Labé, *Louise Labé's Complete Works,* trans. and ed. Edith R. Farrell (Troy, N.Y.: Whitston Publishing, 1986), 114.
176 **In the "Debate . . ."**: Ibid., 36.
176 **"You must be . . ."**: Ibid., 34 and 39.
176 **Men must "do . . ."**: Ibid., 83.
176 **We can only imagine . . .** : Ibid., 67.
176 **André Malraux called . . .** : André Malraux, intro., *Louise de Vilmorin: Poèmes* (Paris: Gallimard, 1970), 14.
177 **Preposterous though it . . .** : Quoted in Jean Bothorel, *Louise ou la vie de Louise de Vilmorin* (Paris: Bernard Gasset, 1993), 290.
177 **"Laughter," she quipped . . .** : Quoted ibid., 41.
177 **Sexual conquest "lights . . ."**: Quoted ibid., 316.
178 **He also fell . . .** : Quoted in Bothorel, *Louise,* 32.
178 **For him, she . . .** : Stacy Schiff, *Saint-Exupéry* (New York: Alfred A. Knopf, 1994), 96, and Christine Sutherland, *Enchantress: Marthe Bibesco and Her World* (New York: Farrar, Straus and Giroux, 1996), 260. Antoine de Saint-Exupéry, *Southern Mail,* trans. Curtis Cate (New York: Harcourt Brace, 1971 [1929]) 28, and Schiff, 98.
178 **First came André . . .** : Quoted in Bothorel, *Louise,* 67.
178 **Her novel sold . . .** : Quoted ibid., 90.
179 **Pali Palffy, count . . .** : Quoted ibid., 114.
179 **There, ensconced as . . .** : Ibid., 173, and Vilmorin, *Julietta,* 42.
179 **Another Hungarian count . . .** : Quoted in Bothorel, *Louise,* 140.
179 **Unlike lesser seductresses . . .** : Vilmorin, *Julietta,* 117.

179 **Afterward, Louise treated** . . . : Quoted in Bothorel, *Louise,* 291 and 159.

179 **"You are a . . .":** Quoted ibid., 160.

180 **When the ménage** . . . : Louise de Vilmorin, *Madame de,* trans. Duff Cooper, intro. Susan Minot (Canada: Helen Marx Books, 1998), 7, 17.

180 **Approaching fifty, she** . . . : Quoted in Bothorel, *Louise,* 230.

180 **"I have no . . .":** Quoted in Schiff, *Saint-Exupéry,* 104.

180 **Welles, a notorious** . . . : Quoted in Bothorel, *Louise,* 230.

180 **One conquest, Pierre** . . . : Quoted ibid., 268 and 269.

181 **She got, however** . . . : Quoted ibid., 312.

181 **After he buried** . . . : Quoted ibid., 290.

181 **Louise returned the** . . . : Quoted ibid., 182. Her view of her own sex stood in blatant contradiction to her life. Having endured female hatred and rivalry since childhood (beginning with her mother), Louise saw women as the archenemy, best kept off her freeway in domestic subjection.

181 **"You are magical"** . . . : Quoted in Bothorel, *Louise,* 302 and 161.

181 **Louise always claimed** . . . : Quoted ibid., 70.

182 **And the original** . . . : Frymer-Kensky, *Wake of the Goddess,* 48.

183 **She loosed the** . . . : Ralph Waldo Emerson quoted on the subject of the comic muse in Paul Lauter, intro., *Theories of Comedy* (Garden City, N.Y.: Anchor Books, 1964), xvi.

183 **An infatuated Samuel Pepys** . . . : Quoted in Bryan Bevan, *Nell Gwyn* (London: Robert Hale, 1969), 52.

183 **In each, she** . . . : This is James Howard's *All Mistaken or, The Mad Couple,* 1667, in which she played Mirida.

183 **"I am the . . .":** Quoted in John W. Wilson, *Nell Gwyn: Royal Mistress* (New York: Dell, 1955), 82 and 83.

184 **Without a trace** . . . : Quoted ibid., 115.

184 **Though women came** . . . : Quoted ibid., 152.

184 **By the end** . . . : Quoted ibid., 115 and 149.

184 **She told his** . . . : Quoted ibid., 103, 120, and 146.

184 **Whenever Charles strayed,** . . . : Quoted ibid., 154.

184 **He also came** . . . : Ibid., 149.

185 **During the conflict** . . . : Quoted ibid., 222.

185 **A "lovely" lieutenant** . . . : Quoted ibid., 203.

185 **"Pray good people . . .":** Quoted ibid., 196.

185 **"Let not poor Nelly . . ."** : Quoted ibid., 215.

185 **Too big for her britches** . . . : Quoted ibid., 188.

186 **Like Inanna, "the . . .":** Frymer-Kensky, *Wake of the Goddess,* 48.

186 **Men trembled and** . . . : Quoted in Rachel M. Brownstein, *Tragic Muse: Rachel of the Comédie Française* (New York: Alfred A. Knopf, 1913), 226, and in Joanna Richardson, *Rachel* (New York: Putnam's, 1957), 121.

186 **A diva of "demonical . . .":** Quoted ibid., 18.

186 **She seemed closer** . . . : Quoted ibid., 57.

187 **"She's my discovery . . .":** Quoted in Brownstein, *Tragic Muse,* 102.

187 **She was nothing** . . . : Quoted in Richardson, *Rachel,* 20.

187 **At the play's** . . . : Quoted ibid., 121.

187 **A steely victrix** . . . : Quoted ibid., 42.

187 **"I am *free*"** . . . : Quoted in Brownstein, *Tragic Muse,* 151.

187 **In common with . . .** : Ibid., 151, and quoted ibid., 103.

188 **Lovers called her . . .** : Quoted ibid., 15.

188 **In 1841, with . . .** : Quoted in Richardson, *Rachel,* 41.

188 **But the "Jewish . . ."**: Quoted in Brownstein, *Tragic Muse,* 207.

189 **"I love to . . ."**: Quoted in Brownstein, *Tragic Muse,* 151.

189 **Deified as a . . .** : Quoted ibid., 136.

189 **"Speak my queen" . . .** : Quoted in Richardson, *Rachel,* 131.

189 **"Watch me light . . ."**: Quoted in Brownstein, *Tragic Muse,* 198.

190 **Alarmed by this . . .** : Quoted in Bernard Falk, *Rachel the Immortal* (London: Hutchinson, 1935), 54.

190 **Biographers pelted her . . .** : Quoted in Brownstein, *Tragic Muse,* xii.

190 **She defiled the . . .** : Quoted ibid., 238 and 176.

190 **George Eliot compared . . .** : Quoted ibid., 228. See her fictionalization in Brontë's *Villette,* ed. Geoffrey Tillotson (Boston: Houghton Mifflin, 1971), Chapter 23, 216–27.

190 **When she was . . .** : Quoted in Richardson, *Rachel,* xi.

190 **Perhaps in her . . .** : Quoted ibid., 60.

191 **The passions aroused . . .** : See a discussion of the scholars who advance this theory of the indelibility of these ancient rites on the subpsyche in Goodrich, *Priestesses,* 9. Ernst Cassirer, for example, claims that a ritual act is "based upon such strong emotion that its underlying meaning seizes [people] in an unforgettable vise of common experience." Goodrich also cites Mircea Eliade, Carl Jung, and Jean Seznec.

191 **With the artist's . . .** : Mihaly Csikszentmihalyi, *Creativity* (New York: HarperPerennial, 1996), 59.

193 **This work, by . . .** : Baudrillard, *Seduction,* 1 and 69.

CHAPTER 7: *MACHTWEIBER:* SEDUCTRESSES IN POLITICS

195 **As John Knox . . .** : Quoted in Fraser, *Warrior Queens,* 204.

196 **Men of course . . .** : Several authors specifically discuss this male dread of female political authority. See Lederer, "On Queens and Amazons," *Fear of Women,* 99–106; Hays, "The Serpent of the Nile," *Dangerous Sex,* 159–67; and Virginia M. Allen, "The *Machtweib,*" *The Femme Fatale* (Troy, N.Y.: Whitston Publishing Company, 1983), 15–37.

197 **In a culture . . .** : See more about Cleopatra's "authority of a goddess," in Guy Weill Goudchaux, "Cleopatra's Subtle Religious Strategy," *Cleopatra of Egypt from History to Myth,* ed. Susan Walker and Peter Higgs (London: British Museum Press, 2001), 129, and Michael Grant, *Cleopatra* (New York: Barnes & Noble, 1972), 118.

197 **Contrary to her . . .** : Ernle Bradford, *Cleopatra* (New York: Harcourt Brace Jovanovich, 1972), 267.

197 **She looked more . . .** : Few contemporary portraits, except a handful of coins, survive. Archaeologists adduce on the basis of contemporary aristocratic female mummies that she was small of stature—under five feet—and full-bodied. See Goudchaux, "Was Cleopatra Beautiful?," *Cleopatra of Egypt from History to Myth,* 210–214.

198 **With her brother's . . .** : See Goudchaux for a good summary of the decline of the empire. In less than fifty years the borders of the Egyptian empire had been steadily eroded by the Roman proconsuls, 18–19.

198 **As the "living . . .":** Quoted in Edith Flamarion, *Cleopatra: The Life and Death of a Pharaoh,* trans. Alexandra Bonfante-Warren (New York: Harry N. Abrams, 1997), 32.

198 **But Cleopatra "spellbound" . . . :** Quoted in Bradford, *Cleopatra,* 69.

198 **Captivated by her . . . :** Flamarion, *Cleopatra,* 34, and quoted ibid., 36.

199 **"I am Isis . . .":** Quoted in Baring and Cashford, *Myth of the Goddess,* 268–69.

199 **Cleopatra's grand opera . . . :** Bradford, *Cleopatra,* 152.

199 **Eight dinners were . . . :** Plutarch, "Mark Antony," *Makers of Rome,* trans. Ian Scott-Kilvert (New York: Penguin, 1965), 295, and Bradford, *Cleopatra,* 116.

200 **She practiced a . . . :** Plutarch, "Mark Antony," 296.

200 **Even Antony's general . . . :** Quoted in Grant, *Cleopatra,* 180 and 195.

201 **Loathed by the . . . :** Ibid., 178.

201 **Even a feminist . . . :** Betty Millan, *Monstrous Regiment: Women Rulers in Men's Worlds* (Berks, U.K.: Kensal Press, 1982), 31.

201 **Antony fell on . . . :** William Shakespeare, *The Tragedy of Antony and Cleopatra,* ed. Barbara Everett (New York: Signet, 1964), act II, scene ii, line 190, and quoted in Judith Thurman, "The Queen Himself," *New Yorker* (May 7, 2001), 75.

201 **"I know I . . .":** Quoted in Paul Johnson, *Elizabeth I* (New York: Holt, Rinehart and Winston, 1974), 320.

201 **Brought to the . . . :** Quoted in "Elizabeth I of England," *Encyclopaedia Britannica* Macropedia (Chicago: Encyclopaedia Britannica, 1997), vol. 18, 244.

202 **Every move was . . . :** Guida M. Jackson, *Women Who Ruled* (New York: Barnes & Noble, 1990), 63.

202 **Early on she learned . . . :** Ibid., 63.

202 **"God hath raised . . .":** Quoted in Anne Somerset, *Elizabeth I* (New York: St. Martin's, 1991), 58 and 60.

202 **Cut to the cleavage . . . :** Quoted in Alison Weir, *The Life of Elizabeth I* (New York: Ballantine Books, 1998), 35 and 237.

202 **During the procession . . . :** Quoted in Somerset, *Elizabeth I,* 71.

202 **Confronting unprecedented hostility . . . :** Quoted in *The Horizon Book of the Elizabethan World,* ed. Richard M. Ketchum and Alvin M. Josephy, Jr. (New York: American Heritage Publishing, 1967), 77.

203 **"Flirtation was her . . .":** Weir, *Life of Elizabeth I,* 18.

203 **Elizabeth astutely safeguarded . . . :** Quoted ibid., 26.

203 **She put men . . . :** Quoted in *Horizon Book,* 77.

203 **Elizabeth's much-touted virginity . . . :** There is some speculation that they consummated the relationship or came close to it since Elizabeth, believing herself to be on her deathbed during a smallpox attack, swore "nothing improper" passed between them but left a lavish pension to the servant who slept in the room. See Elizabeth Jenkins's account in *Elizabeth the Great* (New York: Coward McCann & Geoghegan, 1958), 99–100.

203 **"I will have . . .":** Quoted in Neville Williams, *The Life and Times of Elizabeth I* (Garden City, N.Y.: Doubleday, 1972), 70.

204 **Christopher Hatton, her . . . :** Ibid., 114 and 115.

204 **All the while . . . :** Johnson, *Elizabeth I,* 117.

204 **"To have seen . . .":** Quoted in Williams, 40.

204 **She actively traded . . . :** Quoted in Weir, *Life of Elizabeth,* 30.

205 **They said she . . . :** Quoted in Mrs. Jameson, *Memoirs of Celebrated Female Sovereigns* (New York: Harper & Brothers, 1839), 225.

205 **After dethroning her husband . . . :** Quoted in Millan, *Monstrous Regiment*, 207.

205 **Eighteenth-century Russia, with . . . :** Marija Gimbutas retrieved many of the female cult figurines from Georgia near the Black Sea, the seedbed of the worship of the fertility deities. See her *The Goddesses and Gods of Old Europe*, passim, and Fraser's discussion of its impact on Russian female rulers, *Warrior Queens*, 168–71 and 254–55.

205 **Only the *Machtweib*'s . . . :** Quoted in Gamaliel Bradford, *Daughters of Eve* (Boston: Houghton Mifflin, 1928), 166.

205 **She endured ordeals, . . . :** Quoted in Vincent Cronin, *Catherine: Empress of All the Russias* (New York: William Morrow, 1978), 77.

206 **Her mother disliked . . . :** Henri Troyat, *Catherine the Great*, trans. Joan Pinkham (New York: Berkley Books, 1980), 3.

206 **Retaining her brio . . . :** Joan Haslip, *Catherine the Great* (New York: Putnam's, 1977), 17. Catherine's exact words were "I was never beautiful but I pleased," quoted 19.

206 **In stylish male . . . :** Ian Grey, *The Horizon History of Russia*, ed. Wendy Buehr (New York: American Heritage, 1970), 197.

206 **Warm, gay, and funny . . . :** Quoted in Cronin, *Catherine*, 75.

206 **Robustly sexed, she . . . :** Ibid., 213.

206 **There was the debonair . . . :** Quoted in Cliffe Howe, *Lovers and Libertines* (New York: Ace, 1958), 87.

207 **She called herself . . . :** Robert Bly and Marion Woodman, *The Maiden King* (New York: Henry Holt, 1998), 41, and see the discussion of these Russian goddesses, 35–70 and passim.

207 **"Creation," she announced . . . :** Quoted in Cronin, *Catherine*, 199.

207 **An adept ego . . . :** Quoted ibid., 197.

207 **Rather than direct confrontation . . . :** Quoted ibid., 197.

208 **Yet, all told . . . :** Quoted in Troyat, *Catherine the Great*, 183, and quoted in Fraser, *Warrior Queens*, 255.

208 **After Catherine decommissioned . . . :** Quoted in Howe, *Lovers and Libertines*, 90.

208 **Insisting on her right . . . :** Quoted ibid., 90.

208 **She refused to . . . :** Quoted in Troyat, *Catherine the Great*, 252.

208 **Her last was . . . :** Quoted, ibid., 353.

208 **On her deathbed . . . :** Quoted in Cronin, *Catherine*, 299.

208 **She was a multiple . . . :** Troyat, *Catherine the Great*, 285.

208 **"Autocracy," she said . . . :** Quoted in *A Picture History of Russia*, ed. John Stuart Martin (New York: Bonanza Books, 1968), 103.

208 **As Voltaire put . . . :** Italics mine. Quoted in Troyat, *Catherine the Great*, 183.

209 **Thereafter Inanna, the . . . :** Wolkstein and Kramer, *Inanna*, 105 and 156, and Baring and Cashford, *Myth of the Goddess*, 205.

209 **The only true parts . . . :** Edward Gibbon, *The Decline and Fall of the Roman Empire* (New York: Modern Library, n.d.), vol. 2, 474.

209 **She was the left . . . :** Quoted in Roberts, *Whores in History*, 48.

210 **According to tradition . . . :** Procopius, *The Secret History,* trans. G. A. Williamson (Middlesex, U.K.: Penguin, 1966), 86.

210 **He was then forty, . . . :** Charles Diehl, *Theodora: Empress of Byzantium,* trans. Samuel R. Rosenbaum (New York: Frederick Ungar, 1972), 29.

210 **Beautiful and fine-boned . . . :** Gibbon, *Decline and Fall,* 481.

210 **And she "knew . . .":** Charles Diehl, *Byzantine Empresses,* trans. Harold Bell and Theresa Kerpely (New York: Alfred A. Knopf, 1963), 48.

210 **She percolated with . . . :** Diehl, *Theodora,* 30.

210 **When he assumed . . . :** Ibid., 35. Also see Gibbon for a description of the vast magnitude and wealth of this empire. *Decline and Fall,* 492–93.

210 **Her resplendent apartments . . . :** Diehl, *Theodora,* 47.

210 **When she "wished . . .":** Ibid., 12.

210 **She paired "consummate . . .":** Diehl, *Byzantine Empresses,* 50.

211 **"My dear sir," she . . . :** Quoted in Diehl, *Theodora,* 60.

211 **"Mistress Eagle," she . . . :** Quoted in Meador, *Inanna,* 119.

211 **With a "feel . . .":** Diehl, *Theodora,* 90.

211 **"If flight," she . . . :** Quoted in Gibbon, *Decline and Fall,* 491.

212 **Throughout their twenty-five . . . :** Diehl, *Theodora,* 30.

212 **As heiress of . . . :** Quoted in Meador, *Inanna,* 148, and Robert Browning, *Justinian and Theodora* (New York: Praeger, 1971), 259.

212 **But she, per . . . :** Quoted in Meador, *Inanna,* 136.

212 **He made members . . . :** Procopius, *Secret History,* 90.

212 **Throughout the Middle Ages . . . :** Desmond Seward, *Eleanor of Aquitaine* (New York: Barnes & Noble, 1978), 7, and quoted in Amy Kelly, *Eleanor of Aquitaine* (New York: Vintage, 1950), 127.

212 **Known as the "woman . . .":** Quoted in Regine Pernoud, *Eleanor of Aquitaine* (London: Collins, 1967), 266.

212 **She was born . . . :** Quoted in Alison Weir, *Eleanor of Aquitaine: By the Wrath of God, Queen of England* (London: Pimlico, 2000), 7.

213 **Schooled in the . . . :** Kelly, *Eleanor of Aquitaine,* 10.

213 **Nothing like Eleanor's . . . :** Quoted in Seward, *Eleanor of Aquitaine,* 34 and 35.

213 **Her face paint . . . :** Quoted in Kelly, *Eleanor of Aquitaine,* 28.

214 **Like the divine . . . :** Quoted in Meador, *Inanna,* 153, and quoted in Kelly, *Eleanor of Aquitaine,* 51.

214 **"Why do I . . .":** Quoted in Kelly, *Eleanor of Aquitaine,* 79.

214 **After their return . . . :** Weir, *Eleanor of Aquitaine,* 1.

214 **Although ten years . . . :** Curtis Howe Walker, *Eleanor of Aquitaine* (Chapel Hill: University of North Carolina Press, 1950), 102.

214 **The two had . . . :** Marion Meade, *Eleanor of Aquitaine: A Biography* (New York: Penguin Books, 1977), 140.

214 **Flourishing her learning . . . :** Quoted in Kelly, *Eleanor of Aquitaine,* 114.

215 **When he took her queen . . . :** Quoted in Walker, *Eleanor of Aquitaine,* 103.

215 **Henry never learned . . . :** Quoted in Seward, *Eleanor of Aquitaine,* 147.

215 **Eleanor, by contrast, . . . :** Ibid., 151. Into her seventies she vigorously protected and governed her domains, traveling throughout the Continent to keep her barons in check. She reconciled her feuding sons, made advantageous marriages for her grandchildren, and, at seventy-seven, after Richard's death, retook Anjou and Maine and arranged the truce in which the French king acknowledged John king of England.

215 **Besieged in a** . . . : Quoted in Walker, *Eleanor of Aquitaine*, 234.

216 **If the church fathers** . . . : Quoted in Weir, *Eleanor of Aquitaine*, 354. For more on the myths she inspired, see D. D. R. Owen, *Eleanor of Aquitaine: Queen and Legend* (Oxford, U.K.: Blackwell, 1993).

216 **According to the smears** . . . : Quoted in Pernoud, *Eleanor of Aquitaine*, 266.

216 **The Evita anomaly** . . . : Pamela Druckerman, "Eva Perón Clone: Cecilia Bolocco Has Argentina Clucking," *Wall Street Journal*, August 3, 2001, A8. J. M. Taylor includes a survey of the theories and an explanation of his own for her anomalous rise to power in this male supremacist country in *Eva Perón: The Myths of a Woman* (Chicago: University of Chicago Press, 1979).

217 **She escaped into** . . . : There's no record of Augustin Magaldi's visiting her hometown at the time, and he always traveled with his wife.

217 **In a piece** . . . : Quoted in Alma Guillermoprieto, "Little Eva," *New Yorker* (December 2, 1996), 98, and Nicholas Fraser and Marysa Navarro, *Eva Perón* (New York: Norton, 1980), 25.

217 **While Perón looked** . . . : The extent of her participation in this is a matter of dispute. Three union leaders claim none, while another populist spokesman insists a great deal. See Alicia Dujovne Ortíz, *Eva Perón*, trans. Shawn Fields (New York: St. Martin's, 1996), 125. Nicholas Fraser and Marysa Naverro, on the other hand, argue that she masterminded the October 17 march.

217 **He ended his** . . . : Quoted in John Barnes, *Evita First Lady* (New York: Grove Press, 1978), 100.

218 **"The poor," she** . . . : Quoted in Guillermoprieto, "Little Eva," 102.

218 **Touring the country** . . . : Quoted in Fraser and Navarro, *Eva Perón*, 111.

218 **In the purple prose** . . . : Quoted in Guillermoprieto, "Little Eva," 103, and quoted in Barnes, *Evita First Lady*, 110.

218 **She chanted the** . . . : Quoted in Barnes, *First Lady*, 110. Barnes translates this: "I have dedicated myself fantastically to Perón," 110.

218 **She had a sting** . . . : Quoted in Meador, *Inanna*, 123.

219 **"Women have the** . . .": Quoted in Barnes, *First Lady*, 88.

219 **Diagnosed with cervical** . . . : Certain strains of genital human papilloma virus are associated with carcinoma of the cervix. It's highly likely that she contacted it sexually from him especially since his first wife died of the same disease.

219 **But the transplant** . . . : Quoted in Barnes, *First Lady*, 179. This term of endearment means something like "dark, oriental one." My thanks to Dr. Gabriela Shaw, New York City psychologist and Argentinean, for this insight.

219 **In the end** . . . : Quoted ibid., 137.

220 **These hellcat** *Machtweiber* . . . : Allen, *Femme Fatale*, 196.

220 **With an entrenched** . . . : Quoted in Patai, *Hebrew Goddess*, 242.

220 **The leading ladies** . . . : Quoted in Barbara Goldsmith, *Other Powers: The Age of Suffrage, Spiritualism, and the Scandalous Victoria Woodhull* (New York: Harper Perennial, 1998), 294, and Lois Beachy Underhill, *The Woman Who Ran for President* (Bridgehampton, N.Y.: Bridgeworks Publishing, 1995), 201 and 241.

221 **As Henry James** . . . : Henry James, *The Siege of London: The Novels and Tales of Henry James* (New York: Charles Scribner's, 1936 [1908]), 148.

222 **She was fifteen** . . . : Underhill, *Woman Who Ran for President*, 15.

222 **Laying her hands . . . :** Ishbel Ross, *Charmers and Cranks* (New York: Harper & Row, 1965), 117, and Underhill, *Woman Who Ran for President,* 34.

222 **Unfazed by the . . . :** Victoria Woodhull, "Tried as by Fire," *The Victoria Woodhull Reader,* ed. Madeleine B. Stern (Weston, Mass.: M & S Press, 1974), 25.

222 **He gave them . . . :** Quoted in Mary Gabriel, *Notorious Victoria: The Life of Victoria Woodhull Uncensored* (Chapel Hill, N.C.: Algonquin Books, 1998), 42. In 1870 women were not permitted on the trading floor, another prohibition Victoria gleefully broke, striding "officially and very publicly" onto this male preserve on Wall Street, 41.

223 **A reporter spotted . . . :** Quoted in Underhill, *Woman Who Ran for President,* 56.

223 **With Lilith's "smooth" . . . :** Quoted in Patai, *Hebrew Goddess,* 222.

223 **Feminists and small-town . . . :** Woodhull, "Tried as by Fire," 37 and 39.

223 **If that led women . . . :** Victoria Woodhull, "A Speech on the Principles of Social Freedom," *Victoria Woodhull Reader,* 23.

223 **On a typical evening . . . :** Quoted in Underhill, *Woman Who Ran for President,* 256.

223 **Victoria divorced Blood . . . :** Quoted ibid., 273.

223 **She caught the eye . . . :** Quoted ibid., 280.

223 **"The truth is" . . . :** Quoted ibid., 294.

224 **"Those weeds have . . . :** Quoted ibid., 306.

224 **"Woman," she said . . . :** Quoted in "Which Is to Blame," *Feminism: The Essential Historical Writings,* ed. Miriam Schneir (New York: Vintage, 1972), 149.

224 **She was her . . . :** Patai, *Hebrew Goddess,* 222.

225 **While Victoria identified . . . :** Gloria Steinem, foreword, Jean Shinoda Bolen, M.D., *Goddesses in Everywoman* (New York: Harper Colophon Books, 1984), xi.

225 **Of the two . . . :** Carolyn G. Heilbrun, *The Education of a Woman: The Life of Gloria Steinem* (New York: Dial Press, 1995), xix. As Margaret Hennig and Anne Jardim demonstrate in their study of female superachievers and leaders, this daughter-father bond is unusually common and formative. See *The Managerial Woman* (New York: Pocket Books, 1976), 99–117.

225 **Thanks to this . . . :** Quoted in "Gloria Steinem: Ms. America," A&E Biography, ABC News Production, 1995.

226 **Her mother, too deranged . . . :** Quoted ibid.

226 **Hell-bent on "not . . .":** Quoted in Heilbrun, *Education,* 27.

226 **In her senior year . . . :** Quoted in Sydney Ladensohn Stern, *Gloria Steinem: Her Passions, Politics, and Mystique* (Secaucus, N.J.: Birch Lane Press Book, 1997), 81.

226 **Model pretty with . . . :** Quoted in A&E Biography.

226 **Benton said she . . . :** Quoted in Heilbrun, *Education of a Woman,* 94, 115, and 116; Stern, *Gloria,* 325; and Heilbrun, 111.

227 **By her own . . . :** Quoted in Cynthia Gorney, "Gloria: At 61, Steinem Wants Straight Talk, More Fun, and a New Congress," Motherjones.com/mother jones, 1995.

227 **One New Yorker . . . :** Quoted in Heilbrun, *Education of a Woman,* 121.

227 **She wrote exposés . . . :** Quoted ibid., 170.

227 **The barbed sound bites . . . :** Quoted, A&E Biography.

227 **Throughout the round-the-clock** . . . : Stern, *Gloria Steinem*, 181.
228 **She pooh-poohed her** . . . : Quoted in Leslie Bennetts, "Deconstructing Gloria," *Vanity Fair* (January 1992), 138.
228 **As one critic observed** . . . : Quoted ibid., 140.
228 **She's still in battle** . . . : Robin Finn, "Single No More and Still Wedded to the Cause," *New York Times*, May 23, 2001, B2.
229 **She may wind up** . . . : Gloria Steinem, "Doing Sixty," *Moving Beyond Words* (New York: Simon & Schuster, 1994), 281.
229 **"Dear Goddess," she** . . . : Ibid., 280.
229 **As Jacqueline Kennedy** . . . : Quoted in Stern, *Gloria Steinem*, 184.
229 **Most women who** . . . : See Millan's summary and evaluation, *Monstrous Regiment*, 257–60.
231 **In her comprehensive** . . . : Ibid., 259.
231 **Stateswomen, said the** . . . : See Brantôme, *Fair and Gallant Ladies*, 268–305. Courtier and connoisseur, Brantôme wrote his Fifth Discourse in erotic praise of female leaders, rulers, and warriors. One of the interlocutors of Castiglione's *Book of the Courtier* also speaks well of them. "Don't you believe," he says, "that many women would be found who would now how to govern cities and armies as well as men do?," 212.
231 **Under the czarina's** . . . : Bly and Woodman, *Maiden King*.
231 **Freud thought great** . . . : Becker, *Denial of Death*, 135.

CHAPTER **8**: SIREN-ADVENTURERS

234 **The mythic first** . . . : Baring and Cashford, *The Myth of the Goddess*, 66.
234 **The gods "ben[t]** . . . : Meador, *Inanna*, 17.
234 **As recent studies** . . . : See David P. Barash and Judith Eve Lipton, *The Myth of Monogamy* (New York: W. H. Freeman & Co., 2001); Hrdy, *Woman that Never Evolved;* Fisher, *First Sex;* and Angier, *Woman*, 68, for a summary of this revised view of female sexuality.
235 **When she cruised** . . . : Quoted in Frymer-Kensky, *Wake of the Goddesses*, 28.
236 **The scarlet wretches** . . . : Carla Casagrande, "The Protected Woman," *The Silence of the Middle Ages: A History of Women in the West*, ed. Christiane Klapisch-Zuber (Cambridge, Mass.: Harvard University Press, 1992), 85.
236 **At the height** . . . : This saint was "eyed with disapproval and suspicion" in Agnès's day. "Because she was free and her own mistress (*sui domina et libera*)," she exerted a "bad influence over other women." See Casagrande's discussion, "Protected Woman," 90–91.
236 **At this lively** . . . : Jehanne d'Orliac, *The Lady of Beauty: Agnès Sorel*, trans. M. C. Darnton (Philadelphia: J. B. Lippincott, 1931), 23.
236 **"Her speech," said** . . . : Quoted ibid., 61.
236 **With her "laughing moods"** . . . : M. Capefigue, *A King's Mistress or Charles VII and Agnès Sorel and Chivalry in the XV Century*, trans. Edmund Goldsmid (Edinburgh: privately printed, 1887), 94 and 44.
237 **When Charles VII** . . . : D'Orliac, *Lady of Beauty*, 34.
237 **He suffered fits** . . . : Ibid., 43.
237 **Agnès, though, saw** . . . : Ibid., 47.

237 **She forbade him** . . . : Wismes, *Great Royal Favorites,* 1.

237 **She told him** . . . : Brantôme, *Fair and Gallant Ladies,* 256.

237 **As soon as she became** . . . : Casagrande, "Protected Woman," 100 and 101.

237 **At her insistence** . . . : Quoted in Wismes, *Great Royal Favorites,* 2.

237 **Two other brilliant** . . . : Quoted in d'Orliac, *Lady of Beauty,* 125.

237 **With Étienne, Agnès** . . . : Ibid., 164.

237 **Agnes created the** . . . : Quoted in Wismes, 1.

238 **Her face bore** . . . : Quoted in Casagrande, "Protected Woman," 93.

238 **The clergy published** . . . : Quoted in Capefigue, *King's Mistress,* 14.

238 **Secure in her** . . . : Wismes, *Great Royal Favorites,* 2.

239 **In a pathologic inversion** . . . : D'Orliac, *Lady of Beauty,* 192.

239 **It's easier for** . . . : Voltaire poem quoted ibid., 200.

239 **Agnès's favorite pet** . . . : Quoted ibid., 159.

239 **And for decades** . . . : Quoted in Capefigue, *King's Mistress,* 58.

239 **With her pastel beauty** . . . : Quoted in Mary S. Lovell, *Rebel Heart: The Scandalous Life of Jane Digby* (New York: Norton, 1995), 15.

239 **She became the iconic** . . . : William Wordsworth, "She Was a Phantom of Delight," *English Poetry and Prose of the Romantic Movement,* ed. George Benjamin Woods (Chicago: Scott, Foresman and Co., 1950), 321.

240 **She was taught** . . . : Eva Figes, "Rousseau, Revolution, Romanticism, and Retrogression," *Patriarchal Attitudes* (Greenwich, Conn.: Fawcett, 1970), 94.

240 **Her parents could** . . . : Quoted in Schmidt, *Passion's Child,* 23.

241 **Eventually she had** . . . : Quoted ibid., 82 and 91.

241 **When he saw** . . . : Lovell, *Rebel Heart,* 88.

241 **Jane then divorced Karl,** . . . : Quoted ibid., 125.

242 **She gave Xristo** . . . : Ibid., 146.

242 **Still beautiful at** . . . : Quoted in Schmidt, *Passion's Child,* 153.

242 **Medjuel el Mezrab** . . . : Quoted in Lovell, *Rebel Heart,* 237.

243 **With her eyes** . . . : Quoted ibid., 202.

243 **Medjuel, a renowned** . . . : Schmidt, *Passion's Child,* 213.

243 **She must kiss** . . . : *The Perfumed Garden of the Shaykh Nefzawi,* trans. Sir Richard F. Burton (New York: Putnam's, 1963), 66 and 86.

243 **She was "out** . . .": Quoted in Lovell, *Rebel Heart,* 290.

243 **Impatient with "cooped** . . .": Quoted ibid., 274.

243 **"Oh," Jane exclaimed** . . . : Quoted ibid., 270.

243 **After watching a** . . . : Quoted ibid., 197.

244 **She loved him** . . . : Quoted ibid., 284.

244 **Arabella, he fumes,** . . . : Honoré Balzac, *Lily of the Valley,* trans. Lucienne Hill (New York: Carroll & Graf, 1989), 215 and 201, and Schmidt, *Passion's Child,* 117.

244 **She was a "notorious** . . .": Quoted in Schmidt, *Passion's Child,* 60, and Lovell, *Rebel Heart,* 63.

244 **But like Balzac's minx** . . . : Balzac, *Lily of the Valley,* 213.

244 **All that mattered** . . . : Quoted in Lesley Blanch, *The Wilder Shores of Love* (London: Abacus, 1984), 192.

244 **"This was freedom!** . . .": Byron, "Childe Harold," Canto III, verse 15, and quoted in Lovell, *Rebel Heart,* 141.

245 **The impostor was** . . . : Quoted in Ishbel Ross, *Uncrowned Queen,* 203.

245 **An "insatiable amoureuse"** . . . : Ibid., 1, and quoted in Donna Lawson, intro., Madame Lola Montez, *The Arts and Secrets of Beauty* (New York: Chelsea House, 1964), xviii.

245 **A king abdicated** . . . : Quoted in Bruce Seymour, *Lola Montez: A Life* (New Haven: Yale University Press, 1996), 167.

245 **Teachers decried her** . . . : Quoted ibid., 10 and 13.

246 **Armed with an** . . . : Ross, *Uncrowned Queen*, 17.

246 **She had the** . . . : Quoted ibid., 89.

246 **Men clapped "until** . . . : Quoted in Seymour, *Lola Montez*, 48.

247 **Instantly captivated, he** . . . : Quoted ibid., 70, and Helen Holdredge, *The Woman in Black: The Life of the Fabulous Lola Montez* (New York: Putnam's, 1955), 7.

247 **He wrote a sonata** . . . : Quoted in Seymour, *Lola Montez*, 21.

247 **But the "lightless . . ."**: Quoted ibid., 67.

247 **The next day Ludwig** . . . : Quoted ibid., 89, and quoted in Seymour, *Lola Montez*, 108.

247 **She stroked his** . . . : Quoted in Seymour, *Lola Montez*, 363.

247–48 **She wanted him** . . . : Quoted ibid., 232.

248 **The university closed** . . . : Quoted in Lawson, intro., *Arts*, xiv.

248 **Shattered and deranged** . . . : Quoted in Ross, *Uncrowned Queen*, 110.

249 **Blaming herself, she** . . . : Quoted in Seymour, *Lola Montez*, 363.

249 **In love, she** . . . : Lola Montez, "Gallantry," Charles Burr, *Lectures of Lola Montez: Including Her Autobiography* (Philadelphia: Peterson, 1858), 156.

249 **They just needed** . . . : Lola Montez, "Autobiography," Burr, *Lectures*, 15.

249 **Look at the experts** . . . : "Heroines of History," Burr, *Lectures*, 195.

249 **But true to her contention** . . . : Quoted, Lawson, intro., *Arts*, xviii.

249 **Asked, "Why Lola?"** . . . : Jim Yardley, "Lola, Long Dead Is Still Getting Attention," *New York Times*, April 26, 1998, 3.

249 **As to be expected** . . . : Frederick Brown, "Whatever Lola Wanted," *New Republic* (July 15 and 22, 1996), 37.

249 **Move like the** . . . : Montez, *Arts*, 17, and quoted in Ross, *Uncrowned Queen*, 310.

250 **"Anger," writes Susan** . . . : Brownmiller, *Femininity*, 210.

250 **Not in male** . . . : See, for example, Richard Weber's love poem "Elizabeth in Italy" with the opening line "Suddenly she slapped me," as well as Catullus's and Propertius's celebrations of their mistress's curses. Many books, such as Mario Praz's *Romantic Agony*, 199–300, discuss this theme in literature. See particularly Stoller, *Sexual Excitement;* John Money, *Love and Love Sickness* (Baltimore: Johns Hopkins University Press, 1980), 4 and passim; and Michael R. Liebowitz, *The Chemistry of Love* (New York: Berkley Books, 1983). For a pop example of this male taste, see issues of *Femmes Fatales* (Forest Park, Ill.: Frederick S. Clarke, 1992–present).

250 **Just as the "war . . ."**: Rougemont, *Love in the Western World*, 243.

250 **It was part** . . . : Meador, *Inanna*, 151.

250 **"Manly" and courageous,** . . . : Frymer-Kensky, *Wake of the Goddess*, 29, and quoted in Meador, *Inanna*, 118 and 119.

250 **Seventeenth-century Europe had** . . . : Quoted in Hester W. Chapman, *Privileged Persons: Four Seventeenth-Century Studies* (New York: Reynal and William

Morrow, 1966), 228 and 225, and Cyril Hughes Hartmann, *The Vagabond Duchess: The Life of Hortense Mancini Duchesse Mazarin* (London: George Routledge & Sons, 1926), from title.

250 **She was a macha Hotspur . . . :** Fraser, *Weaker Vessel,* 4 and passim.

250 **When Cardinal Mazarin . . . :** Toivo David Rosvall, *The Mazarin Legacy: The Life of Hortense Mancini, Duchess Mazarin* (New York: Viking, 1969), 40.

251 **"Her mother's darling," . . . :** Chapman, *Privileged Persons,* 183.

251 **She ran riot . . . :** Hartmann, *Vagabond Duchess,* 8.

251 **Her assets included . . . :** Quoted in H. Noel Williams, *Rival Sultanas* (New York: Dodd, Mead, 1915), note 177.

251 **In striking contrast . . . :** Fraser, *Weaker Vessel,* 409.

251 **In five years Armand . . . :** Rosvall, *The Mazarin Legacy,* 65.

252 **But she scorched . . . :** Quoted ibid., 119.

252 **A swashbuckling monarch . . . :** Chapman, *Privileged Persons,* 220.

252 **For three years . . . :** Meador, *Inanna,* 118.

252 **"I have found . . ."**: Quoted in Rosvall, *The Mazarin Legacy,* 140.

252 **After Charles died . . . :** Quoted in Chapman, *Privileged Persons,* 225.

253 **He called her . . . :** Quoted in Rosvall, *Mazarin Legacy,* 179.

253 **At the opening . . . :** Quoted ibid., 182.

253 **"Everything about her," . . . :** Quoted ibid., 174 and 189. The actual quote is "nothing is formed in you which does not turn to love," 174.

253 **Under his guidance . . . :** Hartmann, *Vagabond Duchess,* 197.

253 **Other female admirers . . . :** Quoted in intro, "The History of the Nun or The Fair Vow-Breaker," *The Works of Aphra Behn,* ed. Janet Todd, vol. 3, *The Fair Jilt and Other Short Stories* (Columbus: Ohio State University Press, 1995), 208.

253 **"Each sex," said . . . :** Quoted in Jeanine Delpech, *The Life and Times of the Duchess of Portsmouth* (New York: Roy Publishers, 1953), 109.

254 **"Never have I . . ."**: Quoted in Chapman, *Privileged Persons,* 242.

254 **The court poet . . . :** "Satyr," 1686, from Aphra Behn's commonplace book, Bodleian Library, Ms. Firth c. 16 and BL ms. Harl. 7319. Courtesy of Professor Mary Ann O'Donnell.

254 **She might have deserted . . . :** Meador, *Inanna,* 151.

254 **"She comes, she . . ."**: Ibid., 151, and quoted in Williams, *Rival Sultanas,* 193.

254 **This *über*siren, called . . . :** Quoted in Errol Trzebinski, *The Lives of Beryl Markham* (New York: Norton, 1993), 58, and quoted in Meador, *Inanna,* 125.

255 **In seduction, she . . . :** Quoted in Trzebinski, *Beryl Markham,* 261.

255 **Throughout her childhood . . . :** Quoted in Mary S. Lovell, *Straight On Till Morning: The Biography of Beryl Markham* (New York: St. Martin's, 1987), 18.

255 **At these all-night . . . :** Beryl Markham, *West with the Night* (New York: Farrar, Straus, and Giroux, 1942), 106.

256 **"It was impossible," . . . :** Quoted in Trzebinski, *Beryl Markham,* 53.

256 **The local Masais . . . :** Quoted in Lovell, *Straight On Till Morning,* 59.

256 **When Jock Purvis, . . . :** Quoted in Trzebinski, *Beryl Markham,* 66.

256 **With her blond marcelled . . . :** Quoted in Lovell, *Straight On Till Morning,* 58.

256 **The men "surrounded . . ."**: Quoted in Trzebinski, *Beryl Markham,* 107.

257 **She found the . . . :** Markham, *West with the Night,* 239.

257 Her "delicious sense . . .": Quoted in Trzebinski, *Beryl Markham*, 221.

257 Those who experienced . . . : Quoted ibid., 185.

257 During a two-month . . . : Quoted ibid., 185.

258 Restive in captivity . . . : Quoted in Lovell, *Straight On Till Morning*, 248.

258 When Raoul caught . . . : Quoted in Trzebinski, *Beryl Markham*, 261.

259 Her farm manager, . . . : Quoted in Lovell, *Straight On Till Morning*, 283.

259 In her fifties . . . : Quoted ibid., 289, 292, and 293.

259 The next ten years . . . : Quoted ibid., 283.

259 A fortyish bachelor . . . : Quoted in Trzebinski, *Beryl Markham*, 317.

259 "I ADORE YOU," . . . : Quoted ibid., 342.

259 "I certainly have . . ." : Quoted ibid., 25.

259 She claimed she'd . . . : Markham, *West with the Night*, 239 and 185.

260 Her most terrifying . . . : Ibid., 200.

260 As her enemies . . . : Quoted in Trzebinski, *Beryl Markham*, 157.

260 This woman, she wrote . . . : Quoted ibid., 299.

260 It all originated . . . : Frymer-Kensky, *Wake of the Goddesses*, 28.

261 The "divine hierodule . . .": Husain, *Goddess*, 92.

261 Terrified of the . . . : For a discussion of this abnormal fear of eros, the "Tyrant of Gods and Men," see Bruce S. Thornton's excellent book *Eros*, 11–47 and passim.

261 She jumped ship . . . : Herodotus, *The Histories*, trans. Aubrey de Selincourt (Baltimore: Penguin, 1954), 155, and Hayward, *Dictionary of the Courtesans*, 86.

262 As she grew . . . : Sabrina Mervin and Carol Prunheber, *Women Around the World and Through the Ages* (Wilmington, Del.: Atomium Books, 1990), 90.

262 Her lover, Praxiteles . . . : Hayward, *Dictionary of the Courtesans*, 365–66.

262 As immodest as . . . : Quoted in Basserman, *Oldest Profession*, 21.

262 Filled with the . . . : Licht, *Sexual Life in Ancient Greece*, 349.

262 An avatar of . . . : Friedrich, *Meaning of Aphrodite*, 92.

263 "Phyrne had talents . . .": Quoted in Hayward, *Dictionary of the Courtesans*, 367.

263 If she were loveworthy . . . : John S. Haller, Jr., and Robin M. Haller, *The Physician and Sexuality in Victorian America* (New York: Norton, 1974), 98 and 101.

263 Blanche d'Antigy bathed . . . : Richardson, *Courtesans*, 31.

264 "A love affair . . .": Quoted ibid., 200.

264 One prince said . . . : Quoted in Polly Binder, *The Truth About Cora Pearl* (London: Weidenfeld & Nicolson, 1986), 9.

264 Paris in 1855 . . . : Quoted in Christiansen, *Paris Babylon*, 17. Estimates vary from thirty to a hundred thousand prostitutes. See ibid., 86, and Binder, *Cora Pearl*, 32.

265 For starters, "she . . .": Binder, *Cora Pearl*, 30.

265 She had a round, freckled . . . : Quoted in Richardson, *Courtesans*, 52.

265 Adopting a "new . . .": Binder, *Cora Pearl*, 40.

265 In her company . . . : Havelock Ellis, "Prostitution," *Studies in the Psychology of Sex* (New York: Random House, 1937), vol. 2, part 3, quoted on 299 and 222, and quoted in note, 299.

266 As soon as . . . : Binder, *Cora Pearl*, 35.

266 Men, she believed, . . . : Quoted ibid., 39.

266 She lost her . . . : Quoted ibid., 150.

266 Her "merry disposition" . . . : Richardson, *Courtesans,* 62.

266 She died of . . . : Binder, *Cora Pearl,* 148.

267 But, then, she'd . . . : Binder, *Cora Pearl,* 56.

267 Cora, though, "was . . .": Ibid., 45.

267 Panicked by domestic . . . : Quoted in Bram Dijkstra, *Idols of Perversity: Fantasies of Feminine Evil in Fin-de-Siècle Culture* (New York: Oxford University Press, 1986), 13.

267 She claimed she'd . . . : Quoted in Binder, *Cora Pearl,* 150.

267 "Let us live . . .": Quoted ibid., 123.

267 "Spell sex," said . . . : Quoted in Arthur H. Lewis, *La Belle Otero* (New York: Trident Press, 1967), 4 and 5.

267 Known as the Suicide . . . : Quoted in Cornelia Otis Skinner, *Elegant Wits and Grand Horizontals* (Boston: Houghton Mifflin, 1962), 242.

267 Tangoing around the . . . : Quoted in Lewis, *La Belle Otero,* 34.

267 Her breasts, which . . . : Quoted ibid., 4.

268 Thus began her obsession . . . : Quoted ibid., 194.

268 An American impresario . . . : Ibid., 31.

268 He took her . . . : Quoted ibid., 33.

269 One young Russian . . . : Quoted ibid., 74.

269 A fly-by lover, . . . : Lawrence Durrell, *Justine* (New York: Penguin, 1957), 105, and quoted in Skinner, *Elegant Wits,* 239.

269 The trail of . . . : Quoted in Lewis, *La Belle Otero,* 126.

269 "The flames," she . . . : Quoted ibid., 75.

269 Caparisoned in head-to-toe . . . : Quoted ibid., 182.

270 "I wasn't meant," gibed . . . : Quoted ibid., 193.

270 Like the "advancing . . .": Friedrich, *Meaning of Aphrodite,* 92.

270 After work she . . . : Quoted in Skinner, *Elegant Wits and Grand Horizontals,* 240.

270 "When one has . . .": Quoted in Lewis, *La Belle Otero,* 112.

270 Although besieged with . . . : Quoted ibid., 192.

270 She weekended with . . . : Quoted ibid., 188.

271 Men continued to . . . : Quoted in Lewis, *La Belle Otero,* 243.

271 "The king of . . .": Quoted ibid., 248.

271 She wrote a highly colored . . . : Quoted ibid., 250.

271 Supported by monthly . . . : Quoted ibid., 121.

271 She was snubbed . . . : Quoted ibid., 121.

271 "Think of the . . .": Quoted ibid., 142.

271 Otero was "impossible" . . . : Quoted ibid., 243.

271 Had she known the right . . . : Frymer-Kensky, *Wake of the Goddesses,* 29.

272 The "terrible maneater" . . . : Quoted in Julie Wheelwright, *The Fatal Lover: Mata Hari and the Myth of Women in Espionage* (London: Collins & Brown, 1992), 68.

272 Her true love . . . : As World War I approached and her prospects dimmed, Mata Hari seized on the persona of courtesan spy and boasted to the French Secret Service about an imaginary affair with Crown Prince Wilhelm of Germany and persuaded it to pay her a million francs to extract war secrets from him. Instead she latched on to a minor military attaché, with whom she exchanged worthless gossip while pretending to work for the Germans.

She fooled nobody and cooperated fully in the national witch-hunt for women who renounced domestic responsibilities. (During the war, with the combined threat of women in the workplace and the need for maternal succor and sacrifice, antidomestic sirens involved in politics were targeted as spies and demonized. Hence the myth of the double agent ball breaker in black satin.)

Blunder followed idiotic blunder. As if lured by a fata morgana into the abyss, she demanded more money, invented adventures, and changed the story of her life whenever she found herself in a tight spot. After she was arrested as a German spy, she hired a lawyer with no experience and bungled her way into a death sentence through a web of fibs and weak alibis.

Her one redeeming trait and only link with the siren-adventurers was her classy death. She refused a blindfold, smiled at the firing squad, and blew a kiss as they gunned her down. Victimhood, though, no matter how stylish, didn't belong in the sirens' repertoire. Grand Horizontals preferred conquest, victory parades, and the spoils of war. By the 1920s they'd nearly disappeared, a casualty of postwar prejudices against unhousebound she-swells—except for a few remnants haunting Mediterranean resorts like deposed queens.

One of the last of them, Liane de Pougy, regarded Mata Hari's career from her Nice estate with utter contempt. "She had a loud voice and heavy manner," sneered Liane, "she lied, she dressed badly, she had no notion of shape or colour, and she walked mannishly." She might have also added that she knew less than nothing about seduction. Quoted in Wheelwright, *Fatal Lover,* 35.

272 **The reputed courtesan . . . :** Michael Gross, interview, " 'Basically, I'm a Backroom Girl': Of Lovers, Husbands, Wealth, and Power," Week in Review, *New York Times,* February 16, 1997, 14. Even though she subordinated herself like a "geisha-girl" to men, they had a habit of humiliating and discarding her. Her first husband, Randolph Churchill, philandered in her absence; Averell Harriman and Ed Murrow returned to their wives; Gianni Agnelli jilted her (after having sex with another woman next door while she got an abortion); Elsie de Rothschild ditched her; and both Leland Hayward and Averell Harriman were hard taskmasters, domineering and on occasion insulting. Quoted in Christopher Ogden, *Life of the Party: The Biography of Pamela Digby Churchill Hayward Harriman* (Boston: Little, Brown, 1994), 311.

Instead of escaping the feminine lockup for adventure and an autonomous existence, Pamela embraced the fifties' ethos. She only asked for a man to submerge her identity into, to accept her, and give her entrée into a society where she could follow the script. One socialite told another that the secret of Pamela's success was "merely housekeeping, but housekeeping of the most rarefied sort." She lectured, "We could all learn a thing or two from Pamela's superb example." The "thing or two" might be how to win "best in show" in a good wife competition and how to serve difficult men, but certainly not how to strike out and win the really big prizes of freedom, independence, and the insane adoration of wonderful men. Quoted in Marie Brenner, "The Prime of Pamela Harriman," *Vanity Fair* (July 1988), 77.

272 **And she "didn't . . . :** Ogden, *Life of the Party,* 238. A European man who slept with her often during the fifties corroborated this and said that "her amorous temperament was not very big," 238.

272 **Her contemporary, the . . . :** Aline, Countess de Romanones, *The Spy Wore Red: My Adventures as an Undercover Agent in World War II* (New York: Random House, 1987), 11.

272 **But she too caved . . .** : When Aline married Luis, count of the ancient family of Quintanilla, she underwent a road to Damascus conversion. Submitting to his tutorials with bovine docility, she studiously upclassed herself. When he reproved her for waking unfashionably early, she stayed in bed until ten; when he criticized her "revolting" American table manners, she held her knife the European way; when she did "right and [had] a boy," she obediently gave the child the eight names he dictated. She deferred to his "quiet authority" and strove to fit into the "straitlaced" untraconservative world of the Spanish gentry. When the gaudy Eva Perón arrived in Madrid in heavy maquillage and sexy clothes, Aline winced at her "bawdy sense of humor" and "longed to tell her to tone down." Aline, Countess of Romanones, *The Spy Went Dancing* (New York: Putnam's, 1990), 154 and 155; *The Well-Mannered Assassin* (New York: Jove Books, 1994), 18; and *Spy Went Dancing*, 131.

By toning down, scaling back, and cutting herself to the pattern of a grande dame, Aline earned a big payoff. She dined with movie stars, wore heirloom jewels, and renovated an ancient family ranch and pored over the Romanones archives. She obligingly gave birth to three sons, each with eight names apiece. Her politics, in deference to her husband's views, mirrored the official Romanones position, which wits called "somewhere to the right of Attila the hairdresser." Paul McCarthy, quoted in *Newsweek* (March 25, 1991), 59. The Romanones family represented the extreme right-wing interests in Spain and was severely indicted by the philosopher Ortega y Gasset.

But after Luis's death, Aline loosened her stays and regained a measure of her old independence and swerve. By writing books about her OSS and CIA escapades, she recovered, at least vicariously, the highs of self-sovereignty, action, risk, initiative, and death-defying subterfuge.

272 **Drag race champion . . .** : Interview, Barbara Walters, November 21, 1997, and Kelly Flinn, *Proud to Be* (New York: Random House, 1997), 172.

273 **The cream of . . .** : Quoted in John Connolly, "Hollywood After Heidi," *Swing* (June 1996), 73.

273 **Free spirits everywhere . . .** : See *Rolling Stone* special issue "Women of Rock," (November 13, 1997).

273 **As Leslie Blanch . . .** : Blanch, *Wilder Shores of Love*, 170.

274 **One cultural critic . . .** : William Bolitho, *Twelve Against the Gods* (New York: Viking, 1957), 147.

274 **Wired to move, . . .** : See Liebowitz, *Chemistry of Love*, 77.

274 **As befitted deputies . . .** : See Grace Lichtenstein, Chapter 12, "The Ultimate Playing Field: Sex," *Machisma: Women and Daring* (Garden City, N.Y.: Doubleday, 1981), 279–302 and passim.

275 **"Progress," said one . . .** : Figes, *Patriarchal Attitudes*, 145.

276 **They want identities . . .** : See Stacey D'Erasmo, "Polymorphous Normal," *New York Times Magazine*, October 14, 2001, 104–07. These new "cultural explorers" with fluid sexual lives and identities envisage a future that the siren-adventurers would have endorsed: "a utopia where all the species run free," 106 and 107.

276 **They want—maybe . . .** : Evidence suggests that women are inherently the more nomadic sex. According to a recent archaeological study, women's rates of "intercontinental migrations" have been eight times that of men. Rather than an instinctive masculine impulse to wander, women, it seems, might possess the way-

farer gene. See Natalie Angier, "Man vs. Woman: In History's Travel Olympics, There's No Contest," *New York Times,* October 27, 1998, F5.

276 **"Everybody is an ..."**: Quoted in Pritt J. Vesilind, "Why Explore?," *National Geographic* (February 1998), 41.

276 **She recovered her mythic ...** : Quoted in Frymer-Kensky, *Wake of the Goddesses,* 28.

CHAPTER 9: GODDESS-TRIPPIN': INTO THE FUTURE

277 **Cultural commentators say ...** : Baudrillard, *Seduction,* 95.

277 **"Nobody," writes columnist ...** : "Pretty Mean Woman," *New York Times,* August 1, 1999, 15. The valentine card industry has adapted accordingly, slanting messages away from desire to noncommittal sentiments or suck-me invitations.

277–78 **Sex goddess Jennifer ...** : Bob Morris, "Could This Be Love," *Talk* (March 2000), 149.

278 **She bought décolleté ...** : See this front-page story of the travails of multimillion-dollar lawyer Leslie Friedman. Robert McGough, "If You Can't Get a Man with a Gun, Big Bucks Might Work," *Wall Street Journal,* December 16, 1998, A1–A6.

278 **Memoirs, novels, and ...** : See Ruth La Ferla, who discusses a recent spate of nonfiction dumpee books and lists them. "The Lovelorn Learn to Lash Out," *New York Times,* March 7, 1999, 1–5. Among the other summaries of feminine romantic defeat is Daphne Merkin's account of the "man-crazed helplessness" felt by Everywoman and the pervasive "fear of ending up manless and alone," "Bridget Jones Is Me!," *New Yorker* (August 3, 1998), 74.

Additional nonfiction books include Mary Cantwell, *Speaking with Strangers* (New York: Houghton Mifflin, 1998); Sallie Tisdale, *Talk Dirty to Me* (New York: Doubleday, 1994); Candace Bushnell, *Sex and the City* (New York: Atlantic Monthly Press, 1996); Wurtzel, *Bitch;* Marcelle Clements, *The Improvised Woman* (New York: Norton, 1998); Anka Radakokvich, *The Wild Girls' Club* (New York: Crown, 1994); Katie Roiphe, *The Morning After* (Boston: Little, Brown, 1993); Linda Grant, *Sexing the Millennium* (New York: Grove Press, 1994); Karen Lehrman, *The Lipstick Proviso* (New York: Doubleday, 1997); Danielle Crittenden, *What Our Mothers Didn't Tell Us* (New York: Simon & Schuster, 1999); and Vivian Gornick, *Approaching Eye Level* (Boston: Beacon, 1996).

Fiction is not far behind. Witness the success of Helen Fielding's *Bridget Jones's Diary* (New York: Penguin, 1996), Melissa Bank's *The Girls' Guide to Hunting and Fishing* (New York: Viking, 1999); Sister Souljah's *The Coldest Winter Ever* (New York: Pocket Books, 1999); Karin Goodwin's *Sleeping with Random Beasts* (San Francisco: Chronicle Books, 1998); Amy Sohn's *Run Catch Kiss* (New York: Simon & Schuster, 1999); and Tama Janowitz's *The Male Cross-Dresser Support Group* (New York: Washington Square Press, 1992) and *A Certain Age* (New York: Doubleday, 1999). The one-woman show *Bad Sex with Bud Kemp* had a long run several years ago.

Susan Minot, Mary Gaitskill, and Anita Brookner are three prominent authors who specialize in doormats and losers in love. For sad-sack stories of older women, see Doris Lessing, *Love, Again* (New York: Harper Perennial, 1996) and Marilyn French, *My Summer with George* (New York: Ballantine, 1996).

Kathy Acker in *Don Quixote* (London: Paladin Grafton Books, 1986) writes the ultimate castoffs' lacrimosa. The pathetic narrator says, "About once a year, I see a man whom I actually want and then . . . the usual happens: Either he walks away or, after a day or two he walks away. For me sexuality is rejection," 128.

278 **The younger generation . . . :** Student quoted in Crittenden, *What Our Mothers Didn't Tell Us*, 33. Supporting Crittenden's findings at Georgetown, Princeton, etc., see Patricia Yancey Martin and Robert A. Hummer, "Fraternities and Rape on Campus," *Feminist Frontiers III*, ed. Laurel Richardson and Verta Taylor (New York: McGraw-Hill, 1993), 392–402. Also see Norval Glenn and Elizabeth Marquardt, "Hooking Up, Hanging Out, and Hoping for Mr. Right–College Women on Dating and Mating Today," 2001, Available from Independent Women's Forum, Org/news/010727.shtml, 1-74.

My own interviews at Manhattan College in spring 1995 yielded these responses. Most women on campus, said students, "have very low self-esteem," sleep with guys without desire or purpose (beyond a vague hope of snagging them that way), and "are dumped on." One informant told me of a "100 Club" on campus for high-scoring Romeos.

278 **Nancy Friday foreshadowed . . . :** Nancy Friday, *Women on Top* (New York: Pocket Books, 1991), 67.

278 **France, of all . . . :** Julie Street, "Women: Ooh La La on Saturday Night," *Guardian*, December 6, 1999, 6.

279 **A study finds . . . :** Patricia Sellers, "Women, Sex and Power," *Fortune* (August 5, 1996), 44.

279 **He hunted her . . . :** Quoted in Jean Bond Rafferty, "La Belle Helene," *Town and Country* (September 1998), 176.

279 **If a guy . . . :** "Big Momma Thang," *Hardcore*, and "No Time," *Hardcore/*Sunset Park soundtrack. Unfortunately their private lives haven't caught up with the public braggadocio. Although they give as good as they get in "trade snaps" (rhyming contests reminiscent of Veronica Franco's poetic combats with men during the Italian Renaissance), they tend to sing a different tune in private.

Because of an eight-to-one ratio of African American professional women to men and a gaping disparity of sexual goals–recreational for 42 percent black men and relational for 91 percent women–even the sassiest hip-hop honey may end up, like Lil' Kim, in a humiliating ménage à trois or alone with her girl crew on Saturday night. Also their bluster often just flips the script on black machismo, duplicating an adolescent glamorization of violence, money, status brands, and belt-notching promiscuity.

279 **Female artists have . . . :** Elizabeth Hayt, "The Artist Is a Glamour Puss," *New York Times*, April 18, 1999, section 9, 1.

280 **As trend spotter Faith . . . :** Faith Popcorn, *The Popcorn Report* (New York: HarperCollins, 1991), 58.

281 **They place "all . . .":** Warren Farrell, *The Myth of Male Power* (New York: Berkley Books, 1993), xxv. The needier, more fragile sex, men are "in thrall to women" and their awesome powers. In bed they must surmount primordial womb terrors, stand and deliver, and meet women's rising expectations and voracious orgasmic demands. They know they'll be compared and graded, and they dread an F in sackcraft. On top of these performance fears, men are more emotionally vulnerable. Although they'd swallow hot coals before they'd admit it, the myth of the

lone Romeo on a perpetual journey from kicks to kicks is just that, a myth. Secretly they want the opposite: an anchored existence in perpetual attendance on a
beloved Lady Superior. R. William Betcher, Ph.D, M.D., and William S. Pollack,
In a Time of Fallen Heroes (New York: Atheneum, 1993), 199. For more on this male
vulnerability, see the discussion in chapter 1. The best surveys are Lederer, *Fear of
Women*, Gaylin, *Male Ego*, and Stephen Frosh, *Sexual Difference: Masculinity and
Psychoanalysis* (New York: Routledge, 1994).

Discussions of heightened male romantic susceptibility can be found in Fisher,
First Sex, 275, and Friday, *Men in Love*, 14–16. Both Friday and Robert Bly, among
many others, treat the idealization impulse, and Todd Shackleford, in a famous
study, found that men suffer more from separation anxiety than women, loving
partners more the longer the absence. *Iron John* (New York: Addison-Wesley, 1990),
135, and see a summary of Shackleford's work in *Psychology Today* (January–
February 2000), 12.

Betcher and Pollack have a particularly fine discussion of the deep male longing for home that they call *querencia*, an affection for place and the womblike embrace of the domestic haven, 258. The myth of man the loner appears to be a
counterphobic ploy against this powerful urge.

282 **"Set me free"** . . . : Wolkstein and Kramer, *Inanna*, 48.

282 **Some, like Robert** . . . : In their search for new metaphors of manhood,
many writers on the male role confusion and crisis of confidence recur to older,
prepatriarchal mythic figures. See E. Anthony Rotundo, *American Manhood* (New
York: Basic Books, 1993); Betcher and Pollack, *Fallen Heroes;* William G. Doty,
Myths of Masculinity (New York: Crossroads, 1993); Bly, *Iron John*, 135; and Bly and
Woodman, *Maiden King.*

282 **The entertainment industry** . . . : See Marie Richmond-Abbot, "Early
Socialization into Sex Roles: Language, Media and the Schools," *Masculine and
Feminine: Gender Roles over the Life Cycle* (New York: McGraw-Hill, 1992), 91–117, and
Linda Tschirhart Sanford and Mary Ellen Donovan, *Women and Self-Esteem* (New
York: Penguin, 1984), 177–96.

282 **As Carol Gilligan** . . . : Richmond-Abbott, "Socialization in the Teenage
Years," 119–77; Gilligan, *In a Different Voice*, and Gilligan and Lyn Mikel Brown,
Meeting at the Crossroads (Cambridge, Mass.: Harvard University Press, 1992);
Pipher, *Raising Ophelia;* and Ellyn Kaschak, *Engendered Lives* (New York: Basic
Books, 1992).

283 **Since the whole point** . . . : Paglia, *Sexual Personae*, 91.

284 **Sociologists suggest that** . . . : Asra Q. Nomani, "Stay in Touch," *Wall
Street Journal*, January 1, 2000, R53.

284 **Modern Afrosirens are** . . . : Janis Faye Hutchinson, "The Hip Hop Generation African American Male-Female Relationships in a Nightclub Setting,"
Journal of Black Studies (September 1999), 65.

285 **Although the industry** . . . : Luc Sante, "Different! Be Like Everyone
Else!" *New York Times Magazine*, October 17, 1999, 140.

286 **The ancient Greek** . . . : Friedrich, *Meaning of Aphrodite*, 143–44.

286 **Her entire *ta erotika*** . . . : Henry, *Prisoner of History*, 47 and 49.

286 **Everywhere linguists and** . . . : Bertrand Russell's complaint fifty years
ago that women were "kept artificially stupid and uninteresting" still holds true, as
Deborah Tannen, Robin Lakoff, and other linguists discovered. *Marriage and*

Morals (New York: Bantam, 1959), 17. See Tannen, *That's Not What I Meant* (New York: Ballantine, 1986); Robin Tolmach Lakoff, *Talking Power: The Politics of Language in Our Lives* (New York: Basic Books, 1990) and *Language and Woman's Place* (New York: Harper & Row, 1975); and Laurie P. Arliss and Deborah J. Borisoff, *Women and Men Communicating* (New York: Harcourt, Brace, 1993).

286 **Women, trained as . . .** : Burton, *Anatomy of Melancholy*, 699.

287 **We ratify, demur . . .** : Janet Stone and Jane Bachner, *Speaking Up* (New York: McGraw-Hill, 1977), 19.

287 **We've cut out . . .** : Brownmiller, *Femininity*, 110.

287 **By muzzling ourselves . . .** : See Ernest Becker's analysis of the power inherent in well-mastered speech: "The proper word or phrase, properly delivered, is the highest attainment of human interpersonal power. The easy handling of the verbal context of action gives the only possibility of direct exercise of control of others." And he doesn't even mention the seductive charge of fascinating language! *Birth and Death of Meaning*, 94.

287 **"As a bull's . . ."**: Burton, *Anatomy of Melancholy*, 700.

287 **The chute gates . . .** : Baring and Cashford, *Myth of the Goddess*, 265.

287 **In spite of unparalled . . .** : Faith Popcorn finds a striking "undercurrent of heaviness and gloom" in contemporary society. *Popcorn Report*, 6. Also see Jonathan Eig, "As Good Times Roll What Are Americans Worried About Now?" *Wall Street Journal*, February 8, 2000, A1–B10. Robert H. Frank in *Luxury Fever: Why Money Fails to Satisfy in an Era of Excess* (New York: Simon & Schuster, 2000) notes that levels of personal satisfaction haven't kept pace with the soaring prosperity in the West. Great Britain ranks nine in happiness; the United States, with the highest per capita income, thirteenth. Bertrand Russell observed this characteristic in Americans, however, in the fifties. "Nothing in America," he wrote, "is so painful to the traveler as the lack of joy. Pleasure is frantic and bacchanalian, a matter of momentary oblivion, not of delighted self-expression." *Marriage and Morals*, 200.

287 **But as in the Renaissance . . .** : Castiglione, *Book of the Courtier*, 211.

287 **Passion needs wake-up . . .** : In order to keep love vital, it must be continuously stirred up through creative tension, adventure, and a complex dynamic equilibrium of pain and pleasure, anxiety and security, mystery and certainty, surprise and predictability. This is a given of the *ars amatoria*. See especially Montaigne, "On Some Verses of Virgil," *Complete Essays*, vol. 3, 55–122; Maurois, "Art of Loving," 9–32; Ellis, "Art of Love," *Psychology of Sex*, vol. 2, 507–75; Reik, *Psychology of Sex Relations*, 95 and passim; and Baudrillard, *Seduction*, passim.

288 **Philosopher Jean Baudrillard . . .** : Baudrillard, *Seduction*, 38 and 154.

288 **The call to adventure . . .** : David M. Buss, the neo-Darwinist who champions male supremacy and promiscuity and the primacy of nubile beauties in the mating market nevertheless concedes in a new book that men prefer difficult women. Piquing male jealousy and raising the bar, he now claims, improve a woman's chances in love. See *The Dangerous Passion: Why Jealousy Is as Necessary as Love and Sex* (New York: Free Press, 2000).

288 **Desocialized by cyberspace, . . .** : For the negative impact on social skills created by CMC (computer-mediated communication), see Michael A. Civin's fascinating study *Male, Female, E-Mail: The Struggle for Relatedness in a Paranoid Society* (New York: Other Press, 2000).

288 **According to Daniel** . . . : Daniel Goleman, *Emotional Intelligence* (New York: Bantam, 1995).

288 **A staggering ten** . . . : *PR Newswire*, New York, April 12, 2000, 1, and Gregory Mott, "Don't Be Shy, See Your Doctor," *Washington Post*, March 7, 2000, WH 7. Both these articles note that after depression and alcoholism, social anxiety disorder ranks as the third most common mental affliction.

288 **"Beauty without grace"** . . . : Quoted in Cohen, *Mademoiselle Libertine*, 174.

289 **"Whenever a woman** . . .": Key, *Love and Ethics*, 102.

289 **They're the "goddess** . . .": Meador, *Inanna*, 21.

289 **"Seduction," predicts Baudrillard** . . . : Baudrillard ends *Seduction* with this prediction: "Anatomy is not destiny, nor is politics: seduction is destiny," 180.

290 **They foresee a** . . . : Francis Fukuyama, "The Politics of Women," *Predictions*, ed. Sian Griffiths (New York: Oxford University Press, 1999), 116.

290 **Society, they prophesy** . . . : Richard Carlson and Bruce Goldman, *2020 Visions: A Long View of a Changing World* (Stanford, Calif.: Portable Stanford, 1991), 61.

290 **The "plague years"** . . . : Grant, *Sexing the Millennium*, 6.

290 **A hundred years** . . . : Henry Adams, *The Education of Henry Adams*, ed. Ernest Samuels (Boston: Houghton Mifflin, 1973 [1918]), 385.

290 **They've unleashed backlash** . . . : See Susan Faludi, *Backlash: The Undeclared War Against American Women* (New York: Doubleday, 1991). Defenses of innate male promiscuity and preferences for nubile beauties include Andrew Sullivan, "Why Men Are Different: The Defining Power of Testosterone," *New York Times Magazine*, April 2, 2000, 46–79. Sullivan mounts a new anatomy-as-destiny defense of men's testosterone-driven imperative to fight, philander, and lord it over women. Also see the neo-Darwinian defenses of same in the work of David M. Buss, *The Evolution of Desire* (New York: Basic Books, 1994), E. O. Wilson, et al.

291 **When it came** . . . : Meador, *Inanna*, 19.

291 **Evolutionary psychologist Geoffrey** . . . : Geoffrey E. Miller, *The Mating Mind* (New York: Doubleday, 2000), 258–433 and passim.

291 **Recently** *Esquire* **celebrated** . . . : Ron Rosenbaum, "The Beautiful and the Damned," *Esquire* (March 1996), 106 and 105.

291 *Talk* **ran a** . . . : Michael Cunningham, "Women on Top," *Talk* (April 2000), 172.

291 **What "the lover"** . . . : Ross, *What Men Want*, 200. Or see Dr. William Moulton Marsten's comment "Give them [men] an alluring woman stronger than themselves to submit to and they'll be proud to be her willing slaves." Quoted in Suzy Menkes, "Fearless Heroines with Looks to Match," *New York Times*, June 4, 1995, 51.

SUGGESTED READING

Ackerman, Diane. *A Natural History of Love*. New York: Random House, 1994.
Allen, Virginia M. *The Femme Fatale: Erotic Icon*. Troy, N.Y.: Whitston Publishing Co., 1983.
Angier, Natalie. *Woman: An Intimate Geography*. New York: Random House, 1999.
Baring, Anne, and Jules Cashford. *The Myth of the Goddess*. London: Arkana, 1991.
Batten, Mary. *Sexual Strategies: How Females Chose Their Mates*. New York: G. P. Putnam's Sons, 1992.
Botting, Kate and Douglas. *Sex Appeal: The Art and Science of Sexual Attraction*. New York: St. Martin's Press, 1996.
Baudrillard, Jean. *Seduction*, trans. Brian Singer. New York: St. Martin's Press, 1990.
Beauvoir, Simone de. *The Second Sex*, trans. H. M. Parshley. New York: Bantam, 1952.
Brantôme, Seigneur de. *Lives of Fair and Gallant Ladies*, trans. A. R. Allinson. New York: Liveright, 1933.
Ellis, Havelock. *Studies in the Psychology of Sex*. 2 vols. New York: Random House, 1906.
Fisher, Helen. *Anatomy of Love*. New York: Columbine, 1992.
——. *The First Sex*. New York: Random House, 1999.
French, Marilyn. *Beyond Power: On Women, Men, and Morals*. New York: Ballantine Books, 1985.
Friday, Nancy. *Women on Top: How Real Life Has Changed Women's Sexual Fantasies*. New York: Pocket Books, 1991.
Friedrich, Paul. *The Meaning of Aphrodite*. Chicago: University of Chicago Press, 1978.
Gaylin, Willard, M.D. *The Male Ego*. New York: Viking, 1992.
Gimbutas, Marija. *The Language of the Goddess*. San Francisco: HarperSanFrancisco, 1991.
Goffman, Erving. *The Presentation of Self in Everyday Life*. Garden City, N.Y.: Anchor, 1959.
Greene, Robert. *The Art of Seduction*. New York: Viking, 2001.
Greer, Germaine. *The Whole Woman*. New York: Anchor, 2000.
Haskell, Molly. *From Reverence to Rape: The Treatment of Women in the Movies*. Baltimore: Penguin, 1973.

Hrdy, Sarah. Blaffer. *The Woman that Never Was.* Cambridge, Mass.: Harvard University Press, 1981.

Hufton, Olwen. *The Prospect Before Her.* New York: Vintage, 1995.

Jaskolski, Helmut. *The Labyrinth: Symbol of Fear, Rebirth, and Liberation,* trans. Michael H. Kohn. Boston and London: Shambhala, 1997.

Lawner, Lynne. *Lives of the Courtesans: Portraits of the Renaissance.* New York: Rizzoli, 1987.

Lederer, Wolfgang, M.D. *The Fear of Women.* New York: Grune & Stratton, 1968.

Lerner, Gerda. *The Creation of Patriarchy.* New York: Oxford University Press, 1986.

Lichtenstein, Grace. *Machisma: Women and Daring.* Garden City, N.Y.: Doubleday & Co., 1981.

Liebowitz, Michael R., M.D., *The Chemistry of Love.* New York: Berkley Books, 1983.

Markale, Jean. *The Great Goddess,* trans. July Gladding. Rochester, Vt.: Inner Traditions International, 1999.

Masson, Georgina. *Courtesans of the Italian Renaissance.* New York: St. Martin's Press, 1975.

Meador, Betty De Shong. *Inanna: Lady of the Largest Heart.* Austin: University of Texas, 2000.

Millan, Betty. *Monstrous Regiment: Women Rulers in Men's Worlds.* Berks, U.K.: Kensal Press, 1982.

Miller, Geoffrey F. *The Mating Mind.* New York: Doubleday, 2000.

Neumann, Erich. *The Great Mother,* trans. Ralph Manheim. Princeton: Princeton University Press, 1963.

Orloff, Alexander. *Carnival: Myth and Cult.* Worgl, Austria: Perlinger Verlag, 1981.

Ovid. *The Art of Love,* trans. Rolfe Humphries. Bloomington: Indiana University Press, 1957.

Paglia, Camille. *Sexual Personae.* New York: Vintage, 1990.

Person, Ethel S. *Dreams of Love and Fateful Encounters.* New York: Penguin, 1988.

Reik, Theodor. *Psychology of Sex Relations.* New York: Farrar & Rinehart, 1945.

Richardson, Joanna. *The Courtesans: The Demi-Monde in Nineteenth-Century France.* Cleveland and New York: World Publishing, 1967.

Sherfey, Mary Jane, M.D. *The Nature and Evolution of Female Sexuality.* New York: Vintage, 1966.

Simmel, Georg. "Flirtation," in *Georg Simmel: On Women, Sexuality, and Love,* trans. Guy Oakes. New Haven: Yale University Press, 1984.

Steinem, Gloria. *Revolution from Within.* Boston: Little, Brown, 1992.

Stendhal. *Love,* trans. Gilbert and Suzanne Sale. 1822. Reprint, Harmondswood, U.K.: Penguin, 1975.

Taylor, Timothy. *The Prehistory of Sex.* New York: Bantam, 1996.

Watson, Cynthia Mervis, M.D. *Love Potions: A Guide to Aphrodisiacs and Sexual Pleasures.* Los Angeles: Jeremy P. Tarcher, 1993.

Wolf, Naomi. *Fire with Fire: The New Female Power and How It Will Change the 21st Century.* New York: Random House, 1993.

Wolkstein, Diane, and Samuel Noah Kramer. *Inanna Queen of Heaven and Earth.* New York: Harper & Row, 1983.

Yarnall, J. *Transformations of Circe: The History of an Enchantress.* Urbana and Chicago: University of Illinois Press, 1994.

INDEX

Citations followed by *n* can be found in the notes.

INDEX

Aspasia, 6, 144–46, 147, 286, 290
Asso, Raymond, 72
Astell, Mary, 119
Astraea, 201
Athena, 20, 38
Athenaeus, 99
athletes, 279
Augustine, Saint, 1
Austen, Jane, 328n
Avery, Milton, 159
aviation, 257–58

Bade, Patrick, 311n
Baker, Josephine, 12, 168–73
Bakos, Susan Crain, 314n
Balanchine, George, 170–71
Bale, David, 228
Balzac, Honoré de, 244
Barrington, Bill, 163, 164, 165, 166
Bataille, Maurice, 171
Batten, Mary, 3, 302n
Baudrillard, Jean, xv, 1, 3, 14, 155, 193,
    288, 289, 327n, 352n
Beach, Amy, 331n
Beaujeu, Anne de, 91, 92
beauty:
    adolescent fixation on, 81, 306n,
        313–14n
    African American standards of, 169
    Apollonian ideal of, 40, 306n
    of asymmetry, 50–51, 80, 313n
    audacity vs., 80–82
    current standards of, 52, 80
    evolutionary function of, 50, 51
    geometrical proportions of, 50, 310n
    Italian Renaissance ideal of, 64
    parental love as source of, 79, 313n
    prehistoric sex deities and, 50–51
    as reflection of soul, 64
    seductresses without, 5, 49–82, 280,
        313n
    Stuart English ideal of, 56
    in theater, 76, 312n
Beauvoir, Simone de, 6, 297n, 301n,
    318n
Becker, Ernest, 351n
Beecher, Henry Ward, 223–24
Beers, Charlotte, 24
Behn, Aphra, 253, 328n
belles laides, 49–82, 280
    examples of, 51–79

of literature and film, 81, 313n
as overachievers, 79–80, 81–82
transformational abilities of, 79
Bentivoglio, Ercole, 66
Benton, Robert, 226–27
Berenice, 198
Berenson, Bernard, 55
Berger, Elisabeth, 208
Berle, Milton, 258
Berlioz, Hector, xii, 78
Bernard, Saint, 213
Bernard, Sarah, 295
Bertaut, Jules, 315n
Betcher, R. William, 350n
bird goddesses, 56, 59, 60, 63, 64, 65,
    67–68, 71
Blake, William, 298–99n
Blanch, Leslie, 273
Blier, Bertrand, 81
Blood, James Harvey, 222, 224
blood sacrifice, 33, 305n
blues singers, 169, 331n
Bly, Robert, 231, 282, 350n
body language, 12
Bouillon, Jo, 171
Brady, Robert, 172
Brantôme, Seigneur de, x, 83, 84, 94,
    119, 195, 231, 340n
Brassempouy, Lady, 50
Breze, Louis de, 91
Breze, Pierre de, 237
Briand, Aristide, 270
Briffault, Robert, 299n
Brody, Jane, 314n
Brontë, Charlotte, 186, 190, 191
Brown, Cecily, 279–80
Brown, Norman O., 134, 332n
Browning, Elizabeth Barrett, 99
Brownmiller, Susan, 250, 297n, 298n,
    302n
Brownstein, Rachel, 190
Buckhurst, Sir Charles, 183
Burton, Richard (actor), 19
Burton, Richard (orientalist), 243
Burton, Robert, 109, 300n, 327n
businesswomen, 110, 112–14, 222, 279,
    339n
Buss, David M., 351n
Butler, Benjamin, 223
Byron, George Gordon, Lord, 147
Byzantine Empire, 209–12